HANDBOOK FOR CURATES

MEDIEVAL TEXTS IN TRANSLATION

Guido of Monte Rochen

HANDBOOK
FOR CURATES

A Late Medieval Manual on Pastoral Ministry

*Translated by Anne T. Thayer, with an introduction
by Anne T. Thayer and Katharine J. Lualdi*

The Catholic University of America Press
Washington, D.C.

Library of Congress Cataloging-in-Publication Data
Guido, de Monte Rocherii, 14th cent.
[Manipulus curatorum. English]
Handbook for curates : a late medieval manual on pastoral ministry /
Guido of Monte Rochen ; translated by Anne T. Thayer ; with an
introduction by Anne T. Thayer and Katharine J. Lualdi.
p. cm. — (Medieval texts in translation)
Includes bibliographical references (p.   ) and index.
ISBN 978-0-8132-1869-4 (pbk. : alk. paper)   1. Pastoral theology—
Catholic Church--Early works to 1800.   2. Catholic Church—
Doctrines—Early works to 1800.   I. Thayer, Anne T.
II. Lualdi, Katharine J.   III. Title.
BX1913.G8313 2011
253.088'28209023—dc22
2011012794

Contents

Foreword

Thomas Tentler

To anyone interested in late medieval and early modern religion, from beginning undergraduates to specialists in the field, this translation of Guido of Monte Rochen's *Manipulus curatorum (Handbook for Curates)* is a gift of great value. The extraordinary popularity of this pastoral guide in the centuries before the Reformation is amply demonstrated in the editors' lucid introduction. I urge everyone to begin by reading that introduction because it is an indispensable preparation for appreciating and, yes, enjoying this important book.

I first encountered Guido over forty years ago, in the North Library of the British Museum, looking for material on the theory and practice of confession on the eve of the Reformation. I was not disappointed. As he offered what he thought would be most useful to confessors, Guido's wide-ranging interest in theological fundamentals and his commonsense advice to his priestly readership served me well.

Decades later Katharine Lualdi and Anne Thayer brought about a different and equally rewarding encounter with Guido. And so, encouraged by the editors' infectious enthusiasm for their subject, and armed with an early version of their translation, I consulted the holdings of the *Manipulus* in the rare book room of the Library of Congress. There I began to realize the full extent of this scholarly gift. I admired a translation that achieved clarity while preserving the flavor of Guido's rambling prose. Following their lead, I looked at the marginalia in copies of the *Manipulus* in that library's collection, and I too found medieval and early modern owners using pointing hands and underlining to signal favorite passages, writing brief comments or summaries, and adding pagination or running heads to make it easier to navigate these pages. Eleven of the fourteen copies I consulted were annotated, some extensively, supplying independent corroboration (if one were needed) of the editors' contention that these books did not just occupy shelf space.

But most important of all, the gift of a full English translation made me realize how much of Guido I had neglected and how much I could still learn from him.

Guido was roughly contemporary with literary and theological giants like Meister Eckhart, Dante, Duns Scotus, William of Ockham, Petrarch, and Boccaccio. These authors (and other less famous contemporaries) are remembered, lectured about, and assigned in courses because of the originality of their ideas or their literary accomplishment. Guido was an authoritative pastoral guide for two centuries after the publication of his manual in 1333 because he was not an intellectual or literary pioneer. His fame was earned because he inspired confidence in his safe reliability. Today, historians searching for the ever elusive "lived religion" of late medieval and early modern Europe value him precisely for those mundane qualities.

And yet, as he faithfully represents the teaching of the masters—searching for a theological consensus and filling the text with citations to canon law—an individuality emerges in what he selects and how he presents it. That kind of individuality is also a reason for studying this book. The editors allude to revealing examples—his rule for the requisite consistency of meat broth in a valid, emergency baptism, or his choice of a particularly poignant illustration of the inviolability of the seal of confession. Indeed, the book is replete with such windows on the author and his age. Guido lives in a world charged with spiritual meaning. He speaks un-self-consciously about the confirmation of Christian truth in the natural world. He can find a spiritual sense in every word, movement, and gesture in the celebration of the mass. He produces lists—of virtues, sins, laws, articles of faith, qualities of a good confession—that aim at succinct instruction and suggest to me a touching confidence that ordinary curates might convert them into exhortations to behave, repent, and reform. At the same time, the sympathy of a compassionate pastor is constant, as he warns in many ways against fostering scrupulosity and despair (without using those terms). The ultimate expression of that consolatory impulse is the often invoked principle that necessity knows no law, that in the crisis of death the rules are suspended. And his whole intention in explaining eucharistic mysteries is to give simple priests a certitude that they can convey to the faithful. Surely it is these qualities that in part explain why, as the editors note, so many manuscript editions survive, why a bishop in Switzerland would urge parish priests to seek out one of these manuscripts and copy it for their own use, and why it became a best-selling publication in the early years of printing. It is a commonplace to observe that the Protestant Reformation thrived on print. The *Manipulus curatorum* reminds us that the dissemination of books was central to religious practice in the West long before 1517. The differences in these histories are important—but so are the commonalities. In that context, too, the question of why Guido achieved so commanding a place in pastoral literature gives us something to think about.

My remarks only suggest the richness to students of late medieval and early modern religion of a text at last available in our vernacular. Guido deserves a wider audience and there is now no reason that he shouldn't get it. We have much to learn from him.

Acknowledgments

This project has been years in the making and we owe thanks to many people for helping bring it to fruition.

With her interests in preaching, Anne began reading the *Manipulus curatorum* in the summer of 2004, looking for parish-level catechetical instruction. This dovetailed nicely with Katharine's interests in the vernacular instructions found in the *prône*, a characteristic feature of the parish mass in late medieval and early modern France. Soon both of us realized what an influential source the *Manipulus* was for clerical education and parish life in the fourteenth, fifteenth, and sixteenth centuries. In 2006 Katharine spent a week in Paris hunting down copies of the *Manipulus curatorum* with manuscript annotations. The hunt did not take long; most of the exemplars she examined included annotations. We then spent a week together at the British Library to broaden our sample. As we turned hundreds of well-worn pages filled with annotations, the book came alive for us just as it must have for Guido's late medieval readers. We presented our initial findings at a session organized for this purpose at the Sixteenth Century Studies Conference in 2006 in Salt Lake City. We would like to thank Ronald Rittgers for chairing the session, and Peter Dykema for his presentation and expertise as we immersed ourselves in the world of late medieval *pastoralia*. We also would like to thank Mack Holt, who attended the session and encouraged us to complete the project for publication.

Although this book is the result of close collaboration, Anne assumed the daunting task of translating the text from the original Latin. She would like to thank Thomas Tentler and Beverly Kienzle in particular for their guidance on tricky passages. In addition to taking the lead on the introduction, Katharine was responsible for tracking down Guido's sources; she appreciated the assistance she received with compiling the translation notes and appendix, especially from Thomas Tentler, Russell Friedman, Kenneth Pennington, and the anonymous readers of the manuscript. Katharine also extends her warmest gratitude to the Office of Interlibrary Loan at the University of Southern Maine. We would also both like to thank the editor of this series, Thomas Noble, for guiding and supporting us throughout the process.

Lastly, we would like to thank our families, for whom Guido has become a household name, for their unflagging encouragement and support for this project.

Introduction

In the early 1330s in Teruel, Spain, Guido of Monte Rochen[1] composed a "how-to" manual for simple priests, the *Handbook for Curates (Manipulus curatorum)*, addressing what they must know, do, say, and teach in order to do their job well. As church authorities had spelled out with increasing precision since the thirteenth century, this job centered on the proper administration of the sacraments, especially penance. Guido's manual is structured accordingly, with sections on each of the sacraments, the longest devoted to confession. The book concludes with an overview of basic articles of faith, which every priest was responsible for teaching his congregation. Guido's recipe for pastoral success found a receptive market. More than 250 manuscript copies of the *Handbook for Curates* are still extant,[2] but it truly came into its own with the advent of printing. Between circa 1468 and 1501, some 122 editions of the *Handbook* rolled off European presses both big and small, making it the eleventh most printed title in the period.[3] The large number of

1. The spelling of "Rochen" varies from catalogue to catalogue, from author to author (e.g., Monte Rocherii, Monte Rocherio, Monte Roterio). We have chosen to adopt the spelling used by the Incunabula Short Title Catalogue (ISTC), the single most comprehensive database of fifteenth-century printing. It is available at http://www.bl.uk/catalogues/istc/index.html.

2. Horacio Santiago Otero, "Guido de Monte Roterio y el 'Manipulus curatorum,'" in *Proceedings of the Fifth International Congress of Medieval Canon Law, Salamanca, 21–25 September, 1976,* eds. Stephan Kuttner and Kenneth Pennington (Vatican City: Biblioteca Apostolica Vaticana, 1980), 259–65. Conrado Guardiola, "Los primeros datos documentales sobre Guido de Monte Roquerio, autor del 'Manipulus curatorum,'" *Hispania* 48, no. 170 (1988): 797–826.

3. This figure is based on Michael Milway's statistical study of incunabular printings catalogued in the ISTC. Following other scholars' lead, his rankings are based

surviving incunabular copies (in excess of 1,400) and their location in depositories across Europe and the United States further testify to the book's widespread circulation.[4]

Despite these impressive numbers, Guido and his manual remain largely forgotten by scholars. Admittedly, little is known about Guido himself other than a few tantalizing details. His name appears twice in ecclesiastical records from fourteenth-century Teruel: first in July 1339 as the "magister" adjudicating a dispute over the execution of a bequest for anniversary masses in a local church; and again a few months later as a witness to documents drawn up for the same dispute. This evidence suggests that Guido was an ecclesiastical official and teacher (hence his title "magister") working and living in Teruel. It was a prosperous city of some importance at the time particularly because of its close relationship with the newly established kingdom of Valencia. Guido dedicated his book to Valencia's bishop, Raymond of Gaston, for example, even though Teruel was not under his jurisdiction. In casting himself as Raymond's "devoted servant," Guido acknowledged this relationship along with his own status as a member of the clergy. But secular or regular? Guido never tips his hat in either direction but inferential evidence points to the former.[5]

Regardless of Guido's status, the contents of his manual make readily apparent that he was familiar with the realities of parish practice, as we discuss below. His heavy reliance on canon law and

---

on the estimate that the average print run of incunabula was 500 copies. See Michael Milway, "Forgotten Best-Sellers from the Dawn of the Reformation," in *Continuity and Change: The Harvest of Late Medieval and Reformation History*, ed. Robert J. Bast and Andrew C. Gow (Leiden: Brill, 2000), 113–42. Although the vast majority of printed editions of the *Manipulus* are in Latin, several vernacular translations appeared on the scene as well. These included a French translation printed in Orléans in 1490–1491 and a Castilian translation printed in 1523 in Lisbon.

4. For a list of many of the extant copies and their locations, see *Gesamtkatalog der Wiegendrucke*, Band X, Lieferung 2–3 (Stuttgart: Anton Hiersemann, 1994–1996), col. 282–351.

5. Guardiola, "Los primeros datos documentales sobre Guido de Monte Roquerio." Drawing on newly available ecclesiastical documents, Guardiola's article provides the most detailed biographical sketch of Guido we have found to date.

Scholastic authorities to ground these realities in church teachings also indicates a university education, possibly in Paris. In the early fourteenth century, the University of Paris was the epicenter of Western Scholastic thought; it attracted many influential thinkers to its Faculty of Theology who guided theology in new directions, away from the exhaustive system building of their predecessors toward more selective, in-depth studies of individual issues. Their collective intellectual output found especially dynamic and influential expression in two genres: theological debates on any number of topics—hence the Latin term by which the debates became known, *de quodlibet,* "about anything"—and commentaries on Peter Lombard's *Sentences,* the standard textbook of medieval theology.[6] While composing his manual, Guido explicitly tapped into both genres; in doing so, he revealed his up-to-date theological training and his desire to apply it toward practical ends.

Guido's knowledge of canon law was equally current. Medieval legal studies had their roots in Bologna, where a prestigious school of law had taken shape by the mid-twelfth century. Within fifty years, additional law schools had been established elsewhere in Europe (including Paris). Their importance continued to grow thanks in part to a steady stream of new papal legislation issued as letters known as "decretals." Until the 1320s, decretals were the primary source fueling legal innovation; thus, not surprisingly, they found their way into law school curricula. As his manual reveals, Guido was deeply familiar with Gratian's *Decretum,* the canon law counterpart to Lombard's *Sentences* which had laid the foundations of medieval canon law, as well as with newer decretal collections. He was also versed in Roman law to some extent, although he cites it sparingly in his manual. Assuming he had some type of legal training, his legal know-how would have been a given. It was stan-

6. Russell L. Friedman, "The *Sentences* Commentary, 1250–1320. General Trends, the Impact of the Religious Orders, and the Test Case of Predestination," in *Mediaeval Commentaries on the* Sentences *of Peter Lombard,* ed. G. R. Evans (Leiden: Brill, 2002), 1.41–128; Christopher Schabel, ed., *Theological Quodlibeta in the Middle Ages,* vol. 2, *The Fourteenth Century* (Leiden: Brill, 2007).

dard procedure for medieval law students to memorize vast numbers of laws, with the expectation that they would be able to recall them quickly and accurately when necessary.[7] Guido's use of legal sources reflects just such a concern with precision but, as was the case with his theological background, his aim was to step out of the classroom into the everyday world of pastoral care.

Clearly his approach was in demand at a time when ecclesiastical officials were preoccupied with the need to shape the practice and piety of priest and parishioner through standardized, accessible, hands-on instruction. Their concern had ample precedent, as the profusion of pastoral texts *(pastoralia)* written in the wake of the Fourth Lateran Council in 1215 attests. Indeed, all but one of the council's decrees focused on various dimensions of pastoral care, notably parish priests' sacramental responsibilities toward their parishioners (and vice versa, as reflected in the decree *Omnis utriusque sexus*, requiring all adult Christians to confess at least once a year to their "own" priest). Theologians and church leaders responded in kind; by the 1270s, there was a wide range of literary aids available for the edification of priests and of the souls under their charge: episcopal decrees, manuals on confession, collections of sermons, expositions of the Ten Commandments, and the like.[8] This wave of pastoral instruction continued to build in the fourteenth and fifteenth centuries, bringing Guido's manual right along with it.

The success of the *Handbook* did not protect it from the religious tumult of the sixteenth century. The Spanish Inquisition included Guido's book in its 1559 Index of prohibited books for reasons the inquisitors did not make explicitly clear. Perhaps it fell within the blanket condemnation of books containing "errors" or

7. James A. Brundage, *Medieval Canon Law* (London: Longman, 1995), 44–69.

8. Leonard E. Boyle coined the term *pastoralia* to refer to the large body of literature generated after the Fourth Lateran Council (1215) designed to help a priest in his *cura animarum*. See Leonard E. Boyle, "The Fourth Lateran Council and Manuals of Popular Theology," in *The Popular Literature of Medieval England*, ed. Thomas J. Heffernan (Knoxville: University of Tennessee Press, 1985), 30–43 (see especially the schematic diagram on pp. 38–43).

"frivolous, odd, apocryphal, and superstitious things." This was the first (but not the last) time the *Handbook for Curates* appeared on such an index. Although there is evidence that the book was still in demand at midcentury, its inclusion on the Index brought its heyday to an end.[9]

But until then, Guido's manual was a must-have resource for Catholic clergy. For this reason, it and other *pastoralia* offer a lively window into late medieval parish life, early print culture, and the intersection between the two. From the onset, printers and booksellers were looking to turn a profit and would not have repeatedly invested time and capital into books that didn't sell.[10] And sell they did, with the *Handbook for Curates* at the head of the pack.[11] The immediate success of the *Handbook* suggests that printers capitalized on an existing market and, equally important, on a growing desire to disseminate *pastoralia* more widely among the parish clergy.[12] Despite the proliferation of pastoral manuals in the thirteenth and fourteenth centuries, the expectation that average priests would own one outstripped the reality, due, at least in part, to the cost and labor involved in producing manuscript copies on

9. On Guido and the 1559 index, see J. M. De Bujanda, *Index des Livres Interdits*, vol. 5, *Index de l'Inquisition Espagnole, 1551, 1554, 1559* (Geneva: Librairie Droz, 1984), 197, 408–409, 507. At least one Spanish bookseller had the book in stock on the eve of its condemnation, suggesting that the book still had a market at the time. See William Pettas, "A Sixteenth-Century Spanish Bookstore: The Inventory of Juan de Junta," *Transactions of the American Philosophical Society*, vol. 85, pt. 1 (1995): 1–76.

10. Lucien Febvre and Henri-Jean Martin, *The Coming of the Book: The Impact of Printing 1450–1800*, trans. David Gerard (London: NLB, 1976), 248–61; John L. Flood, "'Volentes sibi comparare infrascriptos libros impressos . . .': Printed Books as a Commercial Commodity in the Fifteenth Century," in *Incunabula and Their Readers: Printing, Selling and Using Books in the Fifteenth Century*, ed. Kristian Jensen (London: British Library, 2003), 139–51.

11. Table 1 in Milway, "Forgotten Bestsellers," 141.

12. Peter A. Dykema, "Handbooks for Pastors: Late Medieval Manuals for Parish Priests and Conrad Porta's *Pastorale Lutheri* (1582)," in *Continuity and Change: The Harvest of Late Medieval and Reformation History*, 143–162; idem, "Conflicting Expectations: Parish Priests in Late Medieval Germany" (Ph.D. diss., University of Arizona, 1998), 118–64, 304–13 (Appendix A, "Manuals for Parish Priests: Printing and Reception History").

a large scale. The advent of printing in the mid-fifteenth century changed this landscape dramatically, not in terms of the types of books the clergy were supposed to have, but rather in their accessibility. By and large, the clergy did not favor trendsetters in their choice of books; the guidance and opinions of *auctoritates* ruled the day.[13] Early printers knew their customer base well, producing already popular texts in increasingly smaller and cheaper formats.[14] The fact that in general these texts remain in the shadows of contemporary scholarship suggests a need to narrow the gap further between what we consider to have been important texts and what people actually bought and, presumably, read in everyday settings across Europe.[15]

Paralleling a trend evident in other genres (e.g., printed sermon collections and liturgical psalters),[16] by the mid-1480s, printers of Guido's manual had largely abandoned the folio format, producing

13. Thomas Tentler makes precisely this point in his descriptive overview of the literature of the forgiveness of sins. Regarding the *Manipulus curatorum* specifically, he argues that its popularity in print suggests that its public "had little sense of history. It is perhaps only a slight exaggeration to say that to readers at the end of the fifteenth century, Guido de Monte Rocherii was a contemporary." See Thomas Tentler, *Sin and Confession on the Eve of the Reformation* (Princeton, N.J.: Princeton University Press, 1977), 30–31.

14. Among the most significant factors driving down costs was the introduction of a new type of paper around 1480 designed for printing, which was less expensive to produce than the paper used for manuscripts. See Flood, "Printed Books as a Commercial Commodity," 141, n. 24. The size of the paper also affected cost. Kristian Jensen provides one striking example: in the 1490s a small folio bible could cost around 2 Rhenish guilder; a one-volume octavo bible cost about half a guilder. See Kristian Jensen, "Printing the Bible in the Fifteenth Century: Devotion, Philology and Commerce," in Jensen, *Incunabula and Their Readers*, 136.

15. Manuals for confessors and manuals for preachers, subgenres of *pastoralia*, have received considerable scholarly attention. See, for example, Tentler, *Sin and Confession*, and Anne T. Thayer, *Penitence, Preaching and the Coming of the Reformation* (Aldershot, U.K.: Ashgate, 2002). By contrast, far less scholarship exists on manuals for parish priests and their increased visibility in the late Middle Ages. Notable exceptions include Peter Dykema and Michael Milway (cited above), and Eric Reiter, who has published a modern edition of the *Stella clericorum* (cited below).

16. Thayer, *Penitence, Preaching and the Coming of the Reformation*, chap. 1; Mary Kay Duggan, "Reading Liturgical Books," in Jensen, *Incunabula and Their Readers*, 72–74.

instead cheaper and more portable quartos, and by the late 1490s octavos dominated the market. As Guido himself reveals, he chose the title of his manual with just such portability and accessibility in mind: "I wanted this little book to be called *Handbook for Curates*, because priests, especially curates, ought to have this little book in their hands, so that they may see the things which ought to be done pertaining to their office."[17]

In explaining his choice of a title, Guido also points to his audience: priests, more specifically "neophyte priests," charged with the care of souls. Guido recognizes a hierarchy of office, learning, and jurisdiction among the clergy, but he endeavors to strengthen those who operate at the parish level. Although by the late fifteenth century, clerics and priests were attending university at rates higher than ever before, many were still educated as apprentices under the tutelage of an experienced cleric.[18] Even so, a common need for practical instruction on the daily responsibilities of pastoral care united the two groups, making them a prime target for manuals such as Guido's. The simple priests he has in mind are not simpletons; nor are they the corrupt clergy of Chaucer's "Pardoner's Tale," or the superstitious ignoramuses of Reformation polemic. They are literate enough to read basic Latin and are addressed by Guido as teachable servants of God.[19] Thus their ignorance was real but not without remedy. Guido views these curates

17. Prologue

18. Dykema, "Conflicting Expectations," 124–27; Kathleen M. Comerford, "Clerical Education, Catechesis, and Catholic Confessionalism: Teaching Religion in the Sixteenth and Seventeenth Centuries," in *Early Modern Catholicism: Essays in Honour of John W. O'Malley, S.J.*, ed. Kathleen M. Comerford and Hilmar M. Pabel (Toronto: University of Toronto Press, 2001), 244–46; Boyle, "Aspects of Clerical Education in Fourteenth-Century England," in *Pastoral Care, Clerical Education, and Canon Law, 1200–1400* (London: Variorum, 1981), 19–32; Reinhold Kiermayr, "On the Education of the Pre-Reformation Clergy," *Church History* 53 (1984): 7–16.

19. Peter Dykema asserts that scholars have consistently mistranslated the term "simplices sacerdotes" which authors of pastoral manuals often used to describe their target audience. By "simple priests," they did not mean simpleminded or stupid but rather those without formal academic training or pastoral experience. See Dykema, "Conflicting Expectations," 230–33.

as essential to the life and health of the church, and it is for their benefit that he aims to be "useful."

As Guido understood, at the most fundamental level, his book's usefulness depended not just on what he wrote, but how he wrote it. For this reason, he aimed to craft his handbook "in a plain but useful style, not caring about ornate words, but about what is fitting and helpful to souls."[20] Even a quick glance at the text reveals that Guido remained true to his intention—his language does, in fact, lack elegance, opting for the direct and unpretentious instead. Metaphors appear only in the occasional introductory paragraph or in exegetical explanation. Phrases like "Know that" or "Concerning this, there are four things to be said," fill the *Handbook.* Although these expressions may appear awkward to the modern reader, they likewise reflect Guido's goal of usefulness. Through this style of presentation, Guido lets the reader know where he is headed and how many steps it will take to get there, providing plenty of signposts and lists along the way.[21]

With that said, content did matter to Guido given his expressed desire to instruct priests in how they should "guide themselves in the execution of their office and how to rightly minister before their God, namely, Christ."[22] He divides his instructions into three major parts. The first takes up the sacraments in general and each sacrament in turn, save penance. By noting the numbers and lengths of chapters in each tract of Part I, it is easy to see that the mass was the sacrament for which Guido provides the most guidance (66 pages). Central to the priest's public ministry, here his sacramental leadership was crucial and various difficulties might arise calling for his judgment. Next comes marriage (33 pages). Marriage was

20. Dedicatory Letter

21. Although this style originated in cathedral schools and universities, by the later Middle Ages, it was pervasive in pastoral literature. See Mary A. Rouse and Richard H. Rouse, "*Statim invenire:* Schools, Preachers, and New Attitudes to the Page," in *Authentic Witnesses: Approaches to Medieval Texts and Manuscripts* (Notre Dame, Ind.: University of Notre Dame Press, 1991), 191–219; David L. d'Avray, *The Preaching of the Friars: Sermons Diffused from Paris before 1300* (Oxford: Clarendon Press, 1985), 64–90.

22. Prologue

increasingly coming under church control and because of its position at the intersection of social, economic, and spiritual concerns,
it offered many complications, adjudicated by civil and canon law.
The sacrament of orders, in contrast, was done by the bishop and
the local priest needed little guidance here (10 pages). Similarly, aside from questions of reiteration, extreme unction was fairly
straightforward (5 pages).

The sacrament of penance was important and complex enough
to merit its own major section in the *Handbook:* it is the longest
of the three main parts.[23] In devoting so much attention to this
sacrament, Guido followed a well-established pattern in pastoral
literature sparked by the Fourth Lateran decree on annual confession.[24] Here the council compared the confessor to a doctor
who must be able to identify the ailments of his patients and de-
vise the most suitable treatment. Such competence required training, which is precisely what manuals for confessors aimed to provide. A foundational work of the genre was the *Summa confessorum*
(or *Summa de casibus conscientiae*) of a fellow Spaniard, Raymond of
Penyafort. Guido relies heavily on Raymond's *Summa* for his treatment of penance[25] but distills its key parts for the benefit of the
novice reader so that, in his words, "if some neophytes or less advanced curates should be uncertain in the forum of penance, this
little work may be an introduction and guide for them."[26] Thus, in
the ensuing discussion of each of the three parts of penance (contrition, confession, and satisfaction), Guido focuses on the practi-
calities of how the priest is to proceed when hearing the confessions of penitents.

Although Parts I and II of the *Handbook for Curates* cast the

23. Tentler ranks Guido as one of the six most authoritative or popular authors
on confession in the late Middle Ages. See Tentler, *Sin and Confession,* 348.
24. Boyle, "The Fourth Lateran Council and Manuals of Popular Theology,"
31–34.
25. Raymond's *Summa* is divided into four books. Book III examines the priesthood, its ordination, and functions. It includes a long section on the sacrament of
penance (chapter 34).
26. Prologue to Part II.

priest above all as the mediator of the sacraments, Part III reveals that he was also the teacher of the people of God.[27] Catechesis was a growing component of pastoral ministry in the late Middle Ages, particularly through preaching at the Sunday parish mass.[28] Within this setting, parish priests were not necessarily expected to deliver formal sermons in the way mendicant preachers did, for example. Rather church leaders admonished pastors to use the weekly liturgy to disseminate basic religious instruction by reciting the *Pater, Ave, Credo*, Ten Commandments, and so on. One can easily imagine Part III of Guido's manual being used to fulfill this role, once again pointing to the book's versatility.[29] Here Guido explains the articles of the faith as found in the Creeds, elaborates on each of the Ten Commandments, and teaches Christians how to pray using the seven petitions of the Lord's Prayer. The final item in this section, the brief "On the gifts of the blessed," rounds out Guido's overarching rubric that the faithful need to be taught "what is to be believed, what is to be asked, what is to be done, what is to be fled, and what is to be hoped for."[30]

Other pastoral works were on the printed book market at the same time and achieved their own measure of popularity.[31] Many were shorter in length than the *Handbook* but provided less practical instruction. For example, the *Cura pastoralis* (ca. 1425) is only 24 oc-

27. Citing the seventh-century theologian John of Damascus, Guido defines the priest's pastoral duties based on the four meanings of *sacerdos* (Prologue). Another popular late medieval manual for parish priests, the anonymous *Cura pastoralis*, defines the care of souls according to the same four meanings. See Dykema, "Conflicting Expectations," 165–67.

28. On the late medieval catechetical movement, see Robert J. Bast, *Honor Your Fathers: Catechisms and the Emergence of a Patriarchal Ideology in Germany, 1400–1600* (Leiden: Brill, 1997), chap. 1. On lay catechesis as part of the parish mass, see Katharine J. Lualdi, "Change and Continuity in the Liturgy of the *Prône* from the Fifteenth to the Seventeenth Century," in *Prédication et liturgie au Moyen Âge*, ed. Nicole Bériou and Franco Morenzoni (Turnhout: Brepols, 2008), 373–89.

29. Anne T. Thayer, "Guido of Monte Rochen's *Manipulus Curatorium* and Sermonic Support," in Ronald J. Stansbury, ed., *A Companion to Pastoral Care in the Late Middle Ages (1200–1500)* (Leiden: Brill, 2010), 123–44.

30. Introduction to Part III

31. Dykema, "Conflicting Expectations," 142–64, 303–13.

tavo leaves in length. It offers definitions and lists designed to answer a bishop's ordination questions.[32] At 17 quarto leaves, *Manuale parochialium sacerdotum,* most likely a thirteenth-century text, gives
relatively little instruction on how to proceed correctly through
routine tasks, but highlights the pitfalls of ministry.[33] In a different vein, another thirteenth-century treatise, the *Stella clericorum*
(34 pages in a modern edition), praises the office of the priesthood and exhorts the clergy to live holy lives.[34] More catechetical in orientation, the *Opusculum Tripartitum* by the early fifteenth-
century pastoral tour-de-force, Jean Gerson, summarizes the Ten
Commandments, how to make a good confession, and the art of
dying well. It is written for the lay reader or hearer, however, and
does not offer direct advice to the priest.[35] Similarly catechetical
in intent is Thomas Aquinas's *De articulis fidei et ecclesiae sacramentis.*
Composed around 1261 at the request of the bishop of Palermo
for a basic pastoral manual, it briefly discusses the Creed and the
seven sacraments.[36]

The *Parochiale curatorum* of Michael Lochmaier offers another interesting basis for comparison. Published around 1493, it is slightly
longer than the *Handbook* but does not have its same range, focus-
ing instead on "issues of parish law."[37] It includes topics such as

32. *Cura pastoralis* ([Ulm: Johann Reger, ca. 1498–1499]; University of Pennsylvania, Van Pelt Library, Inc c-988). See also Dykema, "Conflicting Expectations," 151,
309–11.

33. *Manuale parochialium sacerdotum* ([Strassburg: Printer of the 1483 "Vitus Patrum,"
about 1485]; British Library IA.1325). See also Dykema, "Conflicting Expectations,"
150, 303–304.

34. *Stella clericorum,* ed. Eric H. Reiter, Toronto Medieval Latin Texts 23 (Toronto:
Pontifical Institute of Mediaeval Studies, 1997), 9–11.

35. Jean Gerson, *Opera omnia,* 5 vols. (Antwerp: Sumptibus Societatis, 1706; reprint,
Hildesheim: Olms, 1987), vol. 1, col. 425–50.

36. Thomas Aquinas, *De articulis fidei et ecclesiae sacramentis,* in *Traités: Les Raisons de la
foi, Les articles de la foi et les sacrements de l'Église,* ed. Gilles Emery (Paris: Cerf, 1999), 211–
95. Partial English translation available in *The Catechetical Instructions of St. Thomas Aquinas,* trans. Joseph Collins (New York: Joseph Wagner, 1939), 119–31.

37. Michael Lochmaier, *Parochiale curatorum* ([Nuremberg: Friedrich Creussner, not
before 1493]), aij r (British Library IA.7812). See also Dykema, "Conflicting Expectations," 159, 311–12.

tithes and first fruits owed to churches and the cases in which second marriages may be blessed, devoting far less attention to routine sacramental or catechetical practice. The manual most like Guido's *Handbook* was John Mirk's fourteenth-century *Instructions for Parish Priests*, which covers the sacraments and basic catechesis. It is considerably shorter and presented in rhyme. Because it is in English rather than in Latin, it naturally had a more localized popularity. This may help to explain why—in contrast to the other manuals described above—Mirk's *Instructions* appears never to have made the transition from manuscript to print, thereby posing little threat to Guido's prominence.[38]

Although Guido's manual had much in common with contemporary *pastoralia*, it stood out from the pack by adapting and simplifying the genre's basic features to serve its audience more effectively. The *Handbook* is long enough to be comprehensive, but short enough to be truly useful. Guido was well aware that more expansive, intellectually sophisticated texts could easily overwhelm a neophyte curate or parish priest. These included the various summas for confessors and Aquinas's *Summa Theologiae*, especially Book III and its Supplement. As Guido writes at the end of a chapter on problems that might arise in the mass, "These things concerning the sacrament of the eucharist and its minister and trappings, I have written simply and briefly so that simple priests may find certitude in such things, and in other things which long tracts examine, may they be given occasion to think, question, and ask."[39] Even if Guido did not expect his readers to study "long tracts," he borrowed from the weight of their collective authority to lend credence and depth to his own writing. Thus in good medieval fashion, he repeatedly refers to what the "doctors" "explain," "as-

---

38. According to Susan Powell, the success of John Mirk's sermon collection *Festial* was also a factor. She argues that the *Festial* and *Instructions* were originally intended to work as a unit but as new, more catechetical sermons were added to the *Festial*, the *Instructions* was no longer as relevant. Unlike the *Instructions*, the revised version of the *Festial* had a successful career in print. See Susan Powell, "John Mirk's *Festial* and the Pastoral Programme," *Leeds Studies in English*, n.s., 22 (1991): 85–102.

39. Part I, tract 4, chapter 11

sert," and "say" to address a point. Sometimes he specifies them by name—William Durandus, Aquinas, John Duns Scotus, authorities one would encounter in a university with an up-to-date theological faculty—but often they are cloaked in anonymity.

This is not to say that Guido may not have had more advanced readers in mind. In fact, he combines a fluid use of the "doctors" with a decidedly academic penchant for providing precise citations. With the rise of medieval universities came a greater emphasis on gathering and organizing Christian knowledge in an ordered and accessible way. Given his academic training and ecclesiastical position, Guido was steeped in this body of work and its practical applications. He passed this knowledge and experience onto his readers by providing abundant citations from contemporary works of theology and, especially, of canon law. In doing so, Guido may have envisioned readers with the necessary training and resources to look the citations up themselves, although neither was essential to his book's utility.

Guido's citations, both precise and imprecise, had an added benefit that most likely contributed to his book's popularity. By tethering his directives to Scholastic theology and canon law, he was not simply conveying useful information; he was also conveying a useful way of thinking. University-trained theologians in this period learned the art of *disputatio*, weighing authorities, drawing pertinent distinctions, and systematizing doctrine under guiding principles. Guido is not under any illusion that the users of his book will gain the equivalent of a university education, but he does want to cultivate sensibilities in this direction. Often Guido will explain how he comes to a particular conclusion by following a more fundamental rule over a less essential one, acknowledging disagreement among the doctors along the way. Sometimes he will express his own opinion as to the correct answer; other times he refuses to adjudicate, leaving it up to his readers to draw their own conclusions. In the process, he illuminates a fascinating array of medieval topics. How many hosts can a priest consecrate at one time? Must restitution be made for winnings in illicit games of chance? Should a believer give alms to a Christian stranger or to his own infidel father? When is reading natural signs superstitious and when is it simply good agricultural practice? These are only a sampling of the questions Guido raises for the reader's consideration. Through this approach, he aimed to teach priests to think theologically for themselves and problem-solve accordingly.

Guido's discussion of who should be baptized provides a case in point. Here he walks his readers through a variety of scenarios in a logical and straightforward manner. For example, what if princes and lords of territories in which Jews live want to baptize Jewish children against their parents' will? Guido explains that the authorities are divided on the question and he summarizes the reasoning of each camp. Some doctors assert that since Jews are the servants of princes and lords, they can hand over Jewish children for baptism. The other camp disagrees because of the fear that such children may return to Judaism as adults. These doctors argue that history is on their side because it was most likely this possibility that prevented zealous Christian leaders of the past from forcibly baptizing Jewish children. Guido does not take sides in the debate; he only presents competing points of view. As he concludes: "Which of these is truer, I leave to the judgment of the reader."[40] Although some readers may have had to make this judgment in real life (especially in Guido's native Spain), more still would have benefited from the critical process of decision making Guido encourages, a most useful skill for pastoral ministry.

Usefulness is, of course, at the heart of Guido's educational mission. For this reason, he consciously seeks a workable balance between simple direction and more complex discussion. Once again, his treatment of baptism offers a compelling example. Baptism was understood to be essential to salvation and so was *the* critical sacrament to perform in a timely and correct fashion. All the pastoral literature stresses the importance of getting the words right, "I baptize you in the name of the Father, and of the Son, and of the Holy Spirit." Further, baptism should be done with water, ideally

---

40. Part I, tract 2, chapter 5

by a priest, but by anyone if imminent death is feared. This dual emphasis on the material and verbal composition of the sacrament neatly encapsulates medieval sacramental theology. Borrowing from the philosophy of Aristotle, Scholastic thinkers used the terms "matter" and "form" to explain how sacramental rites worked as vehicles of divine grace. Matter is something that can change or be changed. Form is what the matter gets as the result of change. Thus the "matter" is the material element needed (in this case, water). The words the priest uses comprise the "form" that changes the matter by giving it the capacity to convey the grace of salvation to those being baptized. This is precisely the point Guido hits home later in his manual when he writes, "[s]ince, therefore, according to the Philosopher [Aristotle], the form is that which gives a thing its being and without which a thing cannot exist, it is clear that only those words which are necessary for the sacrament are the form of this sacrament."[41]

Against this backdrop, Guido offers both theological and practical elaborations on the matter of baptism. Because of the necessity of the sacrament to an individual's salvation, its matter should be very easy to come by. Water is neither expensive nor rare; it is available in every country. Water is also fitting because of its cleansing, cooling, and illuminating properties which mirror the spiritual actions of grace. In terms of practice, Guido raises the question, what does one do if one doesn't have plain water on hand? He then evaluates various liquids based on whether or not they include a substantial amount of "elemental water." For instance, he asks,

But can baptism be done in meat broth when other water cannot be found? The answer is that either so much rendering of the meat is done in that broth that it stops being the species of water and becomes another species newly generated, and then baptism cannot be done; or not so much rendering of the meat has been done in it, and then it can be done, and one can be baptized in such broth.[42]

41. Part I, tract 4, chapter 4
42. Part I, tract 2, chapter 2

But how is the priest to know how much cooking is too much? Guido says that it depends on the consistency.

For if the consistency [*spissitudine*] of this broth is like that in meat or a little softer, I do not believe that it is possible to baptize in this broth. But if it is not of such a consistency, but the broth is greasy, I believe that then one can baptize in that broth.[43]

Guido's specific answer is not distinctive. What is, and probably a key to his popular success, is his moderate degree of elaboration on the question. Neither Mirk's *Instructions for Parish Priests* nor the *Manuale parochialium sacerdotum* takes up the question of alternative liquids for baptism. The *Cura pastoralis* simply lists "thick broth already rendered" in a list of prohibited liquids. Thomas Aquinas discussed this question in the *Summa Theologiae.*

Chrism does not destroy the nature of the water by being mixed with it: just as neither is water changed wherein meat and the like are boiled: except the substance boiled be so dissolved that the liquor be of a nature foreign to water; in this we may be guided by the specific gravity [*spissitudine*]. If, however, from the liquor thus thickened plain water be strained, it can be used for baptism.[44]

Guido says nearly the same thing in simpler language. The prescription is clear, but he also provides adequate elaboration to enhance practical understanding.

Although Guido relies heavily on church teachings to shape his discussion, he places one source of authority above all others: Scripture. The *Handbook* is replete with scriptural citations, reflecting the prominence of Scripture in Scholastic theology as well as Guido's own familiarity with both the Old and New Testaments. The church must instruct its pastors, Guido asserts in the dedication, because God has ordered her to do so through His word and Christ's example. Ultimately, these must be a pastor's guide if he is to rightly minister before God.

When viewed as a whole, each of these features of the *Hand-*

43. Ibid.
44. Thomas Aquinas, *Summa Theologiae*, Bk III, q. 66, a. 4.

book for Curates—its practical pastoral guidance, its organized format, its helpful range of theological and legal opinions on contested questions—is key to understanding the manual's phenomenal success in print. Yet if we limit our interpretive lens to print-runs and content description, we miss an equally important part of the picture. Although such information is useful, indeed necessary, to evaluating the book's historical importance, it tells us very little about the real people in real time who read it and if and how they applied its teachings. We know that over the course of the fifteenth century, numerous ecclesiastical authorities urged parish priests to use Guido's manual.[45] And we also know that many priests did, in fact, have the book on hand. But what, if anything, did they make of its instructions and advice?

This is a tricky question that points to the potential disconnect between normative texts and everyday practice. Interestingly, late medieval readers of printed pastoral manuals such as Guido's faced a similar challenge, fueled by a need to understand, remember, and retrieve the information contained therein. In this regard, despite the fact that the printing press allowed for the production and circulation of *pastoralia* on an unprecedented scale, the reading habits and expectations of the buying public followed well-worn grooves. For centuries, readers had marked up manuscripts with mnemonic notes, such as pointing hands, *nota* marks, authority identifications, and the like. By labeling key passages in this way,

---

45. For example, in a letter to the bishop of Coutances, Jean Gerson recommended the *Manipulus curatorum* as one of six books a bishop should make sure his parish clergy study; see Dykema, "Conflicting Expectations," 152. The episcopal synod of Geneva in circa 1435–1445 likewise cited Guido's manual as required reading, which the bishop noted was already widely available among diocesan clergy; see Louis Binz, *Vie religieuse et réforme ecclésiastique dans le diocèse de Genève pendant le grand schisme et la crise conciliaire (1378–1450)* (Geneva: Alex. Jullien, 1973), 1.169. The 1515 episcopal synod of Paris did the same; see V. Angelo, *Les curés de Paris au XVIe siècle* (Paris: Cerf, 2005), 115. Ex-libris in extant copies provide some evidence of ownership, as we discuss. Inventories after death appear to be a less fruitful avenue of research because books intended for hands-on, everyday use such as Guido's were susceptible to loss or damage, particularly when passed down from priest to priest; see Angelo, *Les curés de Paris*, 271–91, 296–303.

a reader was not only more likely to remember their significance; he also made his own trail map for future use. Thus, unlike simple lists ranking the most popular texts, marginalia bear witness to a book's life after it left the printer's shop. More specifically, marginalia expose the ways in which a reader navigated the content and format of a text, leaving tangible evidence in his wake.[46]

Luckily for us, there are hundreds of surviving copies of the *Handbook for Curates.* And better still, they abound with marginalia. In fact, of the seventy copies we reviewed, the overwhelming majority (sixty-two) include marginalia.[47] Our findings appear to reflect the norm. As other scholars have found, books printed before 1501 were very likely to be annotated and, borrowing from a tradition long established in manuscript production, provided sufficient margins expressly for this purpose.[48] Guido was clearly a product and propagator of this mode of interaction between text and reader. As he writes at the end of Part II, tract 4 on satisfaction: "I ask for kindness from the reader for the imperfection of this work,

46. Anthony Grafton, "Is the History of Reading a Marginal Enterprise? Guillaume Budé and His Books," *Papers of the Bibliographical Society of America* 91 (1997): 139–57. See also H. J. Jackson, *Marginalia: Readers Writing in Books* (New Haven, Conn.: Yale University Press, 2001), 50–51; Paul Saenger and Michael Heinlen, "Incunable Description and Its Implication for the Analysis of Fifteenth-Century Reading Habits," in *Printing the Written Word: The Social History of Books, circa 1450–1520,* ed. Sandra Hindman (Ithaca, N.Y.: Cornell University Press, 1991), 225–58; William H. Sherman, *Used Books: Marking Readers in Renaissance England* (Philadelphia: University of Pennsylvania Press, 2008), 7–8; and Bernard Rosenthal, *The Rosenthal Collection of Printed Books with Manuscript Annotations* (New Haven, Conn.: Yale University Press, 1997).

47. Eight included no manuscript notes or marks in the printed text; 17 included fewer than 10; the remainder (45) contained 10 or more, with the vast majority falling at the moderately to heavily annotated end of the spectrum.

48. R. C. Alston, *Books with Manuscript: A Short Title Catalogue of Books with Manuscript Notes in the British Library* (London: British Library, 1994), xiii; Sherman, *Used Books,* xii, 5–9. See also Saenger and Heinlen, who examined eighty-two incunable codices from the Newberry Library's collections. As they write, "The modification of printed texts by reader notes appears to be a frequent feature of the incunable. Over 75 percent of our sample evinces reader annotations in either red or black ink or both"; see Saenger and Heinlen, "Incunable Description and Its Implication for the Analysis of Fifteenth-Century Reading Habits," 244.

so that when he sees what needs to be corrected and added, he may correct and add, not with a malicious spirit, but in a friendly way."[49] Granted, in the case of our sample of the *Handbook for Curates*, the density of annotations often varied widely; some books had less than ten marks while others were brimming with them. Furthermore, the type of annotation was not consistent from one copy to the next. Many readers favored simple checks and pointing hands while others engaged more deeply with the book's content. Even so, regardless of their level of complexity, marginalia bear witness to attentive reading, and as such they offer a compelling point of contact between the text and the flesh and blood of its late medieval readers.

First some caveats. By no means are marginalia in the *Handbook for Curates* perfect evidence of reader response and reception. Typically, it is impossible to identify either the annotator or when he was writing beyond an assessment of his hand. Also, although marginalia mark an individual reader's path through a text, they reveal nothing definitive about if and how the reader assimilated, let alone acted upon, the text's content. That said, marginalia in the *Handbook for Curates* bring to life the human landscape in which the book was embedded. If we ignore this landscape, as rocky as it may be, we risk sanitizing the book in the same way that libraries and booksellers used to do when they reassembled early printed books with an eye toward beauty and uniformity, bleaching away manuscript notes, trimming pages, and so on, in the process.[50]

To trace the contours of this landscape, let us begin with the questions of who was doing the annotating, when, and where. Almost without exception, the annotations in our sample are in Latin, an obvious product of the book's clerical audience, and, based on our best assessment, late fifteenth- and early sixteenth-century hands predominate. As a handful of ownership marks reveals, several copies found their way into monastic libraries while others

49. Part II, tract 4, chapter 6
50. Roger Stoddard, *Marks in Books* (Cambridge, Mass.: Houghton Library, Harvard University, 1985), 2.

stayed closer to Guido's target readers. For example, "Dominus P. Maillot, deacon" clearly inscribed his ex-libris on the back cover of a French translation of the *Handbook for Curates* printed in Orléans in 1490/1491.[51] Two inscriptions in another copy, published a decade earlier in Lyons, are even more revealing.[52] As they record, the book originally belonged to Francisco Parise; upon his death, it passed into the possession of Petri Parise, and then onto Joannus Fallaize from the diocese of Coutances in Normandy (precisely where, decades earlier, Jean Gerson had recommended the book to the newly seated bishop as a must-have for his parish clergy).[53] And finally, in 1517, Guillemus Gaudin, priest-curate, inherited the copy.

This is the most compelling example we found of multiple and successive owners of a single copy of the *Handbook for Curates*—compelling not simply by virtue of its legibility but because of what it suggests about how books circulated at the time. Book ownership was more fluid than it would become in later centuries; books were often read and reread, passing from one clergyman to another over a number of years.[54] Within this context, the fact that approximately 60,000 copies of the book were printed between 1470 and 1501 assumes even greater meaning because a single copy could have multiple owners. And with the book went the visual signposts which subsequent readers often embellished with their own. In fact, the presence of two or more annotators was extremely common in our sample, again mirroring a feature frequently found in other early printed books.[55]

51. Guido de Monterocherio, *Manipulus curatorum* (Orléans: Mathieu Vivian, 1490–1491) (Bibliothèque Sainte-Geneviève 4 OEXV SUP 5 RES).

52. Guido de Monterocherio, *Manipulus curatorum* ([Lyon]: [Nicolas Philippi et Marc Reinhart], [v. 1480]) (Bibliothèque Sainte-Geneviève 4 OEXV SUP 11 RES).

53. See n. 45 above.

54. Incunbular editions of the Latin Vulgate printed in Lyons provide one such example. Ex-libris reveal that they were owned by priests in small parishes in the area, often passing from one curé to the next. See Denise Hillard, "Les éditions de la Bible en France au XVe siècle," in *La Bible imprimée dans l'Europe moderne* (Paris: Bibliothèque nationale de France, 1999), 68–82.

55. Rosenthal, *The Rosenthal Collection of Printed Books*, 12.

So what annotations did readers use to mark their paths through the maze of a text? First and foremost, they worked within the framework of the printed page. Printers of the *Handbook for Curates* consistently provided basic tools for retrievability, including a table of contents, running headlines, and paragraph divisions. Here again, printers were simply following centuries-old techniques of manuscript production aimed at making texts more useable, particularly for clergy charged with ministering to the laity.[56] Yet as helpful as these tools were in visually highlighting the basic divisions of the book, they did nothing to guide the reader through the chapters' specific content. These limitations are especially acute when one considers the fact that some chapters in the *Handbook for Curates* run for multiple pages and include an array of instructions and points of emphasis. As already discussed, Guido's style of presentation provides plenty of signposts and lists but they are buried within the text itself. Complicating things further still, many of the copies we examined did not have numbered pages.

Readers addressed these problems by occasionally hand foliating the book, or more typically by writing convenience notes comprised of a word or summary paraphrasing keyed to the adjacent printed text.[57] Although a few annotators in our sample strayed from this pattern, writing longer, more discursive comments, they were the clear exception to the rule.[58] Despite their simplicity, con-

56. Rouse and Rouse, "New Attitudes to the Page," in *Authentic Witnesses*. Note also that Tentler cites practicality as a key characteristic of literature on confession; it was designed to be used, as revealed in "a host of devices to expedite the retrieval of information. Elaborate tables of contents, exhaustive indices, numerous cross references, careful identification and separation of specific questions, clear and orderly organization. . . . It is worth noting that a table of contents or a long index takes up paper and costs money: we must assume that the gains in usefulness were judged worth it" (p. 49).

57. Rosenthal, *The Rosenthal Collection of Printed Books*, 66.

58. While noting significant continuity over time, Jackson divides the history of marginalia in the English-speaking world into three periods. She argues that discursive notes were far less common in the first period, ending around 1700, because "readers wrote in books as part of the process of learning, whether as students under the authority of teachers or as scholars themselves contributing to the world of

venience notes visually capture and verbally express a moment of
pause in the reader's mental engagement with the book. Through
the physical act of writing the annotation, the reader likely rein-
forced the content of the corresponding text in his mind while simultaneously creating a finding aid. Underscoring, pointing hands,
and *nota* marks are equally prevalent in the *Handbook for Curates* and
likewise allowed readers to chart their course through the book
and to seek out specific information more easily at a later time.

A copy of the *Handbook for Curates* published around 1480 provides an especially interesting example of how one reader used marginalia to create a highly personalized finding device.[59] He hand-
foliated the manual and used his foliation to annotate the table of
contents, writing above certain tracts and chapter titles the corresponding folio numbers. A review of the printed text reveals that,
in turn, the reader annotated the margins of most of these chapters
with a range of visual markers—for instance, enumerating each of
the seven sacraments in the margins of chapter 1, "On the institution of the sacraments," and noting Ambrose, Paul, and Augustine
as authorities on what is required of people receiving the sacrament
of orders. In keying his foliation in the table of contents to his
annotations in the text, this reader reveals that he was not simply
reading in the moment but looking toward future use based on his
own interests and needs.

Not only do the forms of the annotations fall into patterns, so
does the type of information being annotated. Above all, the anno-

---

learning. Ordinary and acceptable additions to books consisted of notes modeled on
those of classical grammarians and editors. . . . Expressions of opinion . . . were rare:
like editors, annotators seem to have been expected to suppress private views in the
interests of cumulative scholarship" (p. 50). In this sense, by and large the annotators in our sample affirmed and stabilized the content of Guido's text and the *auctoritates* upon which it rested. Here we are borrowing from Evelyn Tribble's argument
that the margins and the text can reflect different, and sometimes fluid, relationships
of authority—from the affirmative to contested; see Evelyn B. Tribble, *Margins and
Marginality: The Printed Page in Early Modern England* (Charlottesville: University Press of
Virginia, 1993), 6.

59. Guido de Monte Rochen, *Manipulus curatorum* ([Louvain: Johannes de Westfa-
lia, 1483] [about 1475–1485]) (British Library IA.49262).

tators in our sample aimed for the practical—underlining the words to be used for the act of consecration; enumerating the types of sins priests should include in their interrogation of penitents; highlighting verses listing the circumstances of sin; noting that water is the only acceptable material of baptism. In contrast, Guido's more complex points of discussion are left relatively bare. We can only speculate as to why but would like to suggest one possibility stemming from the very nature of Guido's audience, simple priests. Certainly, as previously discussed, Guido brings his university training to bear on his manual, noting points of debate among *auctoritates*, delving into theological discussions, and the like. But does this mean that these portions of the book were beyond the intellectual grasp of average priests? Louis Binz argues that this was the case in the diocese of Geneva where around 1433, the bishop recommended the book to local clergy. In Binz's view, the bishop's expectation that the clergy would read, let alone use, the *Handbook for Curates* was idealistic at best since it was too long and too encumbered with superfluous details to be useful to priests in general.[60] The form and content of the marginalia in the *Handbook for Curates*, however, reveal how readers disentangled much of the most practical and readily applicable information from the book's more intellectually sophisticated content. As much as Guido may have wanted his readers to understand the broader symbolic and theological context of their actions, in the end, it was largely the actions themselves that seemed to have captured the readers' attention. Was this a result of a lack of training? of interest? both? Impossible to say, especially since we cannot evaluate a reader's interest solely on the basis of the presence of annotations, but at the very least, the marginalia suggest that different readers could have different strategies of engagement. Guido certainly expected as much. In both his opening and closing remarks, he underscores his efforts to simplify the complexities of pastoral care for the benefit of the "ignorant" while allowing more advanced readers to ascend toward higher things.

60. Binz, *Vie religieuse et réforme ecclésiastique*, 169–71, 347–52.

Striking patterns continue to emerge when one considers the distribution of marginalia in the *Handbook for Curates*. As already discussed, basic, practical-minded annotations dominated our sample, indicating not only that clergy read the manual but also, we think, that they intended to use it. Examining the distribution of the marginalia gives us a better sense of where the *Handbook for Curates* appears to have coincided particularly well with readers' pastoral needs. This is not to say that we can equate an unmarked page with an unused page but the predominance of marks in certain sections, and within them in certain chapters, suggests that their content resonated especially loudly among readers.

Based on our initial assessment, Part I, tract 4 on the mass and Part II on penance were the two most frequently annotated parts of the manual. To some extent, the heavy concentration of marginalia here reflects the amount of space each part enjoyed. As described above, Guido reserved his most extended discussion in Part I for the mass, and devoted an entire section exclusively to confession. Even so, when we considered marks per page, in many copies the mass and confession still came out ahead. Notable by comparison was how infrequently Part III was annotated, perhaps because as some synodal statutes attest, priests were expected to recite this information during mass directly from the text.[61]

Narrowing our focus further still, we examined twenty-two copies in our sample with moderate to heavy late fifteenth/early sixteenth-century annotations. The pattern that emerged was still more suggestive: fourteen of the twenty-two copies included manuscript notes in the chapters on who should receive the eucharist and the interrogations to be made in confession, more than in any other chapters.[62]

<hr />

61. This was the case in France, for example. See Angelo, *Les curés de Paris au XVIe siècle*, 115–18, and Nicole Lemaître, "Le catéchisme avant les catéchismes, dans les rituels," in *Aux origines du catéchisme en France* (Paris: Desclée, 1989), 28–44.

62. The closest runner-ups were as follows: 11 of 22 copies had annotations in Part I, tract 4, ch. 10, on the rite of the mass; 10 of 22 had annotations in Part II, tract 3, ch. 4, to whom people should confess; 9 of 22 had annotations in Part I, tract 1, ch. 1 on the institution of the sacraments, Part I, tract 1, ch. 2 on their virtue and

The eucharist and penance were, of course, officially at the heart of the liturgical rhythm of parish life as every adult Christian was required to confess to "his own priest" and receive the eucharist at least once a year. It is thus probably not a coincidence that readers of the *Handbook for Curates* highlighted these two chapters the most frequently because they not only spell out why it is important for priests to know who should be allowed to receive communion and how they are to interrogate penitents; they also describe the face-to-face interaction between priest and communicant, priest and penitent.

And highlight our readers did, in a straightforward, no frills fashion. As in our sample in general, the annotations in these two chapters rarely stray from convenience notes and basic marks, creating functional outlines of the content in the process. Chapter 9 on the eucharist offers a range of representative examples (see figure overleaf). Guido divides the chapter into three major topics—the ways one can receive the eucharist, what is required to do so, and who should receive it—and provides a clear transitional phrase for each. Many readers followed Guido's signposting, marking his transitions with pointing hands or repeated words. Many were also drawn to places where Guido goes beyond technicalities and includes real-life scenarios, scripts and all, which priests might encounter. For example, what should a priest do if a parishioner or subordinate whom he knows is in a state of mortal sin publicly asks to receive communion? He must grant the request, Guido insists, as "it is said that St. Bernard did. . . ." Guido continues with a story of how St. Bernard once faced a similar dilemma when communing his monks; rather than turning back the offender, he gave him the body of Christ, "saying to him in a low voice, 'May the Lord judge between me and you . . . .'" Guido uses the story to support his point while providing his readers with ammunition for their own pastoral challenges. As he concludes, "priests would do well if they tell this example and others like it to their parishioners

---

efficiency, Part I, tract 2, ch. 2 on the matter of baptism, Part I, tract 2, ch. 4 on the minister of baptism, and in Part I, tract 4, ch. 4 on the form of the eucharist.

relicerent.sicut sut multi quibz ceciderut labia et detes/et
sut toti corrosi vsqz ad guttur.Sicut legitur de quoda mo
nacho cisterciensi in vita scti ludouici quonda regis fracie
cui qn ponebatur bolus in oze:cadebat sibi bolus de oze.et
tali sie lep2oso no debet dari cozp⁹ xpi:aliis aut lep2osis be
ne pot dari.Sacerdos etia lep2osus no debet in pntia po̅
puli celeb2are.s3 si ad ptevl̅ i secretovellet:posset.Et ita in
telligo illa cap̅la.extra de cleri.ergo.et de rectozib⁹.z Tua
nos.Hugo etia dicit q̅ sacerdos lep2osus posset celebrare
aliis lep2osis pntibus.   Danatis etia ad mozte p2o crimi
nibus suis(nisi de gratia speciali)non datur vnq̅ cozpus
ch2isti sicut illis qui suspedutur vel submergitur vel com̅
burutur:vel quolibet aliter interficiutur.Illis aut qui p2o
crimine beresis comburutur si cu̅ deuotione. humilitate z
reuere̅tia petat:debet eis dari cozpus ch2isti.vt habet extra
de bere.c.Super eo.li.vi. Sed nu̅q̅d existe̅ti in pcto moz
tali dandu̅ est cozpus ch2isti∻Dicendu̅ est q̅ peccatu̅ aut e̅
notoziu̅ aut occultu̅.si sit notoziu̅ puta quia e̅ notozius vsu
rarius vel notozius concubinarius.vel quolibet alius no
tozius peccator(nisi discedat et secundum statuta ecclesie
condigne peniteat)non est ei dandum cozpus ch2isti qua̅
tu̅cu̅q3 petat:imo est sibi dice̅du̅.Amice no est bonu̅ sume
re pane̅ filiozu̅ et mittere canibus. Si aut est petitii occul̅
tum aut iste petit cozpus ch2isti tempoze quo tenetur coica
re/puta tempoze generalis co̅munionis.vel q3 est infirm⁹/
et sie de aliis casibus in quib⁹tenetur quilibet co̅municare
aut petit alio t̅p̅e.si petat alio tempoze:quantu̅cu̅q3 petat
in publico non tenetur sacerdos dare ipsum sibi: sed debet
ei dicere.Amice non est tempus co̅munieandi/et ideo non
debeo tibi dare cozpus xpi:sed expecta te̅pus statutum.Si
aut petat t̅p̅e quo tenetur co̅municare.aut petit in publico
aut in secreto.si petat in secreto:no est sibi dandu̅. imo est
mone̅dus ne petat in publico.sed si talis pertinax in mali
cia sua petat in publico dari sibi cozpus ch2isti:sacerdos de
bet ipm sibi dare.quia non debet eum p2odere.nec aliquis

Manuscript notes in a 1489 Paris edition of the *Handbook for Curates*, Part I, tract 4, chapter 9, "To whom the eucharist ought to be given," fol. 33v–34r (BnF D-8891).

debet priuari suo iure quousq3 sit declaratu ipsu3 amissise
ius suu. Et ideo cu quilib3 parochianus habeat sus petēti
corpus christi a curato suo:et curatus sit obligat9 ad dadu̅
isto tempore suis parochianis corpus xp̅i et nullus fidelis
paiuetu2 isto iure nisi per petm̅ mortale co̅missu̅ publice. ido
quantu̅cu̅q3 sacerdos sciat subditu̅ suu̅ esse in peccato mortali (nisi petm̅ sit notoriu̅) non debet sibi denegare corpus
xp̅i: si tp̅e statuto z in publico petat ipsu̅ sibi dari. Et ita le-
git fecisse btu̅s bernardus qui cu̅ quada̅ die coicaret mona
chos suos. quida̅ que̅ btu̅s bern̅. sciebat esse i pcto̅ mortali
inter alios accessit ad coicandu̅:et btu̅s bernardus dedit sibi corpus xp̅i dicens ei su̅missa voce. Iudicet dn̅s inter me z
te/quasi vellet dicere. dn̅s scit q̅ tu indigne accedis. et ego
non possum tibi negare :io̅ iudicet inter me et te. et statim
ille miser accepto corpore xp̅i cecidit mortuus. et ideo caue
at sibipnusquisq3 ne indigne accedat. non enim noceret sa
cerdoti:sed sibiipsi. et sacerdotes bene facerent: si illud exe̅-
plum et similia parochianis et subditis nunciarent. Sed
nu̅quid suspectio de crimine debet dari istud sacramenti si
requirant? Dicendum est q̅ triplex e̅ suspicio. queda̅ e̅ violenta. queda̅ probabilis. queda̅ leuis. Suspicio viole̅ta e̅ co̅
tra quam non admittitur probatio. sicut si aliquis inuenitt
cum muliere corrupta in lecto/ solus cum sola:nudus cum
nuda/loco et tempore ad hoc aptis. nec etate nec parentela
nec aliquo alio obstantibus:esset violenta suspicio seu pre-
sumptio q̅ cognouisset eam. ita q̅ no̅ admitteretur probatio in contrarium. Probabilis suspicio est illa que oritur ex
aliquib3 signis et coniecturis probabilibus. sicut si aliquis
inuenietur frequenter cum aliqua loque̅s in loco suspecto
esset probabilis suspicio q̅ aliquod malu̅ ageret. Leuis suspicio est que oritur ex fatua et inordinata suspicione alicu-
ius. Et ista dicitur leuis et fatua suspicio: sicut si videt e̅ ali
quem bonum virum et aliqua̅ bona̅ iuuenculam salutan-
tes se vel sibiinuicem ridentes non in loco vel tp̅e suspectis :
fatuu̅ ee̅t presumere q̅ male agere̅t. Et de tali dicit ialomo̅

c.iii.

By permission of the Bibliothèque nationale de France. See pp. 82–84 for our
translation of this section of Guido's manual.

and subordinates." One of the readers in our sample appears to have appreciated this advice; he marked the opening of the story in red and added a pointing hand for good measure.[63]

The annotations in the chapter on the questions to be asked in confession are equally pragmatic. Since a confessor is a spiritual judge, Guido begins, it is essential that he knows how to recognize what he ought to judge. To this end, the chapter delineates "fixed rules" concerning the seven capital vices and their branches, and includes useful verses to help confessors remember what to ask about, whom to ask, and where to go from there. Again and again, Guido's systematic approach elicited a systematic reader response, which embraced these tools of memory and retrievability. This fact reinforces a point we have already made: what the *Handbook for Curates* (and other pastoral manuals, for that matter) had to offer extended beyond its content per se; it also provided a model for a way of thinking, ordering, and evaluating information. Many readers made note of the mnemonic for capital sins, SALIGIA, for instance, and wrote the name of each vice in the margin of the corresponding discussion. Along similar lines, readers noted with pointing hands, *nota* marks, and underlining (sometimes in red) the verses to remember the circumstances of sin and how a married man can commit the sin of lust with his wife.

So in the end, where do the marginalia leave us in our quest to understand the human impact of the *Handbook for Curates?* At the most fundamental level, they breathe life into the printed page, reminding us that books are about people as much as they are about text. As such, books carry ideas and relationships across time and place, forging bridges between them. The marginalia in the *Handbook for Curates* offer palpable evidence of how readers formed just such bridges, in this case between normative expectations and daily pastoral realities in late fifteenth-century Europe. Even if we can never know if and how Guido's instructions were implemented, the huge number of printed copies in circulation combined with

63. Guido de Monte Rochen, *Manipulus curatorum* (Strassburg: [Martin Flach (printer of Strassburg)], 1499) (British Library IA.2231).

the prevalence of marginalia offer compelling evidence that his ideas mattered—not just in terms of the information they provided but also in terms of how Guido packaged them for his readers. In seeking to cultivate a clerical ethos of pastoral and theological competence in a straightforward, organized fashion, the *Handbook for Curates* stood apart from other medieval pastoral manuals. It provided an accessible and practical model for acting and thinking at a time when the ability of priests to fulfill their pastoral duties was coming under increased scrutiny. It is surely for these reasons that tens of thousands of copies were printed in the late fifteenth century and, as the marginalia attest, found their way into the hands of thousands of curates; Guido's choice of title was apt indeed.

A Note on the Translation

The translation we provide here aims to be a representative presentation of the *Handbook for Curates*. We have chosen a printed model since more readers had access to it in print than in manuscript. It is based on an early printed copy from Lyons, France, housed in the British Library (IA.41534). It is a quarto volume of 104 leaves printed around 1486 by Guillaume LeRoy. As indicated by the listing of incunable printings in *Gesamtkatalog der Wiegendrucke*, there are eleven known variations of the text of the *Manipulus*.[64] Although the differences among these versions are small, such as varied word order or the use of synonyms, the edition we selected for translation comes from the largest textual group, representing nearly half of the extant printings. Approximately two-thirds of incunable editions were printed in France, and Lyons was an early and influential French printing center. We do not know the early provenance of the book, but in the seventeenth century it was owned by Magister Ioannes Huet (Lauduneus), 1658, and Magister Adrianus de Beaurain, curé de La Ferté Superon, 1682. It contains a few marginal notes; the front and back fly leaves have various bits of information written on them that would have been useful

64. See n. 4, above.

for parish priests, such as the seven deadly sins, responsibilities of the priesthood, and the like. On the rare occasions where our chosen edition seems to be missing a sentence or to provide a mistaken reading, we have consulted a copy from another textual family (Strassburg: [Martin Flach], 1499).

Guido's text is in Latin, but his target audience needed an accessible text rather than a rhetorically elegant one. Our translation aims to keep faith with his desire for clarity and intelligibility while at the same time conveying the often plodding and repetitive nature of his wording. Although they may be challenging for the contemporary reader, these features work together in Guido's late medieval pedagogical strategy. He uses many connective words ("and," "nevertheless," "therefore," "indeed") to help the reader see that everything he says follows from what came before it. We have often broken up the resulting long sentences into several shorter ones. Similarly, Guido routinely explains himself for his readers using "namely" and "that is." When these detract from the clarity of the text, they have been omitted. Another characteristic of Guido's style is his frequent use of the passive voice—"it is to be noted that" or "as it is said in." We have often translated such phrases here in the imperative or active voice—"note that" or "as it says in." Our intention is to convey Guido's straightforwardness and authoritative authorial voice while providing a measure of fluidity to the text.

The fundamental reality that Guido wrote as a church leader for a clerical audience is evident in his choice of language. He generally uses masculine pronouns, even when men and women are equally at issue. The translation uses both "he" and "one" for an implied subject or for *homo; persona* is rendered as "person" or "an individual." In Part II on confession, we have sometimes replaced he/him with "the sinner/the one confessing/the penitent" or "the confessor" in an effort to make the text clear.

In typical medieval fashion, Guido draws on many authorities in the course of his handbook. As noted above, Scripture has pride of place, and we have endeavored to identify his scriptural citations.

Quotations are taken from the Vulgate, Catholic Public Domain Version (based on the Douay-Reims).[65] When Guido deviates from the wording of the Vulgate, probably because he is quoting from memory, we have translated Guido's words. Guido (or the printer of the copy we are using), sometimes got the book or chapter wrong when citing a biblical passage. We have let this stand in the text, but given the correct reference in the notes. We also relied on O'Connell, Finberg, and Knox's English translation of the pre–Vatican II Roman missal to guide our own translation of Guido's liturgical language in the various sections on the parts of the mass.[66]

Guido includes many references to canon law in his text. These authoritative decrees concerning church practices, expectations, and governance were gathered in several major collections. The foundational work was Gratian's *Decretum*; it was compiled around 1140 and is in three parts. Guido refers to quotations from Gratian with an abbreviation of the opening words of the section in which it is found (requiring considerable familiarity with this material), preceded by the number of the relevant distinction, canon, question, and chapter.[67] Guido also makes use of the Decretals of Gregory IX (*Liber extra* or *Liber extravagantium*), assembled in 1234 by Raymond of Penyafort,[68] the *Liber sextus* issued by Boniface VIII in 1298,[69] and

65. http://www.sacredbible.org/catholic/index.htm. This includes following the Vulgate numbering of the Psalms.

66. *The Missal in Latin and English*, trans. and ed. J. O'Connell, H. P. R. Finberg, and R. A. Knox (Westminster, Md.: Newman Press, 1959).

67. For example, *de pe.di.vi.Sacerdos*, indicates Gratian, Part II, Cause XXXIII, question III (*Tractatus de penitentia*), distinction 6, canon 2 (which begins *Sacerdos ante omnia caueat . . .*).

68. Citations to this work begin with *extra* and indicate the opening words of the title and chapter being used; *extra de bap.et eius effect.c.maiores* cites material from the Decretals of Gregory IX, Book III, Title XLII (*De baptismo et eius effectu*), chapter 3 (section beginning *Maiores ecclesiae causas . . .*). Guido's tract on marriage is especially dependant on this work.

69. Guido's citations to this work also begin with *extra*, as this work was seen as the "sixth book" of the *Liber extravagantium*, the books of law beyond Gratian; Boniface VIII is often named in the text.

the constitutions of Clement V from the Council of Vienne, promulgated by John XXII in 1317.[70] In the places where Guido cites one of these sources explicitly in his text, we have included the citation in the modern format and corrected it when applicable.[71] In the tract on marriage, Guido also cites several collections of Roman law; these references too are given in modern format.[72]

When it comes to other authorities, again we have sought to retain the character of the *Handbook*. On many topics, Guido's teaching and the questions he raises are quite traditional (e.g., the appropriate age for confirmation). It is often difficult to name particular sources beyond the tradition as a whole. Guido will say, "appropriate reasons are usually given by the doctors. . . ." His readers are expected to value the weight of this tradition, not to actively analyze it. Thus when Guido says, "as the doctors say . . . ," we have not attempted to track down the source. Specific authorities are most often quoted when differing opinions are offered. When Guido cites the author and title of a work from which he has drawn a quotation, we have endeavored to footnote it, directing the reader to Migne's *Patrologia latina* (abbreviated as PL) and/ or to a modern edition.[73] Quite often, Gratian is the source of Guido's quotations. If the quotation comes from an author predating Gratian, we have checked for it in Gratian and included a footnote when found. Guido also lifts quotations from Raymond of Peynafort's *Summa* and various works of Aquinas; again, when we have found a quotation in these sources, we have provided a footnote. For the benefit of contemporary readers who are not familiar with key figures and texts cited in the Scholastic theological tradition, we have compiled a list of those Guido includes with a very brief description of them in the appendix.

70. Guido generally indicates this collection with the phrase "in the constitutions of Lord Clement."

71. The citations that include sets of Roman numerals seem especially prone to typographical errors, quite likely compounded on the part of the printer.

72. For an introduction to the conventions covering canon and Roman law citations, see Brundage, *Medieval Canon Law*, 190–205.

73. Jacques Paul Migne, ed., *Patrologiae cursus completus . . . Series Latina*, 217 vols. 1844–1865. Reproduced Cambridge: Chadwyck-Healey, 1996–2006 (full-text database).

Guido of Monte Rochen

HANDBOOK FOR CURATES

This book is called *Handbook for Curates*.

Author's Letter

To Reverend Father in Christ and the Lord, Lord Raymond, by divine providence Bishop of the holy see of Valencia, Guido of Monte Rochen, the least of your devoted servants, entrusts to you all his services with devout and humble recommendation. The fount of the wisdom ordaining and disposing all things with a miraculous disposition, the word of God, has ordered and disposed the church militant toward the image of the church triumphant. This was figuratively shown by the lawgiver Moses when the command was given to him to build the tabernacle in the desert according to the model which was shown to him on the mountain. The tabernacle constructed in this way in the desert is, in fact, the church militant ordered toward the image of the Jerusalem on high. Indeed, this suggests that the foundations of the church militant are on the mountains of the holy prophets,[1] with high mountains indicating the prelates, the successors to the apostles, who are spiritually at the top of the hierarchy. Those at the top [serve] those in the middle and those in the middle those at the bottom, namely, prelates illuminate, perfect, and cleanse, so that as those in the middle are illuminated by those above them, made holy, perfected with virtues, and purged of errors, in a similar way, they may illuminate, perfect, and cleanse the lesser seculars, namely, laypeople, which they will be unable to do unless they are given instruction in divine doctrine. Therefore, paying attention to these things and examining vigilant practice, I have composed this lit-

---

1. Ephesians 2:20

tle work of instruction for neophyte curates, in a plain but useful style, not caring about ornate words, but about what is fitting and helpful to souls. I have brought forth this little work and dedicated it to you who are a splendid luminary in the most holy church, who shines like a lamp shining in the firmament of the church militant, who with a ray of divine wisdom and the example of a most holy life and the file of correction charitably illuminates, perfects, and cleanses your subordinates, so that it may appear in public polished by the file of your correction, since without that, it would not dare to appear. Therefore, Father, receive with goodwill this little work which humility offers, affection accompanies, and charity prompts, and, corrected and emended, if it seems appropriate in your judgment, share it with neophyte, that is, novice, curates so that those who are ignorant may learn further, and those who do know may rejoice in knowing and ascend to higher things. May the Lord preserve your reverend person, to whom I humbly recommend myself.

Written in Teruel, in the year of our Lord 1333.

Prologue

Because according to what the prophet Malachi says in chapter 2, or rather what the Lord says through Malachi, "the lips of the priest preserve wisdom and knowledge, and they ask for the law from his mouth"[2] (C.11 q.1 c.41). Indeed, "he is an angel of the Lord of hosts."[3] Concerning this, lest that which the Lord threatened to a certain priest of the Mosaic law through the same prophet, saying, "Since you have rejected knowledge, I will drive you away; you do not perform the duties of the priesthood for me,"[4] happen to priests of the evangelical law, I have brought forth in writing something appropriate for the instruction of neophyte priests, especially curates, through which they can guide themselves in the execution of their office and how to rightly minister before their God, namely, Christ. But let no one accuse me of the rashness of presumption that I, an ignorant and uninformed sinner, presume to instruct holy priests who are professors of holy law. Yet confident of the help of him who opened the mouths of the mute and made the eloquent tongues of infants to speak, like a little dog who with its barking incites great hares to run, I will try to write something briefly so that I may give in writing to the more accomplished and skillful material concerning higher and more subtle and more useful things. For I am confident that he who gave speech to Balaam's ass[5] will fill me, his rational creature, with knowledge. And let not venerable priests blush to be taught by me, the least of their servants, but let them consider that word of the outstanding doctor Augustine, which is included in the decretals

2. Malachi 2:7   3. Malachi 2:7
4. Hosea 4:6   5. Numbers 22:28

(C.23 q.3 c.1), "I am already old and sixty years of age, yet I would not blush to be taught by a boy a year old." Indeed as Seneca says, although it may be shameful for old men to learn more, even so it is more shameful for them to be ignorant, because if someone wants to carry out his office rightly, he ought to know those things which pertain to his office. And the office of the priest, and especially of curates, consists in four things according to the fourfold etymology of the name priest [*sacerdos*] offered by the Damascene. Because priests [*sacerdotes*] are the celebrators of mass, priest can mean "saying holy things" [*sacra dicens*]. Because they are ministers of the sacraments, priest can mean "giving holy things" [*sacra dans*]. Because they are hearers of confession, priest can mean "sacred guide" [*sacer dux*]. Because he is the teacher of the people, priest can mean "teaching holy things" [*sacra docens*]. Therefore, on account of the first, they ought to have enough knowledge that they know how to read correctly and clearly those things which are contained in the office of the mass, also how to pronounce and accentuate appropriately, and at least how to understand grammatically. On account of the second, they ought to have enough knowledge that they know the number of the sacraments, and what is the right form and right matter of each sacrament, and the correct way to administer them, especially concerning the sacraments in which they are watched. On account of the third they ought to have enough knowledge that they know how to discern between leprosy and leprosy, that is, between sin and sin, and how to impose salutary penances. On account of the fourth they ought to have enough knowledge that they know at least how to instruct the people in the articles and other rudiments of the faith.

I am setting aside the first because it deals with grammar and I am confident enough that the lord bishops will not promote anyone to the order of priesthood unless he is sufficiently initiated into grammar, and because this will be dealt with when the sacrament of the eucharist is treated. The other three are to be treated in this little book. I wanted this little book to be called *Handbook for Curates*, because priests, especially curates, ought to have this little book in their hands, so that they may see the things which ought to be done pertaining to their office. Here ends the prologue.

The division of this book

This little work is divided into three parts. The first deals with the sacraments and the things which pertain to the administration of the sacraments. The second deals with penance and the things which pertain to the hearing of confession and the imposition of penances. The third deals with the articles of the faith and the things which pertain to the teaching of the people. As for the first part, first some things will be considered about the sacraments in general, next about each one in particular. As for the sacraments in general, first their institution is to be examined, second their efficacy and power, third their number and distinctiveness. Then each one will be taken up individually. First the sacrament of baptism will be examined, second the eucharist, third confirmation, fourth penance, fifth orders, sixth extreme unction, seventh the sacrament of marriage.

PART I: THE SACRAMENTS AND THEIR ADMINISTRATION

Tract 1 of the first principal part is on the sacraments in general.

CHAPTER 1: On the institution of the sacraments

Know that all the sacraments of the new law were directly instituted by Christ, which the doctors prove this way: To whom belongs the giving of any law belongs the instituting of its sacraments. Since Christ was the direct founder, institutor, and giver of the new law, as the Apostle amply proves in the epistle to the Galatians, and is given by Isaiah, saying, "The Lord is our king, the Lord is our lawgiver; he himself will come and save us,"[1] therefore it belongs to Christ alone to institute the sacraments of the new law. Hence he instituted the sacrament of baptism when he received baptism in the Jordan by John.[2] Indeed, as Bede says, "By the touch of his most pure flesh he conferred regenerative power on water."[3] Although he instituted the sacrament of baptism then, no one was obligated to receive baptism until after the resurrection, namely, when on the day of his ascension he said to his apostles and other disciples, "Go forth to the whole world and preach the Gospel to every creature. Whoever will have believed and been baptized will be saved. Yet truly, whoever will not have believed will be condemned."[4]

1. Isaiah 33:22
2. Matthew 3:13; Mark 1:9; Luke 3:21
3. Cf. D.4 de cons. c.10, attributed to John Chrysostom.
4. Mark 16:15–16

He instituted the sacrament of confirmation when he placed his hands on the heads of the children and said to the apostles who would have prevented it, "Allow the little ones to come to me."[5] Although some doctors say that he instituted the sacrament of confirmation on the day of Pentecost when he visibly sent the Holy Spirit on the apostles, I think the first is truer.

He instituted the sacrament of the eucharist on the day of the Last Supper, when, after eating the paschal lamb, he converted bread and wine into his body and blood by his ineffable power, saying, "'Take and eat. This is my body.' And taking the chalice, he said, 'Drink from this, all of you. This is the chalice of my blood.'"[6]

He instituted the sacrament of penance when he began the start of his most life-giving preaching, saying, "Repent for the kingdom of heaven has drawn near."[7] And that sins should be confessed to priests he instituted figuratively when he commanded the ten lepers cleansed by him, saying in Luke 17, "Go show yourselves to the priests."[8] Although sins are forgiven in contrition, by the testimony of the prophet Ezekiel in chapter 18, who says in the person of Christ, "At whatever hour the sinner bewails all his iniquities, I will remember them no more,"[9] nevertheless, sins are still to be confessed to priests if the opportunity arises.

God instituted the sacrament of orders when on the day of the Last Supper after he communed the apostles, he said to them, "Do this in commemoration of me."[10] Indeed then, according to the doctors, he ordained all the apostles. Truly Christ instituted the sacrament of orders in a sevenfold way since there are seven orders. Four are not holy and are minor as are doorkeeper, lector, exorcist, and acolyte; and three are holy and major, as are subdeacon, deacon, and priest. All these are said to be one sacrament because they are ordered principally toward one, namely, the priesthood. He instituted the order of doorkeeper when he made a whip out

5. Mark 10:14
7. Matthew 4:17
9. Cf. Ezekiel 33:12; 18:22

6. Matthew 26:26–28
8. Luke 17:14
10. Luke 22:19; 1 Corinthians 11:24

of cords and threw the buyers and sellers out of the Temple.[11] He instituted the order of lector when, reading the words of Isaiah, he preached, saying, "The Spirit of the Lord is upon me; because of this, he has anointed me. He has sent me to evangelize the poor."[12] The order of exorcist he instituted when he commanded demons to leave those possessed.[13] The order of acolyte he instituted when in preaching he said, "I am the light of the world."[14] And the order of subdeacon he instituted when after supper he washed the feet of his disciples.[15] He instituted the order of deacon when he warned the disciples, just like the Levites, to keep watch.[16] He instituted the order of priest when he supplied his body and blood to his disciples saying, "As often as you do this, do it in memory of me,"[17] and as he offered his body and blood to the Father on the altar of the cross, he himself as the sacrifice.

Truly he instituted the sacrament of extreme unction when he sent the apostles to anoint and heal the sick.[18] Here some doctors say that St. James instituted this sacrament when he said in his letter, "Is anyone ill among you? Let him bring in the priests of the church, and let them pray over him, anointing him with holy oil."[19] But, with all due respect, I do not think they are right for the reason stated at the beginning of this chapter. Indeed I believe that that saying of St. James was not the institution of the sacrament but its promulgation. Hence St. James was not the institutor of this sacrament but only its promulgator.

There is doubt about when the sacrament of marriage was instituted and whether it was instituted by Christ incarnate, since marriage existed in the state of innocence and in the time before the incarnation. Therefore, to resolve these doubts, know that marriage can be considered in three ways—in one way as it is an office of nature; in the second way as it is a remedy for carnal lust,

11. Matthew 21:13; Mark 11:15; Luke 19:45   12. Isaiah 61:1–2; Luke 4:18
13. E.g., Luke 4:33–36   14. John 8:12
15. John 13:4–10
16. Matthew 26:38–43; Mark 14:34–38; Numbers 1:53
17. 1 Corinthians 11:25   18. Matthew 10:1–8; Luke 9:1–6
19. James 5:14

since carnal lust is satisfied in marriage; in the third way as it is
a sign of the union of certain things, namely, of Christ and the
church, which the union of the souls of man and wife signifies,
and the union of human and divine nature in the person of the
son of God which the union of bodies signifies. Marriage, considered in the first and second ways, is not a sacrament as we are
speaking here about the sacrament of marriage. But considered in
the third way, it is a sacrament and was instituted as such by Christ
when, in the Virgin's womb, he wanted to unite our nature with
the divine nature in the unity of his own subject or person, which
union marriage signifies. Just as in the act of marriage the husband
and wife are two in one flesh, so the two natures, namely, human
and divine, are in one person, namely, in the person of the Son.

CHAPTER 2: On the efficacy and power of the sacraments

On the efficacy and power of the sacraments, know that the
power of the sacraments in general (the power of each one in particular will be discussed later) consists in two things, namely, in
removing guilt and in conferring grace. Indeed each of the sacraments of the new law, unless there is an obstacle, that is, an impediment on the part of the recipient, removes guilt if it is found
and confers or augments grace. And by this, the sacraments of the
new law differ from the sacraments of the old law, because the sacraments of the old law, with the exception of the sacrament of
circumcision, had no power with respect to the removal of guilt
and the gathering of grace on the part of the work done [*operis ope-
rati*], but they had all their power and efficacy on the part of the
action of the agent [*operis operantis*]. But the sacraments of the new
law have efficacy not only on the part of the work done [*operis ope-
rati*], but also on the part of the action of the agent [*operis operantis*]. The devotion of the recipient of the sacrament is called the
work of the agent [*opus operantis*]. The action done around the sacraments is called the work done [*opus operatum*], as the work done
[*opus operatum*] in baptism is the sprinkling or immersion in water

and the utterance of words. That the sacraments of the new law, on the part of the one doing the work [*operis operantis*], confer grace and are a cause of grace is clear from the definition of a sacrament offered by the Master of the Sentences in Book iiij, where it is said, "A sacrament is the sign and visible form of an invisible grace in such a manner that it is a sign of the grace of God and the form of invisible grace so that it bears its image and is its cause."[20] But whether the sacraments of the new law are the *sine qua non* cause of grace or the cause *propter quam* requires study with fuller investigation than the present little work requires.

Other powers belong to the sacraments of the new law as well because some of them imprint character on their recipients, namely, the sacraments of baptism, confirmation, and orders. And character is a certain special power through which the recipient of the sacrament can do or receive something which he could not before, as one baptized can receive the other sacraments of the church which the nonbaptized cannot do; and the ordained can exercise the office of his order which the nonordained cannot do; and one confirmed is obligated to boldly confess the faith of Christ in time of persecution for the faith which the nonconfirmed person is not obligated to do, unless perhaps he is particularly scrutinized about the faith.

But the other sacraments, namely, eucharist, penance, marriage, and extreme unction, do not imprint such a character because they can be repeated many times, as a man can communicate, confess, and be anointed many times, and when one wife has died can contract marriage with another. But the sacraments which imprint character should not and cannot be repeated, as no one ought to be baptized or confirmed or ordained to the same order twice. And the reason is that their power always remains, namely, the character which is indelible.

20. Peter Lombard, *Sententiarum Quatuor Libri*, Bk. IV, d. 1, c. 4; see http://www .franciscan-archive.org/lombardus/opera/ls4-01.html.

CHAPTER 3: On the number and distinction of the sacraments

As for the number of the sacraments, know that the sacraments are seven, namely, baptism, confirmation, eucharist, penance, extreme unction, orders, and marriage. The distinction among these sacraments is given by the sufficient [reason] of certain doctors which is this: As it is in bodily life, so, in its own way, it ought to be in spiritual life. And in bodily life, we see that first man is born, second he grows, third he is fed, fourth he comes to such perfection of strength that he can generate children like himself, and thus humankind is multiplied. And because human health can be impeded by infirmity, a person needs a double medicine, one against infirmity, the other against the remnants of the infirmity. And as in bodily life five things are necessary, namely, birth, growth, food, multiplication, and medicine, so in a similar way in the spiritual life, which is the life of the faithful, living in the faith and unity of the church, five things are necessary, namely, spiritual birth which is done in baptism through which one is regenerated in Christ; spiritual growth which happens in confirmation in which baptismal grace is augmented; spiritual food which is given in the eucharist which is spiritual food for the soul. And because the faithful need to multiply spiritually and bodily, for spiritual multiplication the sacrament of orders is received, through which the ministers of the church are multiplied. As for bodily multiplication, the sacrament of matrimony is received which is intended for the bodily multiplication of the faithful. The spiritual medicine against spiritual infirmity, which is sin, is penance; the other spiritual medicine is against the remnants of sin and is extreme unction. And these things are about the sacraments in general.

Tract 2 of the first principal part is on baptism.

CHAPTER 1: What baptism is and why it is so called

Now each sacrament in particular is to be discussed. And first about baptism, concerning which eight things are to be considered. First, what baptism is; second, its matter; third, the form; fourth, the minister; fifth, the recipients; sixth, the rite of baptism; seventh, its effect; eighth, the things added to it.

Baptism is the exterior washing of the body done with the prescribed, that is, fixed, formula of words, so that this material washing which is done on the outside of the body is a sign of the spiritual washing which God does inside on the mind. And it is called baptism from "to baptize" (*baptiso, -as, -are*) which is the same as "to wash" (*abluo, -is, -ere*). Hence "baptism" in Greek is the same as "washing" in Latin.

CHAPTER 2: On the matter of baptism

The matter of baptism is simple elemental water. And you have the whole reason why this water is the proper matter of baptism in the institution of Christ who instituted baptism to be done in water. But if he had instituted baptism in wine or in some other liquid, the wine or the other liquid would be the proper matter of baptism. Nevertheless, some fitting reasons are usually given by the doctors for why Christ instituted baptism to be done in water rather than in another liquid.

The first of these is that the sacrament of greatest necessity ought to have the most common matter, lest on account of lacking the matter someone should be kept from receiving baptism. But baptism is the sacrament of greatest necessity because without baptism, no one can be saved. Therefore, so that no one can excuse himself from receiving baptism on account of lacking the matter or on account of its cost, baptism ought to have the most common matter. And such matter is water, which is found in any land and can be had easily. Indeed someone might excuse himself if the matter of baptism were wine or oil or some other more expensive liquid which is not found in every land, nor could be had easily.

Another fitting reason or explanation is that the nature of water is especially suited to baptism, for water is cleansing for the dirty, cooling for the hot, and clear to the gaze of the eye. Similarly baptism cleans away the dirt of the soul; therefore it is called baptism, because "baptism" in Greek means the same as "washing" in Latin. Hence to baptize is the same as to wash. Again, baptism cools the heat of carnal lust; it also illuminates the eyes of the mind for considering divine knowledge. Therefore the doctors assert thus: That thing is the proper matter of baptism whose nature especially fits baptism; water is this kind of thing, therefore water is the proper matter of baptism.

Whether the water is blessed or not does not matter for baptism because one can be just as well baptized in nonblessed water as in blessed. But the baptismal water in church is blessed on account of the solemnity and great reverence surrounding baptism.

But can baptism be done in rose water or in brandy or in other distilled spirits if elemental water cannot be found? The answer must be no, because such waters are not proper waters, but the humors of the bodies from which they are distilled.

If, however, water cannot be found, baptism may be done in lye, since lye is nothing other than water put through ashes. And for the same reason, some doctors say that baptism may be done in urine when water is lacking, which I do not believe is true, because urine is not water but a humor released from food eaten. And I say the same thing about saliva. But can baptism be done in meat broth when other water cannot be found? The answer is that either so much rendering of the meat is done in that broth that it stops being the species of water and becomes another species newly generated, and then baptism cannot be done; or not so much rendering of the meat has been done in it, and then it can be done, and one can be baptized in such broth. But when such rendering has been done and when it has not can be assessed by the consistency. For if the consistency of this broth is like that in meat or a little softer, I do not believe that it is possible to baptize in this broth. But if it is not of such a consistency, but the broth is greasy, I believe that then one can baptize in that broth. And I say the same thing about mud, namely, if water is squeezed out of it, baptism can be done in that squeezed-out water. Also if snow is melted, baptism can be done in that melted-snow water.

It is customary that this question be asked by some: If there were a child to be baptized near a deep well, and he who ought to baptize him does not have anything with which to draw the water from the well, and cannot get any other water, and the child is in danger of death, should he throw the child into the well, saying, "I baptize you in the name of the Father, and of the Son, and of the Holy Spirit, Amen"? The answer must be no, because according to what St. Paul says, "Evil deeds ought not to be done that good may result."[21] Therefore, although good will come of this because the soul of this child will be saved, nevertheless he who would throw the child would do such evil that he would sin mortally, and, to the degree that he is in his right mind, would damn his own soul. And anyone, according to the beginning of charity, ought to love his own soul more than that of anyone else. And if it is claimed that such a one can confess this sin, and thus would not damn his own soul, the answer is that this is foolish to say because no one is certain of his own life. Hence this person is not sure that he will not die immediately after having thrown the child or even in the act of throwing itself. Hence to have such hope is, strictly speaking, to tempt God, because it is certain that if such a one were to throw the child, he would sin mortally, but it is uncertain if God will give him the time to repent. This is why one should act according to the counsel of St. Augustine, saying, "Hold on to what is certain and let go of the uncertain."[22]

And note that it makes no difference for baptism if the water is

21. Romans 3:8
22. D.7 de pen. c.4; this is from Caesarius of Arles, Sermon 63, "De paenitentia ex dictis sancti Augustini"; see Caesarius of Arles, *Sancti Caesarii Arelatensis Sermones*, vol. 103, Corpus Christianorum Series Latina (Turnhout: Brepols, 1953), 272.

hot or cold, but danger to the one being baptized is always to be avoided.

CHAPTER 3: On the form of baptism

Concerning the form of baptism, know that the Greeks use one form in baptizing, and the Latins another. Indeed the Greeks use this form, "The servant of Christ is baptized in the name of the Father, and of the Son, etc." But the Latins use this form, "I baptize you in the name of the Father, and of the Son, and of the Holy Spirit, Amen." And although baptism results from either form, for the Greeks are baptized as are the Latins, which is clear because those who return to the unity of the Roman church are not rebaptized, nevertheless, the form of the Latins is more appropriate than the form of the Greeks. This point is made clear in two ways.

It is clear in the first way because the more appropriate form of baptism is that which better accords with the words of Christ instituting baptism. But Christ instituting baptism said to the apostles, as St. Matthew recites in his gospel in the last chapter, "Go forth and teach all nations, baptizing them in the name of the Father and of the Son and of the Holy Spirit."[23] And since the words "I baptize" better accord with these words than "is baptized" do, because "I baptize" is active and "is baptized" is passive, and the participle "baptizing" derives from the active and not from the passive, this is why the form of the Latins which says "I baptize" is more appropriate than the form of the Greeks which says "is baptized."

Second, the same thing can be shown this way: That form of baptism is more appropriate in which and through which those things which are necessary in baptism are expressed. But such is the form of the Latins in comparison with the form of the Greeks because in baptism the power of God is necessary, conferring the ef-

23. Matthew 28:19

ficacy of baptism. This is touched on in both forms when "in the name of the Father, and of the Son, and of the Holy Spirit, Amen" is said. It is also necessary to have in it the person receiving baptism, and this is expressed in the form of the Greeks when "servant of Christ" is said, and in the form of the Latins it is expressed when "you" is said. And it is also necessary to have in it the person of the baptizing minister, which is not expressed, at least not explicitly, in the form of the Greeks. But in the form of the Latins, it is expressed explicitly in that "I baptize" is said. This is why the form of the Latins is more appropriate than the form of the Greeks. And the very same form which is used by the Roman church, which is the head and teacher of all the churches as the Lord arranged it (X 3.42.3), is more appropriate than any other. Therefore the obligatory form for baptism is, "I baptize you in the name of the Father, and of the Son, and of the Holy Spirit, Amen."

But should the person to be baptized be named or his name be added or placed before "I," saying, "Peter or Maria, I baptize you in the name of the Father, and of the Son, and of the Holy Spirit, Amen"? This is not essential to the form, because baptism can be done without this. Nevertheless it ought to be put into the form for better expression, although it is not necessary that it be placed there. And this form can be offered in Latin or in any other tongue.

But can anything be changed about this form? Know that he who changes something either intends to change the rite of the church, and then it would not be baptism, or he intends to do the same thing the church does, but out of some ignorance or inattention changes something about this form. In this case, know that such a change can be made in five ways. In one way, by totally omitting its words. Then baptism is not accomplished with such a form, such as if one should say, "I baptize you in the name of the Begetter, and of the Begotten, and of the One proceeding from both." Although in the common way of speaking, "Begetter" means the Father and "Begotten" the Son, and "the One preceding from both" the Holy Spirit, nevertheless, properly speaking about divine beings, "Begetter" and "Begotten" and "One proceeding" expressly signify intellectual conceptions of the persons rather than the persons themselves. But in the form of baptism express mention ought to be made of the persons.

In another way, change can be made in the form of baptism by transposing the words of the form itself, such as if one said, "Baptize you I in the name of the Father, and of the Son, and of the Holy Spirit, Amen," or by any other transposition. And then since the sense of the words remains the same, baptism is not impeded.

In another way, change can be made by adding something to the form itself, and when such an addition corrupts the sense of the words of the form, as Arius changed the form by saying, "I baptize you in the name of the greater Father, and of the lesser Son, and of the Holy Spirit," then baptism is not accomplished.[24] Or, such an addition does not corrupt the sense of the words of the form, so that notwithstanding such an addition the sense of the words remains the same, and then if he who adds something intends to change the form, he accomplishes nothing, since he does not baptize in the faith of the church. But if he does not intend to change the church's form, but out of some foolish devotion adds something like saying, "I baptize you in the name of the Father, etc. and of the Virgin Mary," or "May the Blessed Virgin help you," or something else similar, such an addition does not impede baptism.

In another way, the form of baptism can be changed by leaving something out from it. And then if a whole word is left out, whenever it is one of all these, "I baptize you in the name of the Father, and of the Son, and of the Holy Spirit, Amen," nothing is accomplished, because all these words are essential to the form. But if a whole word is not left out, but a part of a word, then either such an omission is made in the beginning of a word, such as if from this word "of the Father" [*patris*], or some other, the first letter or syllable were removed, such an omission impedes baptism because it takes away the sense of the words. But if such an omis-

---

24. Cf. D.4 de cons. c.109

sion is made from the end of a word, such as if from this word "of the Father" [*patris*] the "s" were removed, or some such, such an omission does not impede baptism since the sense of the words remains the same. As is told in the decretals (D.4 de cons. c.86), a certain priest, not knowing the Latin language, baptized under this form, "I baptize you in the name of the fatherland [*patria*], and the daughter [*filia*], and the Holy Spirit [*Spiritus sancta*]." And the pope says in that decretal that he truly baptized.

In another way, change can be made in the form of baptism by interrupting the words of the form. In this case, if the interruption is such that it changes the intention of the one baptizing, as if in the morning he were to say, "I baptize you," and then he went to conduct his business, and later when he returned he would say, "in the name of the Father, etc.," he would accomplish nothing. But if the interruption is not such that it changes the intention of the one baptizing, as if he were to say, "I baptize you in the name of the Father," and this having been said, he says to those standing there, "Be quiet, pray to God," or some such thing, and then finishes, the baptism is not impeded.

CHAPTER 4: On the minister of baptism

The minister of baptism is twofold. The first is outside the case of necessity, and this is the priest alone. Indeed, outside the case of necessity, it belongs to the priest alone to baptize. The reason for this is given by the doctors this way: He is the proper and ordinary minister of the sacraments who has power over the true body of Christ. But such is the priest. Therefore the priest alone is the proper and ordinary minister of the sacraments. And that the administration of the sacraments belongs to him who has power over the true body of Christ is proved thus: The government of the mystical body of Christ, which is the church, that is, the congregation of the faithful, belongs to him who has power over the true body of Christ. But such is the priest. This is why it belongs to the priest alone to dispense or administer the sacraments.

The other minister of baptism is in case of necessity, and this can be either a man or a woman, either a believer or an infidel. Indeed this distinguishes baptism from the other sacraments, since the minister of baptism, but not the minister of other sacraments, can be someone other than a priest. And the reason for this is that baptism, but not the other sacraments, is the sacrament of greatest necessity, because without baptism no one can be saved. Truly, without the other sacraments many are saved. The doctors, therefore, assert thus: That sacrament which is of such necessity that without its reception no one can be saved ought to have a minister so common that no one may be excused from its reception on account of the lack of a minister. But the sacrament of baptism is of such necessity that without its reception no one can be saved, as Christ our savior says in John, chapter 3, "Unless one has been reborn by water and the Holy Spirit, he is not able to enter into the kingdom of God."[25] Therefore the sacrament ought to have a common minister so that no one on account of the lack of a minister may be excused from receiving baptism. And so in case of necessity, either man or woman, either believer or infidel (like Jew, pagan, heretic) may baptize, as long as he baptizes in water and offers the required words of the form of baptism, and has the intention of doing that which the church does, even though an infidel may believe it does no good. Nevertheless, it is always to be deferred to the more worthy person, other things being equal. Hence an infidel in the presence of a believer ought not to baptize. Also a woman ought not to baptize in the presence of a man. One not promoted to holy orders ought not to baptize in the presence of one promoted. Likewise a layperson ought not to baptize in the presence of a tonsured cleric. And the reason for these things is that he who baptizes, baptizes in the person of Christ and represents his person, which is more perfectly represented by a believer than by an infidel, by a man than by a woman, by one promoted than by one not promoted, and by one tonsured than by one who

25. John 3:5

is not tonsured. Yet know that in the one who baptizes, the intention to baptize, namely, of doing what the church intends or does, is always required; otherwise it is not a baptism even though the other things necessary for baptism are there. It is not required by necessity that the one baptizing intends the baptism to avail for eternal life for the one baptized; indeed with the contrary intention, namely, with the intention that the baptism should avail for nothing, baptism can still be done. Indeed it is required only that the one baptizing intends to do that which the church does, whatever that may be, and it avails as baptism. But what if an actor or someone else in jest should sprinkle water on some unbaptized persons, saying "I baptize you all in the name of the Father, etc."? Are such baptized? The answer is that either he intends to baptize by intending to do what the church does, although he makes his tricks and mockeries about this, and then such a one, although he sins gravely by disrespecting the sacrament, nevertheless truly confers baptism. But, if in his mind he does not intend to do that which the church does, he accomplishes nothing.

In case of necessity, can someone baptize himself? The answer is that this case is discussed in a certain decretal beginning *Debitum* (X 3.42.4) where it tells about a certain Jew who on account of fear of the Jews did not dare to summon a believer, but taking water said, "I baptize myself, etc." On this point, note that baptism is threefold. First, namely, of flowing water, when someone is baptized in water, and this baptism is the sacrament of the church, and it is about this that we speak here. And speaking of this baptism, no one can baptize himself. The reason is given by the pope in that decretal: Because baptism is a certain spiritual birth, and just as no one can give birth to oneself bodily, as St. Augustine says in the book *On the Trinity*, "No one can give birth to himself bodily,"[26] so no one can give birth to himself spiritually by baptizing himself.

And there is another baptism, namely, of fire, when the Holy

---

26. Augustine, *De Trinitate*, Bk. I, c. 1 (PL 42: 820).

Spirit invisibly cleanses and washes someone's soul from sin. And with this baptism, someone (a nonbaptized adult) can baptize himself by disposing himself toward the grace of God and by having the desire for baptism and intending to receive the sacrament of baptism if he should have the opportunity. Hence if he were to die in such an intention, he would be saved. And this is not against the sentence which was cited above, "Unless one has been born again etc.,"[27] because "born again by water" is to be understood as applying to children in actuality, but to adults in actuality or in vow, although with this [baptism] one is not born again by water in actuality, nevertheless one is by vow.

And there is another baptism, namely, of blood, when someone who is not baptized undergoes death for the faith of Christ. And such baptism avails for salvation as long as water baptism is present in vow, if the one who undergoes death is an adult, as was the case in the legend of St. Katherine for the rhetoricians who were converted by her preaching and whom the emperor burned. But if the person is not an adult, such a vow is not required, but death endured for Christ suffices, as it was with the Innocents.[28] And with such a baptism no one can baptize oneself, because no one is allowed to kill oneself for any reason. Nor is this contrary to the examples of Samson[29] and Josiah[30] who killed themselves, because as St. Jerome says, their deed is not to be drawn out to its consequence, because "the privileges of a few do not make common law."[31]

Further, is goodness of life required in the minister of baptism, namely, that he be without mortal sin? It must be said that this question is to be understood as applying to the priest, because, as has been said, he is the proper minister of baptism. Hence, in answer to this, it is to be said that as far as the effect of baptism is concerned, the goodness or badness of the minister makes no difference, because whether he is good or bad, true baptism is con-

---

27. John 3:5
29. Judges 16:28–30
31. C.26 q.2. c.4

28. Matthew 2:16
30. 2 Chronicles 35:20–24

ferred, as has been said. But concerning the minister, does he sin or not by baptizing? The answer is that either the priest baptizes someone in case of necessity without any solemnity, as an old woman would do, and then he does not sin mortally if he baptizes while being in mortal sin. Or, he baptizes outside a case of necessity and with solemnity, and then he sins mortally if he baptizes while being in mortal sin, because he shows irreverence for the sacrament. It is true that Lord Durandus, a certain bishop of Le Puy-en-Velay, who was a doctor of the sacred palace, says in his sacramentary, that any priest baptizing while in mortal sin sins mortally.[32] But whether his opinion is true, I do not know, but I do know that it is very hard.

Know especially that the minister of baptism ought to be one person. And the reason commonly given by the doctors is that the one baptizing baptizes in the person of Christ, who is one, and therefore the person of the baptizer ought to be one. Hence several are not able to baptize one. And if it is claimed that one can baptize several by saying, "I baptize you [plural] in the name of the Father, etc.," say that this is not the same, because when "I baptize you [plural]" is said, it is the same as if "I baptize you and you" were said. But when "We baptize you" is said, it is the same as if "I and you, we baptize you" were said, because there is a difference between "we" and "you [plural]," because "we" is the same as "I and you," and "you [plural]" is the same as "you and you." Therefore by saying "you [plural]," nothing is changed in the form, but by saying "we," something is changed in the form.

But it is customary to pose this case: suppose that here are two [priests], one is mute and the other is maimed, and there is a child to be baptized. The mute one sprinkles him with water and the maimed one offers the words. Is such a child baptized? It must be specified whether these baptize in the form of the Greeks or of the Latins. If they baptize in the form of the Latins, then some doc-

32. Durand of St. Pourçain, *Petri Lombardi Sententias Theologicas Commentariorum*, Bk IV, d. 5, q. 2. A reprint of a 1571 edition is available (Farnborough, Hants, U.K.: Gregg Press, 1964).

tors say that such a child is not baptized, because, as has been said, in whatever form one baptizes, the baptizer baptizes in the person of Christ. As St. John the Baptist says speaking about Christ, "He who sent me to baptize himself said to me, 'the one on whom you see the Spirit descending, he is the one who will baptize.'"[33] But the person of Christ is one. Hence Athanasius, "Not two, but one is Christ,"[34] which is why it is necessary that he who baptizes be one in whatever form he may baptize. But other doctors, like John Scotus and his followers, say that if they baptize in the form of the Greeks, the child is baptized because, as has been said, although he who baptizes baptizes in the person of Christ who is one person, nevertheless he baptizes in the name of the Trinity in which there are several persons, and thus it is not contrary to baptism according to the form of the Greeks if there are several persons baptizing. Which of these opinions is true I know not, but in my judgment, the pope, to whom greater questions, especially those concerning the articles of faith, are to be referred should be consulted about this (X 3.42.3). [But if they baptize in the form of the Latins, these commonly say, like all the doctors, that they do not baptize][35] on account of the above mentioned reason concerning the difference between "we" and "you [plural]," which is the reason of the venerable doctor St. Thomas Aquinas in the last part of his *Summa*.[36]

Such a reason is also given by Master Herveo Britone: In the sacrament of greatest truth nothing ought to be falsified.[37] But baptism is the sacrament of greatest truth, therefore in baptism nothing ought to be falsified. But if these were to use the form of the Latins which the Roman church uses, to those involved, it

33. Cf. John 1:33

34. Athanasian Creed.

35. This phrase is missing in our chosen edition, but is found in the other edition we consulted as a basis of comparison (see the Introduction, p. xlii). We have added it for the sake of clarity.

36. Aquinas, *Summa Theologiae*, Bk. III, q. 67, a. 6; English translation available at http://www.newadvent.org/summa.

37. Hervaeus Natalis, *In quatuor Libros sententiarum commentaria*, Bk IV, d. 3, q. 2. A reprint of a 1647 edition is available (Farnborough, Hants, U.K.: Gregg Press, 1966).

would be a falsified baptism, because if the maimed one said, "I baptize you," that is, "I wash you," he would lie because he does not wash, indeed the mute one does this, which is why it is clear that such a baptism is void. But some doctors endeavor to resolve this issue, saying that if the maimed one did not say "I baptize you," but said, "We baptize you," he would thus not speak a falsehood but the truth, because this prayer, "We baptize you," is true through synecdoche. It is as if there were two writers who wrote one book, so that one wrote one half and the other the other half. One of them could truly say, "We wrote this book." In a similar way, since the mute one in such a baptism sprinkles or pours the water, and the maimed one offers the words, either one can say, "We baptize you." But this does not work, because in order for one of two propositions to be verified via synecdoche, it is necessary that both acts be done for the same reason, for if the acts were done for different reasons, one proposition cannot be verified concerning both. For instance, if one scraped the parchment from which the book was made, and the other wrote the book, this proposition, "We wrote this book," could in no way be verified concerning them. So also it is to be said concerning this phrase, "We baptize you," because to pour the water and to say the words are actions done for different reasons; therefore in no way can the said proposition be verified concerning them.

CHAPTER 5: On those receiving baptism

Both men and women ought to receive baptism, because without baptism, either in actuality or in vow, as has been said, no one can be saved. But it is one way for adults and another for children, because in an adult who receives baptism one's own intention to receive that which the church confers is required, because no one is born again of water and the Holy Spirit, at least in adults, unless one desires it of one's free will (as in D.4 de cons. c.141).[38] But

38. See also D.4 de cons. c.1.

in a child, the faith and intention of those offering him for baptism suffice.

But can someone be baptized in his mother's womb? For instance, if a woman pregnant with a child is in danger of death, should the child be baptized in her womb? The answer is no. The reason for this is given by the doctors thus: Because one who receives baptism ought to receive it from the hands of a minister of the church and be sprinkled with water or immersed, and this cannot be done to one in his mother's womb, thus one who is in his mother's womb ought not nor can be baptized. See the beginning of D.4 de cons. c.115 where it says that he who is not yet born of Adam cannot yet be regenerated according to Christ (and D.4 de cons. c.35).

But suppose that some part of the child should appear outside the womb. If there is fear of the danger that such a child cannot be expected to be fully born, can it be baptized? It depends on that part which appears outside—either it is the head or some other part of the body. If it is the head, it ought to be sprinkled with water saying, "I baptize you in the name of the Father etc.," and the child is truly baptized. And if he should be born later he ought not to be baptized further. And the reason is that the head is the principal part of the body and in it flourish all the senses of the body. But if that part which appears is other than the head, like a hand or a foot, then some doctors say that that part ought to be sprinkled with water and be baptized, and then the child is truly baptized, and if he should be born, he ought not to be baptized further. And the reason is that baptism is done on account of the soul and not on account of the body. And the soul, with respect to its essence, is complete in the whole and complete in whatever part of the body. Therefore when one part of the body is baptized, the whole is baptized, and if the child should be born later, he ought not to be baptized further. But others say that the part that appears outside ought to be sprinkled with water and baptized, but if the child should be born later, he ought to be baptized under this form, "If you are baptized I do not baptize you. But if you are not baptized, I baptize you in the name of the Father, and of Son, and of the Holy Spirit, etc." Which of these speaks more truly, I do not know, but nevertheless I believe that this last is safer.

But, if someone were to be sanctified in his mother's womb, should he be baptized? The answer is yes. Not on account of any guilt he might have, but so that he may be written into the number of the faithful by receiving the character of baptism, and so that he might fulfill the law of Christ concerning the reception of baptism.[39]

But should the little children of the Jews be baptized against the will of their parents? It is to be said that some doctors, like John Scotus and Lord Durandus, bishop of Le Puy-en-Velay, and their followers, say yes. For they say that the princes and lords of the lands in which Jews live can take their children away from them and have them baptized against their will, since the Jews are their servants, and according to the law, the children of servants belong to the lords whose servants they are; thus it is that they can sell or strike them. Therefore they argue thus: It is a greater thing to be able to bind or sentence someone to the servitude of some temporal lord than to servitude to God whom everyone by natural law is obligated to serve. But lords of the lands in which the Jews live can sell the children of the Jews and hand them over to another lord against the will of their parents; therefore they can hand them over to the servitude of Christ against the will of their parents, which is done by the reception of baptism. Truly other doctors, like St. Thomas Aquinas and his followers, say that the little children of the Jews are not to be baptized against their parents' will, and this is on account of the danger which might arise when these children who were baptized against their parents' will become adults. Since offspring naturally follow their parents, perhaps these will deny their baptism and return to Judaism. Indeed it is very likely that if the little children of the Jews were to be bap-

39. Cf. Matthew 3:14–15

tized against the will of their parents, the most Christian emperors and kings who lived earlier and were so zealous for the faith would have forced the children of the Jews to be baptized, and also the highest pontiffs would have induced the kings and princes in whose lands the Jews lived to do this. Which of these is truer, I leave to the judgment of the reader.

But should the mad and the insane be baptized? The answer is that those who are mad either were mad from birth so that they never had the use of reason, or they sometimes had the use of reason but lost it for some reason. If they were mad from birth, they are not to be baptized, because, as has been said, in an adult faith and devotion are required for receiving that which the church confers. But such people cannot have faith or intention since it is supposed that they never have had the use of reason. Therefore such are not able to receive baptism. But if they were mad from birth, but sometimes had the use of reason or sometimes have lucid intervals or times, then, in a time in which they have a lucid interval or the use of reason, if they have faith and devotion for baptism and they ask for it, they should be baptized, even if it is necessary that it be done while they are mad. But if in a time when they have the use of reason or in a time in which they have a lucid interval, they do not have faith and devotion for baptism and do not ask for it, they ought not to be baptized. And I say the same thing about demoniacs, because if before they were demoniacs they had faith and devotion for baptism and asked to be baptized, they ought to be baptized. But if they did not, they ought not to be baptized. The same judgment applies to one who is frantic.

Should someone sleeping be baptized? The answer is that if he can be woken up, he ought not to be baptized in his sleep, but if he cannot be woken up, then it is to be determined as above, because either when he was awake he had devotion for baptism and asked for it and then he ought to be baptized, or he did not have faith or devotion for baptism and then he ought not to be baptized.

But what if there is a monstrosity that has two bodies joined together? Should he be baptized as one person or as two? I say that since baptism is done on account of the soul and not on account of the body, even if there are two bodies, if there is only one soul, he ought to be baptized as one person; but if there are two souls, he ought to be baptized as two persons. But how is it known whether there is one person or two? I say that if there are two bodies and two heads, assume that there are two souls; but if there is one head, there is one soul. And therefore if there are two chests and two heads, assume that there are two souls. But if there is one chest and one head, however many other members are multiplied, there will be one soul.

CHAPTER 6: On the rite of baptism

Baptism is done in two ways; in one way by immersing in water, in the other way by sprinkling with water. But which is better? The answer is that unless there is fear of danger either on account of the weakness of the one baptizing or of the child or something else, it is better done by immersing in water than by sprinkling. The reason for this is that baptism signifies the burial of Christ. Hence the Apostle says, "For through baptism you have been buried with Christ."[40] But burial is better represented when it is done by immersion than when it is done by sprinkling.

Know that everyone ought to observe the rite of the church and ought not to change it. But is immersion or sprinkling required three times or does once suffice? The answer is that once suffices (D.4 de cons. c.85). But other things being equal, it is better done three times (D.4 de cons. c.78 and the gloss), because baptism is given in the name of the whole Trinity which is better represented by three immersions or sprinklings than by one; nevertheless the words are not to be finished before all three are complete. But in this matter of whether it is done once or thrice, each ought to observe the rite of his church.

40. Romans 6:4

CHAPTER 7: On the effect of baptism

The principal effects of baptism are to remove all guilt, original as well as actual, and to confer grace, and to open the entrance of the heavenly kingdom. In this it differs from circumcision, because, although before the passion of Christ circumcision removed original guilt and conferred grace, even so it was not able to open the entrance of the heavenly kingdom. And this is the judgment of the venerable Bede who says in his homily on the circumcision of the Lord, "It should be known among your brotherhood that circumcision once worked the same salvific curing remedy under the law against original sin, which now, in the time of the revelation of grace, baptism is wont to do, with the exception that it could not open the entrance of the heavenly kingdom."[41]

Know that baptism works one way in children and another in adults, because in children nothing is required on their part, but in adults it is required on their part that they not impose an obstacle, that is, that they not have a contrary disposition, namely, that they not come to baptism falsely, but come with due devotion.

And not only does baptism confer grace, but indeed to all receiving it, both children and adults who do not pose an obstacle, it further confers all the virtues, both theological and moral, and if not as far as use, at least as far as habit. And this is the judgment of the general council, and it is found in the constitutions of Lord Clement V (Clem.1.1.un).

And there is yet another effect of baptism, because through it a spiritual relationship is contracted which impedes the contracting of marriage and ends one subsequently contracted;[42] concerning this more will be said when marriage is dealt with. Also, through baptism character is impressed, as was said above; therefore baptism ought not to be repeated. Indeed the penalty according to the law for one who repeats it should be decapitation (Cod. 1.6.2), but,

41. Bede, *Homilies on the Gospels*, 1.11, On the Octave Day of Christmas.
42. See note 234.

according to the canons, the actual penalty is that one may not be promoted to sacred orders.

CHAPTER 8: On the things added to baptism

When baptism is done with due solemnity, catechism and exorcism precede it. Catechism is the same as instruction, because in catechism the one to be baptized is instructed concerning the faith and the reward of faith. Hence the priest asks the one about to be baptized, "What do you ask from the church?" And he, if he is an adult, replies, "Faith." But if he is a child, the godparents respond on his behalf. And then the priest asks, "What will faith offer you?" And they reply, "Eternal life." Then the priest says, "This is eternal life, etc."[43]

And in this catechism, the priest does three things. First, he puts his fingers in the candidate's ears and puts some of his saliva into his mouth, and this signifies that the one to be baptized ought to have ears open for hearing the word of God and the lessons of the faith. The putting in of saliva signifies that he ought to be prompt in speaking about the faith, because speech is done with the help of saliva. Second, he makes the sign of the cross on the candidate's forehead and chest [and mouth] and so signifies that the one to be baptized ought to have and receive the faith of Christ in his heart, which the cross made on the chest signifies, and to confess faith in Christ with his mouth. And he ought not to blush at the faith of Christ, which the cross made on the forehead signifies because shame appears immediately on the forehead, because, according to what the Apostle says in Romans 12, "With the heart, we believe unto justice; but with the mouth, confession is unto salvation."[44] Third, he puts salt in the candidate's mouth which signifies wisdom; according to the teaching of the Apostle in Colossians 3, every word of his ought to be seasoned with the salt of divine wisdom.[45]

43. John 17:3   44. Romans 10:10
45. Colossians 4:6

Exorcism is the same as adjuration, because the demon is adjured to depart from the soul of the one to be baptized and to give place to the coming Holy Spirit. And here the priest does three things to the one to be baptized. First, he makes the cross on his forehead with his thumb and this signifies that the one to be baptized is sealed so that he may be a temple of God or a dwelling place of the Holy Spirit.[46] Second, he makes the cross on him with spit on the ears, nose, and mouth and so signifies that the one to be baptized ought to have the ears of his heart closed, lest he hear the suggestions of the devil. He also ought to have a closed mouth, lest he speak evil words. And he ought to live so that there may be, according to the teaching of the Apostle, "the good odor of Christ"[47] in his life, or this signifies that he ought to send out the smoke of devout prayer through which the demon is put to flight. According to the word of Raphael in Tobit, chapter 4, "Its smoke puts to flight all kinds of demons."[48] And he does this with spit, that is, with the power of Christ which is signified by spit, according to what the gloss says on John 9, "He made mud out of spit."[49] For as spit is sent out from the inner parts of the heart, so the Son of God was begotten out of the substance of the Father. Third, he makes the cross on the candidate with the oil of exorcism on the chest and between the shoulders, and this signifies that the one to be baptized ought to be strong for fighting against the devil and for bearing heavy penances, and that these are done with the help of the oil of divine grace.

After baptism, the priest also does three things to the one baptized. First, he anoints him with chrism and this signifies the strength of the grace of the Holy Spirit which he receives in baptism. Second, he hands him a white garment, and this signifies baptismal innocence. Third, he hands him a burning candle, and this signifies the light of faith which is given in baptism. Further, know that these things do not belong to the essence of baptism,

46. 1 Corinthians 6:19   47. 2 Corinthians 2:15
48. Tobit 6:8
49. John 9:6 (on the gloss, see the appendix).

because without these baptism can well be given in case of necessity. But in such a case, if the one baptized lives, he ought to be brought to the church and there be catechized and exorcised, according to the rite of the church being followed. But he ought not to be baptized again if it is certain that he was rightly baptized. But if it is not certain, he ought to be baptized under this form, "If you are baptized, I do not baptize you. But if you are not baptized, I baptize you in the name of the Father, and of the Son, and of the Holy Spirit, Amen."

And let these remarks suffice about baptism.

Tract 3 of the first principal part is on confirmation.

CHAPTER 1: What confirmation is

Because spiritual growth follows spiritual birth, therefore after having discussed the spiritual birth which happens in baptism, it remains to speak of the spiritual growth which takes place in confirmation. Concerning which seven things are to be considered: First, what confirmation is; second, the matter of confirmation; third, its form; fourth, its minister; fifth, those receiving confirmation; sixth, its rite; seventh, its effect.

Confirmation can be defined thus: Confirmation is a signing done with chrism by the bishop on the forehead of one baptized, with a certain form of words, for the purpose of boldly confessing the name of Christ.

CHAPTER 2: On the matter of confirmation

The matter of confirmation, as is clear from the aforesaid definition, is chrism. In this chrism there are two things, namely, olive oil and balsam. And the reason why these two are the matter of this sacrament is the institution of Christ, who instituted these two things to be the matter of this sacrament. Although indeed it is not found in the gospels that Christ instituted this sacrament, nevertheless St. Peter, who was the vicar of Christ and pastor and rector of the universal church, taught, preached, and promulgated that Christ instituted it. And although this promulgation is not found in the epistles, that is, in the letters of St. Peter, yet the lord pope has it in the decretals of the Roman church, and it can be found in the earliest observance of the whole universal church from the time of St. Peter up until now, which observance exceeds any other authority since the universal church is ruled by the Holy Spirit and cannot err. And if someone grumbles, "Why did the evangelists not put the matter and the form of the sacraments in the gospels?," St. Dionysius responds to this in his book, *On the Celestial Hierarchy*, saying that the evangelists were unwilling to do this lest the matter and form of the sacraments should come under the derision of infidels,[50] because, according to what the Savior says, pearls are not to be thrown before swine.[51] Nevertheless, it is otherwise with baptism because baptism is the sacrament of the greatest necessity, since without baptism no one can be saved. Therefore it was necessary that its form be common and manifest to all. Therefore the evangelists put it expressly in the gospels.

Nevertheless, the reason assigned by the doctors why chrism is the proper matter of this sacrament is that in chrism, as has been said, there are two things, namely, olive oil and balsam. And their properties are especially well suited to this sacrament. Because olive oil is the fuel of brightness and therefore is placed in lamps so that the light can continue there, so oil is the sign of the greater vow and light of faith, which faith the one confirmed ought to have before others, because he is expressly obligated to offer himself to persecutors of the faith and to confess the faith, even without it being required. Hence confirmation is spoken of in the Psalm, "I have found David, my servant," in reception of baptism, "I have anointed him with my holy oil," in confirmation, "for my hand will assist him,"[52] under persecution for the faith. And balsam, by

50. Guido may be confusing the *Celestial Hierarchy* with the *Ecclesiastical Hierarchy*; cf. Aquinas, *Summa Theologiae*, Bk III, q. 72, a. 4.

51. Matthew 7:6

52. Psalm 88:21–22a

reason of its fragrance, signifies the odor of good reputation and esteem, which ought to be found in one confirmed. Hence in Ecclesiasticus, chapter 23, "I gave forth a spicy smell like cinnamon and balsam."[53] Therefore the doctors assert thus: That thing is the proper matter of the sacrament of confirmation whose properties especially fit the effect of the sacrament itself; but these, namely, olive oil and balsam, are of this type, therefore these are the proper matter of the sacrament of confirmation.

And first, know that these ought to be sanctified or blessed by the bishop before they may serve as the proper matter of this sacrament. The reason for this is given by St. Thomas Aquinas in his fourth [book]: For the sacraments which Christ received in his body, sanctification of their matter is not required, because he, by the touch of his most holy body, sanctified them.[54] And therefore because Christ was baptized, it is not required of necessity for the sacrament that the water first be blessed before it may be the matter of baptism, because as Bede says, "Christ, by the touch of his most clean flesh, conferred the power of regeneration on water."[55] And because Christ received the sacrament of the eucharist in himself, it is not required that the bread and wine first be blessed before they may be the matter of the sacrament of the eucharist. But in those sacraments which Christ did not receive in himself, it is required that sanctification of the matter come first. And because Christ did not receive the sacrament of confirmation in himself, therefore, for confirmation, consecration of the matter is required. And I say the same thing concerning the sacrament of orders and the sacrament of extreme unction. Another reason is given by the same doctor in the last part of his *Summa:* Because in those sacraments in which a specially consecrated minister is required, it is required that the matter of the sacrament be con-

53. Ecclesiasticus 24:20 [Ecclesiasticus is also known as Sirach.]

54. Cf. Aquinas, *Scriptum super Sententiis,* Bk 4, d. 7, q. 1, a. 2 (http://www.corpusthomisticum.org/iopera.html); and *Summa Theologiae,* Bk III, q. 72, a. 3. The latter seems to be a better match.

55. Cf. D.4 de cons. c.10, attributed to John Chrysostom.

formed to the minister of the sacrament. But in the sacrament of confirmation, a specially consecrated minister is required, namely, the bishop, which is why in the sacrament of confirmation specially consecrated matter is required.[56] This sacrament cannot be done with other matter.

CHAPTER 3: On the form of confirmation

The form of this sacrament is the words that the bishop says when he makes the cross with chrism on the forehead of the one being confirmed. The words are these, "I sign you with the sign of the cross. I confirm you with the chrism of salvation, in the name of the Father and of the Son, etc." And it is clear that this form is a suitable form for this sacrament, because this form is a suitable form for the sacrament through which and in which those things which are necessary for the sacrament of confirmation are expressed. In confirmation the person of the minister conferring the sacrament is necessary, and this is expressed when "I sign and I confirm, etc." is said. And it is especially necessary to include the person receiving the sacrament, which is expressed when "you" is said. And it is also necessary to include the matter of the sacrament which is expressed when "with chrism" is said. And it is especially necessary to include the power of God conferring efficacy to the sacrament, which is expressed when "in the name of the Father and of the Son, etc." is said. The effect of the sacrament is also expressed in this form, but this will be seen below when its effect is considered. This is why it is clear that this form is the suitable form for this sacrament.

CHAPTER 4: On the minister of confirmation

The minister of this sacrament of confirmation is the bishop alone. The reason for this is assigned by the doctors thus: As it is in a well-ordered corporeal commonwealth, so, in its own way, it

56. Aquinas, *Summa Theologiae*, Bk III, q. 72, a. 3 and a. 11.

ought to be in the spiritual commonwealth. But as it is the case in a well-ordered corporeal commonwealth that to promote someone to a status and degree of excellence over others belongs to him who has charge of the community, namely, to the prince, therefore, because one confirmed by the sacrament of confirmation is placed in a state of excellence above others, since the one confirmed is made a soldier of Christ, it belongs solely to the bishop, who has charge of the whole community in his diocese, to confer the sacrament of confirmation.

But, in case of necessity, can someone other than the bishop confirm? It must be said that in this matter the doctors disagree with one another. Some say that the pope can grant to any Christian permission to administer the sacrament of confirmation. And they give this reason: He who holds the place of Christ on earth and has fullness of power in the church of God can arrange in all the sacraments the things which were not instituted by Christ, but it is not read in the entire canon of the New Testament that Christ instituted the sacrament of confirmation to be given by the bishop alone. Therefore the pope, who has fullness of power in the church and holds the place of Christ, can order that this sacrament be conferred by persons other than bishops.

Other doctors say the opposite, namely, that the pope cannot grant to anyone, unless he be a bishop, permission to confer the sacrament of confirmation. Their reason is that those things which belong to the sacrament by necessity cannot be changed by the pope in any way; but the bishop, of necessity to the sacrament of confirmation, is the minister of this sacrament. Therefore it cannot be done by just anyone, for instance, that someone other than the bishop confer that sacrament. The major premise of this reasoning is conceded by all; the lesser is proved because since it is of necessity that its matter be sanctified, and no one can change this, so it is of necessity for the sacrament that its minister be sanctified, which sanctification is done in spiritual or episcopal consecration. This is why the bishop alone, of necessity, is the minister of this sacrament.

Yet other doctors hold a middle position, saying that the pope cannot grant to just any Christian permission to confer this sacrament, but he can commit it to every priest. And they give the reason for the first statement that it can be committed to no one to have power over the mystical body of Christ, at least for the administration of the sacraments, unless he has power over the true body of Christ, because power over the mystical body of Christ derives from power over the true body of Christ. But only the priest has power over the true body of Christ, therefore to the priest alone can it be granted that he have power over the mystical body of Christ, and this by administering the sacraments. But, in giving the sacrament of confirmation, power is exercised over the mystical body of Christ, which is why permission can be granted only to the priest to be the minister of the sacrament of confirmation. They give the reason for the second statement from a certain decretal in which it is read that Pope Gregory granted to certain English priests that they might anoint those baptized in the faith with chrism.[57] But by such anointing, the sacrament of confirmation is conferred, which is why permission can be granted by the pope to priests to confer this sacrament. And I think this last is truer.

CHAPTER 5: On those receiving confirmation

All the baptized, both men and women, ought to receive the sacrament of confirmation because it is different for spiritual soldiers than for worldly soldiers. Whereas a worldly army ought not to receive women, but only men, because women are not suited for bodily fighting, yet the spiritual army can receive all without distinction, both men and women, because both men and women are suited for fighting spiritually against persecutors of the faith. But spiritual soldiery is given in confirmation, which is why this sacrament can be received by both men and women. And this is what the Apostle says, "In Christ Jesus there is neither male nor fe-

57. D.95 c.1; cf. Aquinas, *Summa Theologiae*, Bk III, q. 72, a. 11.

male,"[58] as if he wanted to say that for Christ there is no difference between male and female.

But are children to be confirmed? The answer is yes, as soon as they begin to have the use of reason, because then they are fit for confessing the faith of Christ. And in this sacrament, the Holy Spirit is given for strength, so that the faith of Christ may be boldly received and confessed.

But can one, without sin, neglect ever to receive the sacrament of confirmation? It must be said that without this sacrament, one can be saved, because many who are not confirmed are saved. But, if the opportunity for receiving the sacrament occurs, everyone ought to receive it. And if one neglects to receive it without reasonable cause, he sins mortally. The reason for this is that anyone, as much as is in him, ought to dispose himself for the reception of grace or its increase, if he is able. But, in the sacrament of confirmation, if it is worthily accepted, grace is conferred or increased. Therefore, whoever has the opportunity, ought to receive this sacrament. For this reason, priests having care of souls ought to prepare their parishioners so that when the bishop comes to the parish they may receive this sacrament.

CHAPTER 6: On the rite of confirmation

The rite of this sacrament of confirmation is that when someone is confirmed, he is anointed with the sign of the cross with chrism by the bishop on his forehead under the form of words given above, namely, "I sign you, etc." And this rite is appropriate. The reason is that in the rite of a sacrament, the power and effect of the sacrament ought to be signified. Now the power and effect of the sacrament of confirmation are that through it the Holy Spirit is given for boldly confessing the faith of Christ, and through it, the one confirmed is made a fighter for Christ. And this is signified in the rite of this sacrament, for through anoint-

58. Galatians 3:28

ing it is signified that by confirmation the one confirmed is made a fighter for Christ, for long ago fighters were anointed.

And through the other [part of the rite], it is signified that the one confirmed ought to boldly confess the faith of Christ. For one can be hindered from confessing Christ on account of two things, namely, on account of shame or on account of fear. Against the first, the cross is made with chrism on the forehead of the one confirmed, so that, it is easy to see, he should not blush to confess the faith of Christ, because shame first appears on the forehead, since when a person is ashamed, the forehead begins to turn red first. Therefore the forehead is anointed against the blush of shame. But against fear, the sign of the cross is also made on the forehead, because when a person is afraid, his forehead and even his whole face begin to turn pale. Therefore, the one confirmed is armed against fear with the sign of the cross.

The slap on the cheek which is given to the one confirmed does not belong to the sacrament of necessity, but is given only to aid the memory. And the place of anointing ought to be wrapped with a clean linen cloth on account of reverence for the sacrament.

CHAPTER 7: On the effect of confirmation

The effect of this sacrament is, as has been said, that the Holy Spirit is given for strength and boldness for confessing the name of Christ and faith in him. Hence, unless there is an obstacle, that is, an impediment on the part of the recipient, in this sacrament new grace is given or old grace is augmented. And there is also another effect of this sacrament, because through it, if it is well and worthily received, forgotten mortal sins and venial sins are forgiven.

Also through this sacrament, character is impressed, as was said above; therefore this sacrament ought not nor can be received twice. Indeed one who knowingly receives it twice deserves decapitation according to the law, as was said above about baptism. And know that the character of confirmation presupposes the character of baptism, because no one can receive this sacrament unless he has been baptized.

Also through this sacrament, a spiritual relationship is contracted, as through baptism, which impedes the contracting of marriage and breaks off one subsequently contracted. This will be discussed below when marriage is dealt with.

And let these remarks about the sacrament of confirmation suffice.

Tract 4 of the first principal part is on the sacrament of the eucharist.

CHAPTER 1: What the eucharist is and why it is so called

After having spoken of the spiritual birth that happens in baptism, and the spiritual growth which happens in confirmation, the spiritual food which is given in the sacrament of the eucharist is to be discussed. Concerning which eleven things are to be considered: First, what the eucharist is; second, concerning the minister of the eucharist or mass, who and of what kind ought he to be; third, concerning the matter of the eucharist, what and of what kind it ought to be; fourth, the form of the eucharist; fifth, in what place the mass ought to be celebrated; sixth, the time at which the mass ought to be celebrated; seventh, how often the mass ought to be celebrated in a day; eighth, the vestments which the priest ought to put on in the mass; ninth, to whom the sacrament of the eucharist ought to be given; tenth, the rite of the mass; lastly, problems which can occur in the mass.

The eucharist can be made known this way: It is the sacrament of the body and blood contained under the species of bread and wine by the power of the words spoken by the priest. It gets its name from "*eu*," which is "good," and "*caros*," "grace," because contained in it is he who is the source of grace, namely, Christ, "from whose fullness we all receive grace,"[59] as it says in John, chapter 2.

---

59. John 1:16

CHAPTER 2: On the minister of the eucharist

The minister of the sacrament of the eucharist, that is, the minister who can and ought to celebrate the mass, is a rightly and lawfully ordained priest, not living in a state of mortal sin, and to whom celebrating has not been prohibited.

I say "who can and ought" because many can celebrate who ought not, like heretical or excommunicated or schismatic or demoted priests, because if they celebrate, they truly confect the body of Christ, yet they sin mortally in saying the mass, and not only those who are celebrating, but also those who hear their mass, if they are notorious as such.

I say "rightly and lawfully ordained" because no one except he who is rightly and lawfully ordained into the priesthood can celebrate the mass. Nevertheless, understand that someone can be not rightly or lawfully ordained in two ways. In one way when in his ordination something which is of the essence of the order or ordination is neglected, such as not being ordained by a bishop, or when they ordained him they did not lay hands on him or the chalice was not handed over to him, or the one ordaining did not say the required and stipulated words or did not have the intention to ordain. Such a person cannot celebrate at all, because such a one is not a priest. In the other way, namely, when in his ordination everything belonging to the essence of the order or the ordination is observed, but something is neglected among those things which belong to the solemnity of the order or the ordination. And such a person can indeed celebrate, yet I believe he ought not to, especially if the omission was due to his own negligence. But what is essential to the order or the ordination and what belongs to the solemnity is not for present consideration, because to know this pertains more to the bishop than to the simple priest.

I also say "not living in a state of mortal sin" because no one living in mortal sin ought to celebrate the mass. Nevertheless, note that someone can be understood to be in mortal sin in two ways; in one way so that he is in notorious sin, in the other way so that he is in hidden mortal sin. In the first way, if he is a notorious heretic, schismatic[or]excommunicate, simoniac, or fornicator, not only does he sin in celebrating, but so do all who hear his mass. And the reason is that these four crimes are especially incompatible with this sacrament. For in this sacrament is the secret of faith; therefore heretics are excluded. And it is the bond of charity; therefore schismatics and the excommunicated are excluded. It is also the vessel of grace, hence it is called the eucharist; therefore simoniacs who buy and sell grace are excluded. In particular, it raises one to a spiritual state; therefore notorious fornicators who are all carnal are excluded. And they are designated notorious fornicators, not on account of suspicion or other probable signs, but because they are condemned of such a crime according to the order of law, or have confessed voluntarily in court, or are canonically convicted, or are so notorious on account of the evidence created when it happened that witnesses are not needed since it cannot be hidden by any subterfuge.

If he is in hidden mortal sin, know that someone can be understood to be in hidden mortal sin in three ways. In one way because he has already committed, or he knows that he has committed in the past, some mortal sin concerning which he is not sorry, does not repent, nor is contrite; and such a one celebrating thus not only sins mortally, but most mortally. And concerning such the Apostle says that "whoever eats and drinks unworthily eats and drinks a sentence," namely, of eternal death, "against himself."[60]

In another way, someone can be in hidden mortal sin because he committed some mortal sin which has not been confessed, but he does not remember this sin. And if such a one diligently examined his conscience before he set himself to celebrate, and was unable to remember this sin at all, and intends to confess the sin if he remembers it and to do penance for it, and is contrite in general over all his forgotten sins, then he does not sin by celebrating. Indeed, by virtue of the sacrament of the mass, he merits mercy and is

60. 1 Corinthians 11:29

absolved of that sin. And thus is that word of the outstanding doctor Augustine to be understood, that this sacrament brings the dead to life,[61] that is, those who celebrate in this way while living in mortal sin. Nevertheless if such a one later remembers the sin, he is obligated to confess it. And therefore anyone, before he sets himself to celebrate, is obligated to diligently examine his conscience to see if he is in mortal sin or not. And so teaches St. Paul, saying, "Let every man test," that is, examine, "himself, and then eat of the bread and drink of the cup."[62] But if one living in mortal sin that he does not remember sets out to celebrate before he has examined his conscience in any way, I believe that he sins, because he is a transgressor as the law of the Apostle already noted, namely, that every man should test himself, etc.

In a third way, someone can be in mortal sin because he remembers clearly that he has committed some mortal sin, but then at the moment he either has the services of a confessor or not. If he does, he is obligated to confess before he celebrates, and unless he confesses, he sins mortally in celebrating. Nor does the general confession made in the beginning of the mass suffice for him, because this confession extends only to venial sins and not to mortal ones, especially to those which a man remembers. But if such a one does not have the services of a priest or if the need to celebrate is immediate, for instance, if he is a curate and it is Sunday or a solemn day and the people committed to him want to hear mass, and there would be a scandal among the people unless he celebrated, or perhaps one of his parishioners is dangerously ill and he asks the priest to give him the body of Christ and he does not have any consecrated hosts which he could give, or if some need to celebrate is immediate for him, like a wedding or some such, in these cases and the like, he is obligated to be contrite and repent of his sin and to intend to confess it when he has the opportunity. Then let him say mass in the name of the Lord, because Christ who is the high priest absolves him, but let him confess later when he has

61. D.2 de cons. c.70
62. 1 Corinthians 11:28

the services of a confessor. But if there is no immediate necessity for this one who is living in mortal sin to celebrate, as has been said, in no way should he set about celebrating, because without a doubt, if he were to celebrate, he would sin most mortally.

But suppose that some priest receives money from someone so that he should say a requiem or some other mass. Does such a priest have such a legitimate need to celebrate that he can celebrate while living in mortal sin without confessing, when he does not have the services of a confessor? I say, saving better judgment, that it seems to me that no priest ought to accept money for saying mass in such a way that his intention is that the mass equals the price in money. Yet according to what the Apostle says, "If we sow spiritual things in you, is it surprising if we harvest from your worldly things?"[63] it is not prohibited when a priest, for the sustenance of his life, not for the price of a mass, receives money from him for whom he says the mass, especially when the priest does not have sufficient pay for the sustenance of his life. But does such reception of money constitute a legitimate need to celebrate, excusing him, so that one who is living in mortal sin can celebrate the mass without sin if he does not have the services of a confessor, even without it being the case that he would confess [if he had the services of a confessor]? I say, saving better judgment, that either this priest is obligated, by reason of the benefice conferred on him by his superior or by him who has the right of patronage in that benefice, to say mass on any day, as are those who have perpetual vicarages in some church. And concerning such, it seems to me that the same thing is to be said that I said above concerning the curate who has an immediate need to celebrate, namely, that he should be contrite and repent of his sin and intend to confess, and then let him celebrate in the name of the Lord and confess when a confessor is available to him. Or, this priest receives money for saying some other individual masses; as there are many who receive money for rogation masses, so too [he may be paid] for one mass, or for many requiem masses, or [for the mass] of the Holy Spirit,

63. 1 Corinthians 9:11

or of the Blessed Virgin, or for the sick, etc. And in this case I say that the one living in mortal sin should in no way set out to say mass before he confesses, because he would sin mortally in saying it. Nor should one in such a case receive money for saying mass right away: indeed he ought to excuse himself by saying, "Friend I am not well disposed at the moment for saying mass, but when God wills that I be disposed, I will willingly do what you ask." And if the other insistently asks him to say mass immediately, if he has received money he ought to return it to him immediately and in no way set about celebrating.

And I said, in the aforesaid description about who and of what kind the minister of the mass ought to be, "to whom celebrating has not been prohibited," which I said on account of some religious, who, according to the statutes of their order, are prevented from celebrating as long as they are doing some penance for their past sins.

But can an angel be the minister of this sacrament, that is, can an angel minister or consecrate? The answer is that no angel, neither good nor bad, can celebrate or consecrate, because it is not able to receive sacerdotal character. Indeed order presupposes baptismal character, hence no one can be ordained into the priesthood unless he is baptized. Therefore the doctors assert thus: No one can receive baptismal character unless he has been baptized. But an angel cannot be baptized, because it is necessary that he who is baptized be sprinkled with water, but an angel cannot be sprinkled with water since it is not a corporeal being. Therefore it cannot be baptized and, as a consequence, cannot be ordained into the priesthood. And if it is claimed that although an angel is not a corporeal being, yet it can assume a body, and thus in that body it could be baptized, just as a rational soul is not a corporeal thing and yet is baptized in the body, answer that this case is not parallel. In one case a soul is united to a body, in the other an angel. A soul is united to a body as the form of the matter, but the angel is not so united, but rather as a mover to something movable. Therefore a soul is baptized in a baptized body, but an angel is not, because soul and body make one subject, but not so the angel with the body it assumes. And since, according to the Philosopher in the beginning of the *Metaphysics*, "Actions belong to their subjects,"[64] the soul is baptized in a baptized body, but an angel is not. And thus, as a consequence, the soul can receive baptismal character, but an angel cannot, which is why an angel cannot consecrate.

But what if an angel were to present a host saying that it was consecrated? Should that host be adored? The answer is that if a bad angel presents it, it should not be adored, unless it is certain that it was rightly consecrated; but if a good angel were to present it, it should be adored. And the reason is that a bad angel, according to the testimony of the Savior, "is a liar and the father of lies,"[65] and always strives to deceive man, which is why it ought never to be believed. But a good angel is always truthful and a pupil of the truth, and always strives for the salvation of man, and therefore ought always to be believed. Because, as the Apostle says, a bad angel often "transforms himself into an angel of light,"[66] a host presented by an angel is to be adored only under the condition that it was rightly consecrated, unless it is certain that it is a good angel.

CHAPTER 3: On the matter of the eucharist

The matter of the sacrament of the mass is twofold, namely, bread and wine. And the reason why these two are the matter of this sacrament is that this sacrament is ordered for spiritual nutrition. And as bodily nutrition consists in bodily food and drink, and bread has most to do with food and wine with drink, thus this spiritual nutrition consists in spiritual food and drink. Therefore in this sacrament, the body of Christ is given under the species of bread as food and the blood of Christ under the species of wine as drink. And so Christ himself says in John 6, "My flesh is true food and my blood is true drink."[67] Nevertheless, know

64. Aristotle, *Metaphysics*, I, 1, 981a16; cf. Aquinas, *Summa Theologiae*, Bk I, q. 39, a. 5 and Bk III, q. 20, a. 1.

65. John 8:44   66. 2 Corinthians 11:14
67. John 6:56

that the bread which is the matter of this sacrament is bread made from wheat and elemental water. I say "bread" because the body of Christ cannot be confected in dough. I also say "of wheat" because with other bread, like in bread made of rye or of barley or any grain other than wheat, the mass cannot be celebrated. I also say "made with elemental water" because I maintain that even if it is made from wheat, if it is made with another water, or with another liquid like wine or milk or rosewater and so on, always, unless it is made with simple water, the body of Christ cannot be confected from such bread. Know too that by the precept and custom of the Roman church, which, by the Lord's determination, is the head and mother and teacher of all the churches (X 2.2.20) and therefore all churches ought to obey her in everything as both mother and teacher, the bread from which the body of Christ is confected ought to be unleavened, because, although by the power of the sacrament the body of Christ can be made from leavened bread, anyone who celebrates with leavened bread sins mortally and is to be severely punished.

Note especially that the wine which is the matter of this sacrament ought to be wine from grapes, because with other wine, like wine made of pomegranates or mulberries or apples or with whatever other wine except wine from grapes, it cannot be celebrated. Consequently note that it cannot be celebrated with vinegar or verjuice. And understand by "vinegar" that which is entirely vinegar, because the mass can be celebrated with wine that is just a bit sour, although one should not do so if other wine can be had. And the reason is that vinegar is not of the same species as wine since it has contrary virtues. Truly the sacrament can be celebrated with new wine, yet I believe that it is better to wait until it is well clarified, since new wine, because of its dregs, can hardly be well drained without some remaining in the vessel.

The most important reason why these two, namely, wheat bread and grape wine, are better matter for the sacrament than some other two is because Christ instituted this sacrament to be celebrated with this matter. Indeed if he had instituted it with other matter then that would be the proper matter of this sacrament. But Christ more fittingly instituted the sacrament to be celebrated with this matter than with another, because the physical effects of bread and wine spiritually suit this sacrament especially well. Indeed bread naturally fortifies, according to the Psalm, "Bread strengthens the human heart."[68] And wine gladdens, according to the same, "Wine gladdens the human heart."[69] And this sacrament, worthily received, spiritually strengthens the recipient lest he grow faint on the path of this world, and therefore it is called the "journey provision" [viaticum], that is, strengthening and gladdening travelers. And it is called eucharist from "eu" which is "good" and "caros" which is "grace," like the good grace which especially gladdens the one who has it. Indeed as bread is made from many grains and wine flows together from many clusters of grapes, so in receiving of the body and blood of the Lord, Christ's faithful are spiritually united, one to another. Therefore it is called communion from "con," which is "together," and "unio," as if "together as one." Also Christ himself compared himself to a grain of wheat, saying in John 12, "Unless a grain of wheat falls into the earth and dies, etc."[70] He also compared himself to a vine, saying in John 5, "I am the true vine."[71] Therefore the sacrament of the body and blood is confected with the wine from grapes and wheat bread.

Know that although water is not included in the essential matter of this sacrament, nevertheless it ought to be mixed with the wine in the chalice, but in a small quantity, because the water signifies the people, according to Jeremiah, chapter 2, "Many waters are many people."[72] Hence the mixing of water with wine in the chalice signifies the spiritual union of Christ and the people which is accomplished by virtue of this sacrament.

But can the priest consecrate this matter in any amount whatsoever? Some doctors say no, but only as much as suffices for him and the people committed to him. The reason is that since the

68. Psalm 103:15   69. Psalm 103:15
70. John 12:24   71. John 15:1
72. Cf. Isaiah 17:12

sacrament is ordered for the use of the faithful, the priest cannot consecrate more than what suffices for the use of the faithful. Other doctors say that the quantity beyond which the priest cannot consecrate is not determined; indeed he can celebrate with whatever quantity of bread and wine is presented to him. Indeed since there is in the form of consecration the demonstrative pronoun "this" (*hic, hec, hoc*), it is necessary that the matter to be consecrated fall under the eye of the priest. Hence they say that the priest at the altar cannot consecrate all the bread and wine that is in the street or all the wine in the cellar, but he can consecrate all the bread and wine that is offered to him in whatever quantity. And the reason is that if the first opinion were true, it would follow that a priest living in the desert could not consecrate as many hosts as one who was in a big city, nor could a simple priest consecrate as many hosts as a curate priest, which are wholly unreasonable claims. And these doctors respond to the other doctors' argument, and they say that there is a difference between this sacrament and other sacraments, because the essence of the other sacraments consists in the dispensing and use of the matter, as the essence of baptism consists in the sprinkling of water and the speaking of the form, and so with the other sacraments. But the essence of the sacrament of the eucharist consists in the consecration of the matter and not in its use, because it is maintained that a consecrated host that is never received is truly the sacrament. And therefore although the priest ought to consecrate only as many hosts as are necessary for him and his people, nevertheless if he were to consecrate a thousand thousands, all would be consecrated.

But some are wont to pose this question concerning this topic. If there were thirteen hosts to be consecrated and the priest only believed there were twelve, would all thirteen be consecrated? Lord Berengar, archbishop of Compostella, teacher of theology in Paris, replies to this in one of his *Quodlibets*.[73] Either this priest

---

73. Berengar of Landorra's collection of *Quodlibets* is not extant; thus Guido's reference to it is an important testimony to an apparently lost work.

intends to consecrate all the hosts which are before him however
many there are, even though he believes there are only twelve, and
then Berengar says that all are consecrated; or, the priest intends
to consecrate precisely twelve and not more, and does not determine which twelve those are, then he says that none are consecrated since each host can still be consecrated (one not more than
another), and the priest does not limit himself to one more than
another. By this reason you might say that this one is not consecrated, by the same reason I might say that that one is not. And so
it may be said of any of the hosts that it is not consecrated either.
Hence when the priest has several hosts to consecrate, he ought
not to limit himself to a certain number, but ought to have the intention to consecrate whatever is before him.

CHAPTER 4: On the form of the eucharist and of the
consecration of the blood

The forms of all the sacraments consist in certain specified
words, and therefore the form of the sacrament of the eucharist
consists in certain limited words. In order to know in which words
the form of the eucharist consists, note that in the mass there are
some words which belong just to the solemnity and some which
are required of necessity. The words which belong to the solemnity are those which only serve to adorn and add to the beauty of
the mass itself, like the *Gloria in excelsis deo* and certain verses which
are said later like the *Sanctus* and the *Agnus dei*. These contribute
nothing to the essence of the mass. Indeed I believe that when
there ought to be a sermon, melodies ought to be completely left
out, or at least be abbreviated, because the sermon accomplishes
more than such songs, since these delight the ears of the body, but
the sermon heals the weaknesses of the heart.

The words which are necessary are those which belong directly
to the office of the mass. Yet note that necessity is twofold, because some necessity is for the sacrament, some necessity is by law.
In the mass, therefore, some words are necessary for the sacrament

and some necessary by law. Necessary by law are all those words which were instituted to be said in the mass by St. Peter the Apostle and by the other high pontiffs, his successors. But necessary for the sacrament are those which Christ offered in the Last Supper when he instituted this sacrament.

And there is a difference between these words, because if someone were to leave out the words which are necessary by law and say those which are necessary for the sacrament and have the intention of consecrating, he would consecrate. Nevertheless, he would sin most mortally and ought to be severely punished. But if he were to say all the words necessary by law and leave out those which are necessary for the sacrament, however much he intended to consecrate, he nevertheless would not consecrate. Since, therefore, according to the Philosopher, the form is that which gives a thing its being and without which a thing cannot exist, it is clear that only those words which are necessary for the sacrament are the form of this sacrament.[74] And those words, as far as the form of the consecration of the body of Christ is concerned, are these: This is my body [*Hoc est corpus meum*].

But know that this phrase is not necessary for the sacrament, because suppose that some priest with the intention of consecrating offers these words, "This is my body"; yet it might not be said that he had truly consecrated, depending on whether it is necessary that these words be preceded by other words which belong to the completeness of the form. Note that the subtle doctor in his fourth book says that all the words from "He, on the day before" [*Qui pridie*], inclusive, to "In like manner" [*Simili modo*], etc., exclusive, are necessary to the form of the consecration of the body of Christ. And his reason is that the consecrating priest offers the words of consecration in the person of Christ; it is therefore necessary that the words of consecration be preceded by some words through which it is made clear that the priest speaks in the person of Christ. But these are, "He, on the day before he suffered death,

74. Cf. Aquinas, *Summa Theologiae,* Bk III, q. 78, a. 5.

etc." [*Qui pridie quam pateretur,* etc.]. Therefore it is required of necessity that words precede [the words of the form].

And [Scotus] demonstrates this through the following example.
If someone were to say, "I declare that Jesus Christ was the minister of circumcision,"[75] it would be uncertain whether this saying
was spoken by St. Paul; but if one were to say, "Paul said, 'I declare
that Jesus Christ, etc.,'" then it would be clear to all hearers that
this saying was spoken by St. Paul. Likewise in the above supposi-
tion, so that it might be specified that the priest says these words,
namely, "This is my body," in the person of Christ, it is necessary
that some other words come first through which one is given to
understand that Christ said these words, "This is my body." And
these words are those given, "He, on the day before, etc."[76]

But other doctors say, as has been said, that necessity is twofold,
namely, for the sacrament and by law. Therefore they say that these
four words are necessary for the sacrament, "This is my body," because with these four words, the consecration is accomplished, if
the priest says them with intention to consecrate. But all the others, nevertheless, are necessary by law, because although someone
omitting them would sin mortally, he would consecrate nevertheless. And they respond to [Scotus's] reasoning when he says that
the consecrating priest speaks in the person of Christ and therefore it is necessary that he should say some words indicating that
he speaks in the person of Christ; they say that of necessity for the
sacrament [such words are] not required, but the intention of the
priest intending to speak in the person of Christ suffices. And on
that account, these words, "This is my body," show clearly enough
that the priest does not speak in his own person, because no one
believes that the priest wants to say that this is his very own body,
but speaks in the person of Christ whose body it is.

Therefore it is to be said that the form of the consecration of
the body of Christ consists precisely in these words, "This is my

75. Romans 15:8
76. John Duns Scotus, *Reportata Parisiensia,* Bk IV, d. 8, q. 2. See John Duns Scotus,
Opera Omnia: Editio minor, vol. II/2, *Opera Theologica* (Alberobello: Editrice, 2001).

body." And concerning this, what does the demonstrative pronoun "this" [*hoc*] designate? Some doctors have said that this pronoun "this" designates the body of Christ. But others say that it does not but rather designates the substance of the bread. But, with all due respect to them, this is not true, and I argue against them thus: According to the judgment of all the doctors, and according to the truth, the sacramental words bring about what they signify. But the aforementioned words, namely, "This is my body," do not cause the body of Christ to be the true body of Christ, because before these words are offered, the body of Christ was already the body of Christ. Nor do they cause the bread to be the body of Christ, because this is false; rather the substance of the bread is the body of Christ. Therefore the pronoun "this" does not designate the body of Christ or the substance of the bread. And on account of this, some others say that the pronoun "this" designates nothing, because the words are said as a quotation by the priest, and therefore the pronoun "this" is not to be considered demonstratively, but materially nevertheless. But this says nothing, because it does not remove the difficulty, since although these words are said as a quotation by the consecrating priest, yet Christ consecrating on the day of the Last Supper did not quote these words, and therefore when he said these words, the pronoun "this" designated something. And therefore I ask what he designated then and if the same difficulty remains as before. Some say that the pronoun "this" designates nothing determined, but designates something indeterminate. Hence, when "This is my body" is said in the person of Christ, it is necessary that some words come first through which [hearers] ought to understand that Christ said these words, "This is my body," and the meaning is that "this" which is contained under those species, whatever it may be, is the body of Christ.

It may be objected that what is contained under those species the whole time the words are being said is bread, because the body of Christ does not begin to be there until after the last syllable has been spoken, namely "um" [in *meum*], and therefore, when "This is" is said, the meaning is that what is contained under those species is the body of Christ, hence meaning that the bread is the body of Christ, which is false. The answer is that this proposition, "This is my body," like any other, is not complete, nor is the full meaning brought forth in the soul of the hearer, until it is fully pronounced. Therefore it is not to be judged on its truth until it is completely pronounced. But it stands, according to the faith, that what is contained under these species after the last syllable has been pronounced is the body of Christ. Therefore it is truly said that the pronoun "this" designates that which is contained under these species, whatever that may be. And [let] these [comments suffice] concerning the consecration of the body.

The form of the consecration of the blood follows.

Concerning the form of the consecration of the blood of Christ, it is to be known in what words it consists. Indeed there is a twofold opinion about this. For St. Thomas Aquinas and his followers say that the form of the consecration of the blood consists in these words, "For this is the chalice of my blood, of the new and everlasting covenant, a mystery of faith. It shall be shed for you and many others so that sins may be forgiven" [*Hic est enim calix sanguinis mei noui et eterni testamenti misterium fidei, qui pro vobis et pro multis effundetur in remissionem peccatorum*]. Thus all these words belong to the essence of the form and one who leaves out something from them would accomplish nothing. And the reason is that not only the subject and the predicate belong to the essence and completeness of any proposition, but also those words which are the boundaries of the subject and the predicate. But these words "of the new and everlasting" [*noui et eterni*] up to "sins may be forgiven" [*peccatorum*] are delimiters of this predicate "this is the chalice of my blood," which is why all the words are essential to the form.

But Master Henry of Ghent and his followers say that the form of the consecration of the blood consists in these words, "This is the chalice of my blood," and that immediately after these words have been said, the blood of Christ is there. But the other words that follow, namely, "of the new and eternal covenant, etc.," do not, according to them, belong to the essence of the form nor are they necessary to the sacrament, but are only necessary by law. Hence, one who leaves out some of these words, such as "of the new and eternal, etc.," although he would sin gravely, truly would consecrate. And their reason is this: Through the sacramental forms nothing is brought about of necessity for the sacrament except that which they effect. But the substance of the blood of Christ in this sacrament is signified rightly and explicitly by these words, therefore, the form of the consecration of the blood of Christ consists precisely in these words.

Which of these opinions is truer, I confess not to know, yet I consider the first to be the safer, and to confirm it, Brother Bernard of Gueraco [Bernard of Auvergne], at one time elected [bishop] of Clermont, bachelor of Paris in theology, in his corrections against Master Henry, brings to bear these two proofs.[77] The first is that the priest does not show the blood of Christ to the people in the mass for adoration until he has completed all the aforesaid words, namely, "This is the chalice" up through "for the remission of sins." And as soon as these words have been said, he elevates the chalice, showing the blood of Christ to the people for adoration, as a sign that now the consecration of the blood is complete and not before. The second proof is that St. Ambrose, who is one of the four principal doctors of the church, wrote all these words in his missal in golden letters, and as he did the forms of all the sacraments. Therefore the intention of St. Ambrose was that all the aforesaid words belonged to the form of the consecration of the blood. Also, in my limited judgment, that seems to be the intention of the decretal X 3.41.6. Indeed the case of the decretal is this. A certain bishop, looking and seeing that in none of the gospels is it found that any of the evangelists gave these words "mystery of faith," wondered who was so audacious that he dared to interpose

---

77. Bernard of Auvergne, *Reprobationes Henrici de Gandavo*, Quodlibet *IX*, Q. 10. We would like to thank Russell Friedman for providing us with a manuscript copy to verify this citation.

these words among the sacramental words. And he consulted the lord pope about this, and it is evident that his intention was that this should belong to the completeness of the form; otherwise his question would be null, because in the same way one could ask about any word in the whole canon. And the pope did not reproach him for his question, indeed he commended him. Therefore it appears that all these words belong to the completeness of the form. And whatever the truth of these opinions may be, I do not know, yet I advise every celebrant that he should say all the aforementioned words as one connected piece and with the actual intention to consecrate, as much as he is able.

Further know that through these words of this form four benefits are touched upon that we receive from the passion of Christ, whose passion this sacrament calls to mind, according to the word of the Apostle to the Corinthians, chapter 9, "As often as you eat this bread and drink this cup, etc."[78] The first effect or first benefit of the passion of Christ is that through it we are liberated from the power of demons. And this is touched on in the form of the sacrament when "This is the cup of my blood" is said, for just as long ago the children of Israel were liberated from the power and slavery of Pharaoh by the blood of the paschal lamb, so the faithful people are liberated from the power of demons through the blood of Christ, according to what John confesses in Revelation, chapter 5, saying of Christ, "You have redeemed us for God by your blood."[79]

The second effect or benefit that we receive from the passion of Christ is that through it we are made heirs of celestial glory, and this is touched on in this form when "new and everlasting covenant" is said. For indeed as a father makes his sons heirs by giving a covenant [or testament],[80] so Christ by setting forth a new covenant, makes us heirs of the glory of paradise. And this covenant

78. 1 Corinthians 11:26
79. Revelation 5:9
80. The Latin *testamentum* may be translated as covenant, as is done in the liturgy, or as testament, as is done in the quotations from Hebrews cited in this paragraph.

was set forth and confirmed in his passion, because "a testament is confirmed by the death of the testator," as the Apostle says in Hebrews, chapter 9.[81] And this is what he offers in the same letter speaking about Christ, "He is the mediator of a new testament, so that, by his death, those who have been called may receive the promise of an eternal inheritance."[82] But know that the gospel law is called "the new and everlasting covenant" to differentiate it from the law of Moses which was the old and transitory covenant. And it is called "new" because it promises new things, namely, celestial goods which are never read to have been promised in the old covenant, but only temporal things [were promised there]. And therefore because temporal goods are transitory, the old covenant was transitory; and because celestial goods are everlasting, the new covenant is called everlasting. It is also called "new" because it was instituted in a new way, namely, by the blood of Christ. For the Mosaic law was instituted with the blood of animals, according to what is read and the Apostle recites in the Letter to the Hebrews, chapter 9, saying that after Moses wrote the law in the book and read it before all the people, he sprinkled his book and the people with the blood of sheep and goats saying, "This is the blood of the covenant, etc."[83] But the gospel law was instituted through the mediation of the blood of Christ, according to what Christ himself says in Luke, chapter 22, "This chalice is the new covenant in my blood, etc."[84] And the Apostle touches on this reason in Hebrews, chapter 9, saying, "Indeed not through the blood of sheep and goats, but through his own blood, he entered once into the [Holy of] Holies, having obtained eternal redemption,"[85] and "thus he is the mediator of the new testament."[86]

The third effect or third benefit that we receive through the passion of Christ is that through it we are formed in the catholic faith. And this is touched on in the form of this most holy sacrament when "mystery of faith" is said. For, according to what Am-

81. Hebrews 9:16–17   82. Hebrews 9:15
83. Hebrews 9:19–20   84. Luke 22:20
85. Hebrews 9:12   86. Hebrews 9:15

brose says in the book that is called the *Hexameron*, "just as blood
extracted from under the right wing of a dove serves to illuminate
corporeal eyes, so the blood of Christ which came out of his right
side while hanging on the cross serves to illuminate the spiritual
eyes of the soul to believe the things that belong to the faith."[87]
And as a figure of this, the veil of the temple which hid those
things which were inside the Holy of Holies was torn in the passion of Christ as a sign that those things which were hidden and
veiled under the shadow of the law and the prophets were now
made manifest and laid open.

The fourth effect or benefit which we receive through the passion of Christ is that we are cleansed from sin by it. And this is
touched on in this form when "for the remission of sins" is said.
And concerning this, St. John the Evangelist speaks in Revelation,
chapter 4, saying, "He has loved us and has washed us from our
sins with his blood."[88]

From these things, it is clear that the form of the consecration
of the body of Christ consists precisely in these words, "This is
my body" (Matthew 26[:26], Mark 14[:22], Luke 22[:19], John 13).
And the form of the consecration of the blood of Christ consists
in these words, "This cup is the new and everlasting covenant in
my blood, a mystery of faith. It shall be shed for you and many
others so that sins may be forgiven."[89] Hence since all the words
of the canon ought to be said with great reverence, contrition, devotion, and mental recollection, these words especially ought to be
said with the greatest devotion and actual intention possible.

And if someone should ask or wonder why in the form of consecration of the blood, "This is my blood" is not said, as "This is
my body" is said in the form of the consecration of the body, answer that the reason is this: Because this sacrament is ordered for
the use of the faithful, which use is the spiritual and sacramental chewing on the part of the body and sacramental and spiri-

---

87. We could not locate this excerpt either in Ambrose's text or in Gratian.
88. Revelation 1:5
89. Cf. Matthew 26:28; Mark 14:24; Luke 22:20

tual drinking on the part of the blood, and because people ab-
hor drinking blood more than eating flesh, therefore to remove
the horror, "This is my blood" is not said in the form of the consecration of the blood, as "This is my body" is said in the form
of the consecration of the body of Christ. And there is a certain
grammatical construction called metonymy, namely, when the con-
tainer is named in place of the contents, as when it is said, "Drink
that vessel of wine." It does not make sense that one would drink
the vessel, but that one would drink the wine which is in the vessel.
Likewise when, "This is the chalice of my blood" is said, it does
not make sense that by the power of the words the cup is there,
because it was there before, but that the blood of Christ is there.

But some may wonder why, in the form of the consecration
of the body of Christ, "This is my body which is given for you"
is not said, since "It shall be shed for you" is said in the form of
consecration of the blood, and the body was given for us just as
the blood was shed. The answer to this is that this sacrament calls
to mind the passion and death of Christ, as the Apostle says in 1
Corinthians, chapter 11, "Whenever you eat this bread and drink
this cup, you proclaim the death of the Lord until he returns,"[90]
namely, in judgment. Also, Christ, instituting this sacrament, said
in Luke 22, as often as you receive, "do this as a commemoration of me,"[91] this means, in memory of my passion. But the passion and death of Christ are better represented by the shedding
of blood than by the handing over of the body. Therefore in the
form of the consecration of the blood "It shall be shed for you so
that sins may be forgiven" is said, and in the form of the consecration of the body "which is given for you" is not said.

And note that although by virtue of the words of the form of
the consecration of the body under the species of bread there is
just the body of Christ and by virtue of the words of the consecration of the blood under the species of wine there is just the
blood of Christ, nevertheless, by a certain concomitance of na-

90. 1 Corinthians 11:26
91. Luke 22:19

tures, under each specie there is the whole Christ, true God and true man, as it is said in the psalm for Corpus Christi where it says, "Flesh from bread, and blood from wine; Yet is Christ, in either sign, All entire confessed to be."[92]

CHAPTER 5: In what place the mass ought to be celebrated

The judgment of all the philosophers bears witness that the influence of particular places is marvelous. And in fact, it is so marvelous that it changes a thing and alters it from its nature. The Philosopher tells in his book, *On Plants,* about Persian apples, named after Persia where they were first found, that those that grow there kill, but those that grow near us are sweet and pleasing to eat.[93] From which it is manifestly clear how much place contributes to changing things. And on account of this, it was taught to the children of Israel in the book of Numbers, chapter 5, that they should not offer sacrifice except in the place that the Lord had chosen.[94] Indeed if the sacrifice of the Israelites which was made of the flesh of goats, calves, and lambs was not to be offered except in a holy and clean place, how much more the catholic sacrifice in which Christ, true God and true man, is offered ought not to be made except in a holy and clean place. Hence the place in which the mass regularly ought to be celebrated is the church. And so says Augustine, "Outside the church is not the place of true sacrifice."[95]

And I say "regularly" because in some cases mass can be celebrated outside the church. Note that in this instance, "the church" can be taken in two ways. In one way, the church is the same as the

92. Aquinas, "Lauda Sion" ("Sion lift thy voice and sing"), a sequence for Corpus Christi composed around 1264. See http://www.ewtn.com/library/PRAYER/LAUDA.txt.

93. *De plantis,* I.7. As did his contemporaries, Guido falsely attributed this text to Aristotle, although scholars now generally believe it was written by Nicolas of Damascus.

94. Deuteronomy 12:13–14

95. C.1 q. 1 c.68, rubric

congregation of the faithful who are gathered in faith and charity; and thus Augustine uses "the church" when he says that outside the church, that is, outside the faith of the church, is not the
place of true sacrifice. In the other way, the church is the same as
the material building in which the hours and the mass are said.
And outside the church so described, the mass can be celebrated
in some cases, such as among a respectable army, or for some festival, or the invocation of some saint, or the funeral of someone
who has died, or some new mass, or some such thing suited to a
great multitude of people and the church is so small that it cannot
accommodate the people. Then one can erect an altar in the cemetery or in some other respectable and clean street, where it ought
to be decently appropriate lest dust or the blowing of the wind or
some other such thing impose a hindrance.

By permission of the bishop of the diocese, on account of
some necessity, the mass can be celebrated in some appropriate
part of someone's house. Even so, let them put a portable altar
blessed by the bishop down on a stone table connected to a supporting post. And this table ought to be whole, for if it is cracked
the mass ought not to be celebrated there, nor even if it is removed
from the support; indeed they would sin who celebrate there. And
this table ought to be made of stone and not of some other material. And one reason for this is that Christ who is sacrificed there is
called "the rock." Hence the Apostle says in 1 Corinthians 10, "And
the rock was Christ."[96] The other reason is that the sepulcher of
Christ, which the altar represents, was made of rock, as the evangelist Mark says.[97] And for this same reason, the corporals ought
to be made of linen, and not of some other material, because in
the tomb Christ was wrapped in clean muslin,[98] that is, in dazzling
white linen; and the corporals signify the linen cloths in which the
dead Christ was wrapped. And the chalice ought not to be made
of glass because it might break easily; nor of wood because wood
is porous, and the blood could seep into the pores; nor of iron or

96. 1 Corinthians 10:4   97. Mark 15:46
98. Mark 15:46

copper or brass because these induce nausea and there would be a danger of vomiting. But it can be made of gold, silver, or tin. But know that when the altar is fully consecrated or blessed, it is not necessary to have another table there.

Note also that altars, whether they are in a church or outside a church, ought always to be set up toward the east [*oriens*], so that he who says mass may have his face toward the east. And the reason is that Christ is called the rising sun [*orientem*] in Luke 1, "He has visited us descending [*oriens*] from on high."[99] And concerning Christ himself, the church sings, "O radiant dawn [*oriens*], splendor of eternal light."[100] Another reason is that, according to what the philosophers say, the eastern part is the right-hand part of heaven, and according to what Christ says in Matthew, chapter 25, God will cause the good to stand at his right hand.[101] Therefore, so that we may merit to be placed at [God's] right hand in the judgment, we ought to pray toward the east. And because the chief of all prayers is the mass, he who says the mass ought to have his face toward the east.

Must the church in which the mass is said be consecrated or not? It contributes nothing to the mass, although with respect to the solemnity of the mass, if possible, it always ought to be said in a consecrated church, since it is very honorable and useful for a church to be consecrated, because when someone enters a consecrated church to pray his venial sins are forgiven him.

Know further that the mass ought never to be celebrated on a ship on account of the danger of spilling the blood.

Also in a church polluted with a spilling of blood or seed the mass ought not to be celebrated; and if someone were to celebrate there, he would sin mortally. Nevertheless, he would not be made irregular from this, as was declared by Lord Boniface VIII in VI 5.11.20. And if a church is polluted in the aforementioned way, mass cannot be celebrated in the cemetery contiguous with it, be-

99. Luke 1:78
100. One of the so-called O Antiphons used in the week before Christmas.
101. Matthew 25:33

cause when a church is polluted, the cemetery contiguous with it is likewise polluted. But if the cemetery is polluted it is not necessarily the case that the church contiguous with it is polluted, since the principal may draw the connection but not the connection the principal, as is found in VI 3.21.un. Hence just as in a cemetery contiguous to a polluted church no one ought to celebrate, so also no one ought to be buried there. It would be otherwise if the cemetery were not contiguous to the church, because given that the church is polluted, even so, a cemetery not contiguous with the church itself would not be polluted, as is clear in the chapter cited above.

And in time of interdict, the mass and the other hours ought not to be said in the church in full voice, nor with the door open, except on four festivals, namely, on the day of the Lord's birth, on the day of the resurrection, on the day of Pentecost, and on the day of the assumption of Blessed Virgin Mary. And lest the churches be defrauded of their due services, and lest the divine offices be neglected, the devotion of the faithful diminish, and the irreverence of the infidels increase, in any time of interdict, the mass and all the other divine offices, both day and night, ought to be said in a low voice in church, with the door closed to the excommunicated, with those under interdict excluded and with the bells not rung, so that they cannot be heard by others who are outside. All these things are found in VI 5.11.24. The one who does otherwise is irregular and ineligible, and he cannot be elected nor can he be absolved, except at the point of death, except by the apostolic see, as is found in VI 5.11.18.

And when someone excommunicated is present, no one ought to celebrate mass in the church or in another place, lest he sin mortally and beyond this be suspended from entering the church; and he cannot be absolved except by him who takes away the sentence of excommunication, as is found in VI 5.7.8. And this ought not to be disregarded because if one so suspended should celebrate, he would become irregular, as is found expressly in VI 5.11.20.

CHAPTER 6: On the time when the mass ought to be celebrated

As Solomon says, "All things have their seasons,"[102] and this is reasonable. Indeed things that go through various seasons require the most ability to change. This appears most clearly in lettuce, which, since the season of its youth is cold and damp, is by nature soothing for fevers and blood ailments, and when it becomes leafy, it is hot and dry and its milk becomes bitter which counteracts jaundice as well as fevers.[103] From this liquid, it is evident how much things that go through a change of season are changed and altered. This was nicely figured in Exodus, chapter 16, where it is read that manna collected at the designated time had every delight and every smell of sweetness. But when it was collected not at the designated time, namely, on the Sabbath day, it rotted and swarmed with worms.[104] This was a figure of the body of Christ as is said in the legend of the body of Christ [*Corpus Christi*] where it says, "A figure of this sacrament came first when the Lord rained manna on the fathers in the desert."[105] Therefore as that manna was not to be gathered except at the designated time, so this most sacred sacrifice ought not to be offered except at the designated time.

Know therefore that the mass ought to be celebrated in the day and not at night, except on the feast of Christ's birth when the mass is celebrated in the middle of the night because Christ was born at that hour. Concerning this more will be said below. In

102. Ecclesiastes 3:1

103. The "milk" that comes from breaking a lettuce stalk was understood to have medicinal properties.

104. Exodus 16:17–20

105. This legend appears to be from the popular thirteenth-century collection of hagiographic stories, *Legenda Aurea* (the *Golden Legend*) compiled by Jacob of Voragine. William Granger Ryan published the first modern translation based on a nineteenth-century Latin text: *The Golden Legend: Readings on the Saints*, trans. William Granger Ryan (Princeton, N.J.: Princeton University Press, 1993). An early English translation also exists, published by William Caxton in 1483. According to Granger, Caxton omitted some of Jacob of Voragine's saints and added others (vol. I, xiv). The legend to which Guido refers is found in Caxton but not in Granger.

earlier times, mass was also said at night during the vigil of the Lord's resurrection. Hence it is still said in the prayer of that mass, "God, who this most holy night, etc." One reason why the mass is celebrated in the day and not at night is that in the mass the passion of Christ is remembered which took place in the day and not at night. Another reason is that the state of sin is represented by night and the state of grace by day, as the gloss says about that text of the Apostle to the Romans 13, "Let us cast off the works of darkness," that is, sin, "and put on the armor of light,"[106] that is, the virtues which are the armor of grace. To portray, therefore, that he who says mass ought to be in a state of grace and without sin, the mass ought to be said in the day and not at night.

But at what hour should the mass be said? Note that there are three principal hours at which the mass ought to be celebrated, namely, terce, sext, and none. And the reason why the mass ought to be said at these hours more than at others is that, as has been frequently said, the mass is said in memory of the passion of Christ, and at these three hours Christ suffered and was crucified. Indeed at the third hour, he was crucified by the tongues of the Jews and the sentence of Pilate, because at the third hour the Jews cried, "Crucify, crucify him!" and at that hour Pilate ruled to satisfy their request.[107] At the sixth hour he was raised on the cross, hence it is said in John, chapter 4, "It was about the sixth hour and they crucified him."[108] At the ninth hour, he gave up his spirit. Hence it is said in Matthew 27, "And about the ninth hour, he cried out with a loud voice," and following this, "he gave up his spirit."[109] And I understand this [requirement] to pertain to a mass which is said solemnly in church because particular masses can be said from the point of dawn until sext, and on days of fasting until none. But after none mass ought not to be celebrated except perhaps on fast days and by reason of orders.

106. Romans 13:12   107. John 19:6, 16
108. Cf. Matthew 27:45; Mark 15:33; Luke 23:44. In John 4, Jesus speaks with the Samaritan woman at the sixth hour. The other edition consulted says Mark 15.
109. Matthew 27:46, 50

But incidentally, note that, not only the mass, but truly the other canonical hours as well, are said and sung in memory of the passion of Christ. For the office of matins is said in memory that Christ, in the early hours of the morning, was taken captive, bound, and mocked in various ways in the house of Ananias, the chief priest, to whom he was led. And matins ought to be said in the middle of the night, according to Psalm 18, "I arose in the middle of the night to confess to you, etc."[110] Prime is said in memory that, at that hour, in the house of Caiaphas, Christ was bound to the column and sorely and most severely whipped, so that according to what Isaiah the prophet had said, "from the sole of the foot even to the head, there is no soundness in it."[111] Terce is said in memory that at that hour Christ was led to Pilate, and was crucified by the tongues of the Jews crying out and saying, "Take him away! Take him away! Crucify him!"[112] And then was fulfilled Psalm 21, "They have opened their mouths over me, just like a lion seizing and roaring."[113] Sext is said in memory that in that hour Christ was stripped and mocked by the soldiers and was nailed to the cross, and then was fulfilled Psalm 21, "They pierced my hands and feet."[114] None is said in memory that at that hour Christ drank gall and vinegar and died, saying, "Father, into your hands I commend my spirit."[115] And then that word of Psalm 68 was fulfilled, "they gave me gall for my food. And in my thirst, they gave me vinegar to drink."[116] Vespers is said in memory that at that hour Christ was given by Pilate to the noble councilor, and was taken down from the cross by Joseph.[117] Compline is said in memory that at that hour, Christ was mourned by his most sorrowful mother and other holy women, preserved with spices and placed in the tomb.[118] And thus it is good and fitting that each of these hours be said at the specified hour. According

110. Psalm 118:62
112. John 19:15
114. Psalm 21:17
116. Psalm 68:22
118. Luke 23:55–56

111. Isaiah 1:6
113. Psalm 21:14
115. Luke 13:46
117. Luke 23:50–53

to the word of Psalm 118, "Seven times a day I uttered praise to you."[119]

Truly on account of occupation with domestic matters or on account of human frailty, it is impossible to keep this. Nevertheless what is mandated in X 3.41.1 ought to be followed, where it says that the priest, having completed the office of matins, namely, in the middle of the night, in the morning may pay his servants to do his tasks, namely, prime, terce, sext, none, and vespers, so that the hours may be completed by competent people, either by himself or by students. And then, with the hours being done and the sick visited, if he wishes, while fasting, he may go out to do rural work. And let them say all these hours in the way in which it is taught in X 3.41.9, where it is taught that the divine office, both day and night, should be said studiously as well as devoutly, and let whoever knowingly transgresses this rule know himself to sin mortally, as is clear since he is a transgressor against the church. Note especially that no one ought to say mass until he has said matins, and it is fitting that prime also be said before the mass. And the other hours, except vespers and compline, can be said before the mass. Note also that the priest ought not to say or perform the office to suit himself, but according to the temporal or sanctoral cycle used in that land.

CHAPTER 7: How often the mass ought to be celebrated in a day

After what has been said about how the mass ought to be celebrated during the day, it remains to discuss how often the mass ought to be celebrated in a day. Know that according to what is said in X 3.41.3, no one ought to say mass more than once a day. Indeed, very happy is the one who worthily celebrates one mass.

The day of the birth of the Lord is an exception; on this day three are celebrated, so that on that day one priest can celebrate

119. Psalm 118:164

three masses, as is found in D.1 de cons. c.48. And one reason why three masses are said on that day is on account of mystery since three states are represented by these three masses, namely, the state before the law, the state under the law, and the state of grace. The mass that is sung in the middle of the night represents the state which was before the law, when the whole world was in darkness. Hence in this mass is sung the prophecy of Isaiah, "The people who walked in darkness have seen a great light."[120] The second mass which is sung at dawn signifies the second state which was under the law, in which state people began to know Christ on account of the sayings of the law and the prophets, but they did not have full knowledge of him. And therefore it is sung at dawn when light begins to appear, but not very brightly. Hence in that mass is sung "Light will shine today, etc." The third mass is said in the bright of day, and signifies the state of grace in which we are. And the office "A child is born to us, etc." is said.

Another reason is to represent the three births of Christ. The first is said to represent his eternal birth by which he was born of the Father. Hence it is said in the introit of that mass, "The Lord has said to me, you are my son, today I have begotten you."[121] And this mass is said in the night when it is hard to see to indicate that this birth is hidden from us. The second mass is said to represent the spiritual birth by which Christ is born in the souls of the righteous by grace. Hence is sung in this mass, "Light will shine upon us today," light, that is, the grace of God. The third mass represents the temporal birth by which he was born of the Virgin Mary for our salvation. Hence is sung, "A child is born to us and a son is given to us, etc."[122]

Further, if the gospels that are read in these masses are considered, the first mass represents the temporal birth by which Christ was born according to the flesh from the Virgin Mary. Hence the gospel that is read in that mass, "a decree went out from Caesar

120. Isaiah 9:2   121. Psalm 2:7
122. Isaiah 9:6

Augustus,"[123] speaks entirely of this birth, as is clear from looking at it. The second represents his spiritual birth, for indeed then is read the gospel, "the shepherds said to one another,"[124] which is to be understood entirely concerning this spiritual birth. The third represents the eternal birth by which he was born of the Father. Hence then is read the gospel of John, "In the beginning was the word,"[125] which speaks entirely of the eternal birth of the son of God.

Note also that on Good Friday the mass ought not to be said. And the reason is that this sacrament is a figure of the passion of Christ, which took place on this day, and with the reality having come, namely, the passion, for that day the figure, namely, the sacrament, ought to cease.

But on other days the priest ought to say only one mass, except in case of necessity when he can celebrate two masses. And one case is if someone were to die and the priest has already celebrated the mass of the day, he can say the mass for the dead, namely, the requiem, provided he is fasting and there is no other priest who might celebrate.

Another case is if someone is in danger of death, asks for the body of Christ to be given to him, and the priest does not have a consecrated host, he can celebrate again, provided that, as I said before, he is fasting and there is no other priest ready to celebrate, because this is always to be understood.

Another case is on account of the necessity of a marriage, namely, when the time for marriage is passing by, if, after the mass has been said, some persons arrive who need to contract their marriage, the priest can celebrate again, as long as he is fasting, as I said above.

Another case is on account of the need of pilgrims, namely, when pilgrims arrive after the mass has been said. And Raymond has this case in his *Summa*.[126] But, with all due respect, this seems

123. Luke 2:1   124. Luke 2:15
125. John 1:1
126. Raymond of Penyafort, *Summa de poenitentia et matrimonio*, Bk III, 24, 13. A reprint of a 1603 edition is available (Farnborough, Hants, U.K.: Gregg Press, 1967).

to be expressly against X 3.41.12. Indeed the case of this chapter is that the archbishop of Sepontina [Sypontus] on the day of the Lord's Supper [Maundy Thursday], by ancient custom, was obligated to make chrism in the church of Sepontina, and the same archbishop went up in the morning according to custom to the Gargarinian church so that there he might receive the pilgrims to that place, and there he was compelled by the clergy and the people to celebrate. Hence he implored the advice of the pope concerning this. The pope responded to him that he only ought to celebrate the mass in the Sepontina church, where he was obligated to consecrate the chrism. From which it is evidently clear that on account of pilgrims the norm of celebrating just one mass per day ought not to be transgressed. Nevertheless, saving a better judgment, I approve of that custom which is observed in some Gallican churches, namely, when some pilgrims come to a church after mass has been said, if there is not another priest there ready to celebrate, the priest dresses himself as if he were to say mass, and says for them the mass of the Blessed Virgin or of the Holy Spirit or of that saint for whom the pilgrimage is made. Nevertheless he does not say the canon or consecrate, but he shows them some relics in the place of the elevation of the body of Christ. And this mass is called a "dry mass." Nevertheless, if elsewhere another custom is followed according to the opinion of Raymond [cited above], I do not disparage it.

Another case is on account of the need of honor or expediency, so that if, after the mass has been said, some great person arrives who wants to hear mass, the priest can celebrate again, as long as he is fasting. This case is found in the gloss on X 3.41.3. Concerning this need I do not know what I should say, because I do not see such great need here that, on account of it, the mandate of celebrating just one mass ought to be transgressed, especially since great persons do not often attend mass in our days, and those who do attend bring their own priests with them.

Another case is on account of the necessity of obligation, as when there are two churches joined together, and someone is the curate, that is, has the care of souls, and they have revenues so meager than they do not suffice for two priests, but only one priest has care of both. In this case, in one day the priest can celebrate in both of those churches on the days in which he is obligated to say mass for his people or administer the sacraments or perform those duties which require the mass. And this case happens in many places and is observed in the region of Toulouse, and also in other parts.

And I believe that in the law the command is not found expressly that just one mass is to be celebrated, since in all the chapters in which mention is made of this matter one finds this phrase, "it suffices," which phrase does not limit power. Nevertheless, the custom of the church, which surpasses any authority whatsoever, holds and maintains this. And therefore no one ought to do otherwise, and if he does, he sins and ought to be punished. But in any case when the priest celebrates several masses, in the first he ought not to drink water or wine after receiving the blood, but only rinse his mouth and take care as best he can lest he swallow anything, because the sacraments are to be received by one fasting. In each mass he may receive the body and blood. And in the final one, he may drink the washing water which is commonly taken after reception of the blood of Christ, but not in the other masses, as I said. This is found in X 3.41.5 and D.5 de cons. c.6.

CHAPTER 8: On the vestments which the priest ought to put on

"Your vestments are to be white at all times,"[127] the word of the Wise One. How much the proper use of vestments contributes to the proper administration of the office and whoever exercises it, the experience of physicians adequately shows. Indeed, it is a fact that a healing salve that alleviates maladies of the eyes, ground by an apothecary wearing inappropriate clothes which he put on the

127. Ecclesiastes 9:8

previous day, put fresh into the eyes torments the patient. If therefore inappropriate clothing does harm in the making of eye salve,
how much more does it do harm in the consecration of the body
of Christ? Hence the commandment of the lawgiver Moses was
figurative in Exodus 28, "You shall make holy vestments for Aaron, in which, having been sanctified, he may minister to me."[128]
Hence know that all vestments which the priest puts on are to be
sanctified and blessed by the bishop. Note, therefore, that the garment which he puts on first, namely, that little shirt or the superpellicium, does not belong to the essence of the mass for a simple
priest, but only to its good practice. I say this on account of bishops and regular canons and chaplains of honor to our lord pope,
to whom such a garment belongs.

Therefore, counting this little shirt, already discussed, or the
superpellicium in its place, there are seven vestments that the priest
wears in the mass, namely, that shirt or in its place the superpellicium, amice, alb, belt, maniple, stole, chasuble. And these seven
vestments signify the seven gifts of the Holy Spirit with which
the priest ought to be imbued. Hence Luke, chapter 24, "You will
be clothed with power," of the Holy Spirit, "from on high."[129]
Or they signify that the priest ought to be defended and armed
against the seven mortal sins, hence the Apostle says in Ephesians
6, "Put on the armor of God so that you may stand against the
wiles of the devil."[130] Or they signify the seven virtues, namely,
three theological and four cardinal, with which he ought to be
adorned. Hence the Apostle says in Romans, chapter 13, "Let us
put on the armor of light,"[131] that is, the armor of virtue, because
"no one dressed in sackcloth," that is, in sin, "is permitted to enter
the king's court,"[132] that is, to enter the kingdom of Christ who
is king, as it says in the book of Esther, chapter 4. Or they signify
that the priest ought to be devoted to the seven works of mercy.
Hence the Apostle, "Be clothed with the Lord Jesus Christ,"[135] "of

128. Exodus 28:2–3   129. Luke 24:49
130. Ephesians 6:11   131. Romans 13:12
132. Esther 7:2   133. Romans 13:14

whose wisdom there is no number,"[134] as it says in the Psalm. Or they signify that the seven petitions of the Lord's Prayer are heard favorably. In sign of which, it is read in the book of Esther that Esther, dressed in royal robes, was heard favorably by Ahasuerus.[135] Or they signify that priests, worthily celebrating in these seven vestments, will have seven gifts in paradise, namely, four on the part of the body and three on the part of the soul. In sign of which it is read in Genesis 27, that Jacob, dressed in the clothing of Esau, got the blessing of his father to great benefit. Or they signify that faithful Jesus will be with us in this sacrament, as long as the world shall last, passed seven days at a time, until the consummation of the age. And thus he "who does not lie promised,"[136] saying, "Behold, I am with you even to the consummation of the age."[137]

And so that something specific may be said about each vestment, know that this shirt or superpellicium signifies that the priest ought to have purity of life. Indeed this shirt is to be made of clean white linen, and on account of this the priest says, "With the pure in heart I will wash my hands clean, and take my place among them at thy altar, Lord."[138] The amice which is placed on the head signifies the elevation of the mind to God which the priest ought to have more than others, especially when he says mass; hence he himself says, "Lift up your hearts," that is, "Let hearts be lifted up to God." The alb which is long signifies the perseverance in good that the priest ought to have, because "whoever will have persevered, even to the end, the same shall be saved."[139] The belt, that is, the girdle that keeps the vestments from falling to the ground, signifies the fear of God which keeps souls from falling through sin, because, as the Wise One says, "Those who fear God will prepare their hearts, and they will sanctify their souls in his sight."[140] The maniple signifies the fruit

134. Psalm 146:5   135. Esther 5:1–3
136. Titus 1:2   137. Matthew 28:20
138. Psalm 25:6; recited in the mass as the priest washes his hands.
139. Matthew 10:22
140. Ecclesiasticus [Sirach] 2:20

of good works which good priests will carry into paradise. Hence concerning these, Psalm 125 says, "But when returning, they will arrive with exultation, carrying their sheaves."[141] The stole signifies the mortification of the flesh, hence it is worn like a cross to show that the priest ought to carry the cross of penitence in his heart or in his body, and thus says the Apostle, "carrying around the mortification of Christ Jesus in your bodies."[142] The chasuble, which covers the other vestments and surpasses all the other vestments, signifies charity which surpasses all other virtues[143] and which "covers a multitude of sins."[144] Therefore "rooted in charity,"[145] "let us live justly."[146] Many other interpretations could be added, but let these suffice for the present.

CHAPTER 9: To whom the eucharist ought to be given

"It is not good to take the bread of the children and give it to the dogs,"[147] and pearls are not to be given to swine.[148] Since in this sacrament are contained the bread and wine "which came down from heaven,"[149] namely, Christ, true God and true man, who is the "most precious pearl, which when a man found it, he hid it and with joy went and sold all he had and bought it,"[150] therefore this sacrament is not to be given to dogs or swine, that is, to unclean sinners.

Therefore, in order to know to whom this sacrament ought to be given, first, the ways of receiving it must be seen. Note that this sacrament can be received corporally, sacramentally, and spiritually, and accordingly, it can be received in four ways. Indeed some receive this sacrament just corporally, like some infidel who does not believe the body of Christ to be truly in this sacrament. If he should receive the consecrated host, he would receive the sacra-

---

141. Psalm 125:7
142. 2 Corinthians 4:10
143. 1 Corinthians 13:13
144. 1 Peter 4:8
145. Ephesians 3:17
146. Titus 2:12
147. Matthew 15:26
148. Matthew 7:6
149. John 6:59
150. Cf. Matthew 13:44, 46

ment only corporally because it is evident that he would not receive it spiritually since he would not receive the fruit of the sacrament. He would also not receive it sacramentally, because one
receives this sacrament sacramentally who truly believes the body
of Christ to be in this sacrament. But this person, as has been said,
does not believe, which is why he does not receive this sacrament
sacramentally, but only corporally. And I say the same thing about
dogs or mice or any other animals if it happens (God forbid!) that
they eat a consecrated host.

Some receive this sacrament only spiritually, like the faithful,
righteous, and holy ones hearing mass with devotion or having the
devotion to hear it, who, although they do not communicate, are
nevertheless participants in the fruit of this sacrament. And thus
is the word of Augustine to be understood, saying, "Believe and
you have eaten,"[151] believe, namely, with firm faith, and you have
eaten, namely, spiritually.

Some receive or eat this sacrament sacramentally and corporally
at the same time, but not spiritually, like false Christians who receive this sacrament in mortal sin. Indeed such receive it corporally, since they receive the consecrated species, and they also receive
it sacramentally since, because they are Christians, they believe the
body of Christ to be truly under these species, and thus they make
use of the sacrament as a sacrament. But, they do not receive spiritually because they do not receive the fruit of the sacrament.

Some receive this sacrament corporally, sacramentally, and spiritually at the same time, like those who receive this sacrament with
devotion and faith, living in charity and the grace of God. From
its reception they receive many good things, namely, grace in the
present and glory in the future.

Second, know what things are required for the proper reception
of this sacrament; these are three, namely, freedom from mortal
sin, elevation of the mind to God, and purity of body. Concerning
the first, this was discussed above in the first chapter, and some-

---

151. D.7 de pen. c.2; D.2 de cons. c.47

thing will be said below. Concerning the second, namely, the elevation of the mind to God, the priest says before the canon, "Lift
up your hearts," as if he says that the one wanting to receive this
sacrament ought to have his heart lifted up to God. Concerning
the third, namely, purity of body, we see that those handling any
sacrament wash their hands, and therefore since in this sacrament
he who is the holy of holies is handled, purity of body is required
in the one receiving it.

Nevertheless note that while freedom from mortal sin is required by necessity for the proper reception of this sacrament, the
other two are required from great fittingness. And therefore, since
some bodily impurity sometimes has mortal sin and dullness of
mind joined with it, as is the case with the pollution which happens in sleep, let us see how this pollution impedes reception of
this sacrament. Know, therefore, that the pollution which happens
in sleep is not a sin in itself, but can be an effect of mortal or
venial sin or no sin, since its cause can be either mortal, venial,
or no sin. Therefore, one should always return to the cause from
which this pollution arises, for it can arise from thinking about
past events, or from drunkenness and intoxication, or from diabolical temptation, or from illness, or from the relief of nature. In
the first two ways, it cannot happen without mortal or venial sin,
because if it comes from deliberate thought with consent, or if
the intoxication was deliberate or habitual, it is a mortal sin. And
therefore such pollution impedes by necessity the reception of this
sacrament. But if the thought did not have deliberate consent, or
the drunkenness or intoxication was not deliberate or habitual, it
is a venial sin; and therefore such pollution does not impede the
reception of this sacrament by necessity. But it does impede it by
fittingness, especially if it was done with a filthy imagination because, as is commonly said, the mind is weighed down by thoughts.
But if there is something which would outweigh it, like respect for
a feast day or fear of a scandal, reception of the body of Christ
ought not to be put off on account of this. And if the pollution
arises from diabolical illusion, I do not believe that it ought to be

put off, especially if it comes at the time of a great feast day or of general communion. And if it arises from illness of nature or relief of nature, reception may be put off on account of respect; this is praiseworthy, unless it be something that reforms sin, as was said above. And that decretal which says that, after such pollution, a man ought to abstain for twenty-four hours is to be understood according to the aforementioned distinction.[152]

Therefore, having seen in how many ways this sacrament can be received and what things are required for the proper reception of the sacrament, it is now to be seen who ought to receive this sacrament. Hence know that this sacrament ought to be received by those who are fasting, as is found in C.7 q.1 c.16; D.5 de cons. c.6. Yet note that fasting is twofold; one is natural, the other ecclesiastical. Natural fasting is canceled by the taking of any food or drink, taken in the manner of food or drink or even medicine. Ecclesiastical fasting is canceled by eating whatever is taken in the manner of food, with the exception of one meal [per day]. Therefore when it is said that the sacrament of the eucharist ought to be received by one fasting, this means natural fasting, because this most holy food ought to enter into the mouth of a Christian before any other food, so he who receives this most holy food should not have taken anything that day in the manner of food or drink or medicine. Even so, because need has no law, and the law is not imposed on the sick, the sick and those who are in a situation of need are not obligated by this. Indeed, at whatever hour of the day or night, whether after breakfast or before, they can receive this sacrament whenever it is necessary for them.

But what if some priest or another person who ought to communicate washes out his mouth in the morning, and perhaps swallows a bit of water? Is he barred from receiving this sacrament? I say that before the reception of this sacrament, it is fitting that one be as corporally and spiritually clean as one can be, and therefore I approve of and praise washing out one's mouth before receiving

152. D.6 c.1, editio romana

this sacrament. Nevertheless, let care be taken lest one swallow water knowingly. Even so, if some (not a large amount) is swallowed with saliva and in the manner of saliva, I do not think that it impedes reception of this sacrament. But suppose that late at night someone ate anise or berries or fennel or something else, and some leftover bits remained between his teeth, and when he washed he swallowed some of what remained between his teeth. Is he barred from receiving this sacrament? I say no because he does not do it knowingly, but swallows in the manner of saliva.

And this sacrament ought not to be received except by one who has use of reason. Hence it ought not to be given to children before they reach the age of discretion, as is found in X 5.38.12, because before that time they do not know how to discern between this food and corporal food and so they do not show the reverence due to such a sacrament.

And for the same reason, this sacrament is not to be given to those out of their minds or insane. Yet a distinction is to be made among these. Either such people were insane from birth and thus never had the use of reason, and I believe that to these the sacrament ought not to be given, because this sacrament requires actual devotion in the recipient and such people cannot have it. Or such people once had the use of reason but lost it for some reason, and they have some lucid periods; and when they have such lucid periods, if they ask for this sacrament with devotion and they want to receive it reverently, it should be given to them. Nevertheless, in a period of insanity, in no way should it be given to them because of the reason already stated. And those who are frantic ought not to be given this sacrament, especially if there is fear of irreverence toward the sacrament, like spitting it out or some such thing. I am speaking about those mad ones in whom the use of reason is entirely bound up. But I believe that it ought to be given to demoniacs if they ask with devotion and reverence, as long as they have the use of reason and actual devotion for this sacrament. And I believe that they can have so much devotion for the sacrament that by the power of the sacrament they are set free from their demon.

And lepers ought not to be given this sacrament. I understand this to apply to lepers so infected that they cannot receive the Lord's body and cannot hold it in their mouths without spitting it back, as there are many who have lost lips and teeth and are eaten away even to the throat. It is read of a certain Cistercian monk in the life of St. Louis, at one time king of France, who when a morsel was placed in his mouth it would fall right back out.[153] To such a leper the body of Christ ought not to be given, but to other lepers it can well be given. And a leprous priest ought not to celebrate in the presence of the people, but if he wants to celebrate for some or in secret, he may. And thus I understand those chapters X 3.6.3 and X 3.6.4. Hugh also says that a leprous priest can also celebrate when other lepers are present.[154]

And the body of Christ is never to be given to those condemned to death for their crimes, except by special grace, like those who are to be hung or drowned or burned or killed in some other way. But the body of Christ ought to be given to those who are to be burned for the crime of heresy, if they ask with devotion, humility, and reverence, as is found in VI 5.2.4.

But is the body of Christ to be given to those living in mortal sin? The answer is that the sin is either notorious or hidden. If it is notorious, suppose that one is a notorious usurer or a notorious keeper of concubines or any other notorious sinner, unless he desists and repents worthily according to the statutes of the church, the body of Christ is not to be given to him, however often he asks. Indeed it should be said to him, "Friend, it is not good to take the bread of the children and throw it to the dogs."[155]

But if the sin is hidden, either he asks for the body of Christ at a time when he is obligated to commune, for instance in a time of general communion or because he is sick and so on in other cases in which everyone is obligated to commune, or he asks at another

153. William of Saint Pathus, *Vie de Saint Louis*, c. 11.
154. This may be a reference to Hugh of Saint Victor's book on the sacraments, which Guido draws on in the next chapter, but we could not locate it therein.
155. Matthew 15:26; Mark 7:27

time. If he asks at another time, however often he asks in public, the priest is not obligated to give it to him, but should say to him, "Friend, it is not the time for communion, and therefore I ought not to give you the body of Christ, but wait for the designated time." But if he asks at the time when he is obliged to commune, he asks either in public or in secret. If he asks in secret, it is not to be given to him; indeed he is to be warned not to ask in public. But if such a one, obstinate in his wickedness, asks in public to be given the body of Christ, the priest ought to give it to him, because he ought not to betray him, nor ought anyone be deprived of what is his by right, until it has been declared that he has lost his right. And therefore, since any parishioner has the right to ask for the body of Christ from his curate, and the curate is obligated to give the body of Christ to his parishioners at this time, and none of the faithful is to be deprived of this right, except through mortal sin committed publicly, therefore as much as the priest may know his subordinate to be in mortal sin, unless the sin is notorious, he ought not to deny him the body of Christ, if he asks in the designated time and in public that it be given to him. And it is said that St. Bernard did this. One day when he was communing his monks, a certain monk whom St. Bernard knew to be in mortal sin approached among the others to communicate. And St. Bernard gave him the body of Christ saying to him in a low voice, "May the Lord judge between me and you," as if he wanted to say, "The Lord knows that you are unworthy to come and that I cannot deny you, therefore let him judge between me and you." And as soon as that wretched man accepted the body of Christ, he fell down dead. And therefore let everyone take care lest he approach unworthily, for indeed he would not cause harm to the priest, but to himself. And priests would do well if they tell this example and others like it to their parishioners and subordinates.

But ought criminal suspects to be given this sacrament if they need it? The answer is that suspicion is threefold—some is strong, some probable, some trivial. Strong suspicion is that against which evidence is not admitted, like if someone is found with a corrupt

woman in bed, one man with one woman, a naked man with a naked woman, in a place and time suited for this, without age, relationship, or anything else standing in the way. The suspicion or
presumption would be strong that he had known her, so that evidence to the contrary would not be admitted. Probable suspicion
is that which originates from some signs or probable conjectures,
like if someone is found frequently with some woman, speaking in a suspicious place. The suspicion would be probable that
something bad was being done. Trivial suspicion is what originates
from someone's foolish and inordinate presumption. And this is
called trivial and foolish suspicion, like if I see some good man
and some good young woman greeting one another or laughing
together, not in a suspect time or place. It would be foolish to presume that they were doing something bad. And concerning such
Solomon says, "Whoever is quick to believe has a trivial heart."[156]

Therefore, when it is asked whether those suspected of some
crime ought to be given the body of Christ, I say that if there is
a strong suspicion concerning some notorious criminal, the body
of Christ ought to be denied him. For example, a strong suspicion may be had about someone that he is a notorious heretic or
usurer or keeper of concubines, and so on. I say that before the
body of Christ is given to him, he ought to purge himself of this
crime (X 5.33.2). But if there is a probable suspicion, the body of
Christ ought not to be denied him until it is proven against him,
even if such suspicion is widely held against him. Nevertheless, he
is to be warned that he should purge himself before he comes to
the sacrament, and if he consents, he does well. But if he remains
steadfast and denies the crime concerning which it is probably presumed against him, I do not believe that, before it is proven, he
is to be deprived of the right which he has to ask for and receive
the body of Christ. Especially since it is his own business, and if
it is received unworthily, it harms him but not others. Nevertheless I believe that the priest can and ought to say some threatening words to him to scare him by saying, "If you worthily receive,

156. Ecclesiasticus [Sirach] 19:4

may it profit you for the salvation of body and soul; if unworthily, may the Lord judge between me and you." But if there is trivial
and foolish suspicion against someone concerning any crime, on
account of such suspicion, since it is trivial and foolish, nothing
in particular ought to be done against him. Nevertheless, in general, it would be good for the priest to say some threatening words,
showing that no one ought to be presumed to be good or bad unless it is established for certain, because many people say many
things and anyone ought to purge himself both before God and
the people before he comes to this sacrament.

But ought this sacrament be given to the excommunicated? I
say no. For as long as they are excommunicated, they are separated from participation in the sacraments and from the communion
of the faithful. But what if someone who is excommunicated is in
danger of death and asks to be given the body of Christ? What
ought to be done? I say that he is excommunicated either by canon
or by law or by a judge. If he is excommunicated by canon or by
law, the priest ought to absolve him if he asks humbly for absolution, because in the case of danger of death, a simple priest can absolve him from whatever sentence of excommunication is brought
to bear by canon, even if the absolution were reserved to the apostolic see. Nevertheless, in whatever case he is absolved, he ought
to be absolved under this form, that if the Lord should offer him
life, immediately, as fast as he reasonably can, he should go to him
who can absolve him and his authority over those things for which
he was excommunicated is humbly to be accepted. And unless he
does this immediately, he will fall back under the same sentence of
excommunication by the same law, as is found in VI 5.11.22. But if
he is excommunicated by a judge, either for great contumacy or for
some other offense, or for some other reason, and whatever it is, he
ought to be absolved if he asks humbly for absolution. Nevertheless, first he should give pledges or an appropriate guarantee that he
will comply with and obey the rules of the church and will repair
the injury suffered. And if he cannot give pledges or a guarantee, let
him swear that he will satisfy as soon as he can.

But what if someone living in mortal sin or excommunication and living in danger of death sends for the priest that he might hear his confession and absolve him and give him the body of Christ, and before the priest comes to him he loses the power of speech? Should he be given the body of Christ? I say that if he understands anything he should be warned that if he is not able to speak he should show some sign of contrition. For instance, he may raise his joined hands to God and strike his chest or through some other signs show that he asks for absolution from sins and from the sentence of excommunication. And his parents and friends, in his place and for his sake, ought to promise and swear faith or give pledges, if they are able, that if the Lord should offer him life he will present himself before the one who can absolve him, and his authority over this will be humbly accepted. And thus the priest ought to absolve and commune him. But if he understands nothing, and if it is evident and can be proven that signs of contrition and repentance came earlier, he ought to be absolved and communed, having first received assurances or pledges or a vow from his parents and friends, in the manner described above.

Note especially that the priest who communes his people ought to warn them about several things. First, that one may not come to this sacrament aware of any mortal sin. Second, that one should leave behind hatred and rancor toward others. Third, that no excommunicated person may come, nor anyone who is not fasting, except in case of necessity. Fourth, that before and after communion they should keep themselves from their wives at least for three days (D.2 de cons. C.21; C.33 q.4. c.1). Fifth, that after receiving the body of Christ, one should not spit in an unclean place or in a place where the spit could be trodden under foot, and this is before eating. Sixth, that as much as possible, they should abstain from vomiting and seasickness. Note that after receiving the body of Christ, a little wine ought to be taken lest some of this sacrament remain in the mouth and be expelled by spitting. Hence in some churches there is the praiseworthy custom that on Easter, after communion, a little bit of wine and bread is given out.

CHAPTER 10: On the rite by which the mass
ought to be celebrated

"Let everything be done respectfully and according to proper
order among you."[157] These are words of the Apostle teaching and
instructing us how we ought to do all our works in proper order
and respectfully, especially those which pertain to the worship of
God, among which the mass is chief. If we ought to do our other works in proper order and respectfully, how much more those
in the mass. Now, therefore, let us consider the rite of the mass,
that is, the way in which the mass ought to be said. The priest,
armed with spiritual armor, that is, dressed in the sacred vestments discussed above, ought to go up to the altar. And because,
as Solomon says, "The wise man accuses himself at the start of
his words,"[158] first, the priest ought to accuse himself, namely, by
offering the general confession which suffices for the remission of
venial sins and also for forgotten mortal sins. But he ought to confess sacramentally the mortal sins which he remembers before he
dresses himself or goes up to the altar; and once this confession
has been made, he may proceed to the mass.

And note why this sacrament is called the mass. According to
Augustine, it is called the mass [missa, from mitto, to send] because
while this sacrament is being confected, a heavenly messenger is
sent [mittitur]. And according to what Pope Innocent explains,[159]
this heavenly messenger is the Angel of Great Counsel,[160] and he
is sent to consecrate. And he is the invisible priest who principally
consecrates and confects this sacrament wherever it is confected.
Hence he is priest and sacrifice, as Augustine says.[161] Hugh gives
another reason, saying that the host itself can be called the mass
because it was first sent from the Father so that he might be with

157. 1 Corinthians 14:40
158. Cf. Proverbs 18:17
159. Cf. Innocent III, De sacro altaris mysterio, Bk IV, c. 6 (PL 217:859).
160. Isaiah 9:6
161. D.2 de cons. c.48

us, and afterward from us to the Father so that he might intercede for us.[162]

Know that the mass is celebrated in three languages, namely, Hebrew, Greek, and Latin. "Alleluia," "Amen," "Hosanna," and "Sabaoth" are taken from Hebrew. "Kyrie eleison, Christe eleison" is taken from Greek. All the rest of the words are Latin. And the mass is said in these three languages, because the title of Christ, when he was hanging on the cross, was written in Hebrew, Greek, and Latin.[163]

The mass is divided into four parts, namely, supplications, prayers, requests, and thanksgivings. The first part pertains to the instruction of the people; the second to the consecration of the matter; the third to the reception of the consecrated matter; the fourth to thanksgiving. The first part extends from the beginning of the mass to the offertory; the second from the offertory to the end of the Lord's Prayer, namely, Our Father etc.; the third to the communion; the fourth to the end of the mass.

The first part contains ten or eleven parts. The first is called the introit because then the priest who is about to serve ought to go up to the altar. And know that long ago, a whole psalm was said in the place of the introit. It was sung by a cleric on the steps [gradus] of the altar, and therefore it is called the gradual. But St. Jerome, who at the command of the Lord in the time of Pope Damasus, set up the ecclesiastical office in large part, instead of the song instituted various introits to fit the variety of festivals and days.[164] And from that psalm which long ago was sung in the place of the introit, he took one verse. Hence on ordinary days, the introit is sung twice to signify that in Christ there are two natures, namely, human and divine. On solemn days, it is said three times to signify three eras, namely, the time which was before the law, the time

162. Hugh of Saint Victor, *De sacramentis Christianae fidei*, Bk. 2, part 8, c. 14 (PL 176:472). English translation, *On the Sacraments of the Christian Faith*, trans. Roy J. Deferrari (Cambridge, Mass.: Medieval Academy of America, 1951).

163. John 19:19–20

164. D.92 c.1

under the law, and the time of grace. Hence the first two times it is said in a low voice, because in the first two eras people did not speak openly and clearly about Christ, but the third time it is said in a full voice, because in the third era, "their sound has gone forth throughout all the earth,"[165] namely, that of the evangelists.

After the introit the "Kyrie eleison" is said; this is the same as "Lord have mercy." "Christe eleison" is truly the same as "Christ have mercy." And it is said three times on account of the Father, Son, and Holy Spirit. And it is said nine times on account of the nine orders of angels with whom we ask to be united by virtue of the mass.

On solemn days, after the Kyrie eleison, the "Glory be to God on high" is said. The angels sang this hymn at Christ's birth up to "of goodwill."[166] The rest of it, namely, "We praise thee, etc." St. Hilary, bishop of Poitiers, added and instituted it to be sung in the mass. And this angelic hymn ought to be sung on the feasts of the apostles, martyrs, confessors, and virgins in whose honor a church is dedicated, and on the feasts of the Blessed Virgin Mary. But when on feast days the mass of the Blessed Virgin is sung, or that of the Holy Spirit, or of some other saint, the angelic hymn or the Creed is not said in it, although it may be chanted in a particular mass. The reason is, as is given in X 3.41.4, to show the difference between commemoration and solemnity. But on Saturday when the mass of the Virgin Mary is sung, I believe that the "Glory be to God on high" ought to be said because that day is dedicated to the Virgin Mary herself on account of many reasons that need not be stated here.

When the angelic hymn has been said, the priest turns to the people and greets them saying, "The Lord be with you." This greeting was taken from the Old Testament, namely, from the book of Ruth, when Boaz said to his reapers, "The Lord be with you."[167] Yet know that a bishop says "Peace be with you" instead

165. Romans 10:18   166. Luke 2:4
167. Ruth 2:4

of "The Lord be with you." And the reason is that the bishop represents the person of Christ, who, when he greeted his disciples, said, "Peace be with you."[168] And know that even if there is only one person in the church, the priest always should say, "the Lord be with you [plural]," because he speaks to the whole church. And to him is replied, "And with your spirit." This response was taken from the Apostle in 2 Timothy, chapter 4.[169]

After the greeting and response, the priest continues with, "Let us pray," speaking in the person of the whole people. Having said "Let us pray," he says the prayer. And this is called the collect, because formerly the bishop or the priest, when all the people were collected, said it over the people. Since indeed in our time we are not able to gather or collect the people this way, we say the prayer which in ancient and general usage is still called the collect. Hence these prayers ought to be said in a certain number, such that one may be said, or three, or five, or seven. When three are said, they signify the Trinity of persons; or three are said because Christ in his passion, which this sacrament calls to mind, is read to have prayed three times. First when he prayed that his hour of passion might be taken from him.[170] Second, when he said, "Father, forgive them, for they do not know what they are doing."[171] Third when he said, "Father, into your hands I commend my spirit."[172] When five prayers are said, they bring to mind the five wounds of Christ. And when seven are said, they signify that the priest, if he worthily says the mass, is favorably heard for all seven petitions which are contained in the Lord's Prayer. Or it signifies that he asks, for himself and for others for whom he says mass, for the seven gifts of the Holy Spirit to be infused by virtue of the mass. And as Master Jean Beleth says, more than seven collects ought not to be said.[173] And when mass is celebrated for the living, no collect

168. Luke 24:36; John 20:26   169. 2 Timothy 4:22
170. Mark 14:35   171. Luke 23:34
172. Luke 23:46

173. Jean Beleth, *Summa de ecclesiasticis officiis*, c. 37. A modern critical edition in Latin is available; see Jean Beleth, *Summa de ecclesiasticis officiis*, ed. Heribert Douteil, vol. 41A, Corpus Christianorum Continuatio Mediaevalis (Turnhout: Brepols, 1976).

for the dead ought to be said. And when mass is said for the dead, none for the living ought to be said, except for the one which applies to both, "Omnipotent and eternal God who rules over the living and the dead, etc." But if in a mass for the living, a collect for the dead is said for some reason, it ought not to be said last but next to last, because the end ought to correspond to the beginning. And when the collects have been said, "Amen" is replied in confirmation.

When the collects are finished, the epistle is read. And it is called the epistle from *"epi,"* which is "in addition to," and *"stolon,"* which is "a sending," as if to say "sent in addition," because the epistles were sent in addition to the gospel. And note that no one ought to say the epistle unless he has been made a subdeacon. Hence it is better that the priest say it than the boy who helps him at mass. After the epistle the responsory is said, which is so named because one ought to respond to the epistle with its verse. "Verse" is so called from "turning" [*vertendo*], because those who say the verse ought to turn themselves to the east.

Then the Alleluia is said with its verse, and this is a song of joy. Hence in a time of fasting, which is a time of sorrow, the alleluia ought not to be said, nor, for the same reason, in a mass for the dead. On great solemnities, after the Alleluia, the sequence, that is, the prose, is said, which is also a song of joy. And these two indicate the joy of the glory of paradise to which we hope to come by virtue of the mass.

Immediately after the prose has been said, the gospel is read. At the beginning he who reads the gospel greets the people so that they may give him attention and hear the gospel. And it is called "gospel" [*evangelium*] from *"ev"* which is "good" and *"angelus"* which is "messenger," as if to say "good messenger," because in the gospel, Christ who is the Angel of Great Counsel is announced.[174] Or, because in it, everything is announced that pertains to our salvation. And note that when the gospel is read from the beginning [of a book], "The beginning of the holy gospel" ought to be

174. Cf. Isaiah 9:6.

said, as in that gospel reading, "The book of the lineage of Jesus Christ."[175] But when the gospel reading is not taken from the beginning, "A passage from the holy gospel" ought to be said, and this means, "the following words are the words of the holy gospel." Note especially that once the title of the gospel has been said, it should be responded, "Glory to thee, Lord," because in the gospel one reads about God's glory and with ours, namely, how Christ defeated the devil and redeemed us and ascended victorious to the glory of the Father. And therefore the hearers of the gospel, rejoicing in praise of their savior, exclaim saying, "Glory to thee, Lord," as if to say, "Lord, may your glory which is preached in the gospel remain with us forever and increase always." Hence when the gospel is read, two candles ought to be lit as a sign that the Lord sent his disciples two by two before his face to preach the gospel.[176] Note that as soon as the gospel is begun, both clergy and laity, both reader and hearers, ought to defend themselves with the sign of the cross on the forehead, mouth, and chest. On the forehead because the forehead is the place of shame. Hence we call shameless people brazen [effrontes], that is, without a forehead [sine fronte]. Therefore, by putting a cross on our foreheads, we signify that we are not ashamed to believe in Christ crucified and to confess him to be true God and true man. And as we sign mouth and chest, it indicates that we boldly confess with our mouths and faithfully and firmly believe in our hearts that Christ crucified, whose book is read, is God and our Lord.[177] And thus the priest or the deacon as he is about to read the gospel, signs himself on the forehead, on the mouth, and on the chest, as if to say, "I am not ashamed to preach his gospel with my mouth and to believe it in my heart." And he also signs the book as if to say, "This is the book of the crucified." And while the gospel is read, all remove their head coverings on account of two things. First, to show that the evangelical teaching removes every covering of the old law. Second, to show that the five senses ought to be uncovered for hearing the gospel.

175. Matthew 1:1   176. Luke 10:1
177. Cf. Romans 10: 9

Hence he who says the gospel ought to have his face to the north as a sign that we ought to defend ourselves with the power of the gospel against "the treachery of the devil"[178] which comes from the north. For as Jeremiah says, "From the north all evil spreads out."[179] When the gospel is finished, each person ought to defend himself with the sign of the cross against the devil, lest he snatch the words of the gospel from mouth or heart.

After the gospel comes the creed, namely, "I believe." And it ought not to be said except on solemn days, and yet not on all of them, but only on those of which mention is made in the creed. Hence it ought to be said on all Sundays, the feast of the Holy Trinity, Christmas, Circumcision, Epiphany, Easter, Ascension, Pentecost, the feasts of the Blessed Virgin Mary, the feast of All Saints, the Transfiguration of the Lord, the feasts of all the Apostles, and the holy cross. But on other feast days, it ought not to be said.

When the creed has been said, the offertory is said, which is named from "offering" [offerendo], because then we offer those things which are necessary for the mass, namely, bread and wine and water. And the priest offering these says, "Holy Trinity, accept, etc." And the priest makes the sign of the cross over the bread and wine so that the Lord may sanctify them. And note that the priest blesses the water and not the wine, because the water signifies the people who need the blessing of God, but the wine signifies Christ who is blessed above all.[180] And with this ends the first part of the mass which is for the instruction of the people and preparation for so great a sacrament.

The second part of the mass follows which concerns the consecration of the matter and it has four parts. The first part is called the secrets, the second the preface, the third the canon, the fourth the Lord's Prayer.

The offering having been received, the priest washes his hands and returning to the altar, bows deeply, saying, "Humbled in spir-

178. Ephesians 6:11   179. Jeremiah 1:14
180. Romans 9:5

it, etc." to show that through purity and innocence of life and humility and contrition of heart, one is made a worthy minister of this sacrament. And standing up he turns to the people saying, "Pray for me brothers, etc." And therefore those who hear the mass ought to pray for him by saying that Psalm, "May the Lord hear you,"[181] or by saying, "May the Lord be in your heart and in your mouth so that he may receive the sacrifice from your mouth and from your hands for your salvation and for all of us." And the laity likewise ought to bow and say devoutly some prayer they know.

After this the priest says the secrets. And as many secrets and in the same order as the collects offered earlier in the opening of the mass before the epistle ought to be said, not more, not less. And this part is called the "secrets" because it is recited secretly, yet formerly it was said in a full voice and so was known by all the laity. But according to what Master Jean Beleth relates in his *Summa*, it happened one day that some shepherds put bread on a certain stone and said the secrets and other words of the canon over the bread which turned into flesh at their utterance. By divine providence, a bitter punishment came among them, for all were struck dead by lightning. Therefore, it was mandated that these secrets among others would be said in silence, so that they would not be known by the laity.[182] The second reason [for saying these prayers in silence] is so that they will not be disdained just as the holy scripture is delivered obscurely.

After this the priest says, "world without end," and they respond, "Amen." The priest greets the people saying, "The Lord be with you." This greeting was discussed above. And because in this sacrament great elevation of mind to God is required, the priest says, "Let us lift up our hearts," as if to say, "Have your hearts lifted up to God," in keeping with the word of the Apostle, saying, "Seek the things that are above."[183] And the people, as if obeying and agreeing, say, "We lift our hearts up to God." And because we

181. Psalm 19:2
182. Beleth, *Summa de ecclesiasticis officiis*, c. 44.
183. Colossians 3:1

ought to extend thanks for all the things God has given to us, the priest adds, "Let us give thanks to the Lord our God." And the people, as if agreeing, respond, "That is just and fitting."

After this the preface is said. And it is called "preface" as if to say "preamble," that is, preparation for the mystery. Thus in the preface some orders of angels are named, because we believe angels to be present in the mass and to assist the priest. When the preface has been said, the song of the angels follows, namely, "Holy, holy, holy Lord God of Sabaoth, etc." that is, of Hosts, "Hosanna," that is, "Save, I beseech you." And "Holy" is said three times to designate the persons of the Trinity, and "Lord God" is said in the singular to show that there is one essence in three persons. And this is taken from Isaiah 6; indeed Isaiah said that he had seen the seraphim and cherubim crying "Holy, etc."[184] Hence we sing the song of the angels because, by this sacrifice, we do not doubt that persons are taken up to the orders of angels; therefore with them we cry out to be saved.

Next, another verse is said, namely, "Blessed is he who comes, etc.," which verse is taken from the gospel, Matthew, chapter 21.[185] While it is sung, the sign of the cross ought to be made as a sign that it is taken from the gospel which is the book of the crucified. Therefore we confess Christ to have come into the world, and we ask to be saved by him.

Then follows the canon and it begins with, "To you, therefore, etc." and lasts until "the peace of the Lord." And it is called the canon, which is a Greek name, and it means the same as rule in Latin, because through these words the consecration of this sacrament is accomplished according to the rule, and because the celebrant ought to conduct himself in all things according to the rule. Hence everything contained in the canon, except the Our Father, ought to be said in silence. And the reason for this is threefold. First, because God does not listen to the clamor of the mouth, but to the heart. Hence St. Bernard says, "Not the voice, but the

184. Isaiah 6:1–3
185. Matthew 21:15.

vow, not the musical string, but the voice; not clamor, but love, sounds in the ear of God." The second reason is lest a minister, who ought to say and offer all the words of the canon with great reverence and devotion and recollection of mind, tired out by long proclamation, be impeded or fail in his devotion. The third reason is lest the words be valued less through daily and frequent use, and be said in inappropriate places, and thus bring about ruin, as I said above about the shepherds. In a certain decretal, it is prohibited under anathema for anyone, except the priest dressed in sacred vestments and [celebrating] by the book and at a consecrated altar, to offer the words of the canon. And therefore because "I am a man of unclean lips,"[186] and these most holy words, which a sinful man is not permitted to speak, are secret, I say nothing of them. No one on his own authority, except the lord pope, is allowed to subtract from or add anything to these words.

Also note that the canon begins expressly with this letter, T, which in olden days was made in the shape of a cross, since the sacrifice which is made by virtue of these words brings to mind the Lord's passion. Hence Christ, who instituted this sacrament, said, "Do this in memory of me," in Luke 22.[187] And because these words have efficacy from the passion of Christ, on account of this, an image of Christ crucified is often depicted there. And in these most holy words prayer is offered for the holy catholic church in general, for the pope, and for the bishop who ordained the celebrant. Prayer is also offered for the king who is the lord of temporal things. Prayer is also offered for all the orthodox, that is, Christians worshipping in the catholic and apostolic faith, whose content is explained in the third part of this work when "I believe in God" is dealt with. Hence by these words schismatics, heretics, Jews, Saracens, and pagans are excluded. And thus note that the excommunicated are not prayed for here.

After this, prayer is offered especially for those to whom the priest is obligated. And I believe that just as he is obligated to

186. Isaiah 6:5
187. Luke 22:19

them in order of charity, so he ought to order them in the mass, so that the priest puts first the one to whom he was obligated first. Nevertheless, if he says a mass specially for someone so that the virtue of the sacrifice may redound to him, even on account of this, it is not as though someone ought to be excluded; he can and should pray for others. And yet concerning this prayer, be warned that it ought to be mental and not vocal. The reason for this is twofold. First, so that the priest may be more recollected and attentive, because sometimes a word distracts his attention. Second, to show that God does not listen to the clamor of the mouth but to the heart, as said above.

And note that none of the faithful who come to mind are to be excluded from this prayer. Indeed whoever comes to mind is always to be commended to God; otherwise the priest sins. Note too that the priest, before he says mass, can offer this prayer, saying out loud to God, "Lord God, in this mass I intend to commend to you this one, etc." Afterwards it suffices that mentally he say in the mass, "Remember, Lord, your servants whom I commended to you earlier." After this many male and female saints are named, all of whom sacrificed themselves for Christ, exposing themselves to death. And let these remarks concerning the words of the canon suffice for the time being.

But something should be said about the signs which are made during the canon. Hence according to what the Lord Pope Innocent says in his book on the mass, "The signs of the cross which are made in the mass are twenty-five in number and are done at seven points which expressly signify the passion of Christ."[188] At the first point, three are made saying these words, "these offerings, these oblations, etc.," and they signify the threefold handing over of Christ. For first he was handed over by God the Father who sent him into the world. Second, by Judas the traitor who sold him. Third, by the Jews who handed him over to Pilate to be crucified. At the second point, five are made saying these words,

188. Innocent III, *De sacro altaris mysterio*, Bk V, c. 14 (PL 217:895–97).

"wholly blessed, a thing consecrated and approved, etc.," and they signify the five people who were involved in the passion of Christ, namely, the person of Christ being sold, the person of Judas selling, and the persons buying who were three, namely, the priests, the Pharisees, and the scribes. At the third point, two are made, saying that phrase "he blessed it." And these two crosses are made first over the bread, second over the wine, on account of the twofold conversion of the matter, namely, of bread and of wine. At the fourth point, five are made saying these words, "a sacrifice that is pure, etc.," and they signify the five wounds of Christ which he bore on the cross. At the fifth point, two are made, one over the body, the other over the blood, saying these words, "sacred body and blood of thy Son, etc." And they signify the bonds with which Christ was bound and the whips with which he was whipped. At the sixth point, three are made, saying these words, "sanctified, endowed with life, etc.," and they signify the three crucifixions of Christ. For first he was crucified by the tongues of the Jews, second by the sentence of Pilate, third by the hands of the soldiers. At the seventh point, five are made, saying these words, "through him, etc.," namely, three with the body over the chalice and two from the side. They signify his three sufferings, namely, of passion, of endurance, and of compassion. The other two signify the water and the blood that flowed from Christ's side.[189] And thus they make twenty-five altogether which is a cubic number to show that however much it may be multiplied, this sacrament is always one. And let this suffice concerning the signs of the canon and consequently about the second part of the mass which pertains to the consecration of the matter of the sacrament, with the exception that when "Peace be with you" is said, three crosses are made.

The third part of the mass comes next, which is for the reception of the consecrated matter. And in this part, first the priest breaks the host into three parts. The first signifies the mystical body of Christ, that is, the faithful who sojourn in this world.

189. John 19:34

The second signifies those who are in purgatory. The third signifies those who are in paradise.

And with "World without end" and its response "Amen" having been said, the priest says, "The peace of the Lord be always with you," making three crosses with one part of the host over the chalice. And these signify that by the death of Christ, peace was restored on earth between God and humanity. Then "Lamb of God" is said three times. "Lamb" [*agnus*] comes from "recognizing" [*agnoscendo*] because as the lamb recognizes its mother by a single bleat, so Christ recognized his mother in his passion. Or it comes from "recognition" [*agnitio*], which is "faithful," because Jesus Christ redeems us by his faithfulness. And "Lamb of God" is said three times because Christ hanging on the cross recognized three people, namely, his Father by obeying him, his virgin mother by entrusting her to a virgin,[190] and the human race by redeeming it. "Have mercy on us" is said twice, and the last time "Give us peace" is said, to show that in this world and in purgatory we need the mercy of God and in paradise we will have the most splendid peace and rest. But in the mass for the dead, "Give them rest" is said because the mass is said for them so that they may come to the rest of paradise.

Then the priest puts one part of the host into the chalice, and this signifies, as has been said, those who are in paradise, who are inebriated with the glory of paradise. As Psalm 125 says, "They will be inebriated with the fruitfulness of your house, and you will give them to drink from the torrent of your enjoyment."[191]

Then the priest gives peace with a kiss, according to some from the eucharist, according to others from the chalice, according to others from the altar, to the deacon, and he to the subdeacon, and thus through these it comes down to others, to signify that "the peace of the Lord, which exceeds all understanding,"[192] comes down through Christ to the prelates, and from the prelates to those under them. It also signifies that all who want to be par-

---

190. John 19:26–27   191. Psalm 35:9
192. Philippians 4:7

ticipants in the fruit of this sacrament ought to be bound together with the bonds of peace and charity.

After two prayers are said, the priest receives the sacrament under the species of bread and wine. But it is not to be given to the laity under the species of wine on account of the danger of spilling. After the reception of the sacrament, the priest ought to take some wine and rinse his mouth, unless he will celebrate another mass that day. And thus ends the third part of the mass which pertains to the reception of the sacrament.

The fourth part of the mass comes next which pertains to thanksgiving. First, it is called communion from "with" [con] which is "together" and "unite" [unio], as if to say "unite together," to indicate that by virtue of this sacrament we are united to God and neighbor through charity. After communion, a certain prayer is said which is called the postcommunion because it is said after communion. And these prayers ought to be said in the same number as the collects. After greeting the people and the response "and with you," the priest says, "Go, this is the dismissal." And this means, "Go after me to Christ and let us follow him," because the host is sent for you to be reconciled to God the Father; or, "Go home," because the mass is ended.

And note that "Go, this is the dismissal" ought not to be said unless the "Glory be to God on high" is said, otherwise "Let us bless the Lord" is said. And in the mass for the dead, "May they rest in peace" is said. If it is asked why "Go, this is the dismissal" is not said at the end of every mass, I say that the mystical body of Christ, which is the church, is threefold, namely, that which is glorified in heaven, that is, the saints who are in paradise; that which still walks on earth, that is, the faithful who are in this world; and that which has already left this world but is not yet in paradise, that is, the faithful who are in purgatory. Therefore although any mass pertains to the whole mystical body of Christ, as is evident in the triple partition of the host, yet according to this threefold distinction, masses ought to be established and appropriated in common. For some masses are celebrated in honor of the saints, and because they are already in the presence of God, in such masses the people are dismissed and "Go, this is the dismissal," is said, as if to say, "Go, hurry to enter into that rest." Some are specially celebrated for the salvation of the living, and because we are not certain of our salvation, we ought to take care lest through our negligence the effectiveness of the mass vanishes from us. Therefore in these masses, "Let us bless the Lord" is said at all times, according to Psalm 23, "I will bless the Lord at all times."[193] Some are celebrated especially for the repose of the dead, and in these, "May they rest in peace" is said.

Note that in the mass the priest turns toward the people five times and greets them seven times. That he turns toward the people five times signifies that Christ appeared five times on the day of his resurrection. First to Mary Magdalene in the garden;[194] second to the women going and returning from the tomb;[195] third, to St. Peter, but when and where is not known,[196] and so when the priest turns for the third time he does not speak in a loud voice; fourth he appeared to the disciples gathered together when he came in to them through the locked door, and Thomas was not with them;[197] fifth, he appeared to two disciples going to Emmaus.[198] And the priest greets the people seven times, signifying that by virtue of the mass we may come to eternal life, in which we will have seven gifts, four on the part of the body and three on the part of the soul.

Note that the priest begins the mass at the right side of the altar and then goes to the left side, and returns again to the right. This signifies that Christ came from the right hand of the Father into the world, and returned again on Ascension Day to the right hand of the Father. According to John, "I went forth from the Father, and I have come into the world. Next I am leaving the world, and I am going to the Father."[199]

193. Psalm 33:2
195. Matthew 28:9–10
197. John 20:19–24
199. John 16:28

194. John 20:14–17
196. 1 Corinthians 15:5
198. Luke 24:13–35

If it is asked whether the canon ought to be said slowly or quickly, that is, whether the priest ought to pause often in the canon or not, the answer is that the priest ought to say every word of the canon with good fullness and great attention. Nevertheless, he ought not to delay there much lest arriving "flies," that is, diabolical temptations, "ruin the sweetness of the ointment,"[200] that is, the sweetness of this sacrament, because the human will is changeable and never remains in the same state. Therefore, as a figure of this, it was said to the children of Israel that they should consume the paschal lamb in haste.[201]

And note that the mass should never be said without light. And let these things suffice concerning the ritual of the mass.

CHAPTER 11: On defects that can occur in the mass

Where greater danger looms, there advice is to be sought more fully. And because in the celebration of the mass, unless it is done in the obligatory way, the greatest danger looms, therefore the greatest care ought to be taken over the defects which can occur in the mass, so that if they happen they can be better corrected. There can be defects in the mass before the consecration or after the consecration or in the consecration itself.

Before the consecration, there can be a defect if it is not administered with the right matter, for instance, if in place of wine water is used. Hence suppose that the priest or the servant who serves him in the mass puts water into the chalice believing it to be white wine. What should the priest do? The answer is that either the priest perceives this error before the consecration or after. If before the consecration, he ought to throw out the water and mix wine with water, and thus he can complete his service. But if he notices it after the consecration of the body, he notices it either before he receives it or after. If before, he ought to mix wine with water in the chalice and begin again from the place, "In like man-

200. Ecclesiastes 10:1
201. Exodus 12:11

ner, etc.," and continue to the end. But if he notices it after the reception of the body, he ought to administer one nonconsecrated host, and put wine with water into the chalice, and start again from the beginning of the canon, according to some. But I believe that it suffices to repeat from that place in the canon, "United in the same holy fellowship," and continue his service. And you may say that perhaps he does not perceive his error until he has consumed the water placed in the chalice instead of wine, and thus he is not fasting and so it would seem that he ought not to celebrate. In this case, I say what is to be kept as a general rule, that whenever two precepts apply to the same thing, the stronger one is more binding. Now concerning the celebration of the mass, there are two precepts. One is that the mass is to be said by one who is fasting. The other is that the sacrament ought to be done completely, that is, the celebrant always should consecrate under both species, namely, bread and wine. It is the case that the precept concerning the integrity of the sacrament is stronger than the precept that it is to be received by one who is fasting, since the former pertains to the essence of the sacrament and the latter to its use. This is why even though he drank water and is not fasting, he still ought to do as was said above, namely, that he should take a nonconsecrated host, wine, and water, and start again at the beginning of the canon, or from that place, "United in the same holy fellowship, etc." and then carry on to the end.

But if he who attends to the wine does not put water there in the chalice, what is to be done in this case? I say that if the priest notices it before the consecration of the blood, he ought to put water in the chalice and thus consecrate. But if he notices it after the consecration of the blood, he ought to confess his negligence and be contrite and proceed with the mass, because wine is the proper matter of this sacrament and not water, as was said above. Nevertheless it ought to be mixed in out of a certain appropriateness.

But what if the priest notices that there is poison in the chalice or that a spider or a fly has fallen in? Should he receive it? Certainly, as far as the poison or the spider goes, I say no, lest the cup of life become a cup of death. But this blood ought to be put among the relics in some clean and suitable vessel, with some written notice [saying] that here is the blood of Christ and that it may not be consumed by anyone, because poison is mixed with this species. And if the priest has not consumed the body of Christ, he ought to put some wine with water in the chalice, and start again from that place, "In like manner, etc." But if he has already consumed the body of Christ, he ought to take another nonconsecrated host, as was said above. As for the fly, I say that on account of a fly, he ought not to throw it out without consuming it. Even so, I do not believe that he ought to swallow the fly, as some say, but it suffices that it be washed and the wash water be consumed. And if he fears vomiting, let him eat something that prevents vomiting. And let the fly be burned and the ashes kept in a shrine. And I say the same thing about a spider, namely, that it ought to be burned and its ashes kept in a shrine.

But suppose that when a priest elevates the host, there should appear the species of a child or of flesh. What should he do? I say that either it appears this way to everyone or just to the priest or just to the people. If it appears thus to everyone, namely, to the people and to the priest, prayers ought to be poured out to God that it be turned back into the species of bread. And if that happens, it ought to be consumed. But if not, other matter ought to be taken and consecrated. But if it does not appear to the priest, but just to the people, it ought to be consumed by the priest.

But what if the chalice falls and the blood is spilled? What is to be done then? I say that what is to be done in this case is taught in a certain decretal, D.2 de cons. c.27, in which it says: "If through negligence some drips onto the ground, it should be licked up with the tongue and the table or ground should be scraped and [the scrapings] burned in fire; and the ashes should be hidden inside the altar. And the priest should do penance for forty days. If the chalice has dripped on the altar, the servant should wipe up the drip and do penance for three days. If the drops get to the third linen cloth, he should do penance for nine days. If to the fourth, he should do penance for twenty days. And placing the chalice to the side, let the servant wash the linen which the drop touched three times in succession, and the washing water is to be taken up and kept in a vessel near the altar."

But if someone, through drunkenness or overeating should vomit the eucharist, if a layperson, he should do penance for forty days; if a clerk, monk, deacon, or priest, he should do penance for eighty days; if a bishop ninety. If he truly vomits because of sickness, he should do penance for seven days. This is found in D.2 de cons. c.27 and D.2 de cons. c.28. And what was vomited up ought to be gathered and burned, and the ashes kept near the altar. What should the penance be for this? Some say that all the days of this penance one ought to fast on bread and water and abstain from communion. Others say that it suffices that one perform some abstinence and say some prayers.

But suppose that a priest dresses himself to celebrate and later, after he has gone forward for the mass, remembers that he has committed some mortal sin which he has not confessed, or he remembers that he is excommunicated. What should he do? If he proceeds [with the mass], it seems that he sins mortally, because "he eats and drinks a sentence against himself."[202] But if he sends everyone away, he would create a great scandal among the people. Some say that such a priest ought not to say the words of consecration, but ought receive a simple host. But this is not true, indeed it is erroneous, because such a one would mock God by showing irreverence toward the sacrament, and he would deceive the people because he would make them commit idolatry. This is found in X 3.41.7. And therefore I say that if this priest cannot delay the mass without scandal, let it suffice that he be sorry and repent and be contrite for his sin. Also let him be sorry that he repented so late, propose to confess as soon as he has the opportunity, and let him consecrate in the name of the Lord, be-

202. 1 Corinthians 11:29

cause in this case, the highest priest, namely, God, absolves him. And although some say the same applies if he is under a sentence of excommunication, nevertheless I believe that in this case, if the priest does not proceed to the consecration, he ought to delay feigning that he is sick or has some other legitimate need. Or if he cannot delay, let him be sorry and repent, and intend to get himself absolved. And I believe that, as for this sin, he is absolved by the highest priest, namely, by God, and this is with respect to guilt. But whether he is absolved with respect to the penalty of irregularity, I will not settle here.

But suppose that the priest omits some of the words of the canon. Should he repeat them? I say that either he has probable [almost certain awareness, or he has trivial or scrupulous awareness. If he has certain or very probable][203] awareness that he left out some of the words, then he ought to repeat them, especially if he knows that they were from the words of consecration. But it is not to be understood that what is doubtfully forgotten should be repeated or what he is unaware of having done, as is said in D.4 de cons. c.113; X 3.43.3.[204] Nevertheless I believe the priest ought to have this intention, "If I said these words, I do not intend to repeat them with the intention of consecrating, but if I did not say them, I say them now." This is argued in X 3.42.2 where it says, "If you are baptized, I do not baptize you, but if you are not baptized, I baptize you in the name of the Father, etc." But these words ought not to be repeated on account of a tender and scrupulous awareness. Therefore the priest ought to be very recollected and attentive when he says these words.

But suppose that when a priest celebrates, while making signs of the cross with the host, perhaps on account of the cold or from carelessness or something else, the host falls into the blood. What ought to be done? I say that he ought to leave it there and not take it out, but he ought to consume it with the blood, because the

203. Omitted in our edition, supplied from the other edition consulted.
204. See also X 3.41.6.

signs of the cross and fractions which are made with the host belong more to the meaning of the mass than to its essence.

Also suppose that on account of the cold, the blood freezes in
the chalice. What is to be done? I say that then the priest ought to
exhale, that is, breathe out, into the chalice so that it melts. Nevertheless I believe that it would be safer if the chalice were wrapped
in hot bread, and if that does not work, it should be placed in boil-
ing hot water, nevertheless taking care that water not get into it.

But suppose that while the priest is saying mass, he dies or comes
down with some illness so that he cannot finish the mass. What is
to be done? I say that concerning this matter there is a general rule
that he who says the mass ought always to finish it and receive the
sacrament if he can. If he cannot, another person ought to receive
and finish it in his place. Therefore in the proposed case, I say that
either the priest dies or is prevented from continuing before the beginning of the canon or after. If before, there is no reason to worry.
If after, it happens either before the consecration or after. If before,
another priest ought to dress himself and begin where the other left
off. But if he dies or is prevented from continuing after the consecration, another priest ought to finish what remains and receive
the sacrament. But suppose he dies after he received the body and
before he received the blood. In this case, I say that another priest
ought to receive the blood and complete the office of the mass.

But suppose that a mouse or some other creature consumes the
consecrated species. What is to be done? I say that if those species
can be taken out of the animal, the animal ought to be opened and
the species reverently placed in a shrine and the animal burned and
the ashes concealed within the altar.

But suppose that the priest reserved the species so long that
they are now rotten and decayed. What ought to be done with
these species? I say that this matter is to be considered according
to the general rule that the body and blood of Christ remain under these species for as long as the substance of bread and wine
would remain under them before consecration, and the body and
blood of Christ stop being under these species as soon as the spe-

cies of bread and wine would stop being there. And therefore if those species were to come to such decay that the substance or appearance of bread and wine does not or could not remain under them, then the body and blood of Christ are no longer present. Therefore they ought not to be received as consecrated. But let the priest, after he has received the body of Christ in the mass, reverently receive them, but not as consecrated. But if they have not reached such a state of decay and the substance of bread and wine can and does remain under them, they ought to be received as consecrated.

But what if worms come from these decayed species? What ought to be done with the worms? I say that they ought to be burned and the ashes concealed inside the altar, and the priest, by whose negligence this happened, ought to be severely punished. Therefore the priest ought to take care lest he reserve the eucharist for too long a time, and that he not keep it in too humid a place so that the species could easily decay.

These things concerning the sacrament of the eucharist and its minister and trappings, I have written simply and briefly so that simple priests may find certitude in such things, and in other things which long tracts examine, may they be given occasion to think, question, and ask.

Tract 5 of the first principal part is on the sacrament of orders.

Following the order laid out in the beginning of this book, having spoken of the sacraments which bring one into the spiritual life, and advance and preserve one, which are baptism, confirmation, and the sacrament of the eucharist, now the sacraments to be discussed are those that allow a person to rise if he falls. And these are penance, which heals one from sin, and extreme unction, which heals the remains of sin. Because the second part of this book will take up hearing confession and imposing penance, the treatment of penance will be delayed for now, lest it be necessary to repeat the same things. And because what is worthy ought to precede what is less worthy, and since the sacrament of orders is greater and more worthy than the sacrament of extreme unction, therefore the sacrament of orders is to be discussed before the sacrament of extreme unction.

Because conferring the sacrament of orders pertains by law and custom only to bishops, who receive the "anointing which teaches them,"[205] according to the witness of St. John, therefore concerning the topic of the sacrament of orders, I will say little. Since I have holy and venerable bishops as fathers and lords, I desire to have them as teachers. Truly because priests are given all their power in the gaining of orders, it is expedient for them to know something about the sacrament of orders which I will cover in a short compendium. And for now these things can be reduced to five points, which are to be taken up in order. First, what order is; second, how many orders there are; third, if character is impressed in any of the orders; fourth, by which action character is impressed; fifth, what things are required in those receiving orders.

CHAPTER 1: What order is

Order is described thus by Hugh of St. Victor: Order is a certain sign by which and through which spiritual power or office is bestowed on the one ordained.[206] And "power" is used here for orders as specifically understood, but "office" is used here for orders as commonly understood.

CHAPTER 2: How many orders there are

The doctors of canon law and theology differ on the number of orders. For the doctors of canon law say that there are nine orders, namely, psalmist, doorkeeper, lector, exorcist, acolyte, subdea-

205. 1 John 2:27
206. Hugh of Saint Victor, *De sacramentis Christianae fidei*, Bk 2, part 3, c. 1 (PL 176:421).

con, deacon, priest, and bishop. And perhaps the reason that persuades them is that since in every order spiritual power or office is
bestowed, spiritual power and spiritual order are present there. But
spiritual power is bestowed on a bishop and a spiritual office on a
psalmist; therefore the episcopate is a spiritual order and so is being a psalmist. Therefore, so that the church militant may correspond to the church triumphant, and since in the church triumphant there are nine orders of angels, in the church militant there
are nine orders of ministers. And this is an apt enough parallel.

But there are many doctors of theology and many of them hold
that there are only seven, because they claim that psalmists do not
constitute an order, nor do bishops, and thus the sevenfold graces
of the Holy Spirit correspond to the seven orders. Whatever one
makes of this, I think that psalmists are not an order just as the
first tonsure is not, which seems to be a greater thing than becoming a psalmist, since it is conferred by a simple priest, but the first
tonsure is ordinarily conferred by the bishop. Hence, as the doctors say, the first tonsure is not an order but a disposition to orders; a disposition, I say, is not necessary, but is fitting. I doubt
whether the episcopate is truly a spiritual order; therefore I leave
this to the decision of greater ones.

But St. Thomas in his fourth book says that "order" is used
in three ways.[207] In one way, it is the name of an office, and thus
psalmist is an order. In the second way, it is the name of a dignity,
and thus the episcopate is an order. In the third way, it is the name
of some spiritual power, and thus there are only seven orders. And
in this way, the doctors can be brought into agreement. And the
number and the sufficiency of these seven orders are commonly
held by the doctors.

Indeed every order is called an order because it is ordered to the
body of Christ as it is contained in the sacrament of the eucharist.
And according to what St. Augustine says, an order is called greater or worthier the more closely it approaches the sacrament of the

207. Cf. Aquinas, *Scriptum super Sententiis*, Bk 4, d. 24, q. 2, a. 1.

eucharist. Therefore, someone can be ordained to an order to consecrate the body of Christ, and this is the priesthood, whose job it is to consecrate the body of Christ. Or [one can be ordained to an order] to administer the consecrated host to the people, and this is the diaconate, whose job it was in olden days to dispense the blood of Christ to the people. Hence St. Lawrence [a deacon] said to St. Sixtus [a priest], "Have you ever found me to be unworthy, to whom you committed the sharing of the Lord's body and blood?" Or one is ordained to present the matter from which the body of Christ itself is confected by the priest, and this is the subdeacon, whose job it is to prepare the bread and the chalice with wine and water. Or one is ordained to bring this matter to the altar, and this is the acolyte, whose job it is to bring the pix with the bread and the vessels with wine and water to the altar. Or one is ordained to cast out the devil lest he impede people from the reception of the sacrament, and this is the exorcist, whose job it is to command demons. Or one is ordained to admit the worthy into the church and exclude the unworthy, and this is the doorkeeper, whose job it is to take care lest any unworthy people should enter. Or one is ordained to relate those things contained in the Old Testament about Christ in this sacrament, and this is the lector, whose job it is to read the prophecies of the Old Testament. And thus here are the number and sufficiency of the seven orders, specifically understood.

Of these orders, some are called minor and not sacred, namely, lector, doorkeeper, exorcist, acolyte. But the other three, namely, subdeacon, deacon, and priest, are called major and sacred.

CHAPTER 3: Whether character is impressed in every order

Since, according to what was said above when dealing with the sacraments in general, character is a certain special power, through which the recipient of a sacrament which impresses character can do or receive something spiritual which one who does not receive this kind of sacrament cannot do. And since the recipient of an order can do something spiritual which one who lacks that order cannot do, for instance, a priest can consecrate, which one who is not a priest cannot do, and so on, therefore, character is impressed in every order. And suppose you say that one who is not ordained can do those things which belong to an order, like one who is not an acolyte can carry the pix with the bread and the pitchers with wine and water to the altar, therefore it is not necessarily the case that character is impressed in every order. I say that this is not a problem, because according to what is commonly said, "We can do what we can do by law," but by law no one can do those things which belong to the ordained without being ordained.

Note that the characters of all the orders presuppose baptismal character, since baptism is the entrance and foundation of all the sacraments. Hence according to the Apostle, "where there is no foundation, one cannot build upon it."[208] Therefore, no one, unless he is baptized, is able to receive this sacrament (X 3.42.3).

But does the character of one order presuppose the character of another order, that is, can he who is not a subdeacon be ordained a deacon, or one who is not a deacon a priest? I say that the character of one order does not of necessity presuppose the character of another order. Hence, one who is not a subdeacon can be ordained a deacon, and one who is not a deacon can be ordained a priest, although this should not be done. Indeed by the letter of the law, one ought to be deposed if out of malice or ignorance he skipped some order. But with the bishop's permission, and with penance being imposed on him who acted negligently or ignorantly in passing over the middle order, one may be promoted, and at the same time be suspended from the performance of higher orders, because according to Gregory, "one should be raised to orders step by step, because he who seeks the highest places should ascend the slope through the designated steps" (D.48 c. 2; X 5.29.un).

But does the character of order presuppose the first tonsure or the character of confirmation? Although Hugh says that no one can be ordained to the priesthood unless he has the first tonsure,

208. Cf. 1 Corinthians 3:9–15

following the reasoning of D.39 [c.2], nevertheless, the doctors of theology commonly say and maintain that the character of orders does not presuppose of necessity the first tonsure or even confirmation. Indeed one who is not tonsured or confirmed can be ordained, although it ought not to be done. Indeed it was said above that the first tonsure is a disposition to orders by fittingness but not by necessity. Nevertheless note that according to those who hold that the episcopate is an order, the character of episcopal order presupposes sacerdotal character, because one who is not a priest can in no way become a bishop. And this seems to be the meaning of that chapter, X 5.31.10. For the sacerdotal order is like the essential foundation for the episcopal order.

CHAPTER 4: By what act character is impressed in every order

Having seen that character is impressed in every order, it is now to be seen by what action it is impressed in every order. And know that since in the sacrament of orders character is the thing itself and the sacrament, it is necessary that, for the impression of character, two things come together which are required in every sacrament, namely, some visible and sensible sign, which is the matter of the sacrament, and some prescribed words which are the [form] of the sacrament. Therefore in the action in which character is impressed in the sacrament of orders it is necessary that there be these two things, namely, the handing over to someone of the instruments assigned to the performance of the order, and the speaking of certain words. Therefore for the order of priest character is impressed, according to St. Thomas, in the handing over of the chalice with bread and wine and the speaking of the words which the bishop then says, namely, "Receive the power to consecrate, etc."[209] Others say that in the anointing of his hands char-

---

209. Aquinas, *De articulis fidei et ecclesiae sacramentis*, pt. 2. In *Traités: Les Raisons de la foi, Les articles de la foi et les sacrements de l'Église*, 211–95; partial English translation: *The Catechetical Instructions of St. Thomas Aquinas*, 119–31.

acter is impressed on him. Nevertheless, I think the first is truer. On the deacon, character is impressed in the handing over of the book of the gospels with the words specified for this. Character is impressed on the subdeacon in the handing over of the chalice, but without the bread and wine, by which he differs from the priest to whom it is given with the bread and wine. Character is impressed on the acolyte, as some say, in the handing over of the candelabrum. Thomas, however, says that it is in the handing over of the pitchers,[210] and this I think is truer because the pitchers bear more directly on the eucharist than the candelabrum does. Character is impressed on the exorcist in the handing over of the books of exorcisms; on the lector in the handing over of the books of the readings of the prophets; on the doorkeeper in the handing over of the keys to the church. In every order the words specified for this should be said with the handing over of the instruments, because without the words, nothing would be accomplished. I also believe that it does not suffice that the bishop hold out these instruments; indeed it is necessary that the one being ordained physically touch them, since the words which the bishop says when he holds out these instruments in this way seem to signify this. Hence he says "Receive." Therefore every one being ordained ought to be warned about this.

CHAPTER 5: What things are required in those receiving orders

Because according to the Philosopher, "The actions of agents take effect in one who can bear them and who is predisposed toward them," therefore, so that orders may be worthily received, know that for orders to be rightly, lawfully, and worthily received, in general four things are required. The first is the obligation of gender, namely, that it be masculine. Hence a woman cannot be ordained nor can she receive the character of any clerical order,

210. Aquinas, *Summa Theologiae*, Supplement to Part III, q. 37, a. 5.

as Ambrose says about the Epistle to Timothy[211] and as found in
C.33 q.5 c.17; X 5.39.33. And the reason why a woman cannot receive
the character of any order is because Christ, who was the institutor of this sacrament, did not promote any woman to any holy
order. Although the most blessed Virgin Mary was more worthy
and more excellent than all of the apostles, nevertheless he did not
commit to her, but to them, the keys of the kingdom of heaven
(X 5.38.10). And if perhaps in some chapter a woman is found to
be called "deaconess" or "priestess," it is to be understood that
she is called "deaconess" based on some blessing which gives some
benefit or spiritual office, perhaps like reading homilies at matins, or something else which is not permitted to other nuns. Or
she is called "priestess" according to the custom of the primitive
church because she was the wife of a priest or perhaps a widow
having charge of the things of the church, resembling the mother
of a family, and so was called "priestess." And thus all the chapters which speak of this topic ought to be explained. The second
thing required is legal age. About this, know that although doctors
of canon law impose many limits in this matter, yet in our times
we see children and those underage promoted to holy orders; indeed we see some promoted to dignities and the like, and even
made bishop or cardinal in less time than is required by law for
reception into the subdiaconate. This, because it is done by dispensation of the apostolic see, which is ruled by the Holy Spirit, ought not to be condemned by anyone. Nevertheless, it ought
to be regularly maintained that, unless it is done in favor of religion, no one ought to be promoted to the subdiaconate unless he
has reached [eighteen years of age, or to the diaconate unless he
has reached][212] twenty years, or to the priesthood unless he has
reached twenty-five years. Yet I believe that the lord bishops can
make exceptions in these cases, and they make exceptions daily ac-

211. 1 Timothy 2:9–10 (PL 17: 467–468). Medieval scholars mistakenly identified
the author of this commentary as Ambrose; scholars now refer to the writer as "Ambrosiaster."
212. Missing words supplied from alternate edition.

cording to the needs of the church which have no law (X 5.41). This is not right, since all these rules ought to be attended to in all cases.

The third thing which is required in one receiving orders is honest behavior, since the doors of dignities or orders ought not to be open to those who are of notorious or doubtful character (D.81.3; X 2.24.10). Required above all things in promotion to orders or to ecclesiastical dignities is that one have a good reputation and be honest in behavior and life. The Apostle shows what the situation of the one being promoted to holy orders ought to be and what character he ought to have in the Epistle to Timothy, and in the Epistle to Titus 5, saying, "it is necessary for a bishop to be without fault, the husband of one wife, sober, prudent, gracious, chaste, hospitable, a teacher, not a drunkard, not combative but restrained well, not quarrelsome, not covetous; but a man who leads his own house well."[213] And although this authority seems to apply to the bishop, nevertheless according to Augustine and Ambrose, this is to be extended to the other orders (D.34 c.14).

And note that many things ought to be said about each of the conditions in the aforesaid authority, yet because they would require a large tract, I will say just a few things, as if going superficially through it. It says "without fault," which is not to be understood as any fault at all since no one lives without fault. And, as Jerome says about 1 Timothy, chapter 3, "It is completely against nature that someone be without sin."[214] Therefore it is to be understood as without enormous, commonplace, notorious, or well-published sin. But one who is in mortal sin, whether hidden or manifest, sins mortally in receiving holy orders, as in receiving the other sacraments (D.40 c.12; D.95. c.3; C.11 q.3 c.21). Therefore anyone ought to confess before he receives holy orders.

Second it says "husband of one wife," and this is to be understood negatively, that is, not of many wives (D.82 c.2), because if it were understood affirmatively, it would follow that virgins and

213. 1 Timothy 3:2–4; Titus 1:5–9
214. D.25 dict. post c.3

those who have never had a wife could not be promoted, which is absurd. And the Apostle speaks according to the custom of the primitive church, in which it was allowed for the ordained to have one wife so long as he had taken her as a virgin, but now it is not allowed since the vow of chastity is joined to holy orders.

But concerning the twice married, why cannot they be promoted, what bigamy is, and in how many ways is it contracted, I will keep silent for the present, because this goes beyond the limits of this tract. And the other conditions, namely, sober, prudent, etc. are familiar enough; therefore I say nothing about them. But note that in various chapters of the decrees and decretals other conditions which ought to be found in one being ordained are collected, namely, he ought not to be doing solemn penance, not belong to the curia, not be a servant or financially obligated, not have a deformed body, not be illegitimate, not be born of a priest, not be an adulterer, not have been baptized in mental illness, not be a pilgrim, not be an unknown person, nor be underage.[215] It would take a bigger tract than this little work to explain any of these.

The fourth thing required in one receiving orders is skill in letters. Hence to be promoted to holy orders or to the direction of souls one ought to have familiarity with scripture in order to be able to teach others. And on account of this, it is mandated that doctors of theology be retained in metropolitan churches, and that clerics leaving the province to study theology should fully collect their stipends, and if these do not suffice for them, the church ought to provide for them and meet their needs (X 5.5.4). Also, one ought to have skill in secular knowledge, and be learned, so that he can discern truth from falsehood, and through this have access to theology. Therefore it is mandated that teachers of the liberal arts be retained in every cathedral church and in other churches to the degree that suffices to provide teachers who can instruct the clerics of those same churches and other poor seculars free of charge. On account of this, a suitable salary is to be allocated to the teacher

---

215. E.g., D.51

in the church (X 5.5.4). And understand this to mean the sciences pertaining to speaking, namely, grammar, logic, and rhetoric, and especially grammar, because the quadrivium, namely arithmetic, geometry, music, and astronomy, contributes little or nothing to the knowledge of piety, as Jerome says (D.37. c.10). Concerning this, namely, what knowledge priests ought to have, look above in the preface to this tract. And although many other things could be said about this topic, yet let these suffice for what this little book can explain.

Tract 6 of the first principal part is on the sacrament of extreme unction.

CHAPTER 1: What its matter is

Now the sacrament of extreme unction is to be discussed, about which there are seven things to be considered. First, what its material is; second, what its form is; third, who its minister is; fourth, what its effect is; fifth, to whom it should be given; sixth, on which parts of the body it ought to be done; seventh, whether it ought to be repeated.

The matter of this sacrament is olive oil blessed by the bishop. And the reason for this is the institution of Christ who instituted it to be done with oil when he sent the apostles to anoint the sick with oil and to heal them.[216] And this fits with the teaching of St. James, saying, "Is anyone ill among you? Let him bring in the priests of the church, and let them pray over him, anointing him with holy oil."[217] And know that when simply "oil" is found in the holy scriptures, it ought to be understood as "olive oil," because that is simply oil, but others are not. They were invented on account of the lack of this oil, such as nut oil, linseed oil, and the like, or on account of some medical treatment, like almond oil and the like.

216. Matthew 10:8; Luke 9:2, 10:9
217. James 5:14

And the fitting reason why such oil is the matter of this sacrament is that the properties of this oil especially suit the effect of this sacrament. Indeed oil is a pain reliever; therefore it is put on wounds. Hence the Samaritan poured oil on the wounds of the man who had been beaten, as is said in Luke.[218] But the effect of this sacrament is to relieve spiritual and corporal pain, as will be said. Note especially on this point that for the oil to be the proper matter of this sacrament, it must first be blessed by the bishop. St. James hints at this when he says "anointing with holy oil," that is, sanctified oil. And the reason why it is necessary that it be sanctified is given in the tract on confirmation, chapter 2.

CHAPTER 2: On the form of extreme unction

The form of this sacrament is the words which the priest says when he anoints the sick person, namely these, "Through this anointing and his most tender mercy, may God forgive you whatever faults you have committed through seeing, hearing, etc." Hence in this form the power of this sacrament is mentioned, which will be discussed below when its effect is taken up.

And know that there is a difference between the forms of the other sacraments and this one because the forms of the other sacraments, according to Ambrose, are indicative, as may be seen by running through each one, but the form of this sacrament is optative, as is clear to the observer. Note that in the Ambrosian missal this form is found, "I anoint your eyes or your ears, etc., and through this anointing etc." Do not worry about this, but the form which the Roman church uses is to be followed. But one may ask, why does the Roman church make greater use of the optative mood in the form of this sacrament than in other forms? The answer is because, as will be said below, this sacrament ought not to be given except to those near death since they are already passing away. Therefore, as is customary for those who are passing away,

218. Luke 10:34

salvation is wished for. Thus the church, in using this form, wishes for salvation for those passing away from this life.

CHAPTER 3: On the minister of extreme unction

The minister of this sacrament is the priest and none other; hence no one, unless he is a priest, can administer this sacrament. This is clear on the aforementioned authority of St. James, "Is anyone ill among you, etc."[219] The reason for this is that it is necessary that he who dispenses the sacraments to the mystical body of Christ should have power over the true body of Christ; but this is the priest alone, which is why only the priest is to administer this sacrament. And it is not like the case of baptism, because baptism is the sacrament of greatest necessity; therefore it is necessary that it should have the most common minister. On this, see above on baptism, chapter 3.

But is it necessary that there be several priests or does one suffice? It would seem from the noted source that there ought to be several because it says "priests" in the plural. But Thomas, in his fourth book, seems to say that if several cannot be had, one will suffice as minister.[220] Nevertheless a priest always ought to anoint and say the words. And if the priest should die or be hindered before he finishes, another ought to finish what remains, namely, the rest of this sacrament of extreme unction. And let these remarks suffice for the present.

CHAPTER 4: On the effect of extreme unction

The effect of this sacrament is this: Indeed as it is with bodily illness, so in its own way it ought to be with spiritual illness. And with bodily illness it is the case that someone may be cured from the illness, yet there still remains a certain bodily weakness coming from the original illness. Therefore one needs a double medi-

219. James 5:14
220. Cf. Aquinas, *Scriptum super Sententiis*, Bk 4, d. 23, q. 1, a. 2.

cine—one which heals or drives out the sickness, another which repairs the remaining weakness. And so it is spiritually. Indeed spiritual illness is sin. Hence the psalmist says in the person of the sinner, "Have mercy on me, Lord, for I am ill."[221] And the healing medicine for this illness is penance. But after one is healed from this illness, there still remains in him a certain spiritual weakness. And this sacrament is appointed against this weakness. Hence the effect of this sacrament is the healing of this spiritual weakness.

And there is another effect, because through this sacrament, venial sins and also forgotten mortal sins are forgiven, and habitual grace is strengthened and new grace is conferred. Understand that this is if it is worthily received.

And there is another effect because, if it is profitable for the soul receiving it, bodily health is restored to it by virtue of this sacrament. All the things said above are proved through the aforementioned authority, James, chapter 5, "Is anyone ill among you? Let him bring in the priests of the Church, and let them pray over him, anointing him with holy oil and the Lord shall alleviate him from his weaknesses. And if he has sins, these shall be forgiven him."[222]

CHAPTER 5: To whom the sacrament of extreme unction ought to be given

From the aforementioned authority, it is also gathered that this sacrament ought not to be given except to the sick, because it says in James 5, "Is anyone ill among you? etc." But it ought not to be given to anyone who is sick, but only to those who are in danger and those close to death who had asked for this sacrament with devotion beforehand, including the insane. Indeed since this sacrament is the sacrament of passing away, it ought not to be given except to those passing away, or to those who are ready to leave this life.

221. Psalm 6:3
222. James 5:14–15

CHAPTER 6: On which parts of the body the sacrament of extreme unction ought to be done

Because purgative medicinal matter ought to be applied to the particular part that is suffering, and since the matter of sin is purged through penance, this sacrament, which is medicine against the weakness remaining after sin, as has been said, ought to be applied to the members, through which the poison of sin enters the soul, which are the sense organs. Hence in this sacrament, the eyes, ears, mouth, nose, hands, feet, and loins ought to be anointed. Thus it is said to the eyes, "Through this holy anointing and through his most tender mercy, may God forgive you whatever faults you have committed by sight." To the ears, "by hearing"; to the mouth, "by taste"; to the nose, "by smell"; to the hands, "by touch"; to the feet, "by walking"; to the loins, "by the heat of lust"; saying before each of these phrases, "Through this holy anointing, etc."

But what is to be done about one blind from birth who has not sinned by sight, or about one deaf from birth who has not sinned by hearing, or about a lame one who has not sinned by walking? Should they be anointed on those members? I say yes, because although the blind man did not sin by seeing, perhaps nevertheless he sinned by inordinately desiring sight. And I say the same about the deaf and the lame. I also think that whenever someone does not have eyes or other members on which anointing can be done, he ought to be anointed in nearby areas on account of the reason I already said.

CHAPTER 7: Whether extreme unction ought to be repeated

Since character is not impressed in this sacrament, it is clear that this sacrament can be repeated, since a person can be sick unto death many times. But can one be anointed multiple times during the same illness? I say that some illnesses last a short time, such as fevers [*synochia* and *causon*], etc. [In these illnesses this sacrament ought not to be repeated.][223] Nevertheless, if someone gets sick again, since the relapse is a separate illness from the first, the person may be anointed again in the relapse. There are other illnesses of long duration, like cough, fever, hectic fever, etc. which last for a year or longer. And since in such illnesses a person can come to the point of death multiple times, in such cases this sacrament can be repeated multiple times. This is the judgment of St. Thomas in his fourth book.[224] Nevertheless he says that if the judgment of some doctor is found to the contrary, that he would not condemn it. But some say that if he who was anointed is cured he ought not to bathe himself afterward; this is rather foolish because it would follow that a bishop whose head is anointed with chrism ought not to wash his head, since his anointing is more worthy than this one. Nevertheless, when someone sick is anointed, there ought to be some servant there who wipes the place of anointing with a linen cloth, and afterward that cloth ought to be burned.

Tract 7 of the first principal part is on the sacrament of marriage.[225]

CHAPTER 1: What engagement is

With the help of God, having explained the sacraments which give birth, enliven, feed, promote, and renew one in the spiritual life, it remains to treat the sacrament which brings forth and gives birth to both being and bodily life, namely, the sacrament of marriage. Because truly this little book is composed for the simple who are not very advanced in canon or civil law, and because more allegations are brought to the courts of both canon and civil law

223. Missing sentence provided from other edition consulted.

224. Aquinas, *Scriptum super Sententiis*, Bk 4, d. 23, q. 2, a. 4.

225. Guido drew much of this material from Raymond of Penyafort's treatise on marriage. For an English translation, see Raymond of Penyafort, *Summa on Marriage*, trans. Pierre Payer (Toronto: Pontifical Institute of Mediaeval Studies, 2005).

from the material in this tract than that in the preceding ones, I will refrain from discussing them, as much as I am able, lest the simple and the less advanced be led into confusion by such allegations, since the simple do not know how to read or understand such allegations.

But since according to the Philosopher, a disposition precedes a form, so engagement precedes marriage. Therefore engagement is to be taken up first. Thus concerning engagement, five things are to be considered. First, what engagement is, and why it is so called; second, how it is contracted; third, at what age it can be contracted; fourth, what the effect of engagement is; fifth, in what cases engagement is dissolved.

Engagement [*sponsalium*] is a promise of future marriage. From this definition, which is common to the canonists and lawyers, it is clear that engagement ought to precede marriage as the present precedes the future. And it gets its name from "pledge" (*spondeo, spondes*) which is the same as "promise" (*promitto, promittis*).

CHAPTER 2: How engagement is contracted

Engagement is contracted in four ways. In one way, by a bare promise, as when "I will take you as my wife," and "I will take you as my husband," are said. In the second way, by giving the engagement deposit, for instance, wealth or some other things. In the third way, by the delivery of a ring. And this is commonly called "betrothal" but it is properly called "delivery of the ring." In the fourth way, through the mediation of an oath, yet always with words in the future tense, as has been said, because if they were words in the present tense already, they would not be words of engagement but of marriage.

CHAPTER 3: At what age engagement is contracted

Because after the seventh year, that is, after the age of seven years, both boys and girls begin to have the discretion which is required for contracting an engagement, therefore, after the seventh year they can contract engagement. But, if before the seventh year, they, or their parents in their place and in their name, contract an engagement, they accomplish nothing, unless when they come to the seventh year, the engagement begins to please them, and from then on the engagement becomes effective. Then, although engaged, he may not know her carnally, nor can [her blood relative] have his blood relative as wife, or vice versa. And note that the age suitable for contracting marriage is twelve years for girls, and fourteen for boys. And if it is contracted before then, it is not marriage, but only engagement, unless they were of marriageable age or so close to it that they could carnally join together, since then the age [requirement] may seem to provide an occasion for wickedness.

CHAPTER 4: What the effect of engagement is

Engagement is contracted in two ways; sometimes it is contracted with conditions attached, sometimes purely. If it is contracted with conditions attached, this can be done in many ways, because the attached condition is possible or impossible or necessary. If it is impossible, for instance, if he were to say, "I will be engaged to you if I have touched heaven with my finger," or if it is necessary, for instance, if he says, "I will be engaged to you if the sun rises tomorrow," or something else similar, these conditions ought not to be used for anything added on, that is, attached. But if the condition is possible, it is either honest or dishonest. If it is honest, for instance, if he says, "I will be engaged to you if my father wishes" or "if you will give me 100 marks," if the condition is not fulfilled, one is not obligated to consummate the marriage until the condition is fulfilled, even if in contracting the engagement there was an oath attached. And always understand this as applying except when carnal copulation has taken place between them, because then it is called true marriage between them, even though it appears to have departed from the attached condition.

However, if the condition is dishonest and against the nature and substance of marriage, for instance, if he says, "I will be engaged to you if you get yourself a sterility drug" or "if you will commit adultery for money" or "until I find someone prettier," such a condition would nullify the contract, so that there is neither engagement nor marriage. If the condition is dishonest, but nevertheless not against the nature of marriage, for instance, if he says, "I will be engaged to you if you kill a person" or "if you steal" or the like, such a condition ought not to be used for anything added on and is to be rejected, and the engagement holds. Note that although it has been said that engagement can be contracted under the condition of a promise of wealth, nevertheless wealth cannot be promised in the way of compensation. And if it was promised, one is not held to the promise of compensation nor can it be asked back again, for instance, if this was said, "If I become engaged to you I will give you 100 marks." Indeed this condition of compensation is not valid since marriage ought to be free, as in Dig. 45.1.12; X 4.1.26.

But if an engagement is contracted purely, that is, without condition, and both persons are fit for contracting marriage and an oath has intervened between those contracting the engagement, they are to be compelled through excommunication to consummate the marriage, unless perhaps there is danger of uxoricide or some other danger. But if one of them should contract himself to another by words in the present tense, let penance be enjoined on him for perjury and breaking faith and let him be released from excommunication. But if an oath does not intervene, they are to be warned to consummate the marriage, but not forced into it, because those reluctant to marry often come to bad ends (C.31 q.2 c.1 and c.2). But if neither one is of marriageable age, they are obliged to wait until they come to the lawful age for contracting marriage. And I say the same thing if one is of lawful age and the other is not, because the one who is of lawful age ought to wait for the other, or if they mutually release one another, they can be separated in the judgment of the church.

CHAPTER 5: In what cases engagement is dissolved

Those who have contracted an engagement together are always bound, so that if a man contracts an engagement later with another woman and has not proceeded to carnal copulation with that second one, he is to be compelled to return to the first. But if he has known the second one carnally, since it may already be called a marriage, he ought to remain with the second and not return to the first. But engagements are dissolved in eight cases.

The first is if one of them wants to enter religious life, which can be done even if the other is unwilling and even if a marriage was contracted by words in the present tense, but was not yet consummated by carnal copulation. And the one who remains in the world remains free; and this is once the other has been professed into religion. This case is found in X 3.32.7; X 4.4.3.

The second case is when the betrothed cannot be found because he has gone to another region; nevertheless the one remaining should first accept penance for perjury or breaking or not keeping faith, if it is the case that the marriage was at least consummated. This case is found in X 4.1.5.

The third case is if either one of them, after the engagement is contracted, gets leprosy or paralysis, or loses eyes, hands, feet or nose, or something else nasty happens to him or her. This case is found in X 4.8.4; X 2.24.25.

The fourth case is if affinity comes up, for instance, if a fiancé has learned that he is consanguineous with his fiancée or vice versa. To prove this, reputation suffices. This case is found in C.27 q.2 c.31; X 4.14.2.

The fifth case is if they mutually release one another. This case is found in X 4.1.2. Nevertheless, some do not accept this case; hence they say that the supporting decretal is not a decretal or that it speaks of comparative promise.

The sixth case is if either one of them commits fornication; this case is found in X 2.24.25.

The seventh case is when the fiancé actually marries another woman, or the fiancée another man, using words in the present tense, or words in the future tense followed by carnal copulation; then the engagement is dissolved on account of the intervening greater bond or agreement. But the offender ought to do penance for perjury or breach of faith. This case is found in X 4.4.1; X 4.1.26.

The eighth case is when a minor comes to lawful age and asks to be released from the bond of engagement and to be given permission to marry another. This case is found in X 4.2.9 and X 4.2.8.

Note that all these cases, after the first, namely, when one wants to enter religious life, are to be understood as applying to a future engagement, which truly and properly is called engagement. And note also that in two of the aforementioned cases, the engagement is dissolved by law itself, namely, when one enters religion and when one contracts marriage with another man or another woman. But in the other cases, it is dissolved through the judgment of the church.

The second part of the seventh tract of the first principal part which is on marriage follows.

CHAPTER 1: What marriage is and why it is so called

After having dealt with engagement, marriage is to be discussed, concerning which there are eight things to be considered. First, what marriage is and why it is so called; second, how marriage is contracted; third, when and where and by which words it was instituted; fourth, why marriage was instituted; fifth, who can contract marriage; sixth, how many kinds of marriage there are; seventh, how many goods of marriage there are; eighth, what things impede marriage.

Marriage is defined by the doctors thus: Marriage is the lawful union of a man and a woman keeping an inseparable way of life.[226] It does not say "of a man and women" or "of men and a

226. C.29 q.1 dict. ante c.1; Inst. 1.9.1. This definition of marriage was first established by the ancient Romans, included in Justinian's codification, and became the basic definition of marriage in canon law through the Middle Ages.

woman," because one man cannot have several wives or one woman several husbands. It says "an inseparable life, etc." This is because neither of them without the consent of the other can profess continence or be free for prayer, [227] because between them, while they live, the conjugal bond remains. In another way, marriage is defined thus: It is the joining of a man and a woman as partners in a common life in accordance with divine and human law.

And it is called "marriage" [*matrimonium*] from "mother" (*mater, matris*) and "duty" (*munio, munis*), since marriage is like the duty, that is, the office, of a mother, because it gives women the chance to be mothers. Or it is named more from "mother" than from "father" because her office is more apparent in marriage than the man's office.

CHAPTER 2: How marriage is contracted

A person contracts marriage by desire or consent, who, if single, abandons others and rejects sexual intercourse with them, even interrupted intercourse. Indeed [a marriage is contracted when] by means of words in the present tense the man consents to the woman in marital affection, and the woman to the man, even without the customary words. Thus if the man says, "I take you as my wife," and she replies, "I take you as my husband," or if the man says, "I want to have you as my wife from among all others," and she replies, "I want to have you as my husband from among all others," or with whatever other words or signs consent is expressed, immediately there is a marriage. Even so, if those marrying are able to speak, words containing or expressing mutual consent are necessary, according to the church.

227. 1 Corinthians 7:5

CHAPTER 3: When, where, and with what words marriage was instituted

Marriage was instituted in the earthly paradise and before sin. With which words was it instituted? Some say with these words in Genesis, chapter 9, "Increase and multiply and fill the earth."[228] But I do not think this is true, for these words were rather a nuptial blessing. Hence I say that it was instituted with the words of Adam placed prophetically in his mouth, when he said, "Now this is bone of my bones and flesh of my flesh. Therefore a man shall leave his father and mother and be joined to his wife, and the two will be as one flesh."[229] Concerning this, see above on the sacraments in general, chapter 1.

CHAPTER 4: Why marriage was instituted

There are two principal reasons for the institution of marriage, although there are many secondary ones. The first principal reason is for raising children. And for this reason, God instituted marriage in paradise before sin between our first parents, to whom he said in Genesis, chapter 9, "Increase and multiply, etc."[230] The second reason is the avoidance of fornication, and this reason comes into play after sin. And concerning this, the Apostle says in 1 Corinthians, chapter 7, "because of fornication, let each man have his own wife, and let each woman have her own husband."[231]

There are many secondary reasons, namely, the restoration of peace, the wife's beauty, wealth, and knowledge. Nevertheless, the principal intention of those who contract marriage should not consider these things, but the two first and foremost ones.

228. Genesis 9:1
230. Genesis 9:1
229. Genesis 2:23–24
231. 1 Corinthians 7:1

CHAPTER 5: Who can contract marriage

Everyone who is able to consent to conjugal affection and perform carnal copulation, unless expressly prohibited, is able to contract marriage. I say "is able to consent" because although a child who is below the [legal] age (this is under fourteen years for a boy and twelve for a girl) may say the appropriate words for contracting a marriage, because they are unable to consent the marriage is null (X 4.1.25). Likewise one who is insane or mad, although he may say the required words for contracting a marriage, does not contract it because he cannot consent (C.32 q.7 c.26). And this is true as long as he is mad, because if sometimes he has a lucid interval and sometimes returns to a sound mind, he can marry and testify. And everything that others can do, he too can do, as is found in Cod. 6.36.5; C.7 q.1 c.14. I also say "who can perform carnal copulation" because he who lacks a virile member or both testicles, or one who is naturally frigid, cannot contract marriage (X 4.14.2). I also say "unless expressly prohibited" because the edict on contracting marriage is prohibitory, therefore all for whom it is not prohibited may contract it (X 4.1.23). Indeed some are prohibited on account of a vow, and also on account of order, and so on with the other impediments which will be discussed below. Note that marriage can be contracted between those who are absent through proxies, as was done between the King of Hungary and Lady Alba, daughter of the king of France.

CHAPTER 6: How many kinds of marriage there are

There are many kinds of marriage, for one is lawful, another clandestine. Lawful marriage is when a wife is requested from those who have power over the woman, and is engaged by her parents, and is provided with a dowry by law, and is blessed by the priests as is customary, and is watched over by bridesmaids and is solemnly accepted. Nevertheless, do not think that without these solemnities it cannot be a true marriage. But as is the case with other sacraments, some things belong to the sacrament by necessity, but some belong only to its solemnity. So too in marriage some things pertain to the substance of marriage, like consent expressed in words in the present tense, and this alone makes the marriage. But other things belong to its solemnity and decorum, like the aforementioned solemnities, without which a marriage is true and lawful with respect to validity, although not with respect to integrity.

Clandestine marriage is when it is done without the aforesaid solemnities. And those who contract it this way expose themselves to great danger. Indeed one might send the other away at will and actually contract with another man or another woman, and thus continue in adultery. Hence such persons are to be advised, in the forum of conscience, to contract anew before the church.

Again, another kind of marriage is initiated, which takes place through words in the present tense, another is completed or consummated, which takes place through carnal copulation. Note that marriage can be completed in two ways, in one way in holiness, in another way by outward sign. Therefore marriage can be completed in holiness before carnal copulation. Hence Augustine said this, among other things, to a certain woman who together with her husband once uttered a vow of chastity, "Not because together you abstained from carnal union, but because your husband desired to be even holier, you remained his wife, and you became holier as you maintained peace and harmony."[232] But marriage is not completed by outward sign before carnal copulation. Indeed the bodily joining of man and woman signifies the joining of the divine and human natures in the person of the Son of God. Concerning this, see above on the sacraments in general, chapter 1. And thus is resolved the question of whether the marriage between the most blessed Virgin Mary and Joseph was a marriage completed in sanctity. Indeed it was completed in holiness, but not by outward sign. Some say that a marriage initiated through engagement in the

232. C.33 q.5 c.4

future tense is ratified through present consent and consummated by carnal copulation.

Again, another kind of marriage is lawful but not ratified, another is ratified and not lawful, another ratified and lawful. Marriage that is lawful and not ratified is that between infidels. It is called lawful because by the legal institutions and the customs of the province it is not contracted against the command of God, but it is not ratified because it is done without faith. Hence Augustine, "A marriage is not ratified which is done without God."[233] Ratified but unlawful marriage is that done between Christians, but contracted without the obligatory solemnity. Ratified and lawful marriage is that contracted between lawful and faithful persons with the obligatory solemnity.

CHAPTER 7: How many goods of marriage there are

The goods of marriage principally are three, namely, faithfulness, children, and sacrament. Faithfulness takes care lest after the conjugal bond there be intercourse with another man or another woman. Second, regarding children, care is taken so that they may be loved, supported, and religiously brought up. Third, regarding sacrament, care is taken so that the marriage may not come apart. And note the first two goods are sometimes present in marriage and sometimes not, but the third belongs inseparably to marriage.

CHAPTER 8: On the impediments to marriage, which contains within it 16 chapters

There are twelve impediments to marriage which impede the contracting of marriage and annul a marriage subsequently contracted.[234] Indeed if one or another of these precedes a marriage,

---

233. C.28 q.1 dict. ante c.17.

234. Guido uses standard, but confusing, legal terminology here and throughout the discussion of impediments to marriage. *Dirimunt iam contractum* means "they

they prevent conjugal consent. But if they follow a marriage, they offer no impediment, as is clear in these examples. A madman cannot contract marriage; if however he becomes mad after he has contracted it, the marriage cannot be dissolved on this account. Likewise, one who has both testicles cut off, that is, is castrated, cannot contract marriage, but if he is cut after he has contracted a marriage, the marriage is not dissolved on this account. And so it is to be understood concerning the other impediments to marriage which are contained in these verses:

> *Error, conditio, votum, cognatio, crimen.*
> *Cultus disparitas, vis, ordo, ligamen, honestas.*
> *Si sis affinis forte coire nequibis.*
> *Hec facienda vetant, connubia facta retractant.*
>
> Error, condition, vow, kinship, crime.
> Difference of religion, force, holy orders, marriage bond,
>   propriety.
> If you are related, if you are unable to have sex,
> These things prevent marriage and annul subsequent
>   marriages.

And these twelve impediments prevent the contracting of marriage and annul a subsequent marriage. There are others which impede contracting a marriage, but which do not annul a subsequent one, namely, feast days and the interdict of the church, as in this verse:

---

break off one already contracted," but, as is clear from the examples that follow, this phrase applies to impediments that annul marriages contracted after the impediment is already in place. A contemporary of Guido, Petrus of Palude, *In quartum sententiarum* (Venice, 1493, 151b), says, "Concerning those impediments which break marriages contracted afterward: they are to be understood so that none of these break a marriage contracted before but only one contracted after. Whence new laws ought to speak more properly that such impediments break marriages 'subsequently contracted' [*dirimunt post contractum*] just as old laws used to say they 'break [marriages] already contracted' [*dirimunt iam contractum*]." We thank our anonymous reader for this explanation and have adjusted our translation accordingly.

Ecclesie vetitum necnon tempus feriarum.
Ista vetant fieri, permittunt facta teneri.

Prohibition of the church and also feast days,
These prevent contracting marriage, but permit contracted
   marriages to continue.

To understand these, each one of them is to be discussed.

CHAPTER 1: On the impediment of error

Having enumerated all the impediments, each one of them is to
be discussed. And first, the impediment of error of person which
by its nature, not by the institution of the church, excludes marital consent, because one who errs does not consent (Dig. 2.1.15)
and the will of one in error is null (Cod. 1.18.8, 9). Hence if a
man or a woman errs in contracting marriage, there is no consent,
which alone makes a marriage. Nevertheless, note that error concerning the person can be threefold. First, concerning the person
himself, as when it is believed about Peter that he is William, so
one errs concerning the person. Another is the error of wealth, as
when it is believed about a pauper that he is rich. Third is the error of character, as when it is believed about one who is ignoble
that he is noble, or about one who is corrupt that she is a virgin.
Now the error of person impedes marriage, so that if one believes
she is contracting with Peter but contracts with William, or one
believes he is contracting with Martha but contracts with Mary,
there is no marriage. But the errors of character and wealth do not
impede marriage. For example, if someone contracts with another
believing her to be a virgin or the daughter of a king, and yet she
is corrupt or the daughter of a peasant, the marriage holds; or if
he believes he is contracting with a rich woman but contracts with
a pauper, the marriage holds (C.29 q.2 c.1).

CHAPTER 2: On the impediment of condition

The impediment of condition was introduced by the church in favor [of those in a condition] of freedom. And concerning this, briefly, it is to be maintained that if a free woman knowingly contracts with a male servant, or a free man with a female servant, the marriage between them holds. But if a free woman contracts unwittingly with a male servant, because she believes him to be free, or a free man with a female servant because he believes her to be free, there is no marriage between them if they did this unwittingly, unless later one comes to know the station of the other to be such and then consents to him or her by word or deed or carnal copulation. Nevertheless, note that error of lower station puts an end to a marriage about to be contracted, and annuls one subsequently contracted, but not error of equal or better station, as when a male servant contracts with a female servant whom he believes to be free, or with a free woman whom he believes to be a servant, because he is not cheated nor has anything to object to about her. Concerning fitting conditions for marriage, see above on engagement, chapter 4, because the judgment is the same here and there.

CHAPTER 3: On the impediment of vow

Regarding the impediment of vow, understand this as meaning a vow of continence or a vow of chastity. Concerning which note that a vow of continence is twofold, for one is simple and the other is solemn. The simple vow impedes contracting a marriage, but does not annul one contracted subsequently. But how can a simple vow be solemn? Although a long time ago there was a disagreement among the doctors, today it has been declared by Lord Boniface VIII in VI 2.15.1 where it says that a vow may be solemnized to the degree that it annuls a marriage in two ways: In one way by the reception of holy orders, namely, subdeacon, deacon, and priest; in the other way, by express or tacit profession made to

someone concerning acceptance as religious. Therefore those promoted to holy orders and the religious cannot contract marriage.
Note the penalty instituted in the constitutions of Lord Clement
the pope against religious who actually contract marriages, namely,
that they are to be excommunicated and removed from their orders, and they cannot be dispensed from this except by the apostolic see (Clem. 3.1.un).

CHAPTER 4: On the impediment of carnal kinship

Kinship is threefold, some is carnal, some spiritual, and some
legal. And the first to be considered is carnal kinship which naturally precedes the others, and this is called consanguinity. Let us
see therefore what consanguinity is, and why it is so called, what a
line of consanguinity is, how many lines there are, how many degrees, and how they are calculated, and up to what degree marriage
is prohibited.

Consanguinity is the bond between persons from the same
stock, established among descendants by carnal propagation. I call
"stock" that person from whom others take their origin, as Adam
was the stock of Cain and Enoch and those who descended from
them. It is called consanguinity from "with" [con] which means
"together" [simul] and "blood" [sanguis] as if to say "having common blood" or "proceeding from one blood."

A line is an ordered collection of persons joined by consanguinity descending from the same stock containing various degrees.
There are three lines, namely, ascending, descending, and transverse. The first, namely, ascending, is the line of those from whom
we derive our origin, like father, mother, grandfather, grandmother, great-grandfather, great-grandmother, great-great grandfather,
great-great grandmother. The second, namely, descending, is the
line of those who derive their origin from us, like son, daughter, grandson, granddaughter, great grandson, great granddaughter, great-great granddaughter, great-great grandson. The third is
transverse or collateral, and this is the line of those from whom

we do not draw our origin, nor they from us, such as brother, sister, the children of two brothers who are called cousins on the father's side, the children of two sisters who are called cousins on the mother's side, and their children and grandchildren to the fourth degree. These are named in C. 35 q.5 c.6. And note that two descending lines make one transverse line, as is clear in this example: The children of two brothers are connected to each other in a transverse line and each of them descends in a direct line from their common grandfather who was the common stock from whom they derived their origin. And thus it is to be understood concerning all the others.

Now, therefore, what a degree is needs to be discussed. Here know that canon lawyers count degrees in one way, jurists another.[235] For according to the canonists, two persons in a transverse line make one degree. But according to the jurists, any one person makes one degree. Suppose there are two brothers. First, according to the canonists, they are in one degree; according to the jurists, they are in two, and so on for each case. But because this contributes little or nothing for the matter at hand, we will let it go and see what a degree is. Degree is customarily the distance between persons by which is known by how many generations' distance two persons differ. And degree is computed in an ascending line this way: Mother and father are in the first degree. Grandfather and grandmother are in the second. Great grandfather and great grandmother are in the third. Great-great grandfather and great-great grandmother are in the fourth. And in the descending line, they are counted this way: Son and daughter are in the first degree; grandson and granddaughter in the second; great grandson and great granddaughter in the third; great-great grandson and great-great granddaughter in the fourth. But in the transverse line, they are counted this way: Two brothers are in the first degree; children of two brothers in the second; their grandchildren, namely, of the two brothers, in the third; their great grandchildren in the fourth

235. I.e., those skilled in Roman law.

degree. Today, beyond this degree, consanguinity is not counted or extended as an impediment to marriage, although in ancient times it was extended to the seventh degree.

Therefore let us see how consanguinity between people is to be computed according to this teaching. If you want to know by how many degrees of consanguinity two persons, say Bartholomew and Bertha, are connected, start with their common stock, from whom both derived their origin. For example, Peter fathered James and John who were brothers; behold the first degree. Or if you do not know who their father is, say instead, James and John are brothers who, as has been said, make the first degree. And I say this because brothers are always to be put in the first degree, as are brother and sister and two sisters. Proceed, therefore, with the counting. James and John were brothers who, as has been said, make the first degree. James fathered Andrew; behold the second degree. Andrew fathered Philip; behold the third degree. Philip fathered Bartholomew; behold the fourth degree for the one we are now considering. Now return to John who was the brother of James, and proceed thus: James and John, as has been said, were brothers. John fathered Thomas; behold the second degree. Thomas fathered Bertha, the one we are now considering; behold the third degree. See, therefore, how Bartholomew and Bertha are connected to each other on one side in the third degree and on the other in the fourth. And this is in the usual way of speaking, because according to the truth, they are not connected to each other except in the fourth degree, and thus there cannot be a marriage between them. This same thing is to be done for those who are more or less close in consanguinity by saying so and so are connected to each other in such a degree. And that the degrees and the persons are to be counted in this way is gathered expressly from these two decretals, X 4.14.7 and X 2.20.47.

But suppose that two persons are connected to each other on one side in the second or third degree and on the other in the fifth. Can they contract marriage between them? I say yes, because the degree of the more remote person will hold good regarding consanguinity and affinity (X 4.14.7). Indeed in this case, the more remote person is beyond the limit of consanguinity, hence they are not connected to each other by the consanguinity that exists between them beyond the fourth degree of consanguinity inclusive, because while in ancient times all consanguinity ended in the seventh degree, today it ends in the fourth.

From what has already been said, it is clear that all consanguinity impedes and annuls marriage up to and including the fourth degree of consanguinity, but not beyond. And understand this for transverse lines, but not ascending ones, because in those inclusive consanguinity extends infinitely, but in transverse ones consanguinity extends to the fourth degree and no further, which means that the fifth degree opens the door to marriage.

CHAPTER 5: On spiritual kinship

Having considered carnal kinship, spiritual kinship is to be discussed. Hence let us see what spiritual kinship is and how many kinds of it there are and how it impedes marriage and in which sacraments it is contracted. Spiritual kinship is a relationship arising from the giving or receiving of a sacrament. For example, a priest baptizes a child, you receive him; both of you become spiritual fathers to the child and you are cofathers as is read in C.30 q.1. c.8.

There are three kinds of spiritual kinship. The first is called copaternity; the second paternity, and this applies between the one who is received [from the font] and the one who receives, that is, between the godparent and the child. The third is called fraternity, and this applies between your spiritual child and your carnal children. Copaternity is so called from "with" [con], which is "together," and "fatherhood" [paternitas], as if to say "simultaneous" or "common fatherhood." For one cofather is always spiritual, and the other carnal.

Therefore it remains to see what the law is concerning the marriage of such persons, and first about copaternity. Note that copaternity is twofold. One is direct, namely, that which I contract by myself, and this impedes marriage, so that if I receive the child of the woman Bertha or if she receives mine, I can never have her as my wife, and if I do take her, the marriage is to be dissolved. Thus it is said in X 4.11.6. The other is called indirect or emergent copaternity, namely, that which one spouse contracts through the action of the other after they have become one flesh, like that which I contract through the action of my wife after she has been carnally known by me. For instance, if my wife receives the child of another, both parents of the child are coparents with me, even though I did not receive the child, because spouses communicate their actions to one another. And concerning this, there is an exceptionally clear example in a certain decretal (X 4.11.4), where it is recounted that Martin married Bertha and Leonard married Brigid. After the marriage, Leonard lifted the son of Martin and Bertha from the holy font. At length Leonard and Bertha died; still alive were Martin and Brigid, whose husband Leonard had acquired copaternity [with Martin] through Martin's son. Can the said Martin contract marriage with the said Brigid? And the lord pope responds, "No way!" And thus it is clear that copaternity, both direct and indirect, impedes the contracting of marriage, and annuls one subsequently contracted.

Now spiritual paternity is to be discussed, which applies between the one receiving and the one received, that is, between the godfather or godmother and the godson or goddaughter. And it is to be said that there can never be a marriage between such persons, and if they have contracted it in fact, they are to be separated (C.30 q.1 c.5; C.33 q.2 c.17).

Lastly spiritual fraternity is to be discussed, which applies between a godson or goddaughter and the carnal son or daughter of the godfather or godmother. And although the ancient doctors said various things about this topic, nevertheless, it is to be held firmly and without any doubt that all children of two coparents, whether born before copaternity or after, can lawfully copulate maritally, except for that person by whom the copaternity came about, because that one can never copulate maritally with any of the children of his spiritual father (C.30 q.3 c.4; X 4.11.1 and X 4.11.7). Likewise note that a cofather can lawfully receive as wife the daughter of his cofather, unless she is the one by whom the copaternity came about (C.30 q.3 c.7).

It is also customary to ask whether someone can have two comothers as wives, namely, one after the other. The answer is that it depends on whether the comaternity precedes or follows the marriage. If it proceeds, one can lawfully have two comothers as wives. For example, Mary and Martha are comothers. Later Martin contracts with Mary and knows her. After she has died, he can contract with Martha. And the reason is that through the subsequent carnal union, nothing is transferred to the preceding spiritual union (C.30 q.4 c.5). But if the comaternity follows the marriage, consummated by carnal copulation, then make a distinction. If your wife receives the child of another, then she whose child is received is made your comother through the action of your wife, and thus after your wife has died you will not be able to have her as wife. And understand that the same copaternity is acquired by the wife through the husband. But if the son of your wife, who was born to another man, was raised from the holy font or held for confirmation before the bishop by another woman, that woman is comother with your wife, but not with you, because no comaternity was acquired there. Hence after your wife has died, you will be able to have her as wife. It is the same if your son, who was born to another woman, was received by another man, because your wife does not acquire copaternity. And in this case, as in the other, a man can have two comothers as wives, and a woman can have two cofathers as husbands, and this can be found in these verses:

> *Qui mihi vel cuius mea natum fonte levavit*
> *Hec mea commater fieri mea non valet uxor.*
> *Si qua mee natum non ex me fonte levavit*
> *Hanc post facta mee non inde vetabor habere.*

> She who lifted from the font one born of me or I one of hers
> She is made my comother and cannot be my wife.
> If she raised from the font one born of my wife but not of me
> This one, after the death of my wife, I am not denied from
>   having.

A man's cofather is not prohibited from marrying one born to his wife. Action makes both comothers, affection never does.

Also note that a layman cannot contract marriage with her whom he baptized. And if he has contracted such a marriage in fact, it is to be dissolved (VI 4.3.un). Likewise note that the son of a priest or another man who baptized a girl cannot contract with that girl (as in the aforementioned chapter VI 4.3.un). Note especially that only through the sacraments of baptism and confirmation is the spiritual kinship contracted which impedes the contracting of marriage and annuls one subsequently contracted. And through catechesis, although a kinship is contracted such as impedes contracting a marriage, nevertheless, it does not contract the kinship that annuls one subsequently contracted (VI 4.3.2).

CHAPTER 6: On legal kinship

Because legal kinship, which is called adoption, is rarely or never in use, and there is little treatment of it in canon law, I will bypass this for now.

CHAPTER 7: On the impediment of crime

Some crimes impede the contracting of marriage but do not annul one subsequently contracted, as is the case with incest, uxoricide, abduction of another's wife, solemn penance, or if someone, undermining his marriage, were to receive his own child from the font so that he might deprive his wife, or a woman her husband, of the conjugal debt and his services. Or again, killing a priest. All these crimes and perhaps many others impede the contracting of marriage, but do not annul one subsequently contracted. Indeed if they are adolescents and there is fear over their lack of self-restraint, the church ought to give them permission to marry (X 4.13.8).

But there are three crimes which not only prevent contracting a marriage but also annul one subsequently contracted. The first is when someone commits adultery with the wife of another, and he or she effectively plots the death of the husband of the adulteress, or the woman with whom the man was adulterous or the adulterer himself plots the death of the wife of the adulterer, so that they might contract marriage together. In this case, they ought not to contract, and if they contract subsequently they are to be separated (C.31 q.1 c.5; X 4.7.1–3). The second is if an adulterer gives his word to an adulteress that he will marry her after the death of her lawful husband, or an adulteress [promises to marry] an adulterer after the death of his wife (C.31 q.1 c.4, and in all the previously mentioned chapters). The third is when he does not give his word to marry her, but basically takes her and contracts with her, because as Pope Celestine says, "It is a greater thing to take than to promise to take" (X 4.7.5 and X 4.7.4). And understand this case to be when the first marriage is true and lawful, because if it were not true, but was thought to be true, it would present no impediment to the second marriage. But if none of the aforementioned cases should arise, someone can rightly contract with her whom he defiled through adultery.

Also note that if a woman who contracts with a married man knows that he is married, then she can never have him, even after the death of his wife. But if she does not know that he is married, indeed believes him to be single, despite the fact that she contracted with him while his wife was living, she can lawfully contract with him after the death of his lawful wife (X 4.7.1; X 4.7.7; X 4.1.18.).

CHAPTER 8: On the impediment of difference in religion

In order for marriage to be ratified and lawful, it is necessary that both spouses be Christian. Indeed a Christian man cannot contract marriage with a Jewish, Saracen, gentile, or pagan woman, and if he has in fact contracted, it is not a marriage. Nevertheless, a Christian can contract engagement with an unbeliever under this form or condition, that the unbeliever be converted to the faith (C.28 q.1 c.15). But one unbeliever can contract marriage with another, as long as they follow the same religious observance, namely, a Jewish man with a Jewish woman, a Saracen man with a Saracen woman. But suppose that one is converted to the faith while the other remains in unbelief. What should be done about these? I say that if the unbeliever does not want to cohabit with the Christian or if he does, but he does not want to do so without affront to the Creator, or without the possibility that he might draw her into unbelief or mortal sin, in these three cases, the affront to the Creator dissolves the law of marriage with respect to the Christian, and the Christian can lawfully contract [another marriage] (X 4.19.7 and X 4.19.8). And it makes no difference here whether the convert was a Jew or a pagan because the law is the same today for both (X 3.33.1). But if the unbeliever wants to live with the Christian, without any of the aforementioned cases, and the Christian wants to live with him, he does well, as the Apostle says in 1 Corinthians 7.[236] If indeed he does not want to live with her, he is not to be compelled to contract marriage, nevertheless while he or she lives, neither one can contract with another, since the marriage still endures, as is clear in the previously cited decretal (X 3.33.1).

But what if a Jew or a pagan contracts with his consanguineous relative according to his own religious observance and later is converted to the faith? Can he remain in such a marriage after his conversion? I say yes, as long as he did not contract within the degrees prohibited by divine law found in Leviticus 18,[237] because unbelievers are not bound by canonical institutions, and through the sacrament of baptism, marriage is not dissolved, but sins are forgiven. Likewise if a pagan having several wives is converted to the faith, can he keep all his wives or only one of them? I say that he can only keep the one who was his wife first, because none of the others was truly his wife. But if one spouse falls into heresy or into unbelief, the one who remains in the faith cannot contract another marriage, but is obligated to hold back, because although in

---

236. 1 Corinthians 7:12–13
237. Leviticus 18:6–18

this case the affront to the Creator seems greater than that at the start of a marriage, yet the marriage is ratified for the believer, and it cannot be dissolved for any subsequent reason, because "those whom God has joined together, let no one separate."[238] But the marriage of an unbeliever is not ratified, therefore it can lawfully be dissolved if the other spouse is converted to the faith (X 4.19.7 near the end, and the chapter cited above).

CHAPTER 9: On the impediment of violence

Violence, by its own nature even without the decree of the church, impedes marriage, because it excludes the free consent which alone makes a marriage. For where fear and coercion are found, consent cannot have a place (X 4.1.14; C.27 q.2 c.2). And because there is a great difference between force and fear, let us see what force or coercion is, and what fear is, and what violence excuses and who fear excuses. Force or coercion or violence (which I take to be the same thing) is assault by a greater thing which cannot be repelled (Dig. 4.2.1). Fear is trepidation of mind over a present or future danger, as is said in the same place (Dig. 4.2.1). Force, coercion, or violence (which I take to be the same thing) is sometimes slight and sometimes violent. Slight force does not exclude marital consent, but violent force does (D.50 c.31; X 4.1.15). Violent coercion is when someone is taken, drawn or led away unwillingly or bound.

Likewise some fear falls on steadfast men, other fear does not. That which falls on steadfast men excuses and excludes marital consent (Dig. 4.2.1; Dig. 4.2.6; X 4.18.1; X 4.1.2). Fear falling on steadfast men is like the fear of death, bodily torture, slavery or sexual violation, as in the following verse:

> Excusare metus hos posse [puta quia nescis].[239]
> Stupri sive status verberis atque necis.

238. Matthew 19:6; Mark 10:9
239. This phrase is from the other edition consulted. It makes better sense than

> For instance, these fears can excuse because you do not know
> [Fear] of sexual violation, or status, or blows and death.

Note that a fear can fall on one person which does not fall on another, as a certain fear might fall on me that does not fall on the king, because it is not likely that men of great dignity would be in dread with fear in a city, or that a king would be afraid of a little army (Dig. 4.2.23). Even so, if there is very appropriate evidence for his fear, the presumption against him is removed, as is said in the same place. And thus the judge will judge according to the status and the diversity of persons, times, and places what kind of fear or violence it is, and according to this will judge for or against the marriage.

Yet note that whatever kind of fear or violence it may be, if a woman who alleges fear or violence has stayed with her husband for a year and a half, or if she has consented to carnal copulation, she ought not to be heard later if she alleges fear or violence (X 4.1.4; X 4.18.4; X. 4.7.6).

CHAPTER 10: On the impediment of order

Some orders, as was said above, are minor, like doorkeeper, lector, exorcist, and acolyte; these do not impede the contracting of marriage nor annul one subsequently contracted. Others are major, namely, subdeacon, deacon, and priest, and these impede the contracting of marriage and annul one subsequently contracted, because a vow of solemn penance is joined to these orders (VI 3.15.un).

CHAPTER 11: On the impediment of bond

The impediment of bond is, namely, when someone is bound to another wife. This has always been the case, even before any decree of the church was issued about this. Never could one bound

---

putaque nostis as found in our text, and it matches the verse found in Raymond's treatise on marriage (Bk IV, 11, 3).

to a wife take another, nor was this ever allowed without a special dispensation of God who was the institutor of marriage, as God dispensed Abraham, Jacob, and the other patriarchs. But because someone can be bound to one person by engagement and yet to another by marriage, let us see what the law is in both cases. Concerning which note that if some man has contracted marriage or engagement with some woman through words in the future tense, he ought not to contract with another woman, nor a woman with another man, but he ought to dismiss the second and return to the first. But if he has contracted engagement with another woman, or a woman with another man, through words in the present tense, or through words in the future tense and this was followed by carnal copulation, then the marriage ought to stand with the second woman or with the second man, even if the engagement contracted with the first was strengthened by an oath. But he ought to do penance for perjury and breaking faith (X 4.4.1 and X 4.1.22).

But if one is bound to another wife in marriage and this was not followed by carnal copulation between them, one can enter into religious life, even if the other is unwilling, and the one who remains in the world can marry another woman or man (X 3.32.7; X 3.32.2; and X 4.4.3). But if there was subsequent carnal copulation between them, never, as long as they live, can they divorce one another except for reason of fornication. And then if they divorce, let them either be reconciled or remain unmarried because, according to the word of the Savior in Matthew 5, if they were to marry others, they would commit adultery.[240]

But suppose a wife believes her husband to be dead and marries another; later he returns. What should be done? I say that as long as she believes that he will not return, let her be excused from adultery and fornication because they were done in ignorance. And let the children, if she has any from her second husband, be judged legitimate. But as soon as the first returns, she ought to leave her second husband and return to the first; if she does not do this,

240. Matthew 5:32

she will be judged as an adulteress (C.34 q.1 and 2 c.1 and c.5). But what if the husband does not return, but his wife believes that he is living? What should she do? She should not demand the conjugal debt from the [second] husband whom she has taken, yet she should pay it if demanded. This advice is given for her in X 4.21.2. Likewise, suppose that a man goes with the army to the Saracens or to a faraway region and does not return; his wife does not know whether he is dead or living. What should she do? I say that however young she is, she cannot marry until she is sure of the death of her husband (X 4.1.19). But how will she be sure? I say that [she will be sure] through the oath of the one under whom he fought, or even of his fellows who knew about his death. And according to the law, she still ought to wait for a year after the oath before she marries, although according to the canons, she can marry immediately after the oath is presented (X 4.21.4). And the Apostle confirms this in 1 Corinthians 7, namely, "with her husband being dead, a woman can marry whomever she likes in the Lord."[241] And Jerome does not condemn even eight marriages, but indeed approves (C.31 q.1 c.11).

CHAPTER 12: On the impediment of the justice of public propriety

The impediment of the justice of public integrity was introduced by the church on account of its propriety. There were two types in ancient times, but now there is just one which is contracted by engagement. Suppose that someone became engaged to a girl seven years old, although he did not know her. Even so, none of his consanguineous relatives could have her as wife, nor he another of her consanguineous relatives (X 4.1.3). I said "seven years old" because before age seven, a pure and proper engagement, that is, one contracted without condition, offers no impediment, nor does it carry any weight, unless she approves it after age sev-

241. 1 Corinthians 7:39

en (X 4.2.4 and X 4.2.5). Note also that it is declared today by a new law that, although an engagement may be nullified by reason of consanguinity, affinity, fraternity, or religion, or frigidity, or whatever other cause, provided that it is not nullified by reason of age, the impediment of the justice of public propriety takes precedence (VI 4.2.un).

CHAPTER 13: On the impediment of affinity

Affinity is the relationship of persons arising from carnal copulation coming to all apart from blood relationship. I said "from carnal copulation," because affinity is contracted both through fornication and marital copulation (C.35 q.2 and q.3 c.10; X 4.13.6 and X 4.14.10). And although there used to be three kinds of affinity, today the first still stands, but the second and third have passed out of use.

Therefore note that the first kind of affinity is contracted by a person in addition to consanguinity through carnal copulation, according to that rule which says, "A person added to a person through carnal propagation changes the degree of relationship, but does not change the type, while a person added to a person through carnal union or copulation changes the type of relationship but does not change the degree." Hence the verse:

> Mutat nupta genus, sed generata gradum.
>
> Marriage changes type, but birth changes degree.

And so that you may better understand, here is an example. Behold I and my sister are one in consanguinity. My sister takes a husband or lover, namely, Peter. This Peter who is a person added to my consanguinity through carnal union changes the type of the relationship, but he is of the first degree of affinity to me, just like my sister. Understand the same thing about all the husbands and lovers of my female blood relations, because by whatever degree of consanguinity they are related to me, in the same degree of affinity their husbands or lovers are related to me. And what I said about the husbands and lovers of my female relatives, understand also about the wives and lovers of my male relatives, because in whatever degree they are consanguineous to me, in the same degree they are affine to me. If someone is consanguineous to me in the second degree, his wife or lover is affine to me in the second degree. I say the same thing about the blood relatives of my wife, because in whatever degree they are consanguineous to her, in the same they are affine to me, and all my blood relatives are affine to my wife in that degree in which they are consanguineous to me. Therefore note that as consanguinity up to the fourth degree impedes the contracting of marriage and annuls one subsequently contracted, so affinity up to the same degree does the same.

Note especially that since degrees of affinity may arise from consanguinity and since there may be doubts about the affinity of some people, recourse is to be made to the person who was the source of the affinity. Find out by how many degrees the person in question is distant from that person, according to the way of assigning degrees of consanguinity given above where it was explained how the degrees of consanguinity are counted, because by however many degrees of consanguinity they are distant, they are separated by the same degrees of affinity. Note also that although the wife of one of my blood relatives is affine to me, nevertheless, the child whom she gets from my blood relative is not affine to me but consanguineous. But if she were to have a child by another man who is not related to me, that child would be neither affine nor consanguineous to me. But a child of a blood relative of my wife will be affine to me like his father, but not in the same degree, because if the father is in the first degree, the son will be in the second. Note further that although my blood relative through whom an affinity was contracted should die, nevertheless the person who survives remains affine to me.

But know that although it may be said that affinity is contracted by the sexual act of a fornicator, understand this to mean if it is done according to the order and way of nature, because if a man knows a woman against nature, meaning, if a man should pollute a woman outside the obligatory vessel, although such pollution is vile, criminal, and damnable, nevertheless, no affinity will be contracted from such sexual intercourse, because such intercourse does not create the mingling or union of flesh through which affinity is contracted. And it seems to me that the same thing should be said if someone should invade the gate of modesty of someone or put his virile member inside the woman's organ but does not complete the act, no affinity is contracted from this. So say Raymond and Hostiensis because mingling of seed is required for the contracting of affinity.[242]

CHAPTER 14: On the impediment of inability for intercourse

Among the other impediments to marriage, inability for intercourse takes center stage because it goes directly against the nature of marriage itself which is intended for the raising of children and the avoidance of fornication; both of these are contradicted by the inability for intercourse. But because not every kind of inability does this, it is to be seen what the inability for intercourse is, how many kinds of it there are, and which ones impede marriage and which do not.

Inability for intercourse is a defect of soul or body or something else by which one is impeded from joining carnally with another. There are many types of this inability, some are natural, others are accidental. Natural ones are like frigidity in a man, tightness in a woman, lack of age in a child. Accidental ones are like castration or bewitchment, which is done through certain spells which are called lots or charms. Likewise, some natural inability is temporary, and some perpetual. Natural inability, if it is temporary, impedes marriage for the time it lasts, like lack of age in a child, because while he is under age he cannot contract marriage (C.30 q.2 c.un; X 4.15.2;

242. Raymond of Penyafort, *Summa*, Bk IV, 15, 4; Hostiensis, *Summa aurea*, Bk IV, "De affinitate," 1. A reprint of a 1537 edition of the *Summa aurea* is available (Aalen: Scientia, 1962).

see above X 4.1.4). Natural inability, like frigidity in a man, if it is perpetual, impedes the contracting of marriage and annuls a marriage subsequently contracted (C.33 q.1 c.2; X 4.15.5). Concerning the tightness of a woman, say that if she can be helped by the benefit of medicine or through continuous practice with a man of suitable size, it does not impede marriage with one by whom she can be carnally known (X 4.15. 3). And note that if on account of the tightness, she separates from him who is not able to know her, and if through assiduous practice with another with whom she can have intercourse she is made suitable for the first, she is to be separated from the second and returned to the first (X 4.15.6). But if the tightness is such that she cannot be helped in any way by the benefit of medicine, it impedes the contracting of marriage and annuls one subsequently contracted, as in the aforementioned case, found in X 4.15.3 and X 4.15.6.

But if the inability is accidental, like castration, it is to be firmly held that such inability impedes the contracting of marriage and annuls one subsequently contracted (X 4.15.2). Concerning bewitchment, a distinction is to be made, because it is either temporary or perpetual. If it is temporary, it does not offer any impediment; if it is perpetual it impedes the contracting of marriage and annuls one subsequently contracted (C.33 q.1 c.4). If someone asks how it can be known if it is temporary or perpetual, I say that from the beginning, all bewitchment may be considered temporary. But if they have lived together for three years, trying hard to achieve carnal copulation, if the impediment of bewitchment still remains, it is considered as a perpetual bewitchment. Nevertheless note that what has been said about castration and bewitchment is to be understood as applying when they precede a marriage, because if they follow a marriage they do not offer any impediment (C.32 q.7 c.25; X 2.6.5; Dig. 23.3.39). Understand the same thing about any other impediment. And understand everything which has been said as being about marriage between Christians, because marriage between unbelievers does not concern us. I say nothing at the moment about the divorce which happens through these impediments because this pertains to officials and prelates, but not to the curates to whom this little book is directed.

CHAPTER 15: On the impediment of festival seasons

Having spoken about the impediments which impede the contracting of marriage and which annul a marriage subsequently contracted, now it is time to speak about impediments which impede contracting a marriage, but do not annul one subsequently contracted. And these are two, namely, festival seasons and the prohibition of the church. Concerning festival seasons, note that engagement and even marriage, which are contracted by consent only, can be contracted during festival seasons, but the transfer of the wife, the wedding solemnities, and carnal copulation are prohibited (C. 33 q.4 c.8–10; X 4.16.2). And note that the festival seasons are from the Advent of the Lord to the octave of Epiphany, and from Septuagesima to the octave of Easter, and from three days before the Ascension of the Lord to the octave of Pentecost inclusive (X 2.9.4). Hence the verse:

> *Coniugium prohibet adventus, hilarique relaxat.*
> *Septuagena vetat, octava pasche relaxat.*
> *Rogamen restat, concedit trina potestas.*

> Advent prohibits marriage, Hilary relaxes.
> Septuagesima denies, Easter week relaxes.
> Rogation restores [prohibition], Trinity concedes permission.

Again:

> *Aspiciens veterem circum quasi quis benedicta*
> *adventus septuagene, vetant rogatio nuptum,*
> *Octava stelle pascheque relaxant.*

> Looking at tradition on how and who may be blessed,
> Advent, Septuagesima, and Rogation deny marriage
> The octaves of Epiphany and Easter relax.

CHAPTER 16: On the prohibition of the church

Concerning the prohibition of the church, maintain firmly that when someone is prohibited from marrying another, perhaps because she is said to be his blood or affine relative or the wife of another, he ought not to marry. But if he does marry, unless he is impeded by some other impediment than the prohibition of the church, they can remain together and are not to be separated. The argument against this in the first case, namely, that the marriage should be ended on account of consanguinity, is given in X 4.14.8. And also in the second case, namely, that they should be separated on account of affinity, in X 4.13.8 and X 4.1.8. And likewise in the third, namely, when the other person contracting marriage is engaged to someone else by words in the present tense, if he contracts later, the second contract is to annulled (X 4.8.2 and X 4.8.3). Solution: it is to be said that they are not to be separated, except for a time so that they might do penance[243] because they held the rule of the church in contempt, and this is said expressly in X 4.1.3; X 4.16.1. Thus all the canons are to be understood which speak of separating them, because it must be explained that it is not for always but only for a time.

Certainly so that various dangers related to this topic of marriage might be avoided, it was ordered by the general council that since marriages are to be contracted in churches, they should be publicly announced by the priests, during a suitable timeframe, so that within that time one who wishes or is in a position to do so may set forth a lawful impediment, and likewise let the priests themselves investigate whether some impediment stands in the way.[244] But when a probable conjecture appears against contracting the marriage, contracting is expressly prohibited to them until what is to be done about it is established with clear proofs. But if the parish priest disdains to do this or if some regular cleric

243. Cf. 1 Corinthians 7:5
244. Constitutions 51 and 52 of the Fourth Lateran Council, 1215; see http://www.piar.hu/councils/ecum12.htm.

took part in a clandestine marriage, let him be suspended from his office for three years. He is to be punished more severely if the nature of his guilt demands it. But also let condign penance be enjoined on those who disdain [the prohibition of the church] and marry anyway, even within the allowable degrees. But if someone maliciously were to set forth an impediment against a lawful marriage, beyond the penance which he ought to do for this sin, he ought not to escape the canonical punishment. And this is best kept in the French churches, where for three Sundays or for three solemn days before a marriage is contracted, it is announced in church that if anyone knows of any impediment on account of which the marriage should not take place, he should offer it. This is called "banns" [*banna*] in France, and those who omit these banns but contract a marriage are both excommunicated; nevertheless the church is generous in its judgment. And let these things suffice concerning marriage.

And thus ends the Part I of this book. I beseech the kindly reader asking for indulgence for those things omitted or less well said, and interposing the shield of prayer against the arrows of detractors, let him correct and emend what was less well said.

Here ends the Part I of this little book, *Handbook for Curates*, which goes over the sacraments and their administration.

PART II: THE SACRAMENT
OF PENANCE

Here begins the second principal part in which penance is dealt with as well as those things which pertain to hearing confession and imposing penances. It is divided into four tracts.

Prologue

Sweet Jesus, the true God and pious Samaritan, who poured wine and oil on the wounds of the injured man who happened among robbers going down from Jerusalem to Jericho, declared the man's state of ruin and sin and its cure and remedy in this parable with signs and wonders.[1] Indeed Jerusalem, which means "vision of peace," is baptismal innocence. Hence Beersheba, which is called the "well of healing," is fittingly represented since the soul of any Christian [washed] in the well of baptismal water is restored by the true, peace-making, and tender Solomon, namely, Jesus who is the true peace, making the two into one,[2] according to the word of the prophet, and is ready to be betrothed in faith. And since Jericho means "the moon" which never remains in the same state, it very clearly prefigures the state of sin in which "the foolish man," that is, the sinner, according to the witness of the Wise One, "changes like the moon."[3] Therefore the man going down from Jerusalem to Jericho is the sinner who, carrying his baptismal innocence through the byways of the vices, will trip

1. Luke 10:30–35   2. Ephesians 2:14
3. Ecclesiasticus [Sirach] 27:12

and fall into ruin. And thus he is robbed by the thieves from hell of his goods, that is, his gifts of grace, and is wounded in his natural gifts. Hence also our Lord Jesus Christ, looking with an eye of tenderness and mercy, descended from the highest heaven into the depths of the world for his healing, and assuming flesh in the womb of the fearless Virgin and binding the wounds of the injured man to the altar of the cross with the cords of charity, he gently poured onto them the tempering or mortifying wine of penance and the oil of kindness. In testimony or sign of this, he marked the beginning of his salvific preaching with this salubrious and most sweet theme, "Repent for the kingdom of heaven draws near."⁴ Here he introduced penance, and for it promised the homeland in return, when at last the work that the Father gave him was finished, namely, healing the injured man. And lest he should abandon him without a caretaker, he commended the injured man to the care of the innkeeper, that is, the curate priest, and he gave him two denarii to use, namely, the two keys of the church which are knowledge for discerning and power for binding and loosing, when he said, "Take care of him."⁵

Therefore, so that priests who are not very advanced in canon law or sacred theology may have some knowledge by which they can discern between leprosy and leprosy, and thus administer healing through salvific penance, in the second part of this work, I have compiled, as well and as briefly as I could, some things out of the opinions of various doctors and the better of my own words for careful study, so that if some neophytes or less advanced curates should be uncertain in the forum of penance, this little work may be an introduction and guide for them. But I have undertaken this, not presuming on my own powers since these are nil, but confident of the mercy of the Savior who, doing all things well, made the deaf to hear and the mute to speak. Hence, reader, considering my goodwill, do not criticize me with a poisoned tongue, but if you find some useful things, attribute them solely to God, but

4. Mark 1:15
5. Luke 10:35

the less useful or utterly useless things attribute to me, and using them, correct and emend with charity.

Tract 1 of the second part is on penance in general, having 4 chapters.

Therefore, concerning penance, in the first tract I will say something about penance in general; later I will say something about each of its parts in particular. First, what penance is and why it is so called, and how many kinds are; second, solemn penance; third, public penance; fourth, private penance.

CHAPTER 1: What penance is and why is it so called and how many kinds of it there are

Penance, according to Ambrose, is defined this way: "It is to mourn over past sins and not to commit again things to be mourned over."[6] According to Augustine, it is defined this way: "Penance is a certain vengeance of sorrow punishing oneself for what one regrets having committed."[7] And it is called penance [penitentia][8] from "pain" (pena, pene) and "to hold" (teneo, tenes), as in "holding in pain" [pene tentio], namely, to the degree that the penitent, through the pain he endures, punishes himself on account of the illicit things he has done. This is proved in D.3 de pen. near the beginning [c.4]. Alternatively, it is defined thus: "Penance is a certain optimal and perfect condition calling every failing back to perfection." Although certainly many and various distinctions concerning penance are offered by the doctors, namely, what its power is and what things cause the sacrament, and many questions con-

6. D.3 de pen. c.1
7. D.3 de pen. c.4
8. *Penitentia* conveys a range of meanings that have to do with ceasing to sin and being restored to grace. It may be translated as penitence (stressing the whole process), penance (meaning especially the sacrament of penance or the satisfaction assigned by the priest in confession), or even repentance.

cerning this topic, omitting all these things which contain more confusion than edification of souls, the definition of penance is to be dealt with. Know therefore that penance in one way is divided like a genus into species; in another way like a whole into parts. The first division is that some penance is solemn, some public, and some private.

CHAPTER 2: On solemn penance

Concerning solemn penance, four things are to be noted. First, what its kind or form is. Know that this penance is not called solemn because it is done in public, but because it is imposed with such solemnity. Hence know that on the Wednesday at the start of the fast, that is, on Ash Wednesday, those who are to do this penance present themselves in church before the bishop and the priests. And the bishop, by offering some warning, shows them the gravity and enormity of their sins. And, dressed in hair shirts, he ejects them from the church, singing that responsory from Genesis, chapter 3, "By the sweat of your face, etc."[9] And thus they are to be outside the church until Maundy Thursday when they will be received and admitted back into the church, but not to communion until they are reconciled by the bishop. This is fully and perfectly discussed in D.50 c.64.

Second, note the reason for this solemnity which is threefold: first as an example and terror to others, then to shame those falling short, then as a sign of the ejection of Adam from paradise.[10] Hence with great sighs and groans, the bishop ought to denounce them because, as Adam was ejected from paradise on account of his sin, so these on account of their sin are ejected from the church. Therefore, as it is given in C.26 q.5 c.14, such penance is not to be repeated. And thus the word of St. Ambrose (D.3 de pen. c.2) is understood who says that "just as there is just one baptism, so there is just one penance," because he speaks of solemn

9. Genesis 3:19
10. Genesis 1:23–24

penance which ought not to be repeated. But if something else ob-tains by the custom of some church, then indeed it can be repeat-ed without danger (D.3 de pen. dict. ante c.22).

Third, note for what crimes and on what persons this penance ought to be imposed. Know that it ought not to be imposed except for grave and enormous and especially well-known crimes which disturb the whole city or community. Nor should it be imposed on a cleric unless he is deposed and who, once he has done it, can-not be promoted to sacred orders or minister in an order already received (D.50 c.55; D.36 c.1). And the reason for this prohibition is fourfold. First is the excellence of order, because those who for-merly were vessels of the vices are not worthy to receive the vessels of the sacraments, that is, orders. Indeed although sin is forgiven through penance, yet there remains some scar, that is, some irregu-larity which impedes him from the reception of holy orders. The second reason is fear of falling from purity through resurgent habit; indeed when bringing the landslide of crime to mind, one does not have the clear dignity befitting the priesthood (D.61 c.2). The third reason is on account of popular scandal. Since such penance is not imposed except for enormous and especially well-known crimes that disturb the whole city, such a one could not minister with-out great scandal (D.50 c.34). The fourth reason is that he does not have the boldness to refute others, since he is conscious that he himself has committed the same or worse than that which he would rebuke (D.25 c.6 and D.50 c.52). But there can be a dispensa-tion for the solemn penitent in minor orders on account of his ne-cessity or utility to the church, as is said in D.50 c.68. And if some-one asks who can grant a dispensation, I say the bishop because it is not specifically prohibited to him (X 5.39.29). And if you say the opposite citing what is said in D.50 c.55, where it says that the bishop who knowingly ordains one doing solemn penance ought to be deprived of the power to ordain, I say that this does not stand in the way, because that is understood as meaning when he ordains without a legitimate reason and without a dispensation or when he gives dispensations too freely (D.51 c.5). Indeed one doing solemn penance cannot contract marriage, but if he does contract it, it will hold; this is proved in D.50 c.65 and C.26 q.6 c.19.

The fourth thing to be noted is by whom solemn penance can be imposed. Know that solemn penance ought not to be imposed except by the bishop or, on his order, by a priest. And only the bishop, or, in case of necessity and on his order, a priest, can reconcile solemn penitents. And if they have repented well, they can be reconciled during Easter week and commune and have entry into the church. But if not, they should remain thus until the end of their lives, and this is given in C.26 q.6 c.14. And because this topic pertains more to the reverend and most holy bishops, whose servant and disciple I am, than to simple priests, I will say no more about this topic.

CHAPTER 3: On public penance

Public penance properly names that which is done in the presence of the church, but not with the aforementioned solemnity, as when pilgrimage through the world is enjoined, with a crutch to lean on or with certain clothing or with some other such thing. And this, as I believe, can be imposed by any confessor on the one confessing to him, because I find no prohibition, unless perhaps it would be contrary to the custom of the church or unless the bishop has reserved it for himself. And note that this penance ought not to be imposed on a cleric unless he is deposed, and it ought not to be imposed on a layperson except for a serious and flagrant crime. And because it belongs to the bishop to judge serious and flagrant crimes, I believe and advise that the one on whom such penance is to be imposed be remitted to the bishop. This is proved in D.6 de pen. c.2. And I believe that such penance can be repeated as many times as the sin for which it is imposed is repeated (D.3 de pen. c. 2, 23, 32).

CHAPTER 4: On private penance

Private penance is that which is done individually and private-
ly when someone regularly confesses his sins secretly to the priest,
and here attention is directed to this in particular. Concerning this,
know that every complete penance has three parts, that is, contrition of heart, confession of mouth, and satisfaction of works, and
this is the second definition of penance. Hence John Chrysostom,
"Complete penance compels the sinner to suffer all things; indeed
in his heart is contrition, in his mouth confession, in his works
satisfaction and total humility, and this is fruitful penance" (D.1
de pen. c.40). Because indeed we offend God in three ways, namely, by thought of pleasure, uncleanness of speech, and pride of
works, and according to the rule of physicians contraries are cured
by contraries, it is necessary that we satisfy in three ways, namely,
by contrition of heart, confession of mouth, and works of satisfaction. Hence such complete penance is that happy and beneficial
three-day period for which the sons of Israel, that is, Christians
seeing God through faith, asked in Egypt, that is, living in the
darkness of sins, when they said, "The God of the Hebrews called
us so that we may go three days' journey," namely, of contrition,
confession, and satisfaction, "into the wilderness," of this world,
"and that we should sacrifice," namely, the sacrifice of penance,
"to the Lord our God; otherwise, a pestilence may befall us," that
is, guilt in the present, "or the sword," that is, pain in the future.[11]
And such complete penance is also that blessed ladder with these
three steps which Jacob saw erected from earth to heaven, and the
Lord leaning upon the ladder,[12] and this is on account of three
things. First, so that the one ascending it might be strongly supported. Second, so that if necessary he might stretch out his hand
to the one ascending it. Third, so that the one ascending it, when
he got tired, might rest in him and put all his confidence in him.
For [the Lord] is not so cruel, as Augustine said, that he would

11. Exodus 5:3
12. Genesis 28:12–13

permit him to fall.[13] In the first step there is sorrow, in the second shame, in the third work. Therefore something is to be said about these three parts of penance in order, and first about contrition.

Tract 2 of the second principal part is on contrition and has 7 chapters.

Concerning contrition, seven things are to be considered in order. First, what contrition is; second, the quantity of contrition; third, its quality; fourth, its duration; fifth, the things for which one ought to be contrite; sixth, what the motives that lead to it are; seventh, its effect.

CHAPTER 1: What contrition is

In order to see what contrition is, note that contrition here is compared with the contrition done to physical things. Hence know that a physical thing is said to be ground up [*conteri*] when it is broken into minute parts, as aromatic spices are ground in a mortar. There is a difference between contrition and breaking, because breaking is when something is broken into large parts and contrition is when it is broken or ground into minute parts. Therefore, the sorrow over sins is called "contrition" [grinding, *contritio*] and not "breaking" [*fractio*] to show that the penitent should not only be contrite over his sins in general, but over each one in particular. But more will be said about this in chapter 5 of this tract.

But why is it called "contrition" rather than "sorrow"? Know that according to what St. Bernard says on the Canticle, "It is therefore called contrition and not sorrow because, as healing ointment is made from many herbs ground in a mortar, so the ointment of compunction or contrition is made from the herbs of many sins born in the soul of the sinner (because as it says in Psalm 62, 'By a deserted land, inaccessible and waterless'),[14] ground in the mortar

13. Cf. C.23 q.5 c.28; D.45. c.16, n. 245
14. Psalm 62:3

of the conscience."[15] And although that is a true and holy saying, nevertheless it does not really answer the question, because according to this, the person is described as grinding rather than being ground, and sin is said to be ground up.

Therefore know that in contrition we should pay attention to three things. First, what is that which is ground up? Second, by whom is it ground up? Third, for what is it ground up, or what is the goal of contrition? What is ground up is the heart of the sinner which is like an earthen vessel full of the poison of sin. And therefore the prophet Joel, by the authority of God, indicating contrition, said, "Be converted to me with your whole heart, in fasting and weeping and mourning, and rend your hearts,"[16] namely, by contrition. That by which the heart of the sinner is ground up is a double millstone, of which one is upward, that is, raising up, and this is the hope of kindness coming from consideration of divine mercy. And the other millstone is downward, weighing down, and this is the fear of penalty coming from consideration of divine justice. And these two millstones ought always to hold the true penitent, and neither one ought to be taken away nor ought they to be handed over to the devil in pledge. As a sign of this, it says in Deuteronomy 3, "You shall not take an upper or lower millstone in pledge,"[17] that is, do not despair over the magnitude and enormity of your sins but always hope in the mercy of God, nor should you be presumptuous but fear the severity of the torments coming from the justice of God. The goal of contrition is that the heart of the sinner, hard as stone, might soften and melt like wax. Therefore it is written, "A hardened heart will have evil in the very end."[18] Therefore the truly contrite can say, "My heart has become like melting wax,"[19] and concerning such a heart it says in Psalm 50, "A contrite and humbled heart, O God, you will not spurn."[20]

15. Cf. Bernard of Clairvaux, *Super Cantica*, Sermon 10:4–5. For a modern English translation, see Bernard of Clairvaux, *On the Song of Songs*, trans. Kilian Walsh (Spencer, Mass.: Cistercian Publications, 1971), 1.61–68.

16. Joel 2:12–13   17. Deuteronomy 24:6

18. Ecclesiasticus [Sirach] 3:27   19. Psalm 21:15

20. Psalm 50:19

Having therefore seen the appropriateness of this name "contrition," let us see what contrition is. Know that contrition is defined by the teachers thus: "Contrition is sorrow for sins, voluntarily assumed with the intention of confessing and satisfying." To clarify this definition, each part offered in this definition is to be considered. Indeed contrition is called "sorrow." Since indeed, according to what has been said, contraries are cured by contraries, and since the medicine ought to be contrary to the illness, and since contrition is the remedy for sin and in sin there was pleasure, it is necessary that there be sorrow in contrition. And thus it is said in Apocalypse 18, "As much as she has glorified herself and lived in pleasure," in committing sins, "so much so give to her torment and grief,"[21] in contrition. Yet note that in contrition there is not only sorrow, but there is also joy. Because when the sinner remembers that through sin he has offended God his creator who created him in his image, and his heavenly father who feeds him bodily and spiritually, and his redeemer who freed him by his own blood from punishment and perpetual damnation, and recalls that through his sin he lost the glory of paradise and incurred the punishment of hell, he ought to sorrow; but when he thinks that through this sorrow he is freed from sin and reconciled to God, he rejoices and not without cause, as indeed one rejoices who once was in peril but avoided shipwreck. Thus the truly contrite ought to rejoice when he sees that he has avoided the shipwreck of sin.

Next comes "voluntarily assumed." Since indeed forced servitude is not pleasing to God, unless the sorrow of contrition is voluntary it will not be acceptable or pleasing to God. And if we commit sin out of coercion, by the testimony of St. Augustine, it is no longer voluntary, and it is not sin.[22] Thus contrition ought to be voluntarily assumed, for if it is not voluntary, then it is not contrition. And the reason for these things is that it is necessary that every meritorious or demeritorious act be elicited or commanded by the will, otherwise it will not be meritorious or demeritorious.

21. Revelation 18:7
22. C.15 q.1 dict. ante c.1 at note 20

Next comes "with the intention of confessing and satisfying." Indeed, the truly contrite person ought to intend to confess and to satisfy when he has the opportunity; otherwise his contrition would be false and void. And the reason is that the integrity of the whole is required for completion, with all its parts coming together. Just as for the completion of a house it is required that the roof, walls, and foundation come together, so truly for the completion of penance, it is required that these three, namely, contrition, confession, and satisfaction, which are the sacrament's integral parts, come together, whether in actuality or in vow.

[Hence in any complete penance there are three parts, namely, contrition of heart, confession of mouth, and works of satisfaction, which the prophet Joel touches on when he says in the person of the Lord, "Be converted to me with your whole heart, etc.,"[23] meaning that contrition and confession are to be made with one's whole heart. And he who is contrite with his whole heart is the one who says with his mouth what he feels in his heart, because when the heart and the tongue do not sound discordant, the symphony is sweet. And when Joel further says, "in fasting, etc.,"[24] he indicates satisfaction. Indeed according to what John says, "For all that is in the world is the desire of the flesh, and the desire of the eyes, etc."[25] Therefore, against the desire of the flesh, Joel says, "in fasting"; against the desire of the eyes, he says, "in weeping and mourning";[26] and against the pride of life he says, "Rend your hearts and not your garments."[27]][28]

CHAPTER 2: On the quantity of contrition

The quantity of contrition is measured in suffering; it is the quantity of sorrow which is essentially contrition itself or the experience caused by contrition. Hence note that in contrition there

23. Joel 2:12   24. Joel 2:12
25. 1 John 2:16   26. Joel 2:12
27. Joel 2:13
28. Missing paragraph provided from other edition consulted.

is a twofold sorrow; accordingly it is called "sorrow" in two ways. For in one way, sorrow is the same as the displeasure of the will, namely, in as much as something which will be or has been done displeases the will. In the other way, it is the same as the suffering resulting or overflowing in sensibility, that is, in the flesh, namely, in as much as some sorrow is felt in one's sensitive part on account of injuring some part, as when a member is cut off or a body is wounded or burned or it suffers from some such thing.

Speaking of sorrow in the first way, where sorrow is displeasure of the will, such sorrow is essentially contrition itself. And thus the sorrow of contrition, namely, true contrition, ought to be and is the greatest sorrow. Hence I say that sin ought to displease the will and the mind, so much so that neither for an agreement nor for convenience nor for inconvenience nor for anything else would you want to consent or to have consented to it. The reason for this is that contrition, if it is true, cannot exist without charity. In order for someone to have charity, however little, it is necessary that he love God above all things, so that for no harm or convenience would he want to offend or to have offended God. And therefore, since sin is an offense against God, your sin ought to displease the will informed by charity, as it ought to be when the will is truly contrite. This is why the will of the truly contrite ought to be such that it in no way, by no chance, for no harm or convenience, wants to commit or to have committed sin. And this is what is said in Jeremiah, chapter 6, where it says, "Make mourning as for an only child,"[29] as the gloss says, "Teach the penitent what he ought to do," and then follows, "Nothing is more sorrowful than the death of an only child, so nothing ought to be more sorrowful than to have offended God through sin." And so I say speaking of sorrow, where sorrow is said to be displeasure of the will, the sorrow of contrition is so great that no sorrow can be greater.

But if one speaks of sorrow as the sorrow created or caused in sensibility, if such sorrow is the effect of contrition in as much as someone who was truly and perfectly contrite by the first sorrow,

29. Jeremiah 6:26

namely, by displeasure of the will and the detestation of sin, and in as much as it is offensive to God, breaks out in weeping, lamentation, and tears (as is read concerning St. Mary Magdalene and St. Peter the Apostle), then I say that it is not necessary that this sorrow in contrition be greater than every other sorrow. Indeed we see many men and women, truly repenting as far as human nature can tell, who cry and weep more over the death of their relatives and friends or over the loss of some temporal thing than they weep or cry over their sins. And the reason for this is that indeed this sorrow is in one's sensible affection and the affection which belongs to sensibility follows experience and sensible cognition, and there are few, indeed very few, who have such sensible or experiential cognition of divine devotion as they have of their corporal pleasures or temporal things. Therefore there are few, indeed very few, who sorrow as sensitively over sin as they sorrow over something temporal or corporal. And if such ones were found, they would be very perfect and worthy of great praise.

It is clear, therefore, that when speaking of sorrow as sorrow names the displeasure of the will, that the sorrow of contrition ought to be maximal, that is, greater than any other sorrow, but when speaking of sorrow as it names the resultant suffering in sensibility, then it is not necessary that the sorrow of contrition be greater than any other sorrow, even though it would be quite fitting.

But must someone truly repentant and contrite prefer to endure any temporal pain, such as illness or death or whatever other pain, than to sin or to have sinned? I say that no one in his right mind ought to pose such a question to himself, nor should anyone pose it to anyone else, because that would be to place oneself or another into temptation. And the human mind is very weak when it comes to sensibility which always flees death and temporal and bodily evils, however perfect a person may be. This is clear in the Savior, our Lord Jesus Christ, who, with the hour of his passion coming close, said, "My soul is sorrowful even unto death,"[30] and this was with respect to sensibility toward death, and explaining

30. Mark 14:34

himself he said, "The Spirit," that is, the rational will, "is willing," to endure death, "but the flesh," that is, sensibility, "is weak," because it flees death.[31] This is why no one ought to put himself in such perplexity, nor ought the confessor to ask this question. But it is required of necessity of anyone doing solemn penance that, where necessity demands, he would rather endure any pain than offend God through sin.

CHAPTER 3: On the quality of contrition

Now the quality of contrition is to be dealt with. About this know that contrition ought to have seven conditions. First, it ought to be discerning; hence it ought to have hope of mercy, so that the truly contrite ought never to despair of mercy, but always ought to hope in the mercy of God, because God is more able to forbear than man to sin. Hence Augustine says on that word which Cain said in Genesis, chapter 4, "My iniquity is too great to deserve kindness,"[32] "You lie, Cain, because the kindness of God is greater than your iniquity." And Ambrose, "Let no one despair because, not the crime which he committed, but his despair, caused Judas the traitor to perish utterly."[33] But because no one knows whether he is worthy of the love or hatred of God, he ought not to presume too much, but always ought to fear because "the fear of the Lord is the beginning of wisdom."[34] And therefore the true penitent ought to grind his grain, that is, his soul, between the two millstones, namely, of fear and of hope, so that from the flour thus ground, cleaned in the sieve of discernment and mixed with the water of tears, that is, of compunction, he may make good bread in the oven of the heart, baked with the fire of charity for his guest, namely, Christ, so that on the day of judgment it may be said to him, "I was hungry and you gave me to eat."[35]

Second, contrition ought to be bitter. Thus that holy King He-

31. Mark 14:38
32. Genesis 4:13
33. C.24 q.1 c.7
34. Psalm 110:10
35. Matthew 25:35

zekiah said in Isaiah, chapter 38, "I will acknowledge to you all my years, in the bitterness of my soul."[36] And if contrition is bitter, it will make peace between God and the sinful soul; hence Hezekiah again, "Behold, in peace my bitterness is most bitter."[37] Therefore contrition ought to be bitter, because the sinner ought to be contrite over that which was loved in illicit thoughts, more bitter because he consented, most bitter because he perpetrated an illicit deed. And if he does so, he will be able to say, as one contrite, that which follows [in Isaiah]. "But you have rescued my soul, so that it would not perish. You have cast all my sins behind your back."[38]

Third, contrition ought to be tearful. Hence the psalmist in Psalm 6, "Every night I will wash my bed," that is, my conscience, "with my tears, I will drench my blanket."[39] And thus did St. Mary Magdalene who washed the feet of our Lord Jesus Christ with her tears, and therefore her sins were forgiven her.[40]

Fourth, contrition ought to be premeditated, as in the aforementioned authority, "I will acknowledge to you all my years,"[41] and concerning this Isaiah says, speaking to the sinful soul, "Take up a stringed instrument," namely of penance. "Circulate through the city," namely, through the health of my soul by considering and remembering each sin, "of the harlot," that is, of the sinful soul who by sinning fornicated with the devil and "who had been forgotten,"[42] that is, by God on account of her sin.

Fifth, contrition ought to be universal, that is, concerning all sins. Sixth, it ought to be long lasting, that is, continual. And these two will be discussed in the next two chapters. Seventh, it ought to be complete, that is, with the intention of confessing and satisfying; otherwise, it would not be contrition but derision. This has been discussed above in chapter 1.

36. Isaiah 38:15
37. Isaiah 38:17a
38. Isaiah 38:17b
39. Psalm 6:6
40. Luke 7:36–50
41. Isaiah 38:15
42. Isaiah 23:16

CHAPTER 4: On the duration of contrition

In order to know how long contrition ought to last, note that according to what was said above in chapter 2, there is a twofold sorrow in contrition. One of these is the detestation or displeasure of the will, and this ought to endure always, as long as a person lives. Nevertheless note that since the commandment concerning contrition is affirmative and an affirmative commandment always obligates (but not forever, only for time and place), the commandment concerning contrition obligates in this way: It is not necessary that a person always be in the act of being contrite, but whenever memory of his sin occurs to him, it should be displeasing to him that he committed that sin. Thus the statement of Augustine in his book, *On Penance*, is understood where it says, "Let one sorrow always and rejoice over the sorrow"; and it continues, "where sorrow has ended, there penance fails."[43] Hence, when he says "Let one sorrow always," "always" means whenever the memory of the sin comes to mind. Likewise when he says, "where sorrow has ended," "always" means either in act or habit. And the reason why contrition ought thus to endure is because no one is certain, at least by common law, if his sin is forgiven through contrition because he does not know if his contrition is sufficient. Hence it is said in Ecclesiasticus, "Do not be willing to be without fear concerning a forgiven sin."[44] Indeed I think that someone might know by divine revelation that his sins have been fully forgiven him; still it ought to displease him to have sinned whenever the memory of his sin occurs to him. Otherwise he would sin a new sin, because as it is an offense to want to sin, so it is an offense to like having sinned.

There is another sorrow in contrition, namely, the sorrow which results and overflows in sensibility, namely, when a person,

43. Augustine, *Liber de vera et falsa poenitentia*, c. 13 (PL 40:1124); D.3 de pen. c.5. Medieval scholars falsely attributed this tract to St. Augustine. It appears almost in full in Gratian's *Decretum* in the *Tractatus de penitentia* (C.33 q.3).
44. Ecclesiasticus [Sirach] 5:5

out of displeasure over sin, breaks out in weeping and tears. And it is not necessary that such sorrow always endure, since there are few, indeed very few, who can cry over their sins for even an hour, let alone through the whole of their lives. And yet it would be a great perfection to be able to weep for sins whenever they were remembered, just as it is read of St. Peter the Apostle that he carried a handkerchief in his breast with which he wiped his tears, because whenever he remembered the sin which he committed when he denied Christ,[45] he was not able to contain his tears, even though he knew well that Christ had forgiven him his sin.

CHAPTER 5: On the things for which one ought to be contrite

Some sin is actual, some original. Actual sin is that committed by one's own action, namely, when one does what one ought not to do, or when one does not do what one ought to do. And in this way, it is defined thus: "Sin is every deed or word or desire against the law of God." Original sin is what man contracted from the beginning in as much as man descends from Adam through his seed, so that formally original sin is nothing other than the lack of original justice. Hence know that Adam at his creation received from God a certain supernatural gift which is called "original justice." This justice so ordered man toward God that the soul of man would obey God in everything, so that he would in no way be moved against the will of God. And, the body so obeyed the soul that it would in no way be moved against the will of the soul or against the rule of reason. And through that gift, all the animals were subjected to man and obeyed him at a nod. According to the psalmist in Psalm 8, "You have subjected all things under his feet, etc."[46] Adam received that gift not only for himself, but also for all his posterity, so that to all who would descend from his seed,

45. Matthew 26:69–75, Mark 15:66–72, Luke 22:54–62, John 18:25–27
46. Psalm 8:8

he would transfer that gift, that is, this original justice. And by his sin, he deprived himself and all his posterity of this gift so that all who descend from his seed lack this gift, and this lack is called original sin.

Now, let us see over what things one ought to be contrite. First, ought one to be contrite over original sin? The answer is no. The reason is that a person only ought to be contrite and sorrow over what is committed by his own action, or what was in his power not to commit. But original sin was not committed by his own action, nor was it in the power of any person not to commit it. This is why one is not obligated to sorrow or be contrite over original sin. And I say that no one needs to be contrite [over original sin] of necessity, yet it would be fitting for an adult who comes to baptism that original sin displease him, not in particular as if it were caused by him, but in general in as much as anything which separates him from God ought to displease him.

But concerning actual sin, how ought one to be contrite over it? Note that actual sin is twofold, some is mortal and some venial. And concerning mortal sins, one ought to be contrite and confess each and every one of them, since contrition does not suffice nor does general confession. Indeed whoever is truly penitent ought diligently to examine and probe his conscience so that he may consider the days, hours, places, times, persons, and all the circumstances in which and with whom the sinner was able to sin and has sinned, and so that as each and every sin which he has committed comes to mind, he may be contrite and confess every mortal sin. Nevertheless, although the truly penitent ought to sorrow greatly and intensely over every mortal sin, yet since one sin is graver than another in deed or intention, one ought to sorrow and be contrite over one more than another.

But what is to be done about forgotten sins? I say that someone can forget his sins in two ways. In one way, he has forgotten in particular but not in general, that is, he remembers well that he has sinned mortally, but does not remember the particular kind of sin, for instance, whether he had stolen something or fornicated, and so on. And such a person is obligated to sorrow and be contrite in general over sin, and in particular, to be contrite over his negligence through which he came to forget his sin. And he is obligated to do what he can about this, namely, so that he might remember his sin in particular, either by thinking back on his ways or by praying to God that he might restore it to his memory.

In the other way, one can forget his sin so that he does not remember either in general or in particular. Here one is still obligated to be contrite in general. And I call for being contrite in general, not under condition, that is, not saying or thinking, "If I have sinned, I am sorry or contrite." Rather I call for being contrite in particular under probable estimation. Indeed a person ought to believe that he has probably offended God in many ways that he does not remember, and so under this estimation, let him sorrow and repent as if he were certain. Then he is contrite and penitent. Hence everyone ought frequently to say the verse of the psalmist in Psalm 30, "Do not remember the offenses of my youth and my ignorances, O Lord."[47]

But how ought one to be contrite over venial sin? Note that there are three kinds of venial sins. One is an unexpected venial sin, committed not through one's own will, but out of a certain impulse, and concerning such a sin one is not obligated to be contrite in particular, except as is fitting. Another kind is a venial sin coming from the will; if one consents to it, one falls into mortal sin. For example, a wayward thought in thinking about the carnal act is a venial sin, but if it is consented to, it is a mortal sin. And when such a venial sin comes to mind, one ought to be contrite over it and repent and diligently avoid it, lest one consent or will consent to it. And there is some venial sin which through its frequency increases one's desire to sin. And here there can be such desire that what was venial by nature is made mortal by this desire. For example, a jesting lie is venial by its nature, but it can be repeated so often that it greatly increases the desire to lie, so that

47. Psalm 24:7

through this desire it can happen that the man will sin mortally as often as he lies in jest. And over this, one ought to be contrite and repent by avoiding it and being careful lest it multiply. Concerning this more will be said below when the confession of venial sins is dealt with, since one is obligated to be contrite over these in the same way that one is obligated to confess them.

CHAPTER 6: What the motives that lead to contrition are

The motives leading to contrition are many. The first and principal one is the love of God. Indeed that which ought principally to draw a man away from sin, and if he has sinned what should correct and amend him, is the love of God and this love as it is begotten in the soul of the sinner. Indeed love follows thinking and [knowing],[48] because as Augustine says, "We love the known, but not the unknown." Therefore when the sinner thinks and recognizes the goodness and justice of God to whom every evil is displeasing and who never leaves any evil unpunished, and he thinks that he has committed many things which displease the divine goodness and on account of which he is worthy to be punished, he is deeply afraid. And when he further thinks of the kindness and mercy of God who is ready to spare all who are sorrowful and penitent and to forgive guilt however great, he hopes for mercy and thus is moved to detest sin. And this movement is called attrition, that is, a certain imperfect contrition. And thus God, who never fails, pours the light of grace into the soul of the sinner, and by that light, the illuminated sinner grows warm in the love of God and in the detestation of sin. Thus servile fear precedes and prepares the heart of the sinner for contrition, but the love and fervor of charity perfect him. And concerning this, Augustine offers an example, saying that as in sewing a seam the pig bristle precedes and makes a way for the thread, yet does not remain in the seam, so fear of punishment precedes contrition, and this fear pre-

48. Corrected from other edition consulted; our text says "love follows thinking and thinking."

pares for the love and charity of God, which, once it is in the soul, expels all fear. And so says St. John in his first epistle, "Perfect love casts out fear,"[49] namely, servile fear which is the fear of punishment, but not filial fear which is the fear of offense.

The second motive is disgrace, that is, shame over sins committed. Hence it says in Proverbs, chapter 12, "Worthy things act with confusion";[50] Job, "Unworthy things act with confusion"; and Numbers, chapter 3, "I will reveal your shame to your face."[51] Indeed when a sinner thinks that all his sins, however secret and hidden they may be, are manifest and open to God, and that, unless he repents and is contrite over them, God will reveal and manifest them to the whole world, he is moved to contrition and penance for his sins. Hence Boethius says, "Great is the necessity enjoined upon our uprightness since everything we do happens before the eyes of the all-seeing judge."

The third motive is detestation, that is, abhorrence, of the vileness of sin. Such indeed is the vileness of sin that it makes a servant of the devil out of a son of God. Hence St. Peter says, "Whoever commits sin is a slave of sin,"[52] since one becomes the slave of the one by whom one is conquered. Since therefore the sinner is conquered by the devil by means of sin, by means of sin he is made a slave of the devil. Hence Anselm says, "You made me, Lord, in your image, and I have covered it over with a horrible image." Hence the sinful soul, seeing and considering the vileness of sin, can say the word which Jeremiah says, "See, Lord, and consider, for I have become vile."[53]

The fourth motive is consideration of the day of judgment and the pains of hell. Indeed as often as the sinner considers that for every word, deed, and thought against the law of God it will be necessary to render an account on the day of judgment, according to the word of the Savior in Matthew, saying, "For every careless word that was spoken on earth, men will give an account on

49. 1 John 4:18
51. Nahum 3:5
53. Lamentations 1:11

50. Cf. Proverbs 12:4
52. John 8:34

the day of judgment"[54] (C.21 q.5 c.21), so often is he moved to contrition and repentance for his sins. Hence Jerome, speaking of the day of judgment, says this, "As often as I consider that day, I tremble with my whole heart," and again, "Whether I eat or drink or do something else, it always seems to me that this terrible trumpet sounds in my ears, 'Arise, dead one, and come to judgment.'" When the sinner considers this with an attentive mind, his whole being trembles in his heart. If, indeed, as St. Peter the Apostle says in 1 Peter, chapter 4, "If the just man shall scarcely be saved, where shall the impious and the sinner appear?"[55] And Gregory, "What will the twig of the desert do," that is, the sinner, "when the cedar of paradise," that is, the righteous, "will be shaken to its foundations?"

The fifth motive is sorrow over the loss of the heavenly kingdom. Indeed when the sinner thinks that he has lost the glory of paradise on account of his sin, it is no wonder if he sorrows; indeed it is surprising if he does not burst in half. If indeed one sorrows and weeps over the loss of wealth, how much more ought one to sorrow and weep over the loss of celestial glory. And therefore St. John said in his Apocalypse in the third chapter, "Hold fast to what you have, lest someone else take your crown."[56]

The sixth motive is sorrow over multiple offenses against the Creator. Indeed when a sinner considers and thinks that he has offended God who created him out of nothing and marked him with his image and redeemed him with his precious blood, it would be strange if he did not sorrow and repent of his sin. Concerning this Bernard says, "Sorrow over sins ought to be bitter, more bitter, and most bitter. Bitter because we offend God, the creator of all. More bitter because we offend our Father who cares for and tends us in many ways. Most bitter because we offend our Redeemer who liberated us by his blood from the bondage of sin, from the cruelty of demons, and from the bitterness of hell."[57]

54. Matthew 12:36   55. 1 Peter 4:18
56. Revelation 3:11

57. Guido most likely borrowed both the quotation and attribution to Bernard from Raymond; see Raymond of Penyafort, *Summa*, Bk III, 34, 8.

Even so, note that although the sinner, as has been said, ought to sorrow and be contrite over his sins, nevertheless, he ought always to hope in the Lord and in his kindness and mercy. Thus he ought to hope for mercy and glory, because, as the Wise One says in Proverbs, chapter 27, "The one who hopes in the Lord will not be confounded,"[58] by confusion, guilt, or punishment.

CHAPTER 7: On the effect of contrition

The effect of contrition is manifold. First, this is clear from the force of its name, for it is called "contrition," as if to say "together or fully ground," which is to be understood thus because in contrition the whole heart of the sinner is literally cut or ground by the great anguish, sorrow, wrath, and indignation which it conceives against sins. Hence the Lord says through the prophet Joel, chapter 2, "Rend your hearts."[59] Likewise, the Psalm, "The sacrifice acceptable to God is a broken spirit, a contrite and humble heart, God, you will not despise."[60] And according to what St. Bernard says, "Contrition cleanses the soul of the accusation of guilt and liberates it from the pains of hell and from the horrible society of demons and from the most vile servitude to sin; it imparts the spiritual goods which the sinner lost through sin, it also restores the society and spiritual communion of the church and all the good things which are accomplished by participation in it. From a child of wrath it makes a child of grace, from a son of the devil it makes a son of God and consequently a participant in the eternal inheritance."[61]

But on whether contrition alone forgives sin, there are various opinions. Indeed some say that as we offend God in three ways, namely, by heart, mouth, and deeds, so it is necessary to satisfy God in three ways, namely, by contrition of heart, confession of

58. Proverbs 28:25   59. Joel 2:13
60. Psalm 50:19

61. Again, Guido appears to have borrowed here from Raymond's *Summa*, although in the reprint we consulted, Raymond provides no attribution; see Raymond of Penyafort, *Summa*, Bk III, 34, 10.

mouth, and satisfaction of deeds; otherwise sin is not forgiven. And these base their judgment on the decretal D.3 de pen. c.8. And these say that all the authorities who say that sin is forgiven in contrition of heart alone are to be understood as applying when the point of necessity excludes oral confession, that is, when someone loses speech or when someone cannot obtain a priest for confession. Others say that sins are forgiven in contrition under the condition, namely, that they confess, and these base their judgment on what is said in D.3 de pen. c.18.

A third group says sin is forgiven in contrition of heart alone for any adult who is truly contrite and intends to abstain from further sin, to confess and satisfy before God according to the command of the church. And these base their judgment on D.1 de pen. c.5: "So great is the kindness of God that he forgives sin at just a promise; although not yet uttered by the mouth, God already hears it in the heart." And this opinion is truer and is more commonly held by the doctors. And it is clear that this opinion is truer from the example of Lazarus whom Christ raised before he was absolved by the disciples.[62] Indeed the dead Lazarus is the sinner who has died by means of sin. According to the word of Ezekiel, chapter 18, saying, "The soul that sins, the same shall die."[63] And he is raised by the Lord when his sin is forgiven him in contrition and afterward he is released by the disciples, that is, released by the priests in confession. It is also clear from the example of the ten lepers cleansed by the Lord who were made clean along the road before they arrived at the priests. Indeed these lepers are sinners who, while they are going to the priests, that is, while they have contrition and the intention to confess, are cleansed from their sins.[64] And so says the psalmist in Psalm 31, "I said, 'I will confess my unrighteousness to the Lord,' and you forgave the impiety of my sin."[65] "I said," that is, I proposed firmly in my soul.

Note that these three are simultaneous in time although they have a natural order among them, namely, justification, contrition,

---

62. John 11:17–44

63. Ezekiel 18:20

64. Luke 17:12–19

65. Psalm 31:5

and the forgiveness of sins. Indeed I must necessarily understand that first someone has grace, then is contrite; grace therefore comes first and love follows since the one who has grace loves. And then contrition follows since the one who loves will be contrite, and forgiveness of sins follows upon contrition. This process is gathered from D.1 de pen. c.37. "Truly whoever [does not] love abides in death."[66] And Augustine, "Without charity, how can someone have true contrition of heart?"[67] It is clear therefore how sin is forgiven by contrition of heart alone. What the absolution of the priest does for the forgiveness of sins will be discussed below when confession is dealt with. Let these remarks suffice concerning contrition.

Tract 3 of the second principal part is on confession, having 11 chapters.

Concerning confession, eleven things are to be considered. First, the institution of confession, second those who are obligated to confess, third the time in which one is obligated to confess, fourth to whom confession is to be made, fifth what things are to be confessed, sixth the conditions which confession ought to have, seventh the repetition of confession, eighth how the priest ought to behave toward the one confessing, ninth the questions to be asked in confession, tenth the power of the keys and the effect of confession, last the seal of confession.

CHAPTER 1: On the institution of confession

As guidance for those things which are to be said about confession, note that in holy scripture "confession" is taken in two ways. In one way, it is the same as the praise of God. Hence to confess in this way is the same as to praise God. It is taken in this

66. 1 John 3:14
67. D.2 de pen. c.14

way when, "Bless," that is, praise, "the Lord for he is good, etc."[68] is said.

In the other way, it is the same as the manifestation of sins before the priest. And this way is defined thus: "Confession is the legitimate declaration of sins before a priest who has the keys and the power to absolve." As a guide to this definition, let us examine its various parts. First, "Confession is the legitimate declaration of sins," is said against those who hide their sins by either excusing or concealing. It is also said against those who recite their good deeds in confession or who confess through a denial of sins, as in "I am not an adulterer, a glutton, etc." "Before a priest who has the keys and the power to absolve" is said so that all the conditions which are required for true confession may be made clear. And it is called "confession" as if to say "together or fully or completely acknowledged." And what is said here applies to confession understood in this way.

Therefore let us see when it was instituted and who the institutor of confession was. As to the first, know that the confession of sins is twofold, namely, mental and vocal. Mental confession of sins belongs to the precepts of the law of nature discerned in some way by faith. Indeed when a person knows and carefully considers that he is offending or has offended God whom he does not see, except by some ray of faith, nature dictates to him that he should humbly ask for mercy for himself from God. And this is never done unless guilt is recognized, which is done through mental confession.

And vocal confession is twofold; some is made to God, some is made to man. Therefore, when speaking of the vocal confession which is made to God, I believe that confession became necessary for salvation immediately after the fall of the first man. And the reason which persuades me is this: In every time in which there is or was sickness, medicine was necessary against that sickness, but immediately after the fall of the first man, there was the sickness

68. E.g., Psalm 105:1, 106:1, 117:1

of sin, not only of original sin, but also of actual sin, at least for many. Therefore confession, even vocal confession, was necessary after the fall of the first man, at least for many. And this is clear from a certain gloss which is offered on that word from Genesis 4, "Adam, where are you?"[69] The gloss says, "These are words of one rebuking and urging to confession, not words of one who is ignorant." And it is evident that this speaks of the vocal confession to be made to God, because then God himself, not man, spoke out loud to Adam. Therefore from that time on, confession, spoken of in this way, was necessary.

But when speaking about the vocal confession to be made to man, I say that it was instituted in the new law by Christ, obviously when he was incarnate, for then, not before, it was fitting that such confession be instituted. And the reason which persuades me of this is twofold, since confession is designed for two purposes, namely, for the manifestation and removal of sin and for accomplishing reconciliation with God and with his church. From this it is clear that confession should have been instituted only under the new law. Also note as evidence for these things which are being said that the state of sin is called "darkness," but the state of grace "light." And so the Apostle said, speaking to the Ephesians after they were converted to the faith and were in a state of grace, in Ephesians, chapter 5, "you were darkness in times past, but now you are light, in the Lord."[70] And in the Epistle to the Romans, chapter 9, "Let us cast aside the works of darkness," according to the gloss, that is, the works of sin, "and be clothed with the armor of light," that is, of virtue.[71] In this law, therefore, the confession to be made to man ought to be instituted, in which "the true light" was rising, the light "which illuminates every man was coming into this world."[72] And this is the new light in Christ, namely, in Christ incarnate. Therefore the confession to be made to man must have been instituted in the new law.

---

69. Genesis 3:9
71. Romans 13:12

70. Ephesians 5:8
72. John 1:9

From the second purpose, namely, from this, that confession is designed for accomplishing reconciliation with God and with his church, it is also clear that it must have been instituted in the new law. Indeed confession is made to man so that a man may be the judge and arbiter between God and the sinner. But an arbiter ought to be such that he is able to reach out his hand to either party. Therefore it is necessary that he to whom confession is to be made is able to reach out his hand to God, to whom the one confessing wants to be reconciled, and to the one who is confessing. But such a one could not exist until God was made man, because then the mediator between God and man was given to us, the man Christ Jesus. And he, after he ascended bodily into heaven, left in the church others whom he appointed in his place as rectors of the church and arbiters to whom he gave authority for reconciling sinners with God and with his church. Therefore confession must have been instituted in the new law by Christ incarnate.

Also, confession is effective through absolution and absolution is effective by the power of the keys, which keys were given to man in the new law by Christ saying to St. Peter the Apostle in Matthew, chapter 16, and in him to all the others, "I will give you the keys of the kingdom of heaven,"[73] and John 20, "Those whose sins you shall forgive, they are forgiven them, and those whose sins you shall retain, they are retained."[74] Therefore it is evident that the confession done in this way was instituted in the new law. Nevertheless, it existed earlier as a figure in the old law in that authority and power were given to the priests to discern between leprosy and leprosy and between profane and holy, but these things were corporal and not spiritual. And Christ showed that this figure had been fulfilled in the new law when he sent the cleansed lepers to the priests, saying, "Go and show yourselves to the priests."[75]

And concerning the second question, who was the institutor of confession? I say that it was Christ himself, and the reason was touched on above in the first part of this work when it dealt with

73. Matthew 16:19   74. John 20:23
75. Luke 17:14

the sacraments in general. And I understand that he was the institutor authoritatively. And I believe that St. James the Less, who was bishop of Jerusalem and who first among the apostles celebrated mass, was the promulgator of this sacrament when he said, "Confess your sins, one to another,"[76] as was said above concerning the sacrament of extreme unction.

CHAPTER 2: On those who are obligated to confess

All adults, after they have arrived at the age of discretion so that they are able to discern between good and evil, are obligated to confess once a year, namely, in Lent, by the statute of the general council that is put forward in *Omnis utriusque sexus* (X 5.38.12). And against the transgressors of that statute, the penalty for such is established in the same place, namely, that contraveners are barred from entering the church and those dying are not to have a Christian burial.

And for this most holy and salubrious ruling, there were three reasons. The first was universal need, "for all have sinned," as the Apostle says, "and are in need of the grace of God."[77] "Indeed there is no one who does good and does not sin," as the Wise One says.[78] Therefore everyone ought to glorify God by confessing himself to be a sinner; indeed he who confesses himself to be a sinner glorifies God by showing himself to need the mercy and grace of God.

The second reason was reverence for holy communion. Since indeed all are obligated to commune at Easter, in order that they may worthily and purely approach such a sacrament, it was necessary to allow the remedy of cleansing and washing away of sin which is done in confession.

The third reason was the discernment of the flock of the Lord, namely, lest wolves who would eat the sheep be hidden among the flock. Therefore [confession] was established, so that the rec-

76. James 5:16   77. Romans 3:23
78. Ecclesiastes 7:21

tors of the churches might know the countenance of their sheep, lest heretics should cover their malice under a fleece of innocence. Therefore all, whoever they are and of whatever condition, are obligated to confess once a year; otherwise they sin mortally and ought to be punished with the above mentioned penalty.

But suppose there is someone who does not have awareness of any mortal sin, but only of venial ones. Since one is not obligated to confess venial sins, therefore, at least such a person is not obligated to confess. I say, without prejudice and the saving judgment or counsel of a better person, that someone can be obligated to confess on account of two things. In one way, on account of the bond of sin; in the other way, on account of the bond of commandment. No one is obligated to confess venial sins on account of the bond of sin since these can be forgiven without confession. Nevertheless they are to be confessed on account of the commandment by which everyone is obligated to confess once a year, even when the one confessing has no sins except venial ones. Hence if he were to have mortal sins which he confessed, he would not be obligated of necessity to confess the venial ones. Nevertheless, this will be discussed more extensively below.

Or further suppose that someone is so attentive to divine things that he does not have a guilty conscience over any sin, either mortal or venial. Is he obligated to confess or not? If not, then not all are obligated and bound to confess, which is contrary to what has been said. But if he is obligated and does not have awareness of any sin, either mortal or venial, then he is obligated to confess and speak against his conscience and so lie, which would be unlawful to say. Therefore at least such a one is not obligated to confess. I say to this that since the Wise One says, "the just one will fall seven times a day,"[79] I believe it is impossible, in this state of earthly pilgrimage, that someone having intellect and the use of reason could go through a day or a week without remorse for some venial sin. But that he could go through a whole year—I consider this

79. Proverbs 24:16

even more impossible. And I do not believe that this gift was given to any saint, except Christ and the Virgin Mary his mother. Nor do I believe that the apostles had this gift, because they sinned venially. As Gregory says, and Augustine in the book *On Nature and Grace*, if all the male and female saints were still living and were asked whether they were able to live without sin, they would all say with one voice, "'If we claim that we have no sin, then we are deceiving ourselves and the truth is not in us.'[80] The Virgin Mary is an exception, concerning whom, when it comes to sin, on account of the honor of the son of God, I want there to be no further question."[81] And Jerome on 1 Timothy, chapter 3, "The thing is nearly against nature that someone may be without sin." Therefore however perfect a person may be, he ought to think in his heart and confess with his mouth himself to be a sinner, because as Gregory says, "It belongs to good minds to acknowledge," that is, to fear, "guilt, where there is no guilt" (X 3.42.6).

Hence by common law all are obligated to confession. And if God, by a special grace, should give the gift to someone that he might not sin mortally or venially, I believe that still, so that he should not disdain the commandment of the church, such a one ought to present himself to his confessor, not because he would call himself a sinner and lie, but he ought to say, "Lord I am not aware of any sin, nevertheless on account of the commandment of the church, I present myself to you." This fits with what I said above, that one sanctified in the uterus ought to receive the sacrament of baptism even though he does not have original sin.

CHAPTER 3: On the time in which one is obligated to confess

According to the testimony of the Wise One, "all things have their time."[82] Therefore now it is to be seen when confession is to

80. 1 John 1:8
81. Augustine, *De natura et gratia*, c. 42 [XXXVI.] (PL 44:267).
82. Ecclesiastes 3:1

be made, namely, whether it is to be done immediately when a person has sinned, or whether it can be deferred to the time stated in the decretal *Omnis utriusque sexus* (X 5.38.12), namely, until Lent. Therefore as guidance for this, know that we can speak of confession either with respect to interior intention or with respect to external words. In the first way, as all the doctors commonly say, one is obligated to intend to confess when one is first obligated to be contrite over sin, because without the intention to confess and satisfy, sin is not forgiven in contrition. And I say "when one is first obligated to be contrite" because, as was said above, always and as soon as a sin comes to mind, one is obligated to be sorry and contrite over it in the way said above, even if one has already confessed. Nevertheless, those things which one duly confessed, one is not obligated to confess again. Concerning this more will be said below when the repetition of confession is dealt with. Therefore, since as soon as a person knows that he has sinned mortally he is obligated to be contrite, he is then obligated to intend to confess.

But if we speak of actual confession, namely, when a person is obligated to actually confess, on this matter the doctors think variously. Indeed some say without distinction that however much and whenever someone sins, he is not obligated to confess before Easter, but he is certainly obligated to be contrite and to be intending to confess. And they base their judgment on two things. First, because the commandment about confessing is affirmative, it therefore does not obligate except for the designated place and time. But the time designated by the church is Lent. Therefore no one is at all obligated to confess before Lent, neither at Christmas nor at Pentecost, according to D.2 de cons. c.19, 21, 15, unless he is in danger of death. Second, because the act of confession is not necessary for justification since justification comes through contrition, confession is necessary only by the commandment and obligation of the church. But the church does not require it before Easter, unless the danger of death is imminent. Therefore, before that time, no one is obligated to confess unless the danger of death is imminent.

Others say that the sinner living in mortal sin is obligated to confess his sin immediately when he has the services of a discrete and suitable confessor and remembers the sins he has committed. The decretal *Omnis utriusque sexus*, X 5.38.12, does not stand in the way because that decretal does not say that it should be deferred until then, but that one should not wait longer than that, as the church prohibits, lest someone remain excommunicated longer than a year. Nevertheless, it does not give permission for remaining [unconfessed] until that time. Besides, that decretal was not issued on behalf of the negligent, but against the negligent. But before it was issued, the sinner was obligated to confess as soon as the opportunity presented itself. Therefore it seems that one would be obligated in the same way after its promulgation.

Which of these opinions is truer, I confess not to know. Nevertheless to say what the first group says seems dangerous to me, but to say what the second group says seems harsh to me.

Truly St. Thomas in a certain quodlibetal question offers some cases in which one living in mortal sin is obligated to confess immediately. The first is when one has an illness from which the danger of death is imminent.[83] And this case is gathered from those things which are said in X 5.38.13. The second case is when one has to do something in which the danger of death is imminent, even though he is healthy at the time, like when one has to cross the sea or make a long journey or fight or some such thing. The third case is if one has to do something which one living in mortal sin cannot do without sinning mortally, for instance, if one must say mass or receive or administer some sacrament of the church. The fourth case is when one commits some sin from which his curate cannot absolve him, and he fears that within the statutory time he will not have the services of a suitable confessor. The fifth case is when his conscience tells him to confess immediately, because then either he is obligated to put conscience aside or to follow it since it is not erroneous but salubrious.

83. Aquinas, *Quodlibet I*, q. 6, a. 2.

Indeed all say that although it is not necessary to confess immediately, nevertheless it is very appropriate. According to the saying of the Wise One, "You should not delay being converted to the Lord, and you should not set it aside from day to day. For his wrath will approach suddenly, and in the time of vindication, he will destroy you."[84] Note that Raymond sets forth in his *Summa* five reasons why it is very useful and appropriate to confess immediately.[85] The first is on account of the uncertainty of the hour of death. Hence the Lord says in the gospel of Luke, chapter 7, "The Lord of that servant will return on a day which he hoped not, and at an hour which he knew not. And he will separate him, and he will place his portion with that of the unfaithful."[86] Likewise it was said to the rich man asking for long life, "Foolish one, this very night demons will require your soul of you. To whom, then, will those things belong, which you have gathered?"[87]

The second reason is that staying in sin always adds sin to sin, and as a consequence, penalty to penalty. Hence the Apostle to the Romans, chapter 2, "Do you not know that the kindness of God should lead you to repentance? But by your hard and impenitent heart, you are storing up for yourself the wrath of God for the day of tribulation and revelation of the just judgment of God, who will give to each one according to his works."[88] It says in Hosea, chapter 4, "Slander, lying, theft, and murder have overflowed, and bloodshed has brought more bloodshed,"[89] that is, sin adds further sin. Hence Gregory, "Sin which is not cleared away through penance is soon drawn to another by its own weight."

The third reason is that when someone spends a longer time in sin, so much further will he be removed from God and, as a consequence, his conversion will be that much more difficult. Accord-

---

84. Ecclesiasticus [Sirach] 5:8–9

85. Raymond of Penyafort, *Summa*, Bk III, 34, 23. Guido copied almost all of the ensuing discussion of Raymond's five reasons why it is fitting to confess immediately directly from this part of Raymond's *Summa*.

86. Luke 12:46   87. Luke 12:20
88. Romans 2:4–6   89. Hosea 4:2

ing to that which is commonly said in Ovid's *Remedy of Love,* "Don't put off till tomorrow [the cure] you can work today. If you are not ready today, tomorrow you will be less so." And Ovid, "Fight against it at the beginning. It is late to get medicine ready when delay has given the disease time to get a hold on you."[90] And the psalmist in Psalm 72, "Lord, those who put themselves far from you will perish."[91]

The fourth reason is that hardly anyone can repent well during a great and painful illness, or even think about his sins. Hence Jerome, "When you are oppressed by illness, you are hardly able to think of anything other than what you are feeling, and the concentration of your mind is taken away where sorrow is strong." Indeed as Augustine says, "Then impediments will abound, for sickness bears down and pain frightens; children, wife, world, and those things he loved illicitly all call to him" (D.7 de pen. c.6). "Therefore hold on to what is certain and let go of the uncertain,"[92] that is, repent and confess while you are healthy and do not put it off until you are sick, according to the counsel of the Wise One saying, "You should confess while you are still alive and healthy."[93]

The fifth reason is that unless the sinner in his lifetime heard the Lord crying out that he should confess and repent, he will cry out to the Lord after the time [for repentance has passed] and will not be favorably heard. On account of the example of the rich feaster who was buried in hell and who was not favorably heard when he asked for a drop of water,[94] confession is not to be deferred or delayed, but it is very appropriate and useful to confess immediately. And Richard, in his fourth book on the *Sentences,* speaking about this topic says that this case is to be judged in one

90. Ovid, *Remedia Amoris,* lines 90–94. Guido copied these lines from Raymond, although in the reprint we consulted, he provides no attribution. See Raymond of Penyafort, *Summa,* Bk III, 34, 23.

91. Psalm 72:27

92. D.7 de pen. c.4; this is from Caesarius of Arles, Sermon 63, "De paenitentia ex dictis sancti Augustini," 272.

93. Ecclesiasticus [Sirach] 17:27

94. Luke 16:19–31

way for a religious, in another for a layperson. For the religious, since the entire time of his life is a time of penance for him, having the services of a suitable priest, if he were to sin mortally, I believe that he is obligated to confess immediately without delay. And "without delay" is understood to mean "as right reason will determine." Truly the layperson can reasonably wait until the time of Lent, which is the time of penitence, since that is a more opportune time for the layperson to confess and satisfy. If they wait for it reasonably, I dare to judge that they do not sin, as long as they firmly intend to confess in that time. But concerning clerics, I do not dare to judge, but I give the sound counsel that all who fall through mortal sin should confess as soon as they can; indeed one does not seem contrite who carries hidden the wound of sin for a long time. These are Richard's words.[95] Whatever else there might be on this topic, I believe that in the cases offered by St. Thomas [in *Quodlibet I* cited above], of necessity, anyone having the opportunity is obligated to confess right away. I also believe that the advice of Richard is sound and salubrious and ought to be followed with diligence and courage.

CHAPTER 4: To whom confession is to be made

Because it is necessary that the one to whom sacramental confession is to be made should have the keys, let us see first about the keys. Here note that this name "keys" is transferred from physical things to spiritual ones. For among physical things a key is a tool for removing some obstacle which was impeding one from having access to a house. So also in spiritual things, that which removes mortal sin, which is an obstacle to entering the heavenly kingdom, is called a key. And this key is threefold. One is the key of author-

---

95. Cf. Richard of Menville, *Super Quatuor Libros Sententiarum*, Bk IV, d. 17, a. 3, q. 6. A reprint of a 1591 edition is available (Frankfurt: Minerva, 1963). Here Richard does raise the issue of when members of a religious order may be obligated to confess immediately when a layperson would not, but he does not provide the examples Guido attributes to him here.

ity, and only God has this. The Jews spoke of this key when they said, "Who can forgive sins, but God alone?"[96] as if to say "no one." And this is true authoritatively. Another is the key of excellence, and the only one who has this is the man Christ. And concerning this key, Isaiah, in the person of God, speaks about Christ, saying, "I will place the key of David upon his shoulder."[97] And the man Christ is said to have the key of excellence in as much as through his passion he satisfied for our sins, "and not only for ours, but for the sins of the whole world,"[98] as St. John says. And this is true with regard to efficacy and sufficiency. Or, the man Christ is said to have the key of excellence in as much as he can give the effect of the sacraments without the sacraments. Third is the key of ministry and priests have this key. It is given to them along with the order of priesthood. And concerning this it was said to St. Peter, "I will give to you the keys of the kingdom of heaven,"[99] and this is the key spoken of here.

Therefore know that the key of ministry is twofold. One is knowledge for discerning, the other is power for loosing and binding. And concerning the knowledge for discerning, there is a great diversity among theological doctors over how it is a key and how not, and whether it is a different key from the power of binding and losing. Therefore I now will say nothing about these topics, particularly since the Lord Pope John speaking in one of his *Extravagantes* which begins, *Quia quorundam* (Extrav. Jo. XXII 14.5), makes mention of this diversity among the doctors and never makes a decision about this. Hence it would be foolhardy to define any of those things which he leaves indeterminate. Nevertheless, it is to be firmly held that these keys are given to every priest in his ordination, but they cannot be put into action until the priest has the matter which he binds. This comes through his commission for the care of souls such as archbishops, bishops, and all those with care of souls have, or through privilege such as the Francis-

96. Mark 2:7; Luke 5:21.   97. Isaiah 22:22.
98. 1 John 2:2   99. Matthew 16:19

cans and Dominicans have, or others who by the privileges of the lord pope or bishops can preach and hear confessions.

From these things, therefore, it is clear to whom sacramental confession is to be made. I say "sacramental confession" to exclude consultative or directive confession, namely, when the sinner confesses his sin to someone, not so he should absolve him, but so he may consult him on it and he may direct him, because such confession can be made to any person who can help or console by praying or instructing. But in speaking of sacramental confession which is done for absolution, I say that, from the aforesaid things, two conclusions are clear. The first is that sacramental confession is to be made to a priest and not to anyone else, that is, it cannot and ought not to be made except to one having the keys, and this is the priest alone. The reason for this is that absolution is done by the power of the keys, thus no one can absolve in the forum of penance unless he has the keys, since the keys are instituted for absolution. This will be better discussed below when the power of the keys is dealt with, but no one has the keys except the priest, since the keys are given along with the order of priesthood. Therefore sacramental confession cannot and ought not to be made to anyone except to the priest. So says Augustine, and it is found in D.6 de pen. c.1, "Whoever wants to confess his sins in order that he may find grace, let him seek the priest."

The second conclusion is that confession is to be made to one's own priest. Although all priests have the keys, as has been said, yet not all have the matter, that is, the parishioners among whom they may exercise the use of the keys, but only those to whom the care of souls is regularly committed, who have the use of the power with respect to those whose care is committed to them. Therefore only to such is confession to be made, and such are penitents' own priests. Therefore confession is to be made to one's own priest.

But someone could ask, Who is one's own priest? Some say that one's own priest is the parish priest who has the job of administering the ecclesiastical sacraments and that confession is to be made to him. And their judgment seems to be based on this reason: Confession ought to be made to him who has the job of administering the sacrament of the eucharist, indeed for this reason the commandment is given to confess in Lent, so that the faithful may worthily come to the sacrament of the eucharist at Easter. Since the parish priest is obligated by his office to give the sacrament of the eucharist to his parishioners, therefore, of necessity, all his parishioners, at least in Lent or at Easter, are obligated to confess to him. And this seems to be the intention of the decretal *Omnis utriusque sexus* (X 5.38.12), and of D.6 de pen. c.3. It also seems to be the intended meaning of the holy scripture in the Old Testament, where it says in Proverbs 27, "Be diligent to know the countenance of your cattle."[100] According to the gloss, "the countenance of your cattle" is knowledge of them which cannot be gained except through confession. Therefore it is necessary that he who has the care of souls should know a confession which cannot happen unless he hears it. Scripture seems to say the same thing in the New Testament, in Hebrews, the last chapter. "Servants obey your leaders in everything. For they watch over you as if to render an account of your souls."[101] If therefore he who has the care is obligated to render an account of the souls of those under him, it seems necessary that he know the state of the souls of those under him. This cannot be done unless he hears their confessions. This is why it is necessary that any subordinate confess to his curate.

Others make a distinction concerning "one's own," and say that "one's own" is used in two ways. In one way, "one's own" is used according to what is distinguished from that of another. In the other way, "one's own" is used according to what is distinguished from what is common. Now these say that everyone is obligated to confess to his own priest according to what is his own as opposed to another's, but not according to what is opposed to the common. For it is evident and certain that if someone were to confess his sin to the lord pope, to the archbishop, or to his bishop,

100. Proverbs 27:23
101. Hebrews 13:17

it would be foolish and rash to say that he is obligated to confess the same sin to his parish curate. Since those who preach and hear confessions by privilege are vicars of the lord pope and the bishops, therefore those confessing to them are not obligated to confess again to their parish priest, since such confessors are like particular penitentiaries. And therefore just as those who confess to penitentiaries of the lord pope or the bishops are not obligated to confess again to their curates, so neither are those who confess to these. And thus today it has been determined by the Lord Pope John XXII in a certain decretal or *extravagante* of his that begins *Vas electionis* (Extrav. Comm. 5.3.2). This also seems to be the intended meaning of that decretal of Boniface, *Super cathedra*, which is found in Extrav. comm. 3.6.2 and in the constitutions of Lord Clement, Clem. 3.7.2, where it is said that Brothers Preachers and Minors have the power of hearing confessions as much as parish priests are recognized to have it by law. But those who have confessed to parish priests are not obligated to confess again, therefore neither are those who confessed to these.

And according to this way [of reasoning], that decretal *Omnis utriusque sexus* (X 5.38.12) speaks of one's own priest as "one's own" as distinguished from that of another, but not as distinguished from or as opposed to the common. The meaning is that one should confess to one's own priest, not to that of another. In any case, if those who hear confessions by privilege of the lord pope would encourage those confessing to them to confess once a year to their own curates, they would do well. And this is encouraged in that decretal of Lord Benedict XI, who was of the Order of Preachers, which begins *Inter cunctas* (Extrav. comm. 5.7.1). And they are obligated to do this, because although that decretal is revoked to the degree that it contradicts the decretal of Boniface which begins, *Super cathedra* (Extrav. comm. 3.6.2), yet it is not revoked regarding those things which it contains by equity and reason.

But can a parish priest absolve his parishioner from every sin? The answer is that Raymond in his *Summa* offers five cases in which the parish priest cannot involve himself unless he was specially commissioned. The first is when a solemn penance is to be enjoined on the sinner. The second is when excommunication is connected with the sin. The third is whenever and wherever he finds irregularity to have occurred. The fourth concerns those who set fires.[102] But to these four cases Hostiensis adds another three cases, so that there are seven. Hence the fifth case concerns a public sinner like a public blasphemer. The sixth concerns forgers of papal letters. The seventh is if it is the custom in a bishopric that certain crimes are referred to the bishop, as obtains by custom in many places and bishoprics for murder, sacrilege, sorcery, forgery, violators of ecclesiastical immunity, sodomites, incestuous persons, perjurers, and other enormous crimes which the bishops reserve for themselves as seems expedient to them.[103] Concerning these no sure rules can be given, but let every curate have his synodal book with which to direct himself in this matter. Lord William Durandus in his *Repertory* says that to specify every case is nothing other than taking away the curate's own power, since he may do all those things by law which are not expressly prohibited to him.[104] This is proved in X 5.39.29, before the end.

Note that Raymond in his *Summa* offers six cases in which a parish priest can absolve and hear the confessions of the subordinates of another priest. The first is when a stranger commits an offense in his parish. The second is if a person has changed his residence, as is the case with scholars studying in Paris or other places. The third is if he is a vagabond, as there are these poor people wandering through the world. The fourth is when someone has an ignorant or malicious and entirely inadequate priest, and wants to go to one with greater knowledge and adequacy with whom he may consult. He can go to him, having first asked and received permission from his own rector or priest; and the priest is obligated to

---

102. Raymond of Penyafort, *Summa*, Bk III, 34, 17. Guido does not discuss Raymond's fifth case, although it is very similar to the seventh case he draws from Hostiensis.

103. Hostiensis, *Summa aurea*, Bk V, "De penitentiis & remissionibus," 14.

104. William Durandus, *Repertorium iuris canonici*, Bk V.

give it to him. The fifth case is if someone wanting to make a long journey, as perhaps to go to St. James or some other pilgrimage or place, having asked permission from his curate to confess on his journey, then whoever can hear confessions can hear his confession. The sixth case is when a sinner is at the point of necessity, because in this case he can confess to anyone.[105] But in the other cases noted before, one cannot confess except to one who is able to hear confessions either by commission or by privilege.

But what is to be done about soldiers and nobles or any others who have various places of residence in various parishes, and for one part of the year live in one place and in another for another? To whom should they confess? The answer is that such people ought to confess to the curate in whose parish they have their principal place of residence, or in whose parish they live for the greater part of the year.

But suppose there is a fragile woman prone to sin whose curate is fickle and deceitful. She fears that if she confesses to him, he would solicit her for sin, or he might reveal her confession. Should she confess to him? I say that if her fear is well grounded or probable concerning these things or some of them, she ought to ask permission from her curate to confess to another, or if she has the services of a superior, such as a bishop or penitentiary or some other religious having the power to hear confessions, let her confess to him. But what if perhaps she cannot have the services of one of these others and the curate is so malicious that he does not want to give her permission to confess to another? What should this woman do? I say that if she fears solicitation, let her commend herself to God by praying that he rescue her from temptation and give her strength and constancy to resist, and let her confess in a public place. And God who, by the testimony of the Apostle, never permits anyone to be tempted beyond what one can bear, will effect his providence, even during temptation and will help her,[106] and thus she will not be troubled.

105. Raymond of Penyafort, *Summa*, Bk III, 34, 15.
106. 1 Corinthians 10:13

But in the case where she fears the revelation of her confession, I believe that if the fear is just and reasonable, not trifling or foolish, that without his permission, if he denies it to her, the law grants her permission to confess to another having the power of hearing confessions, so long as she intends that if she should have an adequate curate, she would confess to him. This is like one who contracts engagement or marriage by applying a dishonest condition against the substance of marriage and so is deprived by law of marriage, as is said in C.22 q.4 c.22; C.32 q.2 c.6, 7; X 4.5.3; X 4.1.14. Thus the priest not serving those things which belong to the substance of confession, indeed acting contrary to them, is deprived by law of the power he had for hearing confessions. Since therefore to maintain secrecy belongs to the substance of confession, on the part of both the one confessing and the confessor, a priest revealing a confession is deprived by law of the power he had for hearing confessions. And therefore if it is justly and reasonably feared that this curate will reveal the confession, no one is obligated to confess to him.

It is true that this argument is not conclusive except against him who has already revealed a confession, and not against him who is about reveal one, but the following argument does this. Indeed according to St. Bernard, "What was instituted for charity, ought not to militate against charity." But confession was instituted for charity, by which everyone is obligated to direct himself to the honor of God, by glorifying him and humbling oneself, and by reconciling oneself to him. Therefore one is not obligated to militate against charity by betraying and defaming the penitent, which would happen if one were obligated to confess to a confessor about whom it is to be feared or presumed, justly and reasonably, that he would reveal the confession. Hence Augustine said to a certain person, exhorting him to confession and penance, "I am not telling you to betray yourself."[107] But if someone knowingly were to confess to someone who would reveal the confession, he would betray himself; therefore he ought not to confess to him.

107. D.1 de pen. dict. post. c.87

But suppose one's own priest is a heretic, or schismatic, or notorious simoniac, or is excommunicated. Ought one confess to him? I say without prejudice, no. And the general reason for all such cases is this: Since indeed it is a mortal sin to participate with the excommunicated in the sacraments, and all such are excommunicated by law, and sacramental confession is a sacrament, whoever confesses to such a confessor would sin mortally. But as far as the heretic is concerned, there is a special reason, because the heretic could more easily put the one confessing to him into error or lead him into despair, as the Pharisees did to Judas who confessed to them saying, "I have sinned in betraying innocent blood." And instead of good counsel, they said to him, "What is that to us? See to it yourself."[108]

Taking another case, indeed it is commonly said and it is true, as will be shown below, that no one ought to defame or accuse another in confession. But it can happen that if someone confesses to his curate it would be necessary to defame another, as in the case when someone sinned with his mother who is well known to the curate or with his daughter or sister whom the curate also knows well. Indeed it is necessary that such a one express the name or person in confession by saying, "I had such a relationship with my mother, or daughter, or with my sister." And since these, as has been said, are known to the curate, thus they will remain defamed before him. It is to be said that he ought to confess, if he has the opportunity, to one who does not have knowledge of the persons. Hence such a one ought to go to his curate, explaining and saying to him, "Lord, I have a reason why I ought not to confess to you, not because you are inadequate, but the reason is such that I ought not to tell you. Therefore I ask permission to confess to another." The priest is obligated to give it to him, and having received it, the penitent is obligated to seek a suitable confessor who has no knowledge of the persons with whom he sinned. And I counsel curate priests that such permission should be readily granted, be-

108. Matthew 27:4

cause two good things arise from this; one that they themselves are freed from the burden, the other that sinners confess better, more suitably, and more securely.

But should a woman who sinned with her curate confess to him? I say that since shame is a great part of satisfaction, and since she would not be as ashamed before one who is aware of the evil deed as she would be before another, this woman ought not to confess to him, nor ought he to hear her. Indeed he ought to say to her, "Go to another." Nevertheless, if she were to confess to him and he were to absolve her, she would be absolved.

The priest or the curate, to whom should he confess? I say that when the care of souls is committed to him by the bishop, if he were to ask for permission to be able to choose his own confessor, or if with the commission to the care of souls the bishop were to say to him, "Lest because you have the care of others' souls you suffer harm to your own soul, we grant you permission to choose a suitable confessor for yourself who has the power to absolve you," this would be very safe.

Nevertheless, it is commonly held that with the commission to the care of souls such permission is implicitly given to them, otherwise the commission of care would be quite detrimental to them. But does this imply that they can confess to simple priests who do not have the authority or power to hear confessions? I say no, according to the rigor of the law. The reason for this is twofold. One is that this is not the way to grant jurisdiction to one who otherwise would not have it. The other is that although curates are given permission to confess, nevertheless, [simple priests] are not given permission to hear them. Nevertheless, I believe, that on account of what they know, curates confess to them and they absolve them. They do not hold back or dissemble; they seem tacitly to give them the power of hearing and absolving them, namely, priests to curates.

Note especially that if someone is in danger of death, and cannot have the services of a priest, he can and should confess to a Christian layperson who is not excommunicated, as is found in D.1

de pen. c.88; D.4 de cons. c.36. And St. Augustine says, "Such is the power of confession that if death is imminent and the priest is absent, one may confess to a neighbor."[109] Nevertheless, such a confession is not a sacrament since it lacks that which belongs formally to the sacrament, namely, the power of the keys. Nevertheless, by reason of the goodwill which extends into the shame which one has in confessing, one is absolved by God. And the one who hears his confession is obligated to pray for him saying [the prayer], "May God have mercy on you, etc.," if he knows it, or the Our Father. Yet if it happens that he avoids death, he is obligated to confess again to one who can absolve him.

CHAPTER 5: On what ought to be confessed

Having dealt somewhat superficially with the one to whom confession is to be made, it remains to see for what things it ought to be made. Know that it ought to be made for sins, as it says in the Psalm, "I said, 'I will confess against myself, my injustice to the Lord.'"[110] It says "injustice," not "justice." And in the epistle of St. James, "Confess your sins to one another,"[111] not good deeds or virtues, as the Pharisee did, saying, "I give thanks to you, O Lord, that I am not like the rest of men: fornicators, adulterers, even as this tax collector chooses to be. I fast twice between Sabbaths. I give tithes from all that I possess."[112] Therefore confession ought to be for sins.

Here note that some sins are venial and some mortal. With respect to venial sins, speaking simply, they do not need to be confessed out of necessity. Since indeed by their nature they are venial, as this word itself conveys, individuals can find pardon either by having interior repentance or contrition in general over them, or through taking up exterior penance, or by striking the chest and the like. Hence note that venial sins are forgiven in many ways, even without sacramental confession. In one way, through the gen-

---

109. D.1 de pen. c.88   110. Psalm 31:5
111. James 5:16   112. Luke 18:11–12

eral confession which is made in prime and compline and at the beginning of the mass. In another way, through episcopal blessing. And I believe this, yet I do not claim this for the priest's blessing given at the end of mass. In another way, through sprinkling with holy water (D.3 de cons. c.20), since all sprinkled with it are blessed and sanctified. In another way, through striking one's chest. In another way, when someone devoutly says the Lord's Prayer, namely, "Our Father, etc." And this is by virtue of these words, "Forgive us our debts, etc." In another way, as some say, by entering a consecrated church, which I understand to mean when one enters in order to pray. In another way, by the giving of alms, as in Daniel, chapter 4, "Redeem your sins with alms"[113] (D.1 de pen. c.76). And I believe they are forgiven through any good work, as in the previously cited decretal. In another way, through the devout reception of any sacrament, especially the eucharist (D.2 de cons. c.7). Nevertheless, understand that when I say such and such venial sins are forgiven, it is when the person has none but venial sins, because if he were to have mortal sins, his venial sins would not be forgiven him until his mortal sins were forgiven. And although by their nature venial sins do not have to be confessed of necessity, nevertheless it is very fitting, especially for accomplished men, such as prelates and religious, to confess them, because the penance for them is much diminished by the power of the keys.

Nevertheless note that in some cases it happens that one is obligated to confess a venial sin, and this is on account of doubt, namely, when one has probable doubt whether a particular sin is mortal or venial, because if one does not repent as if it were mortal, one exposes oneself to risk. Therefore one ought to confess as it lies in his conscience, and leave to the judgment of the priest whether it is mortal or venial. And I advise the priest not be too prone to judge sins to be mortal, but he can say that the sin is great and lead the person to repentance.

One is also obligated to confess a venial sin on account of ec-

---

113. Daniel 4:24

clesiastical statute, namely, when one does not have a guilty conscience over any mortal sin. Because, since by the statute of the church everyone is obligated to confess in Lent, such a one is obligated to confess, and since he does not have mortal sins to confess, it is necessary that he confess his venial sins. Yet some say that it suffices to present oneself to the priest saying, "Lord, I am not aware of any mortal sin, yet I present myself to you, so that you may see my conscience." Therefore it is to be held that it is not necessary to confess venial sins according to what they are, yet it is very useful and profitable. Nor is one obligated to confess them except out of goodness and fairness, except in two cases, namely, when one is bound either by one's own conscience, that is, when one wonders whether it is mortal or venial, or by ecclesiastical mandate, that is, when one does not have mortal sins to confess.

But with respect to mortal sins, I say that every sin, both manifest and hidden, must be confessed separately and singly, and if a sin has slipped from memory, one is obligated to do what one can to remember it. And it is clear that one is obligated to confess even manifest mortal sins to the priest because in order for the priest to absolve the sinner, it is necessary that he know the sins as God, whose place he holds and by whose authority he absolves. But he cannot know them as God unless they are told to him in confession. Therefore, however manifest a sin may be, the sinner ought to tell his confessor his sin in confession. Just as in the judicial forum it does not suffice for the judge to know the case as a private person, indeed it is necessary that he know it as a judge; likewise in the penitential forum, it does not suffice for the confessor to know the sin as a man, indeed it is necessary that he know the sin as God, that is, that it be told to him in confession.

One is also obligated to confess sins however hidden they may be. The reason for this is that as a doctor of the body cannot give a healing remedy unless he knows the illness, so it is that the confessor, who is a doctor of the soul, can never impose salutary penance unless he knows the sin, but he cannot know a hidden sin unless it is revealed to him in confession. Therefore it is necessary that one confess the sin, however hidden. Indeed this is just, so that the sinner who did not blush to sin in the sight of God from whom nothing can be hidden, may not blush to confess to a sinful man. It is evident, therefore, that all mortal sins whatever they may be, whether manifest or hidden, are to be confessed individually, separately, and singly.

But are the circumstances of sin to be confessed? The answer is that the circumstances of sin which are to be considered in confession are contained in this verse:

> *Quis quid ubi quos quotiens cur quomodo quando.*
> Who, what, where, whom, how often, why, how, and when.

Whoever attends to the soul by giving medicine, seeks to know "who" the sinner is, whether male or female; old or young; noble or not noble; free or servant; established in a dignity or office, or a prelate; of sound mind or insane; learned or not learned; single or married; cloistered, cleric, or lay; blood relative, affine relative, or stranger; Christian, heretic, Jew, or pagan; etc.

"What," that is, whether the sinner committed adultery, fornication, debauchery, murder, sacrilege, or the like. Likewise whether what he committed is huge, medium, or small. Likewise whether it is manifest or hidden, a long time ago or recent, and the like.

"Where," namely, whether [the sin was committed] in a profane or sacred location, whether in the house of the Lord or in another place.

"Whom," namely, through whose mediation and information, because all such are made participants in the crime and its condemnation, and the sinner himself is liable for their sins. Likewise, through "whom," that is, with whom and for whom and against whom.

"How often," namely, how often did he know his partner in adultery or fornication, whether once or many times; how often did he say injurious or lying words to his neighbor; and how often did he repeat injuries and the like, for a repeated wound is healed more slowly.

"Why," namely, by what kind of temptation or on what occasion did the sinner do this, and whether he might have avoided this temptation or occasion or was overtaken by it. Likewise whether it was done freely or was coerced, and with what coercion, whether conditional or absolute. Likewise whether out of greed or poverty, whether by stealing or injuring another.

"How," that is, by what mode of action or suffering, which is better understood by the deed than by reading or speaking.

"When," namely, whether in a holy time, such as on feast days or in Lent, or on other days. Likewise whether before penance was received, or afterward, and thus breaking it.

These, therefore, are the circumstances which are to be considered for every sin. Among them, one considers the person of the sinner himself, or the person to whom the iniquity was done, and this is "who." Some consider the sin itself, either with respect to the substance of the deed, this is "what"; or with respect to the mode of action, this is "how"; or with respect to its final cause, this is "why"; or with respect to the injurious cause, this is through "whom"; or with respect to the frequency of the deed, this is "how often." One considers time, this is "when"; one considers place, this is "where."

But some of the circumstances change the type of sin. For example, to take the goods of another against the owner's will is the sin of theft. Now to this sin is added to the circumstance "where," namely, that it is taken from a holy place. Now the type of sin is changed since it is no longer just theft but sacrilege. Likewise to know a woman who is not one's own wife is fornication. The circumstance "who" is added, namely, that she is already married, and it is now adultery;[114] or that she is a virgin, now it is debauchery; or that she is his blood relative, now it is incest. Or the circumstance "how" is added, that is, he did not know her in the proper way, and the type of sin is changed because it is now the sin against nature. Likewise, drunkenness by its own nature is not

114. Sentence clarified from other edition consulted; our text reads, "The circumstance is added, namely, that she is not his wife, and it is now adultery."

a mortal sin; the circumstance "how often" is added, that is, that one already is in the habit of getting drunk, now it is a mortal sin. Likewise to strike another injuriously is a sin; the circumstance of "who" is added, namely, that the person one struck is a cleric, now the type of sin is changed, because now it results in excommunication. And so with the other circumstances.

But some circumstances do not change the type of sin, rather they aggravate the sin. For example, to know a single woman, not one's own, is fornication. The circumstance "when" is added, that is, that he knows her in a holy time, although it does not change the type of sin, nevertheless the sin is aggravated; or the circumstance "how" is added, that is, publicly and openly, certainly the sin is now aggravated. And so with the other circumstances.

Indeed there are some circumstances which alleviate sin. For instance, to strike a cleric is a sin; the circumstance "why" is added, namely, that someone strikes him in play, now the sin is diminished. Similarly, to take something that belongs to someone else is a sin; the circumstance "when" is added, that is, when someone takes it in a time of great necessity, certainly the sin is diminished. And so with the others.

It is clear therefore that some circumstances change the type of sin, some aggravate but do not change it, some alleviate it. Now concerning the circumstances that change the type of sin, the doctors agree in saying that they are to be confessed of necessity. Hence it does not suffice to say in confession, "I took the property of another." Indeed if it was taken from a holy place, it is necessary that this be expressed by saying, "I took it from the church or from some such a place." Nor does it suffice to say, "I sinned with a woman"; indeed it is necessary to indicate whether she was a married woman, a virgin, a female relative, or a nun. And so with all the circumstances. But concerning the circumstances which aggravate but do not change the type of sin, there is diversity among the doctors. For some say that they are to be confessed of necessity, but others say that they need not be confessed of necessity, but only out of appropriateness, and this is especially useful for accomplished and intelligent men. And I believe that confessors ought to ask about these kinds of circumstances, and especially among the simple, concerning which more will be said below. But concerning alleviating circumstances, the doctors say that they ought not to be confessed except if one is asked about them.

From what has been said, it is clear how both mortal and venial sins are to be confessed. But which sins are mortal will be discussed below when the questions to be asked in confession will be dealt with, because if they were discussed here, it would be necessary to discuss them again there.

CHAPTER 6: What confession ought to be like

In order to know what confession ought to be like, note that David the prophet, in the second penitential Psalm, which is 30th in order, offers a summary of the conditions of confession, saying, "I said, 'I will confess against myself, my injustice to the Lord,' and you forgave the impiety of my sin."[115] Here he indicates that confession ought to be premeditated when he says, "I said," that is, I determined in my heart. Second, it ought to be open and not veiled, therefore he says, "I will confess," that is, I will not be silent or veiled by excusing or defending myself. Third, it ought to be accusatory, therefore he says "against myself," that is, to my detriment. Fourth, it ought to be shameful, therefore he says "injustice," that is, sin over which a person blushes. Fifth, it ought to be one's own, therefore he says "my," and not another's. Sixth, it ought to be meritorious, for next comes, "and you forgave the impiety of my sin."

But so that we may proceed more specifically, note that in order for confession to avail, it ought to have the sixteen conditions which are contained in this verse:

> Sit simplex humilis confessio pura fidelis,
> Atque frequens nuda discreta libens verecunda,

115. Psalm 31:5

Integra secreta lachrimabilis accelerata,
Fortis et accusans et sit parere parata.

Let confession be simple, humble, pure, faithful;
And frequent, direct, discerning, free, shameful;
Complete, secret, tearful, quick;
Forceful and accusing and ready to comply.

Therefore the first condition is that it be simple, indeed simple as in without layers; hence confession ought to be without the layers of any falsehood, so that the truth may not be silenced nor falsehood be mixed in, even for reason of humility. Hence Augustine, "When you lie for reason of humility, even if you do not err before you lie, you will be made a sinner by lying."[116] Hence a sinner ought not to conceal what he has done nor say what he did not do, but simply and plainly he ought to tell all of his sins, because as the Wise One says, "He who walks in simplicity, walks in confidence."[117]

The second condition is that it be humble. Indeed such was the confession of the tax collector about whom Christ says in Luke that he did not dare "to lift his eyes to heaven, but struck his chest saying, 'Lord, have mercy on me, a sinner,'" and therefore he went home justified.[118] Therefore St. Peter says, "Be humbled under the powerful hand of God, so that he may exalt you in the time of visitation,"[119] because as Job says, "Glory shall uphold the humble in spirit."[120]

The third condition is that it be pure and not done on account of hypocrisy or vain glory. Rather let it be done purely on account of God, and not done in servile fear, that is, fear of the punishments of hell, but in filial fear, that is, fear of offending the divine majesty, as was said above on contrition. And let it be done without any fiction, because such a confession would be the confession of a wolf. About which a fable is told that once a wolf confessed

116. C.22 q.2 c.9
118. Luke 18:13–14
120. Proverbs 29:23

117. Proverbs 10:9
119. 1 Peter 5:6

and the confessor said to him, "Make the sign of peace, since I think your soul is crooked and false. You hardly lay down your life, you are in the habit of snatching away, you are hardly a friend to the sheep, whatever you may say." It is as if he said, "Although you pretend repentance and contrition in your external appearance, you hold malice in your internal soul, that is, in your heart."

The fourth condition is that it be faithful, namely, that both the one confessing and the confessor are within the catholic faith, and that it is done according to the teaching of the church and not according to the teaching of the heretics. And it should be done with the hope of mercy, lest it be like the confession of the traitor Judas, who after he had rightly confessed, saying, "I have sinned in betraying innocent blood,"[121] despaired of mercy and hung himself with a noose. This is proved in D.1 de pen. c.88 and D.6 de pen. c.1.

The fifth condition is that it be frequent, which is understood in two ways. In one way, the one who frequently falls into mortal sin may rise frequently through penance. And this is found in D.3 de pen. c.2, c.23 and c.32. In the other way, it means that the same sin should be frequently confessed. Hence Augustine, "As often as one confesses the disgrace of his many crimes, the more easily will the mercy of forgiveness reach him."[122] Nevertheless, concerning this, when one is obligated to do this will be discussed below when repetition of confession is dealt with.

The sixth condition is that it be direct, because one ought not to confess through a messenger or through a letter, but out loud from one's own mouth and face to face or in person, so that the one who sinned on his own may blush on his own. Likewise one ought not to confess with the words or names of the crimes veiled, but any sin, however disgraceful, ought to be honestly expressed by its proper name. And all the circumstances, however disgraceful and abominable, are to be expressed, so that all the pus from the ulcer may be expelled. But concerning the circumstances which

121. Matthew 27:4
122. C.26 q.6 dict. post c.11

are to be confessed, we have written above in the preceding chapter. And note that a mute can and ought to confess through signs. And one who speaks another language and its idioms, so that his confessor does not understand him, ought to confess through an interpreter. And the interpreter, like the priest, is obligated to keep the confession secret. And note that if someone writes his sins in a list in order to remember them better, and reads the list before the priest, he does well.

The seventh condition is that it be discerning, namely, that one should confess his sins distinctly and separately, not confusedly. According to the Psalm, "Every night, with my tears, I will wash my bed,"[123] saying, "I will wash every night," that is, wash every sin, "my bed," that is, my conscience. Again [it is to be discerning] so one may choose an expert judge, as Augustine says, "Seek a priest who knows how to bind and loose you."[124] Concerning this, see above in the chapter "To whom confession is to be made."

The eighth condition is that it be free, that is, voluntary, so that it is not like the confession of Achor who was coerced into confession and stoned,[125] but it should be like the confession of the thief hanging on the cross on the right.[126] Indeed although one ought to sorrow over the sins one has committed, yet one ought to rejoice on account of the life which one recovers, hence it happens that joy and sorrow are simultaneous and together in the same place. Hence the psalmist, "According to the multitude of my sorrows in my heart, your consolations have given joy to my soul."[127]

The ninth condition is that it be shameful, since a sinner ought to confess with great shame, and thus merit mercy. Hence Augustine, "The mind labors by suffering the blush of shame. And since shame itself is a great penalty, the one who blushes for Christ is worthy of mercy" (D.1 de pen. c.88). Nevertheless there ought not

123. Psalm 6:7
124. D.6 de pen. c.1
125. Achan was stoned in the Valley of Achor; Joshua 7:19–26.
126. Luke 23:41
127. Psalm 93:19

to be so much shame that, on account of it, one fails to tell the truth. Hence the Wise One in Ecclesiasticus, chapter 3, "For the sake of your soul, you should not be ashamed to speak the truth. Indeed there is confession that brings glory or mercy."[128]

The tenth condition is that it be complete, namely, that the sinner tells all his sins, not by telling them to two priests, but that he tells them all to one, omitting nothing. Indeed God is complete in the highest degree and he does not accept an incomplete work; indeed he heals the whole person or nothing. Hence the verse:

> Summa dei pietas, veniam non dimidiabit,
> Aut nihil aut totum te penitente dabit.

> The highest kindness of God, will not divide mercy in half,
> Either nothing or all, he will give to you as you repent.

Augustine says, "Be careful lest, led by shame, you divide your confession."[129]

The eleventh condition is that it be secret, both on the part of the one confessing and on the part of the confessor. On the part of the one confessing so that he should not tell or announce his sins in the streets, lest others be scandalized by his sin, and lest those with whom he did evil brag about it. And how it ought to be secret on the part of the confessor will be discussed below when the seal of confession is dealt with.

The twelfth condition is that it be tearful. And concerning this Jerome says, "Day and night, do not give yourself rest or let the pupils of your eyes be still." And John Chrysostom, "Tears wash away the offense which it is a shame to confess."[130] And in truth, tears are a great sign of contrition, especially in an adult man, for in a child or a woman, tears do not mean much. For concerning women, Ovid says, "They teach their eyes to weep."

The thirteenth condition is that it be quick, that is, rapid. And concerning this condition, look above in the chapter on when confession is to be done.

128. Ecclesiasticus [Sirach] 4:24–25   129. D.5 de pen. c.1 paragraph 7
130. D.1 de pen. c.2

The fourteenth condition is that it be forceful, as in the example of St. Mary Magdalene, who was so forceful in repenting on account of her bitter interior compunction, that without shame getting in the way, she publicly confessed of the disgrace of her sins.[131] Thus the sinner ought to be forceful in repenting and confessing his sin so that he is not at all held back from confessing them, because it is written, "love is strong as death."[132]

The fifteenth condition is that is be accusatory, namely, that one says that he has committed sin by his own malice, accusing himself forcefully, not offering excuses for his sins, as our first parents did.[133] Hence the Wise One, "The just accuses himself at the beginning, his friend will arrive and excuse him."[134] This friend is God, and unless the sinner now accuses himself before this friend and before the priest, the vicar of God, he will have many accusers in the future, namely, God, his own conscience, the devil, sin, and even the whole world, because, as the Wise One says, "He will fight with all the world against the irrational,"[135] that is, sinners. But if the sinner accuses himself now, God will excuse him in the future.

The sixteenth condition is that one be ready to comply, that is, be obedient. Augustine says, "Let the penitent put himself entirely in the power of the judge, that is, into the judgment of the priest, holding back nothing, so that, with everything having been judged, he may be ready to do for the recovery of the life of the soul whatever he would do to avoid the death of the body, and to do this eagerly because he will regain infinite life. Indeed he ought to do with joy for an immortal future what he would do to delay the death he is about to die."[136]

And Raymond in his *Summa* adds another two conditions. The first is that confession be one's own, namely, that the sinner accuses himself and not another.[137] As the Psalm says, "God, I have an-

131. Cf. Luke 7:36–50, 8:2   132. Song of Solomon 8:6
133. Genesis 3:12–13   134. Proverbs 18:17
135. Wisdom 5:21   136. D.5 de pen. c.1 paragraph 7
137. Raymond of Penyafort, *Summa*, Bk III, 34, 24.

nounced my life to you,"[138] it says "my life," not "another's." Otherwise, if he should betray the crime or sin of another, he would not be the corrector of this crime, but its betrayer or detractor. Hence no one ought to name another in confession, nor ought the priest to ask him for a name. But sometimes it happens that the circumstance of the sin is such that the sin could otherwise not be confessed, for instance if one knew one's mother or daughter. But what is to be done and how this case is to be handled were discussed above in the chapter, "To whom confession ought to be made."

The second condition of confession that Raymond adds is that it be careful so that sins are not said in passing, like bankers reckoning numbers, but with ripe understanding and careful deliberation, so that as a result, attention may be paid to devotion and one may have greater contrition and shame.[139] Therefore let the sinner confess according to the aforementioned pattern. And having forgiveness of sins, one will have the rewards of the saints.

CHAPTER 7: On repeating confession

Even though, as was said above, it is very useful and fruitful to confess frequently, sometimes it is also necessary. Note therefore that the doctors offer various cases in which confession is to be repeated of necessity for salvation. The first is on account of the enormity of the evil deed. When someone has a case from which his confessor cannot absolve him and he sends him on to his superior, the sinner ought to repeat the confession which he made to the inferior to the superior, so that he may know what penance is to be imposed on him, unless perhaps the superior in this case redirects it back to his inferior. This case is proved in C.33 q.2 c.7; X 5.38.3.

The second case is on account of the ignorance of the confessor. If indeed the confessor is inexperienced and does not know how to impose penance for the sins confessed to him, he ought

138. Psalm 55:9
139. Raymond of Penyafort, *Summa*, Bk III, 34, 26.

to send the sinner to an experienced confessor who knows how to impose a salutary penance on him. The sinner is obligated to confess again the sins confessed the first time. Hence Augustine, "Seek a priest who knows how to loose and bind you."[140]

The third case is on account of contempt of satisfaction. When someone confessed his sins, disdained to do the penance imposed on him, and removed from his memory what that penance was, he is obligated to confess that as well as the same sins if he remembers them. This case is proved in D.3 de pen. c.5. Nevertheless, a distinction is to be made in this case, because either he will confess to the same confessor to whom he confessed first, or to another one. If he confesses to the same one, and this confessor remembers the sins confessed before, then he is not obligated to confess them to him again unless he wants to. It suffices to say, "Lord, I already confessed to you and you remember and know about my sins. Because I disdained to do the penance which you imposed on me, and I do not remember what it was, I come to you so that you may impose it or another penance on me." But if the confessor does not remember the sins confessed to him the first time, I believe that the sinner is obligated to confess again. And I say the same thing if he confesses to another.

The fourth case is on account of the sinner's deceptive malice. When someone knowingly holds back some mortal sin in confession, even though he confesses all his other sins, he is obligated to confess the one he held back and all the others again. And the reason is that the first confession was not done in charity, since he remained in mortal sin. Therefore it was impossible for the other sins to be forgiven him. If they were not forgiven, he is obligated to confess them again. Hence Augustine, "I know the Lord is the enemy of every wrongdoer. How, therefore, if one holds back a sin, will he receive mercy for the others?" (D.3 de pen. c.42). But note the distinction made in the preceding case, because if he confesses to the same priest, it would suffice for him to say, "When

140. D.6 de pen. c.1 paragraph 6

I confessed to you, I maliciously held back this sin," and this is if the confessor remembers the other sins. But if he does not remember, the sinner is obligated to confess them all again. And I say the same thing if he confesses to another.

All the doctors agree that in these four cases confession is to be repeated of necessity. But there are other cases in which the doctors differ. The first is on account of remembering a forgotten sin. The second is on account of backsliding. Indeed some doctors say that when someone remembers a certain mortal sin which was not confessed or when one relapses into some sin which was already confessed, for instance when one who confessed to adultery commits it again and falls back into adultery, he is obligated to confess again all the sins confessed before. And as for the first case, the reason is that otherwise the confession would not be complete. As for the second case, their reason is that they say that all sins, even if previously forgiven, return on account of ingratitude and backsliding. Others say that it suffices to say in general that one has committed other sins, and recently has remembered this sin, or recently has committed this sin. A third group of doctors says, as a middle way, that in the previous two cases, sins of the same type ought to be confessed again in particular, but it suffices to confess sin of another type in general. For example, someone now remembers that he committed a sin, namely, theft; if he confessed theft previously, he is obligated to confess the same theft in particular, as the first opinion says. But concerning his other sins, it suffices to confess in general, as the second opinion says. And I say the same about backsliding. Which of these opinions is better and truer, I leave to the judgment of better men, and each may choose as he wishes.

Master Godfrey of Fontaines, a master of theology in Paris, in a certain one of his quodlibets adds another case, namely, when someone confesses some sin and neither sorrows over nor repents of the sin or of previous sin nor proposes to keep himself from it in the future; such a one is obligated to confess again.[141] And

---

141. Godfrey of Fontaines, *Quodlibet IX*, Q. 10. For a printed edition, see Godefroid de Fontaines, *Le huitième [-dixième] quodlibet de Godefroid de Fontaines*, vol. 4, Les

among the many reasons which lead to this conclusion, one is this: Something of a subsequent order cannot exist essentially without the prior order, and much less can stand in opposition to what came first, just as someone cannot be confirmed unless he has been baptized, because baptism and confirmation have a necessary and essential order between them. But confession and contrition have an essential order between them, which is why in order for confession to be efficacious in this way, it is necessary that contrition precede confession or at least be simultaneous with it. But in the proposed case, contrition does not precede, nor is it simultaneous with, confession. Indeed its opposite, namely, pleasure and contentment in sin, is simultaneous with confession, which is why this confession is worth nothing. Therefore it is necessary that it be repeated. It is true that Brother Bernard of Gannat [aka Bernard of Auvergne], a bachelor in theology and once bishop elect of Clermont, in his correction against the said Master Godfrey, says that such a one is not obligated of necessity to confess again, but is obligated to be contrite again over those sins previously confessed falsely and the fiction itself. By virtue of the confession already made and contrition in the present, his sins are forgiven him. Therefore he argues thus: Contrition is and can be efficacious as much by virtue of confession already made as it is and can be by virtue of confession about to be made. But contrition deletes all sins by virtue of confession, as the doctrine of the faith holds, and therefore also by virtue of confession already made. Indeed confession already made has real existence, and therefore its power can work better than that of confession not yet made.[142] Which of these opinions is truer, I do not know. Nevertheless I believe that one is obligated to confess, at least in general, that many sins were confessed previously from which one neither repented nor intended to abstain, but now is

philosophes belges: Textes et études (Louvain: Institut supérieur de philosophie de l'Université, 1924), 242–46.

142. Bernard of Auvergne, *Reprobationes Godefridus de Fontibus, Quodlibet IX*, Q. 10. The Cathedral Chapter at Clermont elected Bernard to be bishop in 1304 but Pope Clement V annulled the election in 1307, hence Guido's reference to Bernard as "bishop elect."

contrite over them and is ready to do the penance enjoined, unless one has already done it. And I believe that if one were to confess all his sins in particular, he would do well. And Raymond seems to think this in his *Summa*.[143] See also the reason for it in the chapter mentioned in the fourth case [D.3 de pen. c.42].

CHAPTER 8: How the priest ought to conduct himself toward the one confessing

Having shown what confession is and what it ought to be like, it remains to shed light on the confessor, and first, how he ought to conduct himself toward the one confessing. Note here that the confessor priest ought to take the place of a spiritual doctor and the sinner the place of the spiritually ill. A doctor of the body coming to a sick person first soothes the patient, and has compassion on him by addressing himself skillfully to the sick one. He speaks with flattering words; he promises health so that the patient may disclose more confidently the magnitude of the illness and the intensity of the pain. Just so, the priest as a spiritual doctor, when the sinner, who is like one spiritually ill, comes to him, ought to win over the sinner with words and appease him with flatteries, so that the sick one, that is, the sinner, may more confidently disclose his illness, that is, his sin. Therefore the confessor ought to teach and admonish the sinner to sit humbly at his feet, and not allow him to sit as his equal. And if the sinner is a woman, he ought to teach her to sit sideways, lest the priest look at the woman's face, because, as it says in Habakkuk, "The face of a woman is like the face of a lion and a burning wind."[144] Nor should he look anyone confessing in the face because then the penitent will confess more boldly.

Then with kind, sweet, and soothing conversation, he ought to lead the one confessing to compunction, relating the benefits which Christ conferred on him, especially in his passion, namely, when he

---

143. Raymond of Penyafort, *Summa*, Bk III, 34, 51.
144. Cf. Habakkuk 1:9

was willing to suffer such pain for the salvation of sinners. Likewise because he said, "I did not come to call the righteous, but sinners."[145] Likewise the priest may show him that those who have sinned more, if they repent well, afterward are more loved and exalted by God. This is clear in David, Peter, Paul, Mary Magdalene, and the thief, who all were the greatest of sinners, and because they repented well of their sins, later they were loved and especially exalted by God. Let him also set forth to him the kindness, mercy, charity, and gentleness in Christ by which he is ready to receive sinners. Let the confessor also urge the penitent not to be ashamed to confess to him, because he is a sinner just like the one who is confessing, indeed perhaps even more so than he, and that he will not be confessing to him as to a man, but as to one holding the place of God, and that he would more quickly give himself up to be killed than reveal the penitent's sins.

And if perhaps after all of these [encouragements], the sinner does not want to confess, let the confessor set before him the terror of judgment and the punishments of hell, and how many evils are prepared for sinners, and that as much as God severely punishes those who are unwilling to repent, so much he mercifully spares those who do repent. And with all of these things having been laid out, let him simply hear his confession. But let the confessor beware lest he spit or show some sign of disgust even though the sinner confesses some disgraceful and enormous sin, but let him hear everything with kindness and gentleness.

CHAPTER 9: On the questions to be
asked during confession

Although some say that questions are not to be asked in confession, because the asking of them is very dangerous on account of human simplicity and shame, I believe the contrary, namely, that questions are to be asked in confession. Hence Augustine, on the

145. Matthew 9:13; Mark 2:17; Luke 5:32

text, "Whoever is without sin, let him cast the first stone,"[146] said, "Let the spiritual judge take care that just as he has not committed a crime of wickedness, so he does not lack the gift of knowledge; indeed it is necessary that he know how to learn whatever he ought to judge. Indeed judicial power demands that he learn what he ought to judge. Therefore let the diligent inquisitor elicit from the sinner, and let the subtle investigator wisely and, as it were, shrewdly, ask him what perhaps he does not know or in shame wants to hide. Therefore to learn crimes and their varieties, let him not hesitate to investigate place, time, etc. Having learned these things, let the confessor be ready and willing to lift and bear the burden himself; let him have sweetness in affection, kindness toward the crimes of another, discernment of their variety." These and many other things are given in D.6 de pen. c.1. Also Gregory says, "The key of loosing is the word of correction, because by asking and reproving he uncovers guilt, which often even the one who committed it does not know" (D.43 c.1). And also according to the words of blessed Job, "The winding serpent is to be brought forth subtly," from the chest of the sinner, "by the birthing hand,"[147] that is, by the industry of the confessor.

Seeing, therefore, that questions are to be asked in confession, now we must see what they are to cover and in what order. Thus know that questions are to be asked about mortal sins and their circumstances. Therefore in order to know about what things questions are to be asked, it is necessary to know what the mortal sins are. Here note that a sin can be mortal in two ways. In one way, by its nature; for example, fornication is a mortal sin by its nature. In the other way, any deed can be a mortal sin as a result of intention. For example, singing in church is not a mortal sin, indeed it can be meritorious; but to sing in order to please a woman and draw her into sin is a mortal sin. And because human intentions are almost infinite, fixed rules cannot be given about those things which are mortal sins due to intention. Therefore we will speak of those sins which are mortal by their nature.

146. John 8:7   147. Job 26:13

Hence know that all transgressions of the commandments of the Decalogue are mortal sins. These will be discussed in Part III of this work when the Ten Commandments of the Decalogue are dealt with. Some mortal sins are listed by the Apostle in Romans 13, such as idolatry, vice against nature, iniquity, malice, fornication, avarice, wickedness, envy, murder, contention, deceit, spite, usury, theft, detraction, lying, pride, elation, evil intentions, disobedience, folly, disorder. And to these he adds those who are without affection, without fidelity, without mercy. That all these things are mortal sins is clear from what follows, namely, that "those who do such things are worthy of death."[148] But no one is worthy of death except through mortal sin, therefore all the aforementioned are mortal sins.

But in order to have fixed rules concerning mortal sins, note that all mortal sins may be reduced to the seven capital vices which are contained in this expression, *saligia*. Note that in this expression *saligia*, there are seven letters, of which each one stands for a mortal sin. So, by the letter s, *superbia* [pride] is understood; by the first a, *avaritia* [avarice]; by l, *luxuria* [lust]; by the first i, *ira* [anger]; by g, *gula* [gluttony]; by the second i, *invidia* [envy]; by the second a, *accidia* [sloth]. Hence the verse,

> *Das septem vitia per hoc dictum saligia.*
>
> Give the seven vices through this word—*saligia.*

And these are the seven evil roots which take root "in the deserted land, inaccessible and waterless,"[149] of sinful man, of which I am one. Truly from each of these roots, many branches sprout forth, as Gregory conveys in *On Job*, "For from this evil root which is pride arise the seven worst branches, namely, disobedience, boasting, hypocrisy, stubbornness, contention, discord, presumption."[150] And note that these are called mortal, because on account of these, man incurs spiritual judgment.

The first and chief among these is pride, that is, inordinate love

---

148. Romans 1:25–32   149. Psalm 62:3
150. Gregory I, *Moralia in Job*, Bk XXXI, c. 45 (PL 76:621).

of oneself, namely, of one's own excellence and honor, by not redi-
recting it to the honor of God, either in deed or in habit, or to the
edification of one's neighbor. And there are four modes of pride.
The first is when one desires to be seen and regarded by another as
better than he is, and presumes about himself that he is good, even
though he is bad and a sinner, or that he has some good quality
which he does not have. The second mode is when a person considers himself to have the good qualities which he has, not from
God, but from himself. The third mode of pride is when a person
considers himself to have that which he has from God by his own
merits and not through the grace of God. Fourth, when someone
through nobility or wealth or something else wants to appear inordinately more excellent than others and beyond what his own status calls for.

And note that the branches of pride that were mentioned above
are called daughters by some. They are to be described somehow
on account of the simple. Hence disobedience is contempt for the
commands of superiors, namely, of God or of whatever person
one is obligated to obey, so that through this contempt the disobedient person may seem not to be subject to another person or not
to be a subject. Hypocrisy is falsely showing outward devotion in
order to have the praise of others. Contention is to contend with
or resist others through words and to want not to be outdone by
others in words and disputes, so that through this one may seem
more excellent. Stubbornness is when one relies much too much
on one's own opinion or knowledge, being unwilling to believe the
counsel of one's betters, so that through this one may appear wis-
er. Discord is when someone rebels and contradicts the will of
his betters impudently and out of pride of heart. Presumption
is when someone through inordinate clothing and whatever other wonderful things wants to be noticed and take pride in himself
and be considered by others as more worthy than they.

Six things are born of the root of avarice, namely, betray-
al, fraud, falsehood, perjury, mental disquiet, hardness of heart
against mercy. Treachery is deceit in interior things. Fraud is de-

ception in exterior things on account of a defect in something sold or bought. Falsehood is deception and deceit by word in order to trick a neighbor in either selling or buying. Perjury is a word against conscience advanced with an oath, or a lying oath proffered or affirmed. Mental disquiet is worry about acquiring riches and the like. Hardness of heart is when a greedy person hardens his heart and determines that he will give nothing to the poor nor mercifully assist another. Avarice is the inordinate appetite for having undue riches or whatever can be bought or sold with money. And avarice is twofold. One kind is when a person guards his goods too closely, but does not take them unjustly from others. And this avarice is a mortal sin in two cases. The first is when one loves one's riches and occupies oneself with them so much that one slights the honor of God and his commandments. The second is when one does not assist one's poor neighbor who is in need, because then avarice is a mortal sin. The other kind of avarice is when someone desires to take the goods of another or to withhold them unjustly in some way with a deliberate intention. And such avarice is always a mortal sin, except when the thing taken is insignificant. Perhaps to steal a tiny morsel of bread or some such thing is not a mortal sin.

And beyond these daughters of avarice, there are others which are added on by some, namely, plunder, theft, treachery, and usury. Plunder is taking something belonging to another with violence. Theft is the unjust and secret taking of something belonging to another against the will of the owner. Treachery is deceit concerning persons, for instance, when one person betrays or hands over another, as is well known concerning Judas the traitor. Usury is when, through extending the length or the terms of a loan, something beyond the principal is received, at least regarding things where the use and consumption of the thing do not differ, like bread.

From the corrupt root of lust, eight daughters are born, namely, mental blindness, thoughtlessness, inconstancy, rashness, self-love, hatred of God, love of the present world, despair or abhorrence of the future world. Mental blindness is when on account of the pleasure of this mode of sexual appetite one is hindered and withdrawn in mind. Thoughtlessness is when human reason is impeded and put to sleep on account of vigorous lust. Inconstancy is when on account of the pleasure of this mode of sexual appetite one is held back from doing or completing good deeds which one began to do or proposed to do. Rashness is when on account of the pleasure of this mode careful consideration of what is to be done is impeded. Self-love and hatred of God come from the will, namely, when one is more eager to carry through with lust and incur the hatred of God than to abstain or withdraw from lust. Love of the present world and abhorrence of the future judgment is when a lustful person is so delighted to remain in lust that he wants to stay and live here forever and does not care about eternal life.

Lust is an inordinate appetite for sexual pleasure, and it has six types. First is the sin against nature, namely, when sex is done in a way which is not consistent with human generation. Fornication generally is all sexual intercourse between a single man and a single woman outside the law of marriage. Adultery is sexual intercourse done within marriage, namely, when at least one or the other is married. Incest is sexual intercourse with a blood relative. Debauchery is the deflowering of a virgin. Rape is when a woman is violently taken against the will of her parents. And note that all sexual intercourse done outside the law of marriage is mortal sin because it is against the law of nature, against the commandment of God, and against justice for the neighbor. Likewise all impure touching done with the intention of provoking the act of lust is mortal sin, or at least the cause of mortal sin.

From the pestiferous root of anger grow six branches, namely, quarreling, mental commotion, stubbornness, clamor, indignation, blasphemy. Anger is a movement of blood around the heart on account of the desire for vengeance. Hence know that anger is sometimes virtuous and not a sin, namely, when the desire for vengeance is according to the due order of justice and with charity, as when one seeks the correction of sin and not one's own vindication or the harm of one's neighbor, but only seeks vindication for the guilt of an offense. Such anger is called zeal. But when such a desire for vengeance is for the vindication of one's own injury and for the harm of one's neighbor, it is already a sin. It is not permitted for one to take such vengeance, unless one has the authority. And it is a mortal sin when such a desire for vengeance brings harm to someone, because it is against love of neighbor. But to the degree that it is an impulse of feeling preceding reason and is not deliberate, it is a venial sin. Indignation is when one despises in his heart another who wronged him and judges him unworthy and despicable considering his failure. Mental commotion is when an angry man, as if inflated with anger, thinks about the way and means of harming the one who did him wrong. Blasphemy is speaking against God, saying that he permitted such a wrong to be done or happen to him. Clamor is insulting speech against a neighbor without naming a particular wrong, and in the gospel, this is called *"racha"* ["idiot"], that is, a sign of derision.[151] Indignation is speaking against a neighbor with the naming of a wrong, for instance, when someone out of anger calls another a thief or murderer or such like. Quarreling is anger taken into outward deeds, namely, beating, cutting, wounding, and the like.

From the voracious root of gluttony five things are born, namely, improper joy, scurrility, uncleanness, loquacity, dullness of the senses. Gluttony is an inordinate and immoderate desire for eating and drinking against the rule of right reason, namely, consuming more food and drink than suits the nature and physical constitution of the one consuming and the way of life of those among whom he lives. Yet know that gluttony is not a mortal sin by its nature except in two cases. One is when one does not withdraw oneself from the sin of gluttony on account of fear or love of God, but desires food or drink so much that one is not drawn back even on account of divine command. Second is when one willingly drinks oneself into such a state that one does not know

151. Matthew 5:22

how to conduct oneself, and then gluttony is a mortal sin. Dullness of mind is the separation of the intellect from visible and tangible things on account of consuming too much food and drink. Improper joy is the disordering of the will concerning love of food and drink, namely, when one rejoices over an excess of such things in a wandering, disorderly fashion. Loquacity is when with an excess of disordered words and wild laughter one fails to regulate oneself. Scurrility is when a man is too much like a buffoon in his outward actions. Uncleanness is vomiting after inordinate eating or drinking, or even pollution of seed arising from being too full.

From the false root of envy five things are born, namely, hatred, murmuring, disparaging, exultation in the adversity of a neighbor, and torment in his prosperity. Envy is sadness over the good of another to the degree that it is an impediment to one's own superiority. Hatred is to wish evil on another and through this to diminish the good of the neighbor. Murmuring is diminishing the reputation of another through hidden words and not through openly expressing his malice or infamy. Disparaging is defamation of another through plain words, but in his absence. Derision is demeaning the words or deeds of another through mockery and laughter. Exaltation in the adversity of a neighbor is when someone rejoices in the adversity and loss of a neighbor. Torment in prosperity is sorrow and displeasure over the goods and prosperity of others which one cannot impede.

From the vile root of sloth six things proceed, namely, malice, rancor, faintheartedness, despair, sluggishness concerning the commandments, wandering of the mind toward illicit things. Sloth or laziness is tedium or aversion toward divine blessings, namely, when one does not have good devotion or delight in the love of God, but rather tedium and aversion and mental retreat. And this is contrary to the charity which everyone ought to have in loving God above all things, and one ought to cling to him with delightful love. And such laziness is caused by the rebellion of the flesh against the spirit. Wandering of the mind toward illicit things is when someone does not find delight in spiritual things and has leisure for carnal delights and seeks them, for instance, by too much playing or too much lying around. Despair is retreat from the divine goodness to which one is firmly to cling. Sluggishness concerning the commandments is, on account of sloth, to neglect and disdain the divine commandments which are to be kept of necessity for salvation. Rancor is the indignation which a lazy person has against those who rightly warn him to do those things which he is rightly obligated to do. Malice is the hatred and indignation which a lazy person has against those who teach the lazy to have spiritual goods in as much as they are impediments to corporal pleasures. Lukewarmness is slight love for God and his commandments. Weakness is when a lazy person does not want to endure any penance for the love of God, nor do anything good thing which he is obligated to do. Sleepiness is sleeping too much in the manner of beasts and laziness about getting up to do well the things one is obligated to do when one is obligated to do them. Faintheartedness is [putting off] the arduous good deeds that fall under the counsels, for instance, confessing late, repenting late. Idleness is stopping doing the good works which one is obligated to do when one is obligated to do them and attending to useless and noxious things. And beyond these six branches or daughters of sloth, four more were added which are very helpful in the explanation of the material.

These, therefore, are the seven roots with their little branches, which number forty-three all together, and thus these added with the seven roots make fifty in total. Concerning which fifty the prophet Elijah says, "If I am a servant of God, let fire descend from heaven and devour you and your fifty."[152] Thus the confessor ought to say to the one confessing, "If because I am a servant of God," that is, because I am in the place of God, "let fire descend from heaven," that is, let the fire of the Holy Spirit descend into your soul, "and devour you," that is, the old or erring man, "and your fifty," that is, the roots and branches [of sin].

152. 2 Kings 1: 10, 12

Now, therefore, let us see how the priest ought to ask questions about these things. If indeed the sinner, on his own or at the questioning of the priest, should confess to pride saying, "I have sinned with the sin of pride," the priest ought to ask how, saying, "In what way were you proud? Were you ever disobedient to the orders of your superiors, such as those of the church or prelates or your parents or a lord or magistrate?" And this always ought to take the sinner's condition into consideration. If he says yes, let him ask against which orders, how, how often, why, when, and where, which are the circumstances that, as was said above, are to be paid attention to and considered with respect to all sins. Then let him ask, "Have you ever boasted of the good things bestowed on you by God, whether they are goods of nature, like beauty, fortitude, ability, nobility, and the like, or whether they are goods of fortune like riches, money, clothing, jewels, horses, fields, possessions, and similar temporal goods, or whether they are goods of grace like wisdom, eloquence, knowledge, virtues, and the like?" The confessor, accordingly, ought to say, "Have you ever been exalted in your mind or ever prided yourself on your fortitude, beauty, ability, nobility, riches, wisdom, eloquence, virtues, and other good things bestowed on you by God, so that you have not humbled yourself before God for these good things as much as you should have? Or have you believed that you have these things by your own merits and not purely by the grace of God? Or on account of these things have you believed yourself to be worth more than another so that you disdain the deeds and words of others and refuse to consider them as equals?" If he says yes, let the confessor ask how often and in what way, and so on with the others. Then let him ask further about this, "In order to be commended and honored above others, were you ever a hypocrite, so that you would show holiness and goodness on the outside, but keep malice and iniquity on the inside?" If the one confessing says yes, let the confessor ask how often, in what way, when, etc. Then let him ask, "Because you were not honored or preferred before others, have you sometimes provoked controversies and disagreements in a city, village, society, or college?" If he says yes, ask if evil deeds came out of it, because if so, he is responsible for all of them. Then let the confessor ask, "On account of pride, lest you seem to be outdone by others, were you obstinate in maintaining, against the truth and justice, your own judgment and your opinion and your word?" If he says yes, ask whether some loss resulted, because, if so, he is obligated to make good on it. Then let the confessor ask him, "Have you ever presumed to do something which would exceed your military strength, your situation, and your condition and that of your men?" If he says yes, let him ask if anyone was killed or injured as a result, because if so, he is obligated to make reparation. And thus the evil root of pride can be pulled out from the heart of the sinner.

In the same way, the root of avarice is to be discussed, since if the sinner on his own or at the questioning of the priest should confess to the sin of avarice, let the priest ask him how, saying, "Have you ever committed fraud or deceit, or ever told a lie or committed perjury either in buying or selling or making some other contract?" If he says yes, let the confessor ask which fraud or deceit, but the priest himself should not specify it for him. Indeed, this is to be kept as a general rule, that in these questionings, the priest ought not to descend to particular sins or particular circumstances of sins, because perhaps many, after such questionings, would transgress since the ways and means of sins were shown to them that they themselves did not even know to consider. And therefore the confessor should always ask in general, saying, as has been said, "Have you ever committed fraud or deceit?" And if the penitent says yes, let the confessor ask which, and why, and in what ways, against whom, how often, and in what cases. Then let him ask him, saying, "Have you ever, on account of your avarice, neglected to fulfill the seven works of mercy?" And he should specify these for him saying, "Have you ever seen a hungry person to whom you did not give anything to eat?" And so with the other works of mercy, which will be discussed below in Part III of this work. If he says yes, let the confessor ask him about the circumstances, as has been said. Also concerning the sin of avarice, let him ask about gaming, theft, plunder, usury, concerning which something will be said below.

Concerning the extremely foul root of lust, note that there are seven types of lust. The first is fornication, the second adultery, the third debauchery, the fourth incest, the fifth rape, the sixth sacrilege, the seventh is the sin against nature. Fornication is sexual intercourse between a single man and a single woman. Adultery is the violation of another's spouse. Debauchery is the illicit deflowering of a virgin. Incest is abuse of affine or blood relatives. Rape is when a girl is violently taken from the house of her parents so that, once corrupted, she may be kept as a wife or concubine. Sacrilege, in this context, is the sexual intercourse of monks or nuns or those promoted to holy orders. The sin against nature is done in many ways. In one way, when species is not preserved, as when it is done with an animal; and this is called bestiality. And concerning this, it says in the law of Moses, "The one who has sexual intercourse with an animal shall be put to death."[153] In another way, when species is preserved, but not sex, as when a man lies with a man or a woman with a woman; and this is properly called the sin of the Sodomites because the Sodomites were troubled by this sin, and therefore were turned to ashes by sulphurous fire (Genesis 19).[154] And four other cities perished on account of their proximity (D.1 de pen. c.46). In another way, when the right vessel or the right way is not preserved, although the sex is preserved, as when a man misuses the woman's vessel or when he does not know her in the natural way. In another way, it is done when it is the same person acting and receiving, as when a man corrupts himself or a woman herself. And this is called the sin of effeminacy, as the Apostle says, "Nor the effeminate, nor males who sleep with males shall possess the kingdom of God."[155]

Therefore, concerning this accursed sin of lust, the priest ought to proceed extremely cautiously so that he does not descend too much into the particulars, since frequently both men and women

153. Exodus 22:19   154. Genesis 19:1–29
155. 1 Corinthians 6:10

have thus discovered, through too much explicit naming and questioning of crimes, sins which they had not known could be committed. Hence if a sinner on his own or at the questioning of the priest says that he has sinned with the sin of lust, let the priest ask him if he is single or not, and whether he sinned with the sin of fornication or adultery or debauchery or incest or rape or sacrilege or the sin against nature. That is, let him ask him if the woman with whom he sinned was single, a widow, a wife, an affine or blood relative, a nun, or a virgin, and whether he took her through violence or not. And this suffices if the person confessing has understanding. But if he is a simple person, let the priest ask whether he knew her in the natural way, yet not descending to particulars, that is, he should not ask whether he knew her from the front or the back, and so with the other questions. But let him ask about the number of persons, that is, if the one confessing knew one or many, but he should not ask the names of the persons. Let him ask especially about the number of incidents, that is, whether once or twice or several times. And let him also ask about the time, that is, if it was done in a holy time, and also about the place and by what temptation he sinned, and whether he anticipated the temptation or was overtaken by it, and whether he sinned spontaneously or under coercion, and under what coercion, whether it was conditional or absolute, and whether he sinned out of sensual desire or out of poverty (this takes place especially among women). And so concerning many other things which experience will teach him.

But because this most wicked root of lust sends out its shoots, it even overwhelms the bed of spouses under the law of marriage. Know that a married man can sin with the sin of lust with his wife in many ways, even mortally. These ways are contained in these verses:

> *Tempore mente loco conditione modo.*
>
> In time, in mind, in place, in condition, in manner.

The abusing married man sins with his wife in five ways. In time, that is, if he knows her during the time of her menstruation, because if he knowingly did this he would sin mortally, and in the old law it was mandated that he be killed. But what about the menstruating woman, does she sin like the man? I say that if the husband asks for the [conjugal] debt to be rendered to him by his wife during her menstrual period, to the degree that she can, she ought to persuade him not to ask by saying that she is sick and not ready for this act at the moment. Nevertheless, she ought not to say that she is in that condition unless it would suit his self-possession and prudence or his discretion, because he might take such great offense at her that he might send her away. But if it would suit the husband's discretion and prudence she can reveal it to him. And if he is unwilling to desist, let her give herself to him, but with sorrow and bitterness of heart.

He can also sin in time, that is, if he knows his wife during a time of fasting or on saints' days or days of communion, or in time of childbirth. I do not think that in this case it is a mortal sin since the boundaries of marriage are not transgressed, as will be said right away, although they are to be warned that they should abstain from the carnal act during such times. And concerning this there is C.33 q.4 c.1 and c.2.

In mind, that is, in intention. Indeed a man can come to his wife in three ways. In one way, in order to beget offspring from her, which is for the service and worship of God. In another way, so that he renders the conjugal debt which is claimed by her. And if he comes to her with such an intention, he does not sin mortally or venially, indeed it is meritorious as long as he does not commit anything else thereupon. In another way, with carnal concupiscence. And if such concupiscence remains within the boundaries of marriage, namely, that he would in no way come to her except that she is his wife, it is only a venial sin. But if this concupiscence transgresses the boundaries of marriage, so that he does not come to her just as wife, but as a woman, such that, if he had another at the ready, he would just as well come to her, this is a mortal sin.

In place, that is, if he knows her in a church, or in a cemetery, or in another holy place. And in this case I believe that both sin mortally. In condition, that is, if he knows her under a dishonest or even illicit condition, as was seen above when marriage was treated. In manner, that is, if the man knows her in a way contrary to that instituted by nature, and that is the worst sin with one's wife. Hence, according to what Augustine says, "The use which is contrary to nature is detestable with a prostitute, but it is even more detestable with one's wife" (C.32 q.7 c.11). According to this, therefore, the priest can adapt his questions concerning the sin of lust between man and wife, yet let him not descend to particulars.

Concerning the sin of anger, if the sinner on his own or at the questioning of the priest confesses to it, the priest can ask, "On account of anger did you speak blasphemy against God or against his saints?" If he says yes, let the confessor ask him when, how often, why, and so on with the others. Then let him ask, "Have you ever, on account of anger, spoken insolent words to a neighbor?" If he says yes, let him ask which words, why, how often, where, and in front of whom. Let him also ask if he was injurious to his neighbor, namely, striking or beating someone in anger. If the penitent says yes, let the confessor ask him who it was, and whether it was a cleric or a layperson, religious or secular, and where and why, and so on concerning the other circumstances of person. Let him also ask how often he repeated the injuries and where and why, etc.

Concerning the sin of gluttony, if the sinner on his own or at the questioning of the priest confesses to it, let the confessor ask if, on account of gluttony, he ever broke a fast of the church or if he ate meat during them, and why, and how often, and if he got drunk, and if he has the habit of getting drunk, and if on account of drunkenness he said insulting, dishonest, or injurious words, and how often and to whom he said them, etc. And note that according to what Gregory says, "Man sins in five ways through gluttony,"[156] which ways are contained in these verses:

> Certum stat quod quinque modis gula damnat edentem.
> Dum nimium comedit, comedendi prevenit horam.

156. D.5 de cons. c.22

Querit delicias, parat escas deliciose.
Aut sumit auide quid non erat deliciosum.

It is certain that gluttony damns the eater in five ways.
While he eats too much, eats before meal time.
Seeks delicacies, prepares delicious foods.
Or takes greedily what is not delicious.

Note that to eat a lot because of physical constitution or age or labor is not a sin; nevertheless, it ought not to be consumed with eagerness, ardor, or greed. Likewise to enjoy moderate amounts of expensive foods is not a sin, especially among the rich who are accustomed to such things; nevertheless they ought not to be consumed too greedily or to be unsuited to one's status. And because mention has been made of drunkenness, note that drunkenness is used in three ways. In one way it names complete forgetfulness of mind, and thus it is not a sin (C.15 q.1 c.2). In a second way drunkenness names the action of drinking frequently. And this, as Augustine says, "is a venial sin, unless it is incessant, because then it is a mortal sin, especially if one knows the strength of the wine and does not want to add water" (D.25 dict. post c.3 §4). In a third way, drunkenness names a certain disposition and eagerness for getting drunk and as such is always a mortal sin (D.35 c.9).

Concerning the sin of envy, if a sinner on his own or at the questioning of the priest confesses to it, let the priest ask him if the harm or misfortune of a neighbor pleases him, and if the neighbor's good or advantage displeases him, and if out of envy he has ever disparaged his neighbor by imputing a false crime to him or by downplaying or hiding the good which was in him, or by exaggerating what was in him or making it known to those who did not know it. Likewise, how often has he done this, and why, and so with the other circumstances. Likewise if he bears hatred or rancor or ill will against his neighbor, and why, and so with the others.

Concerning sloth, let the priest ask if the sinner could have done many good things which he did not do, said what he did not say, thought what he did not think, and avoided many evils which he did not avoid. Likewise if out of negligence he failed to go to mass, to the sermon, and to other good works, etc.

Therefore, the priest will be able to shape his questions according to this teaching, and regarding these, the unction which he receives from God and experience will teach more than further reading.

Truly the priest should vary his questions according to the variety of those confessing. Hence, if the one confessing is a religious he should be asked about the three vows of the rule, namely, about obedience, poverty and chastity. He also should be asked about observances of the rule, and especially about the abuses of the cloister which frequently corrupt the state of the religious. These are twelve, namely, a negligent prelate, a disobedient disciple, a lazy youth, an obstinate old man, a monk of the curia, a monk or regular canon who is an advocate, costly habit, exquisite food, rumor in the cloister, strife in chapter, dissolution in choir, irreverence toward the altar. And according to these and other regular observances, the confessor ought to shape his questions.

And concerning secular clerics, questions are to be asked about simony, business, and other things which pertain to simony and to avarice. And if they have administrative responsibilities or an office or benefice, they should be asked about the squandering of goods or whether they have spent the goods of the church for evil purposes. Likewise ask whether they have been present at the divine offices and canonical hours, whether they wear a suitable tonsure and habit, if they sing the divine office wholly and completely. Likewise let them be asked about lust, hunting, irregularity, playing with dice, and the like, in which they are accustomed to sin often.

For princes, questions are to be asked about justice. For soldiers, about pillaging. For merchants and other officials exercising mechanical arts, about fraud, deceit, lying, perjury, etc. For burghers and citizens, commonly ask about usury and pledges. For peasants and farmers, about envy and theft, and especially about tithes, first fruits, tributes, assessments. Hence note that although the aforementioned general pattern is to be observed for all, yet according to the diversity of persons and duties, insist more zealously and particularly upon specific crimes.

When these questions have been asked, if the one confessing is a simple person, let the priest ask him if he knows the Our Father, Ave Maria, Creed, and if he knows how to sign himself. And if he does not know, let him instruct him or warn him that he should learn more. Then let the confessor ask if he is tempted by any temptation, and by which one, and how he is doing at resisting; and let him teach him how. If indeed he is tempted by pride, let him think about the humility of the son of God by which "he humbled himself, becoming obedient even unto death."[157] Also let him think about the case of the devil who, on account of his pride, fell from paradise into hell, and from an angel became a devil. If the one confessing is tempted by avarice, let him think about the brevity of life and the instability and vanity of the world, and that he will be able to take none of his riches with him from here. If he is tempted by lust, let him think about death and how he will be after death, since, "there is no better way to subdue the living flesh of a person than to consider in advance how it will be when dead." Let him also think about the punishments of hell and the joys of paradise. These things and many others the confessor ought to show and tell him.

When this is done, let the confessor summarize and repeat the penitent's confession in general, saying, "Friend, you have confessed this sin," and let him show him the gravity of the sins by severely rebuking him and leading him to tears of compunction and contrition. And to this end, it avails much if the priest shows a sorrowful and tearful face to the sinner. As it is read of St. Ambrose that when someone confessed his failing to him, he wept bitterly, so that however stubborn the one confessing was, he would provoke him to weeping and tears. And thus also the priest ought to do, and so the sinner led by shame may be summoned to tears, so that tears of admonition may arouse tears of repentance. Therefore, let the

157. Philippians 2:8

priest take exceeding care lest he fawn over the penitent in confession; rather to the degree that a person is great and to be revered, let him rebuke and correct him severely. Nevertheless, let him take care that he not be too irritating or that he not be too harsh in his words. But if the sinner wants to repent well, let the confessor promise him eternal life and mercy for his sins, so that the sinner always may leave consoled by him. Having duly done these things, let the confessor have him say the general confession, warning him that if he remembers any other sin, he should return to confession. And after having imposed penance on him, let the confessor absolve him in the name of the Lord. But if the penitent is excommunicated with the major excommunication, the confessor in no way ought to absolve him until he is absolved from that excommunication. But according to common teaching, any curate having the care of souls can absolve from the minor excommunication. Therefore before he absolves him from his sins, let him absolve him from the minor excommunication, saying, "By the authority of God granted to me I absolve you from the bond of minor excommunication, if you incurred it through participation with the excommunicated." And afterward let him absolve the penitent of his confessed and forgotten sins.

But suppose a curate has some deaf, or mute, or blind, or insane, or demon-possessed parishioners and perhaps he knows that these are in mortal sin. What should he do about them? For if he should warn a deaf person to repent, it would not be useful because he does not hear. If he is mute, he is not able to confess. A blind person cannot see signs, nor even read like a mute. An insane person is not capable of reason, nor the demon-possessed either. I say that the priest ought to do his duty so that he may lead them to contrition, repentance, and compunction, according to what is possible for them, namely, by words, or writing, or nods, or signs, and all other means by which he can. And if he cannot, let the priest pray to God, and let him have his people pray, that God might illuminate their hearts toward repentance. If he omits no effort reaching out, it will not be imputed against him. But concerning how the priest should deal with the sick person who loses the power of speech and cannot confess, see above in Part I, tract on the eucharist, chapter 9.

CHAPTER 10: On the power of the keys

Because it was said above when treating penance that sins are forgiven in contrition, doubt exists about what the priest forgives by the power of the keys in absolution, since he does not forgive guilt, because, as has been said, that is forgiven in contrition, or penalty, because even after the penitent is absolved he remains obligated to [pay his] penalty. Concerning this matter, this is what seems to me ought to be said. Indeed the one who comes to confession is either perfectly contrite, or not. If he is perfectly contrite, then God, by virtue of contrition, forgives him his sin, according to the testimony of Ezekiel, who says in the person of God, "At whatever hour the sinner cries out, I will not remember all his iniquities."[158] And so before he comes to confession he is cleansed from guilt.

But if he is not perfectly contrite, then by virtue of confession, this imperfect contrition is restored to perfect contrition, so that from being attrite, by virtue of confession, he is made contrite. And thus by virtue of confession his sins are forgiven with respect to guilt. Nevertheless note that when it is said that sin is forgiven in confession or in contrition, it is to be understood that God, not the contrition or the confession, forgives the sin. Hence Ambrose, as is given in D.1 de pen. c.51, "The word of God forgives sin." And Augustine, as is given in D.4 de cons. c.141, "No one takes away sin except Christ alone, who is the lamb who takes away the sin of the world. But he takes it away by forgiving sins which have been committed, and by helping prevent them, and by leading one into the life where sins cannot be committed." And when he says "Christ alone," he does not exclude the Father or the Holy Spirit, since the works of the Trinity are indivisible, and this is true as far as the works which are done outside [the Trinity].

158. Cf. Ezekiel 33:12, 18:22

So what do the keys or the absolution of the priest do here? According to some, the answer is that God cleanses the soul in contrition from the stain of guilt and the priest absolves him from the bond of eternal punishment. I admit that I do not understand them, because I do not see how someone, after he has been cleansed from the stain of mortal guilt, can be obligated to eternal punishment, since this punishment is not due except for guilt or mortal sin. If therefore God cleanses the soul from mortal guilt in contrition, as a consequence, God absolves him from the bond of eternal punishment.

And therefore others say that although sin is forgiven in contrition as far as guilt and the sentence of eternal punishment are concerned, nevertheless, the sinner still remains obligated to do two things, namely, to confess his sin and to do some satisfaction for sin. And therefore the priest, by virtue of the keys, absolves him from the bond by which he was obligated to confess and binds him to satisfaction. And thus the priest is said to loose and to bind by the power of the keys. Although it is true that the sinner is obligated to do those two things, nevertheless it does not seem, according to this way of thinking, that the words of the form of sacramental absolution can be verified well, for the priest says, "I absolve you from sins," and not "I absolve you from confession." Therefore according to this way of thinking, it is necessary that somehow he absolve from sins.

And therefore some say that the sinner through sin is not only obligated to God whom he offends, but also to the church from which he alienates himself by sinning. And therefore, although in contrition he is reconciled to God, nevertheless he still remains to be reconciled to the church by making confession to the one who is the leader of the church. And although this is true, nevertheless it does not seem to suffice, since the keys extend not only to loosing and binding on earth, but also in heaven, according to Christ's saying, "Whatever you bind on earth, etc."[159]

And therefore some others say that the priest by the power of

159. Matthew 16:19

the keys does not accomplish anything except ostensively; hence they say that he absolves, that is, he shows the penitent to be absolved. Hence when he says, "I absolve you," it means, "I show you to be absolved." And these seem to base their conclusion on the authority of Ambrose, saying, "The priest indeed exhibits his office but does not exercise any power of judgment."[160] But their conclusion seems to attribute too little to the keys. And the word of Ambrose is to be understood to mean that the priest exercises no power of judgment authoritatively, but he certainly does ministerially.

And therefore others say that the priest, by the power of the keys, absolves from guilt if he finds it, as long as the one confessing does not pose an obstacle, and he absolves from the punishment of purgatory, to which the sinner was obligated, not by relaxing it, but by commuting it into temporal or corporal punishment. And this is done under the condition, namely, that the sinner should fulfill his enjoined penance, so that if the enjoined penance is adequate, he will be absolved from all the punishments of purgatory, and if it is not adequate, he will not be absolved from all the punishments of purgatory, but from a certain amount. And therefore if he should die having completed adequate penance, he will not be punished in purgatory. But if the penance was not adequate, or if it was adequate, but he did not complete it during his lifetime, he will complete it in purgatory. And this opinion seems reasonable enough to me.

Others say that since every mortal sin is offensive to the divine goodness which is infinite, the obligatory punishment for mortal sin is infinite, and as a consequence it is disproportionate to us as human beings. But by the power of the keys it is made proportionate to us insofar as by the power of the keys the passion of Christ, which gives efficacy to all the sacraments and which was sufficient to satisfy for the sins of the whole world, is communicated to the one confessing. Hence according to this way of think-

160. D.1 de pen. c.51

ing, the power of the keys is such that by their power, the passion of Christ is communicated to the one confessing, in whose power one can satisfy for sins, which one could not do before. Hence I believe that one Our Father imposed as penance by the priest is more efficacious to satisfy for sins than if someone were to say a hundred thousand on his own, because the former has merit from the passion of Christ, but the latter from the merit of the one saying it. And this opinion is very reasonable.

CHAPTER 11: On the seal of confession

The seal of confession ought to be secret, because in no way, by no pact, for no reason should it be broken. Indeed the priest ought to endure any pain before he would reveal a confession, not by word, or by writing, or by a nod, or by a sign. And concerning this seal, Gregory says, as is given in D.6 de pen. c.2, where it says, "And let the priest take great care lest he reveal anything to anyone about those sins which were confessed to him, not to neighbors or strangers, and not (God forbid!) by any temptation. For if he were to do it, let him be deposed, and all the days of his life let him wander ignominious as a pilgrim." Likewise *Omnius utriusque sexus* (X 5.38.12), "Let every priest beware lest by word or sign or some other way he betray the sinner to any extent, but if he needs the counsel of one more experienced, let him seek it cautiously without any mention of the person. Because we decree that the one who dares to reveal the sin disclosed to him in the tribunal of penance, not only is to be deposed from the sacerdotal office, also he is to be driven away to do perpetual penance perpetually in a strict monastery." Thus in this decretal the confessor is instructed about what he ought to do and of what he ought to beware.

If indeed a case should come to a priest in confession about which he does not know how to counsel the penitent well, he ought to consult one who is more experienced than himself on this, so that he may see what he ought to do. But under what form will he reveal to this experienced person the sin which another confessed to him? I believe under this one: "If such a case were to happen, what should be done?" Or, "If someone were to confess such a sin, how should he be counseled?" But I believe he ought not to say, "I heard this in confession," because by saying this he would lie, because he did not hear it as himself, but as the vicar holding the place of God. And even less should he say, "Someone confessed to me," because by saying so, in general and implicitly he reveals the confession and so lies because the confession was made to God and not to him, except as to one holding the place of God.

But suppose a priest is brought forward as a witness and is compelled to swear about a crime which he heard in confession. What should he do? If he speaks so that he reveals the confession, he will be punished; if he denies it, he commits perjury. I say that if he only knows about it through confession he ought to swear that he knows nothing about this matter about which he is questioned, and he does not commit perjury because he himself knows nothing about it. Indeed it is true that he knows that a crime was confessed to him, but he does not know whether the one confessing spoke truly or falsely in confessing, and therefore he can truly say that he knows nothing. But what if the judge presses him, and asks him on oath whether he has heard anything about the crime at issue? The answer is that an oath does not bind him to say anything in this matter, since the oath was not invented to be a bond of iniquity (X 2.24.23). Taking an oath is not obligatory in anything done against the commandment of God. Hence since to reveal a confession is against the commandment of God, namely, against "Do not bear false witness,"[161] no oath is obligatory here. Hence such a one can legitimately swear to have heard nothing, and let him understand that he heard nothing as a man or in such a way that he ought to testify.

Alternatively, suppose that a priest knows through confession that there is some heretic in his parish or elsewhere who is leading other children to heresy. What should this priest do? Ray-

---

161. Exodus 20:16; Deuteronomy 5:20

mond, in his *Summa*, seems to say that in this case the confession can be revealed, and his reason is that the offender does not keep the faith of the church since he is a heretic and an infidel, therefore faith is not to be kept with him (C.23 q.1 c.3). Nevertheless, with all due respect, another opinion seems more consonant with the truth, which Raymond himself also recounts, namely, that the priest ought not to reveal the confession himself, but ought to go to the bishop or inquisitor and say, "I care for and keep watch over your sheep; there is a wolf in your flock." And what Raymond says is that since the heretic does not belong to the faith, faith is not to be kept with him.[162] I say that by revealing the confession, faith is not broken with the person, but with God "who is faithful in all his ways."[163]

But can the one confessing give permission to the confessor to tell what he told him in confession? I say that the one confessing can make it so that what the confessor knows as God, he also knows as a man, namely, by telling him outside of confession the same thing he told in confession, and thus the confessor can say that which he heard as a man outside of confession. But does it suffice that the one confessing should tell the confessor by saying, "I give you permission to tell those things which I said in confession," or is it necessary that he repeat everything to him outside of confession? Some doctors say that it suffices for him to give permission to the confessor. Yet Durandus in his fourth book says no, rather he is obligated to repeat everything to the confessor outside confession.[164] And his reason for opposing it is because no one can dispense with the things which belong to the sacrament of necessity, not even the pope, concerning whom more will be seen. But to keep confession secret belongs to sacramental confession of necessity, as is variously proved; therefore no one can give a dispensation from this. And as a consequence, no one can give

162. Raymond of Penyafort, *Summa*, Bk III, 34, 60.
163. Psalm 144:17
164. Durand of St. Pourçain, *Petri Lombardi Sententias Theologicas Commentariorum*, Bk IV, d. 21, q. 4.

permission that those things which were said by him in confession may be revealed. Therefore in order that they may be revealed, it is necessary that they be known otherwise than through confession. From these considerations, it is clear that if someone knows something through confession and outside of confession, he can reveal it and testify to it in the same way as whatever he knows outside of confession. Note that the seal of confession directly and principally pertains to sin, as is clear from the decretal cited above, *Omnis utriusque sexus* (X 5.38.12), where it says, "Let every priest beware." Nevertheless as a consequence, by a certain appropriateness, it also pertains to other things.

And let these things suffice concerning confession.

Tract 4 of the second principal part is on satisfaction, having 6 main chapters.

Having explained, by the grace of God, two parts of penance, namely contrition and confession, the third, namely, satisfaction, remains to be taken up. About which there are six things to be noted. First, what satisfaction is and in what things it consists; second, almsgiving which is the first part of satisfaction; third, fasting which is the second part; fourth, prayer which is the third part; fifth, the measure of satisfaction, namely, what penance is to be imposed for one or another sin; sixth, whether one can satisfy for another.

CHAPTER 1: What satisfaction is

Satisfaction, according to Gregory, "is to remove the causes of sins and not to indulge further in their enticements."[165] Thus in this definition two things are touched upon which ought to be in every satisfaction. Just as good and complete medicine ought to cure past illness and protect for the future, so too satisfaction

---

165. D.3 de pen. c.3; attributed by Gratian to Augustine.

ought to be a remedy for past sins and a precaution for the future. The first thing is touched on when it says, "to remove the causes of sins." The second when it says, "not to indulge further in its enticements." Indeed a medicine, if it is to be suitable, ought to be appropriate for the illness and targeted directly against it, by the testimony of St. Jerome who says, "Medicine is to be applied to the particular disease,"[166] for what heals the heel does not heal the eye. And according to what Jerome says in his first epistle, "All that is in the world, is either the desire of the flesh, or the desire of the eyes, or the arrogance of life."[167] And this means that there are three roots of all sin, namely, avarice, which is what is meant by "the lust of the eyes," lust, which is what is meant by "the desire of the flesh," and pride, by that which is called "the arrogance of life." Therefore against these three roots of sin are targeted the three parts of satisfaction, namely, almsgiving which is targeted against avarice, fasting against lust, and prayer against pride. And thus there are three parts of satisfaction, namely, almsgiving, fasting, and prayer. And these three parts will be taken up in order.

CHAPTER 2: On alms, which has 4 little chapters within it

Although many, various, and diverse things have been written by the holy doctors about the virtue of almsgiving, yet all these are comprehended in the brief discussion of St. Tobias, saying, "Almsgiving liberates the soul from death and sin, and it will not suffer the soul to go into darkness."[168] Almsgiving is three-fold. First, it consists in contrition of heart, namely, when someone offers himself as a sacrifice to God. About this it is said in the Psalm, "A crushed spirit is a sacrifice to God."[169] And about almsgiving, the Wise One says this, "Show mercy so that your soul may be pleasing to God."[170] And the almsgiving mentioned here

166. Cf. c.1 q.1 c.18
168. Tobit 4:11
170. Cf. Wisdom 4:10

167. 1 John 2:16
169. Psalm 50:19

is not part of satisfaction, rather it is an integral part of contrition, divided from satisfaction to the degree that penance is said to have three parts, namely, contrition, confession, and satisfaction. Another is almsgiving which consists in compassion for the neighbor in which we have compassion for the sufferings of others just as we do for our own. And concerning this Job says, "From the beginning, mercy grew strong with me and it came out with me from my mother's womb."[171] The third consists in generosity of hand, namely, when someone offers to the needy something of one's temporal substance on account of God. And this is what we are giving attention to here. And concerning this the Savior says in Luke, "Give alms and behold all things are clean to you."[172] And Ambrose says, "Feed those dying of hunger, lest you kill the poor" (D.86 c.21). And under this kind of almsgiving the seven works of mercy are contained, which will be discussed in Part III. But for now consider four things about alms. First, from what ought they to be given; second, who can give them; third, to whom they ought to be given; fourth, how should it be done.

First consideration on alms, namely, from what alms ought to be given

Omitting the distinction between necessary and superfluous, it is to be said that in this all the doctors commonly agree that alms ought to be given neither from others' goods nor from things illicitly gotten. Hence Tobias showing his son from what things alms ought to be given says, "Honor God with your substance."[173] He says, "with your," not "with another's." And Gregory says, "It is not to be considered almsgiving if the things dispensed to the poor come from things illicitly acquired."[174] Nevertheless, note here that acquiring something illicitly can be done in three ways. Indeed some things are illicitly acquired for which the right of ownership is not transferred to the recipient, as in pillage and

171. Job 31:18
172. Luke 11:41
173. Cf. Tobit 4:7
174. C.1 q.1 c.27

theft. And there are other cases for which the right of ownership is transferred, but demanding it back goes along with it, as in usury and simony; and in these cases, alms cannot be given. There are others for which right of ownership is transferred and its return is not expected, as with money and other things acquired by stage acting or harlotry. In the first two cases, when right of ownership is not transferred, or it is transferred and its return is expected, alms cannot be given, but one ought to make restitution according to the method that will be discussed below. Hence from goods acquired by theft, pillage, usury, and simony, alms cannot be given. But in the third case, namely, when the right of ownership is transferred, and its return is not expected, as with things acquired by stage acting or harlotry, alms can be given out of these things. And Ambrose approves this distinction at the end of C.14 q.5 c.15.

But can alms be given from things which are acquired from a game of chance or dice or some other game? The answer is that when I speak of a game, I do not mean by "game" what is done for comfort or recreation, because such a game is lawful as long as it is honest and covered by proper circumstances. Rather, I mean by "game" that which is done for greed, which is entirely and always illicit, and many sins accompany it. First, indeed, here there is the desire to get rich, behold "greed which is the root of all evils."[175] Second, here there is the desire to despoil one's neighbor, behold pillage. Third, here there is great usury, namely, eleven for ten, not only in a year or in a month, but in the same day. Fourth, here lying and hurtful and vain words are multiplied. Fifth, here there is blasphemy, behold heresy. Sixth, here there is manifold corruption of the neighbors who watch the game. Seventh, here good people are scandalized. Eighth, here there is contempt of the prohibition of holy mother church. Ninth, here there is loss of time and of the other good deeds which one was obligated to do in that time. From which it is clear how much they sin who make time for such games. And concerning the penalties for clerics who make time

175. 1 Timothy 6:10

for such games, it is read in the Canons of the Apostles thus, "If a bishop, presbyter, or deacon is devoting himself to a game of chance or to getting drunk, either let him stop or let him be certainly damned. And a subdeacon, lector, or cantor doing similar things, either let him stop or be barred from communion."[176]

It is clear therefore that what is acquired in such a game is acquired illicitly. But can it be demanded back? Some doctors say no, but he who is made rich ought to spend it on the poor, by the argument in C.14 q.5 c.15, since indeed baseness dwells on both sides, and the situation of the occupier or possessor is better. Others, and nearly all the canonists, say that it can be demanded back. And this is proved in Dig. 11.5.2. And the Greek Constitution says that it can be demanded back for up to fifty years.[177] And according to these, alms cannot be given out of what was acquired in a game. Indeed, Raymond, with whom St. Thomas and almost all the doctors of theology agree, says that a distinction is to be made. Either someone plays voluntarily and out of greed, not coerced by anyone, and then if he loses, he cannot demand back what he lost; but he who wins is obligated to spend it on the poor or restore it, according to the judgment of his soul. Or, someone plays drawn in by force or through the pleading of another, and then if he loses, he can demand it back. But if in fact he wins, he is not obligated to give it back, but to spend on the poor what he has won.[178] This judgment is proved by many laws, and is adequately consonant with reason and equity.

Note that there are some persons to whom one is always obligated to restore whatever was won from them in a game, like the mad, prodigies, orphans, those under age fifteen, the mentally ill, the deaf, the blind, mutes, and those who labor under a perpetual illness. Because such people are not able to oversee their possessions, therefore tutors and caregivers are given to them. The same

176. D.35 c.1
177. Guido's reference to the Greek Constitution is from Raymond of Penyafort, *Summa*, II, 8, 7.
178. Raymond of Penyafort, *Summa*, II, 8, 12.

is true for monks and other religious and for sons who do not have private property while soldiering or the like. It is also true for a wife who does not have personal property, and also for the administration of ecclesiastical property which belongs to the poor, and similar cases. Hence neither prelates nor curates can remit such winnings to their debtors, lest they should be seen as wasters or squanderers. For since the acquisition of wealth from such people, according to many laws, is criminal and vicious, I say it is not to be restored to the one who lost it in a game, but to the tutor or the caretaker or the husband or the father or the church or the monastery.

Second consideration on alms, namely, who can give alms

Alms can be given by anyone who owns his own property or who has right of ownership or administration of another's temporal goods. Can a monk or other religious give alms? I say that such a person either has administration or not. If he has administration, he can and ought to spend on pious causes whatever extra he has, once the needs of the church have been met. As St. Bernard says, "The goods of the church are the goods of the poor, and whatever is retained by the ministers of the church, beyond food and clothing, is all sacrilege and pillage." But if he does not have administration, saving the judgment or counsel of someone better, I believe that he cannot and ought not to give alms unless he asks and obtains permission from his prelate. Indeed a monk cannot manage the profits of his monastery, except at the command of his abbot (C.16 q.1 c.11, rubric; D.5 de cons. c.36). And I understand this to mean unless the one who asks for alms is at the point of extreme need, that is, he is needy unto death, because in that case, he ought to give to him if he can, unless his prelate would expressly forbid him, because in such a case every person is obligated by the commandment of God to help his neighbor, according to the rule, "Feed those dying of hunger, etc." (D.86 c.21). And also in such a case, all things are considered common property (D.47 c.2). Note that if a monk not having administration goes on a pilgrimage or to study at the command of his abbot, he can give alms without any restriction. For to the one to whom the prelate gave permission to abide among scholars or to go on pilgrimage, it seems he also gave permission to do all that honest scholars and pilgrims are accustomed to do. Nevertheless let him do it moderately for everyone ought to conform himself to the ways of those among whom he lives (D.41 c.1).

But can a wife give alms without the permission of her husband? The answer is that if the wife has personal belongings [*parafernales*], that is, her own property by gift, so called from *"para"* which is "according to" and *"ferna"* which is "gift," as if to say, "according to her gift," she can give alms from these things, even against her husband's will (Cod. 5.14). And from the things belonging to her husband, like bread and wine and other things, which by good and approved and laudable custom are commonly under the management of the wife, she can give alms moderately and according to the capability of her husband and according to the greater or lesser need and number of the poor. And she ought to adjust her conscience so that she does not displease her husband in his heart even if sometimes he prohibited her by mouth. For husbands are accustomed to give such a prohibition to their wives, not to restrain them from giving anything, but from giving an excess which they suspect they might give, if they were given too free a hand. She can also adjust her conscience according to the condition and misery of the pauper, thinking that if her husband were to see him, it would please him in every way that she should give him alms. But if she is repeatedly and explicitly told that it would displease her husband, let her resign her conscience if she can; if she cannot, let her not give and mourn that she cannot give. And so I understand C.33 q.5 c.17, where it is said that a wife ought not to give alms when it causes scandal to her husband, and I understand this to mean unless the poor person is at the point of extreme need, because then she ought to give fearlessly, otherwise she would sin. And what I said about the husband's belongings, I also meant about the dowry gifts. For the undiminished right of ownership of dowry gifts belongs to the husband (Cod. 5.12.30). And Lord Albert says that if a woman is rich, that is, if she becomes rich by her own business or service, and does not have personal belongings, she can give alms out of what she earned without the mandate or consent of her husband.

Also the son of the family cannot give alms from his father's belongings without his permission and mandate, unless he supposes that it would please his father, as I said above concerning the wife. And I understand this to be the case unless such a son has his own property from soldiering or something like soldiering; indeed from such property he can give alms, even against his father's will. Property from soldiering is what he acquired from military service. Property from something like soldiering is what he acquired by skill or honest employment. And I understand this to mean unless he should see a poor person in extreme need. Also concerning the son going on pilgrimage or studying, apply what I said above concerning the monk.

And even less can a servant or serving girl give alms from the belongings of their lords, unless perhaps the administration of goods was committed to them, because then they can, although moderately, knowing that it will not displease the lord.

Third consideration on alms, namely, to whom
alms ought to be given.

Alms ought not to be given except to the needy, and this is heard in the name "almsgiving." Hence almsgiving [*elemosina*], as Eberhard says, is so called from *"eloys"* which is "the poor," and *"moys"* which is "water," as if to say "the water of the poor," that is, of the needy.[179] Among those who ask for alms, some ask as if collecting a debt, like the religious mendicants who preach the word of God and celebrate daily for their benefactors. And these, provided it is established that they have that office, are to be preferred over others. And these are said to ask as if collecting a debt because

179. Cf. Eberhard of Béthune, *Graecismus,* c. 10.

not only are temporal things to be given to them, but also spiritual things are received from them. Hence in the person of such a one the Apostle says, "If we have sown spiritual things among you, is it any wonder if we harvest from your temporal things?"[180]

Others ask for the sustenance of their life, like those paupers who beg. And in this case, either one can give to everyone or one cannot. If one can give to everyone, then one ought to give to all without any distinction. This is shown in the example of Abraham and Lot who received all indiscriminately as guests; they even received angels as guests.[181] If indeed they had rejected some, perhaps they would have rejected the angels among them. And in this case John Chrysostom says, "Let us abstain from the absurd, that is, from the abominable diabolical curiosity, namely, of discerning between pauper and pauper, for it is not from their life that they receive, or you give a reward to them and God pays you back, but from goodwill and much honoring, and from mercy and goodness" (D.42 c.2). Likewise Gregory says at the end of C.11 q.3 c.103 that alms are to be given even to one who is excommunicated, and this I understand to apply as much to one excommunicated as to any other notorious sinner, meaning, give unless because of their fullness they would neglect their own righteousness and would be made worse, because in such a case alms are not to be given to them, as Augustine says (C.5 q.5 c.2). And understand this to apply unless he is hungry unto death, indeed then, however much they neglect righteousness, they ought to be fed, unless perhaps a secular judge has condemned them to die of hunger for their evil deeds.

In the second case, in which one cannot give alms to everyone, given that all may be equally needy, Ambrose says ten things are to be considered here, namely, faith, cause, place, time, [mode], need, blood relationship, age, debility, condition or nobility. Faith, because a Christian is to be preferred over an infidel. Cause, because if two are held captive, one on account of his guilt, the oth-

180. 1 Corinthians 9:11
181. Genesis 18:1–8

er without guilt, this one is to be preferred over the other. Place, because a captive or one detained in prison is to be preferred over one who can go freely wherever he likes. Time, because if one suffered in a time of persecution, he is to be preferred over one who has never suffered persecution. Mode, so that all is not diverted to one, nor are all resources poured out simultaneously, but they are to be dispensed separately, unless perhaps someone wants to leave the world completely. Need, so that the needier one is preferred over the less needy. Blood relationship, so that the relative is preferred over the stranger. Age, because the old are to be preferred over the young. Debility, so that the sick one is preferred over the healthy and the weak over the strong. Nobility, so that the noble is preferred over the non-noble. And this is to be understood for other pairs.

Yet there could be such a condition on one part that it would alter the stipulation into the opposite. For example, suppose someone has an infidel father who needs alms and a Christian stranger also needs alms, and he cannot help both but only one. Whom should he help by offering food, the infidel father or the Christian stranger? In this case, some say that the infidel father is to be preferred to the Christian stranger in offering food, but the Christian stranger is to be preferred to the infidel father in love (D.30 c.1). And this opinion is founded on the commandment, "Honor your father,"[182] and this is understood to mean if they are equally needy. But if the stranger is needy unto death and the father is not, then the stranger is to be preferred over the father. Others say the opposite, namely, that good strangers are to be preferred. Which of these speaks better, I leave to the judgment of the reader.

Fourth consideration on alms, namely, how alms ought to be given

Because according to what the Philosopher says in *Ethics*, mode imposes a type of act or action,[183] which I understand as a type

182. Exodus 20:12; Deuteronomy 5:16
183. Guido most likely is quoting from Aquinas here, although we were unable to locate the source.

of behavior; indeed it does not suffice to do good unless it is done rightly. Hence the Lord commanded Moses, "You shall justly pursue what is just."[184] Therefore in order for almsgiving to be meritorious, it is required that it be done in the proper way. Hence alms ought to be given gratefully or joyfully, as the Apostle says in 2 Corinthians 21, "Let the one who gives give joyfully, neither out of sadness or obligation. For God loves a cheerful giver."[185] Second, it ought to be done secretly. Hence the Savior, "When you give alms, do not sound a trumpet before you as the hypocrites do"; and then follows, "But when you give alms, do not let your left hand know what your right hand is doing."[186] Third, it ought to be done generously, and this is according to the ability of the giver. Hence Tobit 4, "Son, if you have much, distribute abundantly. If you have little, nevertheless strive to bestow a little freely."[187] Fourth, it ought to be done prudently, so that it is done according to the pattern given in the previous chapter. Fifth, it ought to be done quickly. Hence the Wise One, "The one who gives quickly, gives twice." Sixth, it ought to be done zealously, that is, with right intention, namely, so that it is done for God and not for vain glory. Hence, as Gregory says, "In order that he may merit heaven, let him not seek the wind of transitory favor."

CHAPTER 3 [of Tract 4] of the second principal part is on fasting which is the second part of satisfaction, having 4 little chapters.

The second part of satisfaction is fasting, concerning which it says in Tobit, "Almsgiving is good with fasting."[188] Four things are to be considered here. First, how many types of fasting there are; second, when it was instituted; third, how many things are required for fasting to be meritorious; fourth, how many good things fasting accomplishes.

184. Deuteronomy 16:20
186. Matthew 6:2–3
188. Tobit 12:8

185. 2 Corinthians 9:7
187. Tobit 4:9

First consideration on fasting, namely, how many
types of fasting there are

Note that fasting is threefold. The first is bodily, from material food and drink. The second is afflictive, from temporal joy. The third is to abstain from mortal sin. And with this threefold fasting we ought to punish the beast of burden, that is, our body; indeed it is useless to fast from food unless one also fasts from sin. Hence Isaiah says, "Why have we fasted, and you have not taken notice? Why have we humbled our souls, and you have not acknowledged it?"[189] Isaiah speaks in the person of one fasting in mortal sin. And he adds a response in the person of God, saying, "Behold, you fast with strife and contention, and you strike with the fist impiously." And then follows, "Is this the fast such as I have chosen?" as if he would say, No. Rather it is this, "Release the constraints of impiety, relieve the burdens that oppress, and break apart every burden," namely, sins. "Break your bread with the hungry, and lead the destitute and the homeless into your house. When you see someone naked, cover him, and do not despise your own flesh."[190]

Second consideration on fasting, namely,
when fasting was instituted

The Lord instituted fasting in the earthly paradise when he ordered our first parents not to eat from the tree of the knowledge of good and evil.[191] But later, he sanctified it in the desert when he fasted for forty days and forty nights.[192]

Third consideration on fasting, namely, how many things
are required for fasting

In order for fasting to be meritorious, four things are required which ought to go along with it, namely, generosity, joy, hour, and measure. Concerning generosity, Jerome says, "You will be what you eat if you do not fast; give to the poor so that your fasting

189. Isaiah 58:3
191. Genesis 2:17

190. Isaiah 58:5–7
192. Matthew 4:2; Luke 4:2

may be fullness for your soul, not wealth for your purse." "God approves of that fasting," as Gregory says, "which raises the hand of almsgiving to another; therefore that which you take away from yourself enriches another, so that as your flesh is afflicted, the flesh of your needy neighbor is relieved." Concerning joy, Christ said, "And when you fast, do not choose to become gloomy, like the hypocrites. For they alter their faces, so that their fasting may be apparent to men."[193] Concerning the third thing, namely, hour, note that the hour for eating on fast days is the ninth hour, or thereabouts. Nevertheless, according to what Thomas says in his fourth book, "It is not necessary to look at an astrolabe, but it suffices not to anticipate noticeably the stated hour by too much."[194] Hence it is read in 1 Kings 14 that Jonathan, who anticipated the hour of eating, was sentenced to death.[195] Concerning the fourth thing, namely, measure, note that the one fasting ought to eat very moderately. Hence St. Peter says in 1 Peter 5, "Be sober, etc."[196] And this moderation is to be observed in both the quality and quantity of food. In the quality of food, so that a person does not eat forbidden foods like meat or milk products. And likewise, choice foods prepared in exquisite ways are not to be sought. Concerning this, see the above chapter on the questions to be asked in confession. Moderation also is to be observed in quantity, so that one does not take food beyond what suffices for natural sustenance. Indeed an excess of food does many bad things because it provokes lust and dissipates all good works. A figure of this is read in 4 Kings 25, where Nebuchadnezzar, which means prince of cooks, through whom is understood the gluttony of the belly, destroyed the walls of Jerusalem,[197] through which are understood the virtues of the faithful soul. Hence Augustine, "The mind made lax by a great appetite for food loses the power of prayer." And Jerome, "The belly heated with wine more easily bursts forth in lust."[198]

193. Matthew 6:16
194. Aquinas, *Scriptum super Sententiis*, Bk IV, d. 15, q. 3, a. 4.
195. 1 Samuel 14:24–45   196. 1 Peter 5:8
197. 2 Kings 25:1–10   198. D.35 c.5

Fourth consideration on fasting, namely, how many good things
it accomplishes

Fasting, observed in the obligatory way, accomplishes three good things. First, it curbs the stimulation of carnal vices. Second, it raises the mind to the contemplation of divine things. Third, it obtains the rewards of grace, virtue, and heaven. And these three are touched on in the preface for Lent in which it is said, "You who by our bodily fasting restrains our vices, elevates our minds, and bestows virtue and reward." Note especially that by "fasting" all bodily afflictions are understood, such as vigils, pilgrimages, flagellations, etc.

CHAPTER 4: On prayer, which is the third part of satisfaction

Prayer, which is the third part of satisfaction, is thus defined by the Damascene, "Prayer is the pious raising of one's state of mind toward God frequently lest the soul be sluggish to break out in voice." Or thus, "Prayer is the gathering of voices reaching out to beseech God." Note therefore that in prayer one ought not to ask for temporal things, at least, not first of all, but ought to ask for spiritual things pertaining to salvation, according to that word of the Savior, "Seek first the kingdom of God and his righteousness, and all these things will be added unto you,"[199] namely, temporal things. What things ought to be asked for in prayer Christ makes clear when his disciples were saying to him, "Teacher, teach us to pray." He said, "When you pray, say, 'Our Father.'"[200] And this will be discussed in Part III where this material will be treated in particular.

For prayer to be entirely meritorious and effective as satisfaction, it is required to have thirteen conditions, namely, that it be faithful, untroubled, humble, discrete, shameful, devout, secret, pure, tearful, attentive, fervent, painstaking, and constant. We will

199. Matthew 6:33
200. Luke 11:1–2

not pursue these further because there are notes about them for whoever wants to direct his attention to them.

Finally, prayer avails especially against spiritual vices. Hence Jerome on the text, "this kind of demon is not cast out except by prayer and fasting,"[201] says this, "Medicine is to be applied to the particular disease," for what heals the heel does not heal the eye. Bodily plagues are healed by fasting. Plagues of the soul or mind are healed by prayer.

If one asks which of the three parts of satisfaction is better, namely, prayer, almsgiving, or fasting, the answer is that if they are compared with respect to the object to which they look immediately or with respect to the matter concerning which they exist, then prayer is more worthy and better than the other two. Indeed prayer has God as its immediate object, as is clear from its definition. For prayer is the pious raising of one's state of mind toward God. Almsgiving has for its immediate object the suffering of the neighbor; indeed it is established for relieving it. Fasting has as its immediate object the desire of the flesh, because it is ordered and established for curbing this. Indeed prayer concerns spiritual things, but almsgiving and fasting concern corporal things, which is why it is clear that prayer is more worthy and better than almsgiving and fasting, etc. But if they are compared with respect to what they encompass, then almsgiving is better than prayer and fasting, because almsgiving contains in itself prayer and fasting. Indeed the one who gives alms to the needy obligates the recipient to pray to God for him, and thus prayer is included in almsgiving. Indeed the one who gives alms is a participant in the fasting and abstinence of the one who receives them, and thus fasting is contained in almsgiving. Hence I believe that almsgiving is more useful and better for satisfaction than fasting and prayer. And this seems to be the intention of St. Paul the Apostle in his first letter to Timothy, chapter II, where he speaks thus, "Exercise yourself so as to advance in piety," that is, in almsgiving, "for the exercise of the body," that is, fasting, "is somewhat useful, but piety is useful

201. Mark 9:28

in all things, holding the promise of life, in the present and in the future."[202]

CHAPTER 5: On the measure of penance

The more serious a sin is, the greater the penance or satisfaction that should be imposed and done for it compared with other comparable sins. And I say "with other comparable sins" because there can be such circumstances on the part of the person sinning, or even on the part of the sin, that for a less serious sin a heavier penance or satisfaction ought to be imposed. For example, it is well known that to kill one's mother is a greater sin than to kill one's wife, and nevertheless, by law a heavier penance is to be imposed for uxoricide than for matricide. And the reason is that the penance ought to be such that it is a remedy for past sin and a precaution against future sin. And since men are more prone to uxoricide than to matricide, so that they may be better restrained, a greater penance ought to be imposed for uxoricide than matricide. And for the same reason, a greater penance ought to be imposed on the young for deceit than on the old. But other things being equal, as much as a sin is greater, so much greater a penance is to be imposed for it.

To see therefore what penance ought to be imposed for what sin, the degrees of sin are to be considered, namely, which sin is greater than another. Here know that the gravity of sins can be considered in three ways. In one way, with respect to the sin itself, and this is done in two ways. In one way, on the part of the cause leading to the sin, for according to what Gregory says, "Sin is committed in three ways, namely, it is perpetrated out of ignorance, or weakness, or by intentional knowledge, study, or malice. Now sin which is perpetrated out of weakness is worse than that perpetrated out of ignorance, but it is much worse if it is perpetrated out of intentional knowledge" (D.2 de pen. c.22). Hence a greater penance is to be imposed for a sin perpetrated out of weakness,

202. 1 Timothy 4:7–8

that is, out of temptation or frailty, than for a sin perpetrated out of ignorance, but a much greater one for a sin perpetrated out of intentional malice. And this does not contradict what Ambrose says, "He who promises himself impunity sins gravely, he who disdains [more gravely], but the one who does not know most gravely." "Most gravely" is to be explained as "most dangerously," because penance is not to be done in particular for a sin about which one was ignorant. Hence John Chrysostom, or "Golden Mouth," "No better remedy is found against sins than the continual memory of them" (D.3 de pen. c.36), and understand this to be when a man remembers his sin with contrition, not with delight.

The gravity of a sin with respect to the sin itself can be considered in another way. For as Augustine says, "As one arrives at sin by three stages, namely, by suggestion, delight, and consent, so there are three different kinds of sin itself, namely, sin in the heart, sin in deed and in mouth, and sin in habit."[203] Thus it is that sin in deed is worse than sin in the heart, but the worst is sin in habit. Hence the three different kinds of sin are understood through the three dead ones whom Christ is read to have raised, namely, the daughter of the leader of the synagogue,[204] the son of the widow,[205] and Lazarus.[206] He raised the girl at home, behold the sin of thought; the boy at the gate of the city, behold the sin of deed; Lazarus after four days in the tomb, behold habitual sin. Again, he raised the girl by word alone, the boy by word and gesture, and Lazarus by word, weeping, and tears. This was to show that a greater penance is to be imposed for a sin of deeds than for a sin of thought, but a much greater one for habitual sin.

In a second way, the gravity of various sins can be considered with respect to their own kind. As Augustine says about the sin of lust, "The evil of adultery surpasses fornication; adultery is surpassed by incest. Indeed it is worse to lie with one's mother than

---

203. D.2 de pen. c.21. The three resurrections performed by Christ are mentioned briefly here.

204. Mark 5:22–43, Luke 8:40–56   205. Luke 7:12–15

206. John 11:1–44

with another woman. But the worst of all is that which is done against nature" [C.32 q.7 c.11].

The gravity among sins can be considered in a third way, and this is among different kinds of sins, as Augustine says, "Homicide is worse than adultery" (C.33 q.2 c.9). And in general, all sins which are committed directly against God, such as idolatry, heresy, blasphemy, and the like, are worse than other sins. This will be discussed in Part III when the Ten Commandments are taken up.

Having seen the degrees among sins, let us see how the priest ought to conduct himself concerning the imposition of penance. Concerning this, know that the consensus of the doctors holds that all penances are arbitrary, that is, they are to be assigned at the discretion of the priest, taking into consideration the quality and quantity of the crimes, as well as the person, dignity, office, poverty, weakness or debility, physical constitution, custom, society, tears, devotion, religion, and quality of time, and all the circumstances mentioned above.

And note that for the imposition of penances, it is good to know the penitential cases which I Iostiensis gives in his *Summa* entitled "On Penance," where he says that the one who does not know these cases is not worthy to have the name of priest.[207] And the priest ought to declare to the confessing sinner, and he ought to be discerning about this since he can moderate the penance as to quality and thus he can say for the benefit of any sinner, "You ought to do such and such a penance, but perhaps your lifetime will not suffice; therefore I give you such and such a penance. For all your sins I grant to you that indulgences held will avail for you, and I enjoin on you as penance all the good things which you will do and the evils which you will endure for the love of God." Hence Pope Leo, "The durations of repentance, that is, of penances, are to be established by your judgment with habitual moderation, to the degree that the converts, that is, the souls of the penitents you examine, are devout." Again in the 8th synod, it was given over to the judg-

207. Hostiensis, *Summa aurea*, Bk V, "De penitentiis & remissionibus," 60.

ment of those who preside [to decide] how long or in what way those who err ought to repent (C.26 q.7 c.2 and c.8). Jerome says the same thing (D.1 de pen. c.86), "The measure, namely, the time of penance, ought to be left to the decision of the priest."

But so that simple priests especially may know more particularly how to proceed with the imposition of penances, know that according to the rules seven years of penance should be imposed for perjury, adultery, fornication, voluntary homicide, and other capital crimes. This is for two reasons. One is because God commanded Miriam, the sister of Moses and Aaron, who was struck with leprosy, meaning the leprosy of any mortal sin, to remain outside the camp for seven days, and after her cleansing to return to the camp.[208] This reason is given in C.33 q.2 c.11. According to this, by a day we understand a year, according to the word of the Lord saying through the prophet, "One day for each year, I have given to you."[209] The other reason is that just as a sinner through mortal sin loses the sevenfold grace of the Holy Spirit, so through a seven-year penance, he may regain it. Note that although it is said that seven years' penance is to be imposed for such crimes, nevertheless more or less severe penances ought to be imposed to the degree that greater or lesser crimes demand, taking other circumstances into account, as will appear in what follows.

There are many cases in which, on account of the dignity of the sinner or the enormity of the sin, a greater penance is to be imposed; or in some cases, a lesser one. For if a priest should commit fornication, he ought to do penance for ten years, according to the pattern handed down in D.82 c.5. And some understand this to mean for simple fornication. But others understand this, perhaps better, for incest or adultery, and for one who knew a blood or affine relative. Likewise if a priest knew his spiritual daughter whom he had baptized or raised from the holy font, or whose confession he had heard, or whom he had held in confirmation, he ought to do penance for twelve years and be deposed. And also she ought

208. Numbers 12:13
209. Ezekiel 4:6

to leave her goods to the poor and serve God in a monastery until her death (C.30 q.1 c.9). Likewise one who knew a nun ought to do penance for ten years, and she likewise, according to the pattern given in C.27 q.1 c.26, 27. One who kills his mother ought to do penance for ten years with adequate severity according to the pattern given in C.33 q.2 c.15. Still, a greater penance should be imposed on one who kills his wife (C.33 q.2 c.8).

Note also that for parents in whose beds children are found dead, if the one by whose fault it happened is to be forgiven, he ought to be persuaded to enter a monastery in the same bishopric where he may deplore his sin in perpetual penance. But if he cannot be persuaded to do this on account of the frailty of the flesh, permission to remain married is to be given to him and a heavy penance is to be imposed on him while he remains in the world. Likewise, one ought not to be persuaded to enter a monastery in two other cases, one of which is when the other spouse lives, unless perhaps the spouse likewise wants to enter. The other case is if one has young children, from whom one cannot depart, unless someone who fears God and is above suspicion would bring them up. But if it happened without one's knowing it, for instance if one negligently put the child in bed with oneself, and in the morning found it dead, one ought, as some doctors say, to do penance for three years, one of which should be on bread and water (X 5.10.2,3 and C.3 q.5 c.20).

For accidental homicide, five years penance is to be imposed when guilt precedes the accident, otherwise, nothing, except perhaps as a warning (D.50 c.42 and the two following chapters). And I think the judgment is the same for unavoidable homicide. This topic will be considered in Part III on the Ten Commandments.

Concerning the vice of sodomy, Augustine makes clear how detestable it is, saying that it is a greater crime by far than knowing one's mother.[210] And this is clear through the punishment inflicted on the Sodomites who perished in fire and sulfur sent from

---

210. C.32 q.7 c.11

heaven.[211] This sin also cries out especially to God for vengeance. Hence in Genesis the Lord says, "The outcry from Sodom and Gomorrah has reached me,"[212] because, as Augustine says, "the fellowship which ought to exist between us and God is violated by this sin, since that very nature, whose author he is, is polluted by perversity of lust" (C.32 q.7 c.13). Also concerning this sin, Augustine says, "God, seeing in human nature heinous deeds against nature being committed, almost did not become incarnate, and endless evils can be named from this heinous crime. It is indeed so much of a curse, that not only the act but even uttering or naming it pollutes the mouth of the speaker and the ears of the hearers in some way." And the Spanish think about this badly. For children in cradles and also women disregarding womanly shame mix this heinous and vile word, *castella,* in with all their words. Hence I believe that for this most heinous crime the heaviest penance should be enjoined.

Many other crimes are given in various chapters in the body of the decretals for which a penance greater than seven years is to be imposed, which I omit here because such crimes, by law and custom, are reserved to the judgment of bishops, who I believe know such laws better than I do.

And nevertheless, I believe all penances today without exception are arbitrary, that is, assessed at the judgment of the priest, weighing the contrition and condition of the sinners and all other circumstances. It is possible that the one confessing could have so much contrition that for a very grave sin a moderate penance or rather almost nothing should be imposed. The Lord Pope Clement IV did this. One day, while riding through Rome, a certain woman, who came from remote parts, came to him carrying a little boy in her arms, and in a loud voice with great tears, cried, "Holy Father, have mercy on me, a sinner, and give me penance, for I had my son whom I carry here by my son." And the pope, in front of all, absolved her from the sin, and imposed on her the

211. Genesis 19:24
212. Genesis 18:20–21

penance that she should fast six days a year on bread and water. And the woman, departing and mulling over the gravity of the sin and the smallness of the penance believed that the pope had not understood her well. In the morning she approached the pope and confessed as before, and the pope absolved her, imposing on her the penance that she should say three Our Fathers. And so the woman, again departing and mulling over the sin and its penance as before, again returned to the pope, and in front of all, confessed as she had done before. The pope absolved her, imposing on her the penance that she should say one Our Father. And when the pope was asked why he had imposed such a light penance, the pope replied that she grew more in contrition, sorrow, and shame by publicly confessing her sin than if she had fasted all the days of her life on bread and water. In keeping with this example, therefore, the confessor, when imposing penance, ought to pay attention to the contrition, sorrow, and shame of the one confessing, and as he sees more or less contrition he ought to impose more or less penance.

Yet note that for a sin where a report ought to be made, as in simony, or restitution made, as in theft, pillage, depredation, arson, usury, fraud, deceitful business, and gambling, according to the distinction noted above [in the first consideration on almsgiving], the penance ought to be imposed that one should renounce or restore, if one can. Or, if one cannot, let him have the intention to restore and sorrow that he cannot, and let him promise that if God gives the wherewithal, he will make restitution. Otherwise he should not be absolved, nor have penance imposed on him.

Note that the priest always ought to impose penance through the contrary corresponding to the sin itself, such as prayer for the proud, alms for the greedy, fasting for the lustful, and if it seems expedient, pilgrimage or a change of location, so that one may chastise the flesh and be restrained from delight as a result of remembering the deed, or seeing the person with whom or the place in which one sinned and the sin was perpetrated (D.81 c.9; C.15 q.1 c.4).

Note especially that the priest ought to beware lest he impose a penance on a servant that puts him at a disadvantage with his lord, or on a disciple that puts him at a disadvantage with his master, or vice versa. And even more especially let him beware concerning husbands and wives that he not impose such a penance on one by which the other can figure out the spouse's sin.

But suppose someone confesses his sins and says he repents. Yet he does not want to submit to the burden of penance, saying he is delicate, ill or poorly constituted, or the like. What should be done with him? I say that if he says he repents of his sins and intends to abstain from further sins, when he claims illness or frailty or recoils from the severity of satisfaction, the priest ought to induce him to have a spirit ready for any satisfaction by showing him the magnitude of his sins, and what and how many good things he lost on account of them, all of which he would regain through penance, and by showing what and how much Christ suffered for our sins who nevertheless was most delicate, and what and how much the saints, martyrs, and holy virgins suffered although tender and delicate and free from sin. Let the priest add, "This much penance is owed for all the sins you have committed," and the priest ought to show him many such things. And if he cannot induce him to do penance by all these things, let him impose on him such as he truly believes the penitent is able to bear. And to such a practice the example of Christ invites us who never imposed a greater penance than "Go and sin no more."[213] Hence John Chrysostom on the text, "They tie on heavy burdens, etc.,"[214] says, "If we err by imposing too little penance, is this not better by reason of the mercy of God than to overcome the penitent with too much cruelty?" (C.26 q.7 c.12). Augustine says, "If the priest cannot rejoice over the complete purgation of the sinner, let him at least rejoice because he is liberated from hell and send him to purgatory." From which it is clear that if penance is not adequate, it will be completed in purgatory.

Referring to what was said above which we want to mark dili-

213. John 8:11
214. Matthew 23:4

gently, suppose again that someone confesses his sins, and truly wants to abstain from one of them, but not from another. Should he be admitted to penance? I say that the priest ought to hear and receive his confession. Even so, he ought not to absolve him, but give salutary counsel concerning the sins confessed to him. He can offer and advise that the one confessing do some penance for his sins, and influence him to his advantage as much as he can. And all the good deeds which he does on the advice of the priest, to the degree that they are unformed, that is, done without charity, although they do not serve him directly for obtaining eternal life, nevertheless they avail for four things, or for some of them. First, for the punishment of the last judgment to be undergone more tolerably (D.3 de pen. c.49). Second, to obtain temporal prosperity (D.3 de pen. c.47; C.22 q.2 c.20). Third, so that his heart may be illuminated for penance (D.5 de pen. c.6 at the end). Fourth, because the devil cannot harm him, as is clear in the Jew about whom Gregory tells in *The Dialogues* that because he signed himself with the sign of the cross, demons were not able to harm him.[215]

From what has been said, it is clear that in order for penance to be satisfying and meritorious, it is necessary that it be done in charity, that is, that the one who does it be without mortal sin. But suppose penance was enjoined on someone and before he completes his penance, he falls into mortal sin, and while in sin he completes his enjoined penance. Afterward, he returns to a state of grace. Does this penance avail or is he obligated to repeat it? To this, St. Thomas says in his fourth book that there are some satisfactory works whose effect remains after they are done, as after alms are given, the effect still remains, namely, the diminution of the temporal substance of the giver. Likewise after someone has fasted, the effect of the fast still remains, which is the bodily weakness of the one fasting.[216] And even though these were done in mortal sin, it is not necessary to repeat them. There are other

---

215. Gregory I, *Dialogorum Libri*, Bk III, c. 7 (PL 77:229–32).
216. Aquinas, *Scriptum super Sententiis*, Bk IV, d. 15, q. 1, a. 3.

satisfactory works which after they are done, nothing remains of them, like prayer. And therefore, if they are done in mortal sin, it is necessary to repeat them. Hence if the penance enjoined on someone was to say one hundred Our Fathers, if he says them while in mortal sin, he would not complete his penance. Rather it would be necessary that he repeat his penance while living in grace. It is otherwise with almsgiving and fasting, as has been said. Concerning this, know that works done in charity are put to death through subsequent mortal sin, and are brought to life later after true penance, if it follows. But those things which never were alive, that is, those things which were done in mortal sin, never can be brought to life. Hence the verse:

> *Illa reviviscunt que mortificata fuerunt.*
> *Sed non reviviscunt que mortua facta fuerunt.*

> Those things come back to life which were put to death;
> But not those things which were made dead.

CHAPTER 6: Whether one can satisfy for another

Now it remains to see whether one can satisfy for another. Concerning this, note that the one for whom another satisfies is either living or dead. If he is living, either he can satisfy for himself or he cannot. If he can, I say that the one cannot satisfy for the other. And the reason that persuades me of this is this: The equity of justice demands that the one who sinned should satisfy and this is if he can. But this one sinned and is able to satisfy for himself, therefore it is necessary that he should satisfy. But if he cannot satisfy for himself, then I say that another can satisfy for him. But many things are required for this, some on the part of the one who satisfies, some on the part of the one for whom he satisfies, some on the part of both, some on the part of the work of satisfaction. On the part of the one who satisfies, relationship is required, namely, that he who satisfies be obligated by a blood relationship to him for whom he satisfies. So I believe that if a father were powerless to satisfy, with the other conditions being met, his son could satisfy for him. And the reason is that the father and the son are almost one person. And on the part of the one for whom he satisfies, necessity is required, namely, that he needs it, and also impossibility, namely, that he is not able to satisfy for himself. On the part of both, charity is required, namely, that both be in charity because charity is the root of merit, and without this no work is satisfactory. And on the part of the work of satisfaction, it is required that the one who satisfies for another should satisfy more than he for whom he satisfies. For instance, if the one for whom he satisfies were obligated to fast six days, it would be necessary that he who satisfies for him fast longer. I believe also that it is necessary that it be done on the authority of a superior.

But if the one for whom he satisfies is dead, either he is in paradise, and then he does not need anyone to satisfy for him, because as Augustine says, "He does injury to the martyr who prays for the martyr," which is to be understood to mean anyone living in paradise, as is said expressly in X 3.41.6, or he is in hell, and then, according to the opinion of all the theologians, nothing done for him profits him, because in hell there is no redemption. Or, he is in purgatory, and then a living person can satisfy for him. And so says Augustine in the book *On the Care of the Dead* where he says, "Let us not reckon that anything reaches the dead for whom we care, except what may be implored for them by masses, or alms, or prayers of suffrage" (C.13 q.2 c.19).[217] And Gregory says, "The souls of the dead are released in four ways: by priestly offerings or the prayers of the saints or alms of the beloved living or fasts of relatives."[218]

Although, many things should be said about penance, nevertheless let these which have been said suffice for the sake of brevity. I ask for kindness from the reader for the imperfection of this work, so that when he sees what needs to be corrected and added, he may correct and add, not with a malicious spirit, but in a friendly way.

Here ends the second principal part of this book.

217. Augustine, *De cura pro mortuis*, c. 22 (PL 40:609).
218. C.13 q.2 c.22

PART III: BASIC CATECHESIS

Here begins the third part about the articles of the faith and those things which pertain to the teaching of the people.

Because our Lord and master Jesus Christ was about to ascend from the world to the Father, he said, instructing his disciples how to conduct themselves toward the faithful whom he had redeemed with his blood, "Go into the whole world and teach all nations."[1] With these words, he instructed and admonished the leaders of churches, the disciples' successors, that they should teach his salvific doctrine to their subordinates. This was beautifully figured in the old law, where it is read that on the breastplate of judgment which the priest wore on his chest, doctrine and truth were sculpted.[2] By this, it is given to be understood that the angelic priests ought to bear in themselves the doctrine of truth and announce it to their subordinates. Otherwise they incur a judgment of cursing, as the Lord threatens them through Isaiah saying, "Woe to you mute dogs unwilling to bark!"[3] Rightly, therefore, the church leader is called a dog, because by the barking of preaching and evangelical doctrine he ought to keep wolves, that is, demons, away from the flock of the Lord and arouse souls sleeping in sin. But he is made mute when he becomes listless through idleness or remains silent out of ignorance. Therefore he deserves to be reproved by the Lord because he ought to labor especially with his mouth, and wisely and carefully keep watch over his soul, lest he be ignorant of divine knowledge. Rather he is obligated to know those things that he should know in order rightly to perform his

1. Matthew 28:19   2. Exodus 28:30
3. Isaiah 56:10

office and teach the people committed to him. And this extends at least to the things the people ought to know. For present purposes, these can be reduced to five things, namely, what is to be believed, what is to be asked, what is to be done, what is to be fled, and what is to be hoped for. Therefore the church leader ought to teach those under him what is to be believed, what is to be asked, what is to be done, what is to be fled, and what is to be hoped for. The first is contained in the articles of faith; the second in the petitions of the Lord's Prayer; the third and fourth in the commandments of the Decalogue; the fifth in the gifts of the glory of paradise. And these things are to be treated in this third part. And accordingly, this third part is divided into four chapters. Chapter 1 will be about the articles of faith; the second about the petitions of the Lord's Prayer; the third about the Ten Commandments; the fourth about the gifts of the blessed.

CHAPTER 1: On the articles of the faith

By the testimony of the Apostle, "without faith it is impossible to please God."[4] Indeed faith is the foundation of all good works without which every building built will perish and fall. But this faith is most fully contained in the articles of faith, and the articles are contained in the creed. Note, therefore, that there are four creeds which, although they vary in words, yet are one in sense and meaning.

The first is called the Apostles' Creed, namely, "I believe" [credo], which is said during compline and prime. It is called the Apostles' Creed because the apostles, having received the grace of the Holy Spirit, composed it. And so it is called "the symbol" [symbolum] from "one at a time" [singulis] and "choice bit" [bolus] because each one of them offered his own bit. Hence St. Peter began by saying, "I believe in God the Father almighty, Creator, etc." And the other apostles followed in turn.

4. Hebrews 11:6

The second creed is called the Nicene Creed because the holy fathers at the Nicene Synod composed it. And it is sung in mass, as was said in Part I in the tract on the eucharist, chapter 10.

The third is called the Athanasian Creed because St. Athanasius composed it himself. And it, namely, "Whoever wishes to be saved," is said in the first service of the day.

The fourth can be called the Innocentian or Lateran Creed because it was composed under Innocent [III] at the Lateran Council. And it is given in Clem. 1.1.un.

And as the whole truth of doctrine and Christian faith is comprehended in four gospels, so all the articles of faith are contained in four creeds. And as the same doctrine is in each of the four gospels, so there is one meaning and faith in each of the four creeds, so that according to the vision of Ezekiel, "the wheel is within a wheel."[5] The topic, therefore, of these four creeds is the articles of the faith, which are said by some to be twelve and by others fourteen. Those who say there are twelve divide them according to the number of the twelve apostles, who, as has been said, composed the creed and preached the catholic faith and founded the church. Those who say there are fourteen divide them according to their subject matter. Since the matter with which the articles of faith deal is the divinity and the humanity by which our Lord Jesus Christ is true God and true man, therefore, according to those people, there are seven articles pertaining to the divinity and seven pertaining to the humanity. The articles pertaining to the divinity are divided this way: one considers the essence, three consider the persons, and three consider the works of the persons.

The article which considers the essence is to believe in God as three and one, namely, one in essence and three in persons. And against this article erred Mani who posited two gods, one good and the other evil. And to remove this error, since in the Apostles' Creed it only says "I believe in God," in the Nicene Creed "in one God" was added. And concerning this article in the Athanasian

5. Ezekiel 1:16

Creed it says, "And this is the catholic faith, that we worship one God in trinity and trinity in unity," as if to say, "We believe God to be one in essence, and triune in persons."

And the articles pertaining to the persons are three. The first is to believe in the person of the Father. And concerning this article it is said in both creeds, "Father almighty," so that the Father is the first person in the Trinity, not by any priority of nature or time, but only by priority of origin. This is because the person of the Father originated from nothing, but the other persons originated from him. And this is touched on in the Athanasian Creed when it is says, "The Father was made from no one, nor was he created or begotten."

The second article of these that pertain to the persons is to believe in the person of the Son. And concerning this it is said in both creeds, "And in Jesus Christ his only Son our Lord," so that we ought to believe that the person of the Son was not made or created, but was begotten by the Father. And this is touched on in the Athanasian Creed when it says, "The Son is from the Father only, not made, not created, but begotten." Against this article erred Arius who said that the Son of God was created and is less than the Father. Therefore against this error of Arius, it was added in the Nicene Creed, "God from God, light from light, true God from true God, begotten not made." Indeed, although Christ is less than the Father in as much as he is a man, in as much as he is God he is equal to the Father. Thus Athanasius says, "Equal to the Father according to divinity, less than the Father according to humanity." Indeed there were some heretics called Ambrites who said the Son was begotten of the Father in time, and was not from eternity; against this error it was added in the Nicene Creed, "And was begotten of the Father before all worlds."[6]

The third article of those which pertain to the persons is to believe in the person of the Holy Spirit. And concerning this article, it says in the Apostles' Creed, "I believe in the Holy Spirit," so that

6. The reference here is to the Athanasian Creed.

we ought to believe the Holy Spirit to be truly God, proceeding from the Father and the Son. Thus says Athanasius, "The Holy Spirit is from the Father and the Son, not made or created or begotten but proceeding." Against this article the Greeks err, saying the Holy Spirit proceeds from the Father alone. And against their error, the Roman church added in the Nicene Creed, "who proceeds from the Father and the Son." And there were other heretics who said the Holy Spirit was a creature and not God; hence against their error it was added in the Nicene Creed, "who with the Father and the Son together is worshiped and glorified." For no creature ought to be worshipped with a worship equal to that of God.

Against these three articles concerning the trinity of persons erred Sabellius who posited the confusion of persons, saying that the same person was sometimes the Father, sometimes the Son, sometimes the Holy Spirit. Against which error Athanasius says, "For there is one person of the Father, another of the Son, another of the Holy Spirit." Hence know that one person is another with respect to another, nevertheless is not other. Hence this is true: the Father is another [alius] with respect to the Son; but this is heretical and false: the Father is other [aliud] than the Son, because this word "another" [alius], which is masculine, names diversity in persons, but this word "other" [aliud], which is neuter, names diversity in essence.

The other three articles pertain to the works of the Trinity. Some of these works pertain to the work of nature, namely, to the work of creation. And concerning this, there is one article which says that we ought to believe God to be the creator of all creatures. And concerning this article, it says in the Apostles' Creed, "creator of heaven and earth." Against this article erred Mani who said that the good god created good invisible things, but the bad god created visible things. Hence against his error it was added in the Nicene Creed, "all things visible and invisible." Nevertheless, note that in the Apostles' Creed "creator" is said, but in the Nicene Creed "maker" is said. And there is a difference between "to create" and "to make." For "to create" is to produce something out of nothing, but "to make" is to produce something out of something else. Therefore, because in the beginning God created angels and all matter, both celestial and terrestrial, from which he later made other things, he is called "creator." But, because later, out of that matter he made all other creatures, he is called "maker."

And some works of God pertain to the work of grace, namely, to the work of justification. And concerning this, there is one article by which we ought to believe that by grace the faithful are spiritually united and sins are forgiven the faithful who are united in the unity of the church and the catholic faith. And concerning this, it says in the Apostles' Creed, "the holy catholic," that is, universal, "church, the communion of saints, the forgiveness of sins." And in this article, all the sacraments of the church are comprehended. And whatever the most holy Roman church instructs and teaches about baptism and eucharist and the other sacraments of the church, in which the faithful of the church in turn participate and communicate and through which forgiveness of sins is accomplished, is to be believed. Against this article erred Pelagius who posited that through the act of free will alone, without the grace of God, the forgiveness of sins could be achieved. Also against this article erred the Jacobites, Nicolatians, Jovinians, Waldensians, and universally all heretics, Jews, Saracens, Gentiles, pagans, and whoever believes otherwise than the holy Roman church about baptism, eucharist, and the other sacraments. Also against this article err especially the Greeks and all other schismatics who deny the most holy Roman church to be the head and teacher of all the churches. Hence against this error was added in the Nicene Creed "one apostolic church." Also against the error of Donatus, who posited the repetition of baptism, was added in the Nicene Creed, "I confess one baptism, etc."

Some of the works of God also pertain to the work of glory, namely, to the work of glorification. And concerning this there is one article, namely, that we believe all will be resurrected by the power of God, both the good and the bad; and the good will be rewarded, but the bad punished. And concerning this article, it says in the Apostles' Creed, "the resurrection of the body and life everlasting." And in the Nicene Creed, "And I look for the resurrection of the dead and the life of the world to come." Against this article erred the Sadducees who denied a future resurrection. Also against this article erred Plato who posited resurrection to be natural and thus done by the power of nature, namely, at the end of the great year which will be completed, as he said, in 36,000 years. Also against this article erred Origen who posited that the bad ones in hell are punished only until the day of judgment. Hence against those errors, it says in the Athanasian Creed, "at whose coming," meaning, by whose power, against the error of Plato; "all men will rise with their bodies," against the error of the Sadducees; "and they shall give an account of their own deeds, and those who have done good will go to eternal life, but truly those who have done evil to eternal fire," against the error of Origen.

These, therefore, are the seven articles pertaining to the divinity. The other seven pertain to the humanity. The first concerns the conception of the Son, namely, to believe that the Son of God was conceived in the uterus of his mother, the Blessed Virgin Mary, by the power of the Holy Spirit. And concerning this it says in the Apostles' Creed, "who was conceived by the Holy Spirit." And in the Nicene Creed, "who for us men and for our salvation came down from heaven and was incarnate by the Holy Spirit." Against this article Mani erred, saying that the Son of God had not assumed true, but rather phantom, flesh. And against this error it says in the Athanasian Creed, "perfect God, perfect man, subsisting of a rational soul and human flesh."

The second article of those pertaining to the humanity concerns the nativity of Christ, namely, to believe that the Son of God was born of the Father from eternity and born of the Virgin Mary in time, who existed as a virgin before giving birth, while giving birth and after giving birth. And concerning this article, it is said in both creeds, "born of the Virgin Mary." Against this article the perfidious Jews err, denying that the Son of God was born of the Virgin Mary. Also against this article that heinous Jovinian erred, saying that although the Blessed Virgin conceived, nevertheless, she was corrupted in giving birth. And against this error it is said, "born of the Virgin Mary."

The third article concerns the passion of Christ, namely, that we believe the Son of God, for our salvation, suffered, was crucified, died, and was buried, and this is with respect to his human nature because the divine nature suffered nothing. And concerning this article it says in both creeds, "suffered under Pontius Pilate, was crucified, died, and was buried." Against this article erred the extremely foul Muhammad, who, although he says in one of his writings that Christ was born of the Virgin Mary, nevertheless, denies that Christ suffered or was crucified, but another did so in his place. Against this article Origen erred, saying that Christ suffered not only for men, but even for the demons in the air when he ascended into heaven. And against this error, it says in the Nicene Creed, "who for us men and for our salvation came down from heaven."

The fourth article pertaining to the humanity concerns the descent into hell, namely, that we believe that the soul of Christ, which in death was separated from his body, yet [remained] united to his divinity (and with the body remaining in the tomb also united to divinity), descended to the limbo of the holy fathers, which is a certain part of hell, and liberated from there the holy fathers who died in faith that Christ would become incarnate and in charity, leaving sinners damned in hell. Concerning this article, it says in both creeds, "he descended into hell."

The fifth article concerns the resurrection, namely, that we believe the Son of God to have been resurrected from the dead on the third day, according to what the writings of the prophets predicted. And concerning this article it says in the Nicene Creed, "on the third day he rose from the dead." Here note that Christ was in the tomb forty hours, but it says that he was there three days, which according to Augustine is to be understood through synecdoche, so that part of a day is given for the whole day. Hence

Christ himself was there through the last part of Friday, because at the end of that day he was put in the tomb, and was there through the whole Sabbath day, and through the first part of the Lord's day, because he arose at dawn.

The sixth article concerns the ascent to heaven, namely, that we believe that forty days after his resurrection, Christ ascended to heaven with a great retinue of angels and the souls of the holy fathers which he had drawn out from hell. And concerning this article, it is found in both creeds, "He ascended into heaven and is seated at the right hand of God the Father almighty."

The seventh article concerns his coming in judgment, namely, to believe that at the end of the world, Christ will appear in human form with great strength and power in the Valley of Jehosaphat, and there he will judge the good and the bad. And concerning this article it says in both creeds, "from thence he shall come to judge the living and the dead."

These, therefore, are the fourteen articles, of which seven pertain to the divinity and seven to the humanity. And priests ought to teach these articles to their subordinates and especially those that pertain to the humanity, and most especially those about things which the church solemnizes, such as the article on the conception, concerning which the feast of the Annunciation to Blessed Mary is celebrated; and the article on the nativity, concerning which the feast of Christmas is celebrated; and the article on the passion, concerning which the feast of Good Friday is celebrated; and the article on the resurrection, concerning which the feast of Easter is celebrated; and the article on the ascension, concerning which the feast of the Ascension of the Lord is celebrated. And those articles, along with the article on the coming in judgment, every Christian, after arriving at the age of discretion, is obligated to know explicitly. And concerning these articles pertaining to the humanity, there is a verse:

Nascitur abluitur patitur descendit ad ima,
Surgit et ascendit, veniet discernere cuncta.

He was born, washed, suffered, descended to the depths,
He arose and ascended, he will come to separate all.

This is the catholic faith which I believe in my heart and confess with my mouth, in which faith I want to live and die, testifying that I believe in all things as the most holy Roman church believes. And if I have not said something well, I retract the whole, so that it may not be taken as well spoken.

CHAPTER 2: On the petitions of the Lord's Prayer

Delivering the mode and form for praying, the Savior said in Matthew 6 and Luke 12, "When you pray say, Our Father who art in heaven, etc."[7] Here note that this prayer surpasses all other prayers in three ways. First, by reason of the teacher who composed it, who was Christ, true God and true man, "in whom all the treasures of wisdom and the knowledge of God are hidden."[8] Therefore, as much as the teacher who composed this prayer surpasses all other teachers, so much does this prayer surpass all other prayers. Hence this prayer is called the Lord's Prayer, because the sovereign Lord composed and arranged it. Second, it surpasses all other prayers by reason of form. Indeed it is a most pleasing and very short prayer so that no one can excuse himself and say that it gives rise to boredom or aversion because of its long-windedness. And although it is short in words, it is nevertheless very profound in meaning and most effective in gaining results. Hence the Wise One says concerning it, "A short prayer penetrates the heavens." Third, it surpasses all other prayers by reason of the material it covers, for in it is contained everything necessary both for his life and the next.

Hence note that in this prayer the Savior proceeds thus: first he teaches us to seek to gain God's favor, second he teaches us the mode and form for praying. The first he does when he says,

7. Matthew 6:9–15; Luke 11:2–4; Guido and the liturgy follow Matthew's version more closely.
8. Colossians 2:3

"Our Father, etc." The second he does when he says, "Thy king-dom come, etc." Concerning the first, he does two things. First he teaches us to seek to gain God's favor. Second he teaches us to seek to gain the efficacy of the prayer where he says, "Hallowed be thy name, etc." Therefore let us say, "Our Father who art in heaven."

First, we confess God to be the origin of all things, because he is "Father." Second we set forth our privilege, because we say "our." Third, we name his own name, because we say "who art." Fourth we assign a certain home to him, because we say "in heav-en." Let us therefore say, "Our Father, who art in heaven."

Here know that according to what Eberhard says, "Father" may be taken in five ways. In the first way, God is called Father by rea-son of care, second by reason of birth, third by reason of age, fourth by reason of honor, fifth by reason of creation.[9] God is Father in all these five ways. First, by reason of care. Thus Paul the Apostle asserts, saying, "Cast all your cares on God, for he cares for everyone."[10] And Christ himself says in Matthew, "Don't be anxious, saying, what shall we eat or what shall we drink or with what shall we be clothed? For your heavenly Father knows that you need all these things."[11] Second, God is Father of all by reason of birth. Hence the Apostle says concerning him, "By his own will he produced us through the Word of truth, so that we might be a kind of beginning among his creatures."[12] Hence any-one can say what the psalmist says, "The Lord said to me, you are my son, today I have begotten you."[13] And God says about anyone in 2 Kings, "I will be as a Father to him and he will be as a son to me."[14] Third, God is Father by reason of age and antiquity. Hence Daniel says concerning him, "The ancient of days sat, and the books," namely, of conscience, "were open before him."[15] Hence we all can say what the Apostle says, "We have one father, God."[16]

9. Eberhard of Béthune, *Graecismus*, c. 9.
10. 1 Peter 5:7
11. Matthew 6:31–32
12. James 1:18
13. Psalm 2:7
14. 2 Samuel 7:14
15. Daniel 7:9–10
16. John 8:41

Fourth, God is Father of all by reason of honor, because we ought to honor God with a special honor and reverence which is called "worship" by the doctors. This honor ought not to be shown to any creature, nor is it proper. Hence, anyone can say what is said in Matthew, "I confess you as Lord God, Father of heaven and earth,"[17] since here to confess is the same as to praise or to honor. Fifth, God is Father of all by reason of creation. Hence Moses, "Is he himself not your father, who has possessed you, and made you, and created you?"[18]

Hence, because we say "Father," we have confidence in him that we will obtain what we ask in this prayer. Hence we can assert thus: The Father gives to the Son that which he asks from him, if that which is requested is just and necessary for the Son. But God is the Father of all and that which we ask in this prayer is most just and truly necessary for us. So we have confidence that God will give all things to us. And this reasoning is founded on the word of the Savior in Luke, where it is said, "If you who are evil know how to give good things to your children, how much more the heavenly Father will give a spirit of goodness to those who ask him."[19] It is as if he says that indeed he will give.

Second, in this prayer we set forth our privilege, when we say "our." Here note that although it was said above that God is the Father of all in these five ways, yet he is especially father to us who are regenerated in the water of baptism. Hence we who are baptized and regenerated in Christ can say, "our Father," because we are more mercifully liberated, more specifically adopted, more nobly nourished, and more profitably taught by him. I say, therefore, that God is especially our Father, because we Christians are more mercifully redeemed and liberated by him. Hence we can say to God what is said in the Apocalypse, "God, you have redeemed us by your blood."[20] About this redemption St. Peter says, "You have not been redeemed with corruptible gold or silver from your vain ways, but with the precious blood of the immaculate lamb our

17. Matthew 11:25
19. Luke 11:13

18. Deuteronomy 32:6
20. Revelation 5:9

Lord Jesus Christ."²¹ Second, I say that God is especially our Father, because we Christians are specifically adopted by him. And concerning this, the Apostle says, "God sent the spirit of his Son into our hearts in whom we cry, Abba Father,"²² so that we may receive adoption as sons of God. Third, I say that God is especially our Father, because we Christians are more nobly nourished by him. Indeed in the sacrament of the eucharist, God feeds us with the body and blood of Christ. Thus Jesus himself says in John, "My flesh is true food, and my blood is true drink."²³ About this food the Psalmist says, "Man ate the bread of angels."²⁴ Concerning this bread Christ says, "Whoever eats of this bread will live forever."²⁵ Hence the church, recognizing the benefit, breaking forth in a voice of gratitude, says, "O Lord, how sweet is your spirit, you who, that you might show your sweetness to your children, have given the bread of heaven, filling the humble hungry you fill with good things, but sending the disdainful rich away empty."²⁶ Fourth, I say that God is especially our father because we Christians are more profitably taught by him, and this takes place through evangelical teaching, which alone is salvific and profitable teaching. And David asked for this teaching when he said, "Teach me goodness and discipline and knowledge."²⁷ About this teaching, the Wise One says, "My son, listen to the teaching of your father."²⁸

And because we say, "Our Father," we may have confidence that what we ask from God in this prayer, he will give to us. So we assert thus: The original draws to itself the less original and the accessory (VI 3.21.un), but God gave himself to us, and therefore we call him ours, and in his sight all things are accessory. Therefore we are certain that all these things will be given to us by God. And

21. 1 Peter 1:18   22. Galatians 4:6
23. John 6:56   24. Psalm 77:25
25. John 6:59
26. This is the gospel antiphon used during second vespers in the celebration of the feast of Corpus Christi, drawing on Wisdom 12:1, Wisdom 16:20, and Luke 1:53.
27. Psalm 118:6
28. Proverbs 1:8

this reasoning is founded on the word of the Apostle, saying in the Epistle to the Romans, "If God is for us, who can be against us, who did not spare even his own son, but handed him over for all of us. Will he not also give us all things with him?"[29] It is as if he answers, "Indeed!"

Third, in this prayer we name God's own name when we say "who art." About this, know that although, according to the doctors, in this life we may not know the proper name of God, yet among all the other names which are spoken of God, this name "who art" is the most proper to him, which is clear from this: When Moses was asking how he should answer the sons of Israel if they should ask what God's proper name was, God said, "speak thus to the children of Israel, 'He who is' sent me to you."[30] We therefore call God "who art," because God is the sure being, never failing but completing all things, the highest goodness sufficing for all, the pure truth teaching all, the true charity refreshing all. I say that we call God "who art," because he is the sure being, never failing. Hence he says of himself in Exodus, "I am who I am."[31] And the psalmist says, "from ages past, even to all ages, you are."[32] Second we call God "who art," because God is the highest goodness sufficing for all. Hence God said to one calling him good, "No one is good but God alone."[33] And concerning him the Psalm said, "You are good, so in your goodness teach me your justifications."[34] And the Apostle says, "Our sufficiency is from God."[35] Third we call God "who art" because God is the pure truth, teaching all. Hence Christ says in John, "I am the way, the truth and the life."[36] And in Matthew, "Teacher we know that you are truthful, and teach the way of God in truth."[37] Fourth, we call God "who art" because he is the true charity, refreshing all. Hence in the first letter of John, "God is love. And he who abides in love, abides in God, and God in him."[38] And he himself says in Mat-

29. Romans 8:31–32

31. Exodus 3:14

33. Mark 10:18; Luke 18:19

35. 2 Corinthians 3:5

37. Matthew 22:16

30. Exodus 3:13–14

32. Psalm 89:2

34. Psalm 118:68

36. John 14:6

38. 1 John 4:16

thew, "Come to me all who labor and are heavily burdened and I will refresh you."[39]

Therefore by saying "who art," we have confidence that God who is the sure being will fail no one, but will bring him to completion; because he is the highest goodness, he will suffice for all; because he is the pure truth, he will teach all; because he is the true charity, he will refresh all.

Fourth, I say that in this prayer, in seeking to gain God's favor, we assign a certain home to him, when we say, "in heaven." Concerning which, note that for present purposes, heaven is fourfold, because heaven is supernatural, material, spiritual, and intellectual. Supernatural heaven is the Trinity itself. And concerning this heaven it is said in Genesis, "Take in," that is, look to, "heaven," that is, the Trinity, "and number the stars," that is, its perfections, "if you can."[40] For present purposes, material heaven is the celestial empyrean, concerning which it says in Genesis, "In the beginning God created heaven and earth."[41] When heaven is described as "starry" or "holy" it means the celestial empyrean. Spiritual heaven is the devout soul, concerning which it says in the Psalm, "The Lord's throne is in heaven."[42] Intellectual heaven is the angelic nature, concerning which it says in the same place, "The heavens are made firm by the word of the Lord,"[43] that is, the angels are confirmed in good. And God is in all of these heavens, because in the first heaven, that is, in the Trinity, he is undivided in essence. In the second heaven, namely, in the empyrean, he is clearly seen in glory. In the third heaven, that is, in the devout soul, he is living through grace. In the fourth heaven, that is, in the angelic nature, he himself is lifting it up through excellence. About the first, it is said in the first letter of John, "Three are those who give testimony in heaven, the Father, the Word, and the Holy Spirit,"[44] and these three are one in essence. About the second, it is said in the Apocalypse, "And the sacrifice of God was opened in heaven,

39. Matthew 11:28
40. Genesis 15:5
41. Genesis 1:1
42. Psalm 10:5
43. Psalm 32:6
44. Cf. 1 John 5:8

and the ark of his covenant was seen."[45] The ark of the covenant is God, who, as the Apostle says "is the mediator of the new covenant."[46] About the third heaven, it is said in the Psalm, "I have lifted up my eyes to you, who dwells in the heavens,"[47] that is, in devout souls. About the fourth it is said in the Psalm, "Your magnificence is raised above the heavens,"[48] that is, according to the gloss, above the nine choirs of angels.

Therefore by saying "in heaven" we have confidence that because God is in the first heaven, we will be transformed in him; because in the second, we will be inhabited by him; because in the third, we will be made alive through him; because in the fourth, we will be raised up through him. And thus ends the first part of the Lord's Prayer, in which we seek to gain God's favor.

The second part of the Lord's Prayer follows in which we desire or ask for the prayer to be effective by saying, "Hallowed be thy name." And this is the first petition in order, but it is the last in content or intention.

Here note that in order for our prayer to be effective, that is, in order that our prayer may be heard favorably by God, four things are required, namely, that it be made with firmness of faith, with goodness of content, with devotion of soul, and that it be done in the name of Christ. First, I say that in order for the prayer to be effective, it is necessary that it be made with firmness of faith. For, just as a document is not effective unless it is signed in the proper way, so prayer is ineffective unless it is signed with the signature of faith. And therefore Christ said, "Whatever you ask in prayer, believe," that is, sign with the signature of faith, "and you will receive it and it will be done for you."[49] Hence it says in John, "We know that God does not hear sinners."[50] Also as the Apostle says, "Everything which is not from faith is sin."[51] And therefore as Christ says, "True worshippers will worship the Father in spirit and in truth,"[52] namely, of faith.

45. Revelation 11:19
46. Hebrews 9:15
47. Psalm 122:1
48. Psalm 8:2
49. Matthew 21:22
50. John 9:31
51. Romans 14:23
52. John 4:23

Second, it is necessary that it be done with goodness of content, that is, that in prayer, useful, not foolish, things are requested. Just as an improper petition is nothing, so an improper prayer is nothing. In indication of which Christ said, "You ask but you do not receive because you ask wrongly."[53]

Third, it is necessary that it be done with devotion of soul. Just as it is necessary for there to be fire for smoke to ascend from a censer, so in order for prayer to ascend to God it is necessary that it ascend from the fire of charity. In indication of which it is read in the Apocalypse, "The angel of the Lord stood before the altar of the temple, having a golden censer in his hand, and much incense was given to him, which is the prayers of the saints. And the aromatic smoke ascends in the sight of God from the hand of the angel."[54] Thus David asked in the Psalm, "Lord, let my prayer be directed to you as incense in your sight."[55]

Fourth, [it is necessary] that it be done in the name of Christ. Indeed as a manager ought not to act except in the name of the management, otherwise what he does is not valid, so, since when praying we are managers of Christ, if we want to be heard favorably, it is necessary that we ask in the name of Christ. Hence Christ says, "Whatever you will ask the Father in my name will be given to you."[56]

Thus we desire these four things to be in our prayer when we say, "Hallowed be thy name." Three are touched on when "hallowed" is said since holy can be understood in three ways. In the first way, it is the same as firm, designating the firmness of faith. In the second way, it is the same as without earthliness, designating the usefulness of the thing. In the third way, it is the same as tinged with blood, in which the devotion of soul is designated. The fourth thing is touched on when we say, "thy name." Concerning which name, it says in Mark, "In my name demons will be cast out, new tongues will be spoken, serpents will be taken up, and if some drink poison, it will not harm them, they will lay

53. James 4:3   54. Revelation 8:3
55. Psalm 140:2   56. John 15:7

hands on the sick and they will be well."[57] And thus ends the second part of the Lord's Prayer, in which we desire or ask for the effectiveness of the prayer.

The third principal part of the Lord's Prayer follows in which we are taught the form and mode for praying when "Thy kingdom come" is said. Here know that from this point to the end, there are six petitions in which we ask for everything that is necessary for us both in this life and the next.

Since indeed all human perfection consists in two things, namely, in turning away from evil and in seeking good, according to the Psalm, "Turn from evil and do good,"[58] in this prayer we ask God to confer on us all good things and take away all evil. For the gathering of good things, three petitions are offered. Since indeed good is threefold, namely, the good of glory, the good of grace, and the good of nature, we ask to be given this threefold good. For we ask for the good of glory to be given to us when we say, "thy kingdom come," namely, the kingdom of paradise. And the meaning is, "O, our Father who art in heaven, we ask that your kingdom may come, that is, may come to us." But why do we say, "thy kingdom come" rather than "may we come into thy kingdom"? I say it is to specify that the glory of paradise is not gained by one's own merits, but by the sheer grace of God. According to the word of the Apostle saying, "Not by works of justice which we had done, but according to his mercy, he saved us."[59] Therefore, "thy kingdom come," is said, that is, by your grace may it come to us; but we do not say, "may we come," because as has been said, we cannot arrive there by our own merits. "For no one can come to me unless my Father has drawn him,"[60] as it says in John. Concerning this kingdom, Augustine says, speaking in the person of Christ, "What do I have to sell? The kingdom of heaven, how is it purchased? The kingdom with poverty, [glory with contempt,][61] rest with labor, joy with sadness, life with death."

57. Mark 16:17–18   58. Psalm 33:15, 36:27
59. Titus 3:5   60. John 6:44
61. Missing phrase supplied from other edition consulted.

We ask for the good of grace when we say, "thy will be done on earth as in heaven." As evidence for this, know that man is called "earth" in holy Scripture. Hence the Psalm, "My soul is like earth without water before you."[62] Hence it is said about the righteous person in the same place, "Lord, you are blessed in the earth."[63] And the angels and saints standing in paradise are called "heaven." Hence the Psalm, "The heavens are telling the glory of God."[64] Therefore the meaning is, "O, our Father, who art in heaven, may your will be done on earth," that is, among earthly people, "as it is done in heaven," that is, as it is done among the angels and saints. Or, "earth" may be understood as the church militant and "heaven" as the church triumphant, so that the meaning is, "just as your will is done in the church triumphant, so we ask that it may be done in the church militant." And what this will is, the Apostle teaches us saying, "This is the will of God, your sanctification."[65] And "thy will be done" is said, but not "our will," because, as Christ says, "Not everyone who calls me 'Lord, Lord' will enter the kingdom of heaven but the one who does the will of my Father who is in heaven, he will enter the kingdom of heaven."[66]

We ask for the good of nature when we say, "Give us today our daily bread." Here know that bread [*panis*] is named from the Greek *"pan"* which means "all" in Latin. Here, therefore, when we ask for bread, we ask for all things that are necessary for sustaining this most miserable and transitory life. And this does not contradict what was said above in Part II, tract 4, in the chapter on prayer where it was said that in prayer temporal things should not be requested, which means that in prayer temporal things are not to be asked for directly and for themselves. But to the degree that they are necessary to attain heavenly and eternal things, they may be appropriately requested. Hence Gregory in a collect, "Thus let us so pass through temporal goods that we do not lose eternal goods."[67] Or, it means that temporal goods are not to be request-

62. Psalm 142:6   63. Psalm 40:3
64. Psalm 18:2   65. 1 Thessalonians 4:3
66. Matthew 7:21
67. Gregory I, *Liber sacramentorum*, "Hebdomada V Post Pentecosten" (PL 78:176).

ed in superabundance, but for sustenance. And we ask for them in this way here when we say "today," because we only ask for as much as is necessary for today. And thus Solomon asked when he said, "Give me neither poverty, nor wealth. Apportion to me only the necessities of my life."[68] And Paul, "Having food and something to wear, with these we are satisfied."[69]

Also note that the bread we ask for in this prayer is threefold. The first is the spiritual bread of austere penance. This is the barley bread about which it is said in John, "A boy is here who has five barley loaves."[70] The five loaves are the five parts of perfect penance, namely, contrition, confession, prayer, alms, and fasting, which were discussed above in Part II. The second bread is the sacramental bread of the eucharist, about which bread it is said in John, "Here is the bread who came down from heaven. If anyone eats from this bread, he shall live in eternity."[71] In the strength of this bread, the faithful walk to the mountain of paradise. The third is the material bread of temporal substance. About this bread, it is said in Genesis, "by the sweat of your face you will eat your bread."[72] And we ask for these three breads in this prayer, according to the word of the Savior in Luke, saying, "Friend, lend me three loaves."[73] Therefore these three petitions provide for the gathering of good things.

There are other petitions which provide for the removal of evil. Concerning which note that evil is twofold, namely, the evil of guilt and the evil of punishment. The evil of guilt is twofold, namely, past and future. Therefore accordingly there are three petitions for the removal of evil. In the first we ask to be forgiven the evil of past guilt when we say, "forgive us our debts as we also forgive our debtors." These debts are sins, according to Christ's parable which he told to Simon the leper, saying, "A certain manager had two debtors, etc."[74] This parable, according to the gloss, is to

68. Proverbs 30:8
70. John 6:9
72. Genesis 3:19
74. Luke 7:41

69. 1 Timothy 6:8
71. John 6:51–52
73. Luke 11:5

be understood concerning the debt of sin. We ask this debt to be forgiven us by God as we forgive our debtors, that is, those who have sinned against us. And this is understood as the debt of injury which we ought to forgive. Otherwise, unless we forgive, God will not forgive us; as Christ says, "Your heavenly Father will not forgive you, unless you forgive one another from your hearts."[75] "Indeed with whatever measure you measure out, so shall it be measured back to you."[76] If therefore you want God to forgive you your sins, forgive those who have sinned against you. Otherwise it may be said to you, "'Out of your own mouth, I judge you, worthless servant.'[77] Indeed you say, 'forgive me as I forgive,' but you do not forgive, therefore you say that I ought not to forgive you."

But does someone who hates his brother sin in saying this prayer? I say no, because he does not say it in his own person, but in the person of the church. This is clear because it says "us" and not "me." And therefore, since the universal church which is ruled by the Holy Spirit cannot err, no one ever errs in saying this prayer.

In the second petition, we ask to be guarded against the evil of [future] guilt when we say, "And lead us not into temptation." Here know that sometimes temptation results in good, as is clear in Genesis, when it says, "God tempted Abraham."[78] And in the book of Wisdom, "God tempted them and found them worthy of him."[79] And God is said to tempt in two ways. In one way permissively, so that he allows it to happen. And this is taken up when it says, "God tempted them," that is, he permitted them to be tempted. And in this way God tempted Job. In the other way, God is said to tempt so that he might show others an example of virtue. And in this way God tempted Abraham so that he might show the virtue of his obedience. But this temptation is not what is meant here.

75. Matthew 18:35
76. Matthew 7:2; Mark 4:24; Luke 6:38
77. Luke 19:22   78. Genesis 22:1
79. Wisdom 3:5

Sometimes temptation results in evil, and this is twofold, for some temptation comes from enemies, that is, from demons, and some from the flesh, namely, in as much as the flesh rises up against the spirit. Temptation which comes from enemies is not a sin, unless it is consented to; but if it is resisted, it is very meritorious. And in this way Christ was tempted, as Matthew says, "Jesus was led into the desert by the Spirit, so that he might be tempted by the devil."[80] Temptation which comes from the flesh always arises from sin, in as much as this rebellion of the flesh against the spirit originates in us from the sin of our parents, and is itself materially original sin. Now this rebellion at its beginning is not under our control, just as it is said that first movements are not in our power. But to resist this rebellion or to consent to those first movements is well within our power. And therefore to consent to temptation, whether it comes from enemies or from the flesh, is always a sin. If the consent is made with deliberation, it is a mortal sin; if the consent is sudden and almost surreptitious, it is only a venial sin. Therefore, we do not ask in this petition not to be tempted, but we ask not to be led into temptation, for when we are led into temptation we consent to temptation. Therefore in this petition, we ask nothing else from God except that he may give to us strength for resisting temptation, which the Apostle promises will come to pass, saying, "God is faithful, and he will not permit you to be tempted beyond your ability. Instead, he will effect his providence, even during temptation, so that you may be able to bear it."[81]

In the last petition we ask to be delivered from the evil of punishment when we say, "But deliver us from evil." This is understood to mean from the evil of eternal punishment, which is simply evil. For the evil of temporal punishment can be and sometimes is good, as it was good for the holy martyrs to suffer and sustain many punishments and many torments. Hence from such evil we do not ask to be delivered, but from the evil of eternal punishment. Ac-

80. Matthew 4:1
81. 1 Corinthians 10:13

cordingly the church asks, saying, "Deliver me, Lord, from eternal death."[82]

At the end of all the petitions, "Amen" is added on, that is, "Let it be so," as a confirmation of all the petitions.

Thus there are seven petitions in the Lord's Prayer. In the first of which we ask for the effectiveness of the prayer, when we say, "hallowed be thy name," as if we were saying, "your name is holy and sure," so that what we ask in this prayer may be sure. Therefore although this petition is the first in order, it is last in intention. In the other six petitions, we ask that all good things be conferred on us and all evils be taken away from us. May the Lord grant that all these things be vouchsafed to us. And let these remarks suffice for the present because perhaps we will speak further about this matter another time.

CHAPTER 3: On the Ten Commandments of the law

When a young man asked, "What must I do to gain eternal life?" Jesus replied, "If you wish to enter into life, keep the commandments."[83] It was as if he said, "The entry into eternal life is the keeping of the precepts and commandments," the commandments being the precepts of the Decalogue. And the "decalogue" is so called from *"decas"* which is "ten" and *"logos"* which is "word," as if to say, the word of the Ten Commandments. Therefore there are ten commandments of the law,[84] of which some order man toward God and some toward his neighbor. The commandments which order man toward God are three, since man owes God three things. Indeed just as a vassal owes his lord three things, namely, faithfulness, so that he does not recognize another lord; reverence, so that he does not give him offense; and servitude, so that he devotes due obedience to him; so too everyone owes God these three things by

82. This is a responsory sung in the office of the dead and in the prayers offered after a funeral mass but before burial.

83. Matthew 19:16–17

84. Exodus 20:2–27; Deuteronomy 5:6–21

the dictates of natural law. And therefore, as far as the first is concerned, there is this commandment, "You shall not have strange gods before me."[85] As for the second, there is this, "You shall not take the name of your God in vain."[86] As for the third, there is this, "Remember that you are to sanctify the day of the Sabbath."[87]

The commandments which order a man toward his neighbor are seven. Indeed they order man toward his neighbor in two ways, namely, that he should do good to him and that he should not harm him. As for the first, there is one commandment, namely, "Honor your father and your mother."[88] As for the second, there are six. A man can harm his neighbor in three ways; in one way by deed, in another way by word, in another way by desire. By deed, he can harm him in three ways, namely, in his own person, or in a person joined to him, or in his own wealth. As for the first, there is this commandment, "You shall not murder."[89] As for the second, "You shall not commit adultery."[90] As for the third, "You shall not steal."[91] That a man should not harm his neighbor by word, there is this, "You shall not speak false testimony."[92] That a man should not harm his neighbor by his will, there are two others. So that he may not harm him by the desire of lust, there is this, "You shall not covet your neighbor's wife."[93] And lest he harm him by the desire of greed, there is this, "You shall not covet the goods of another, namely, neither servant nor serving girl, neither ox nor donkey,"[94] lest he should harm him by the desire of greed. These, therefore, are the ten commandments of the law; something about each one will be said in order.

On the first commandment

The first commandment is, "You shall not have strange gods before me."[95] Thus by this commandment are prohibited all idol-

85. Exodus 20:3
87. Exodus 20:8
89. Exodus 20:13
91. Exodus 20:15
93. Deuteronomy 5:21
95. Exodus 20:3

86. Exodus 20:7
88. Exodus 20:12
90. Exodus 20:14
92. Exodus 20:16; Deuteronomy 5:20
94. Exodus 20:17; Deuteronomy 5:21

atries, all heresies, and all kinds of witchcraft or divination, however they may be done, whether by fire or air, whether by water or
earth, whether using the bodies of the dead or observing the chat-
tering or the flight of birds, whether by magical signs or vain in-
spection of the psalms or gospels or other scriptures. As a general
rule, all divination, whether it is done by the aforesaid means or
however else, is prohibited by this commandment and is cursed by
God and by holy mother church as so much idolatry and repro-
bate infidelity. Since indeed some work to discover the things of
the future, which belong to God alone, through such superstitions,
they attribute the rights of deity to creatures. Thus claims Isaiah
saying, "Announce to me the prior things and the things to come,
and I will say that you are gods."[96] And Augustine, "You shall
not observe the so-called Egyptian days or the calends of Janu-
ary, which they keep with vulgar songs, certain events, and foods
one after another; gifts are given as at the beginning of the year,
auguries are made for fate, or for certain months, days, and times
or years, or the course of the moon or the sun. The one who does
these or any divinations or auguries whatsoever, or observes or attends or consents to such observations, or believes in such, or goes
to their house or lets [a diviner] into his house or inquires of one,
should know that he has violated the Christian faith and baptism,
and has become a pagan and an apostate enemy of God, and has
gravely incurred the wrath of God forever, unless, after being corrected by ecclesiastical penance, he is reconciled to God."[97]

But note that farmers who observe the times for sowing or cutting trees or similar things which have a reliable natural cause or a
natural reason, and doctors who observe certain days and times for
giving medicines or performing blood-letting and the like, are not
condemned here. Since all these inferior things are with respect to
their corporal nature under the influence of celestial bodies, this is
not prohibited; indeed it is necessary and proper to examine these
things and pay attention to the flux of the stars and the planets.

96. Cf. Isaiah 41:22–23
97. C.26 q.7 c.16

But since the rational soul is in no way under the influence of celestial bodies, as Solomon and Ptolemy say, "the wise soul shall
rule over the stars,"[98] it is superstitious and vain to look for such
things among those things which proceed from free will. Hence
to predict future rain from the clamor of crows is not superstitious, since such animals, from the direction of the winds and the
change of season, can feel change in their bodies. Note also that if
some man or woman collects some herb while saying the Creed or
the Lord's Prayer in order to put it on a sick person with the intention that, by this, God, the Creator of all, should be honored as
God, he or she is not reproved as long as no superstitious practice
is observed or mixed in (C.26 q.7 c.13 and q.7 c.16).

And this is to be kept as a general rule in this matter, that every
inquiry which is made through the tacit or explicit invocation of
demons, in whatever way it is done, whether through magical signs
or through shapes or in some other way, is prohibited by this commandment. But what about those conjurers who use and recite the
name of God and the angels and use many good words? I say that
care is to be taken with such, lest evil may lie under the appearance of good. Hence this is diligently to be avoided lest among
those names, unknown names may be mixed which are more likely
to be the names of demons than of angels. Since indeed according to what Bede says, "There is no false doctrine which does not
have some truth mixed in with the false," it is impossible that in
these superstitions there is nothing true mixed in with the false,
nor some good with the bad. And because "a little leaven corrupts
the whole mass,"[99] even though much good is present, if there is
also some bad, the whole is corrupt and suspect. Because even the
evil angel "presents himself as if he were an angel of light,"[100] do
not believe these visionaries who claim to have seen angels or various saints. As [Augustine] says, "Test the spirits to see if they are
of God."[101]

98. Cf. Proverbs 17:2   99. Galatians 5:9, 1 Corinthians 5:6
100. 2 Corinthians 11:14   101. 1 John 4:1

On the second commandment

The second commandment is, "Do not take the name of your God in vain."[102] Thus by this commandment are prohibited, first and especially, all kinds of perjury, and there are many. As evidence for this, know that for swearing to be lawful, it is necessary that it have three things, namely, truth, judgment, and justice. Thus the Lord says through Hosea the prophet, "They will swear, says the Lord, in truth and justice and judgment"[103] (C.22 q.2 c.2). Indeed truth always ought to be in the consciousness of the one swearing, so that he knows for sure that it is as he swears it to be. Otherwise, if he only believes and does not know for sure that it is so, he ought not to swear to certain knowledge but to credulity. Judgment here means specific deliberation, so that no one may swear even the truth except on account of necessity, that is, when one says something true to someone which helps this person or is useful to believe, and the person does not want to believe it on just a simple assertion. Justice means that what is sworn is lawful and honest (X 2.24.26). Therefore in whatever way one swears, whether the oath is assertive or promissory, if one of these is missing—if it is sworn to be false or true when the one swearing believes he swears falsely, or it is sworn without any necessity, or he swears something illicit—it is always perjury and is directly contrary to this commandment.

But what about those daily oaths which are made out of a certain levity or some bad habit? Is there perjury since judgment is missing? I say yes, but if it was about something lawful and without the intention to deceive or swear falsely, then it is only a venial sin. But if it is made about something illicit or with the intention to deceive or swear falsely, it is a mortal sin. Note that since swearing was not instituted to be a bond of iniquity, an oath which is made about some illicit thing or against charity, and which cannot be kept without the destruction of one's eternal salvation, for in-

102. Exodus 20:7
103. Jeremiah 4:2

stance, if I swear that I will kill someone or will not give alms or some such thing, is perjury and not to be kept in certain respects. Hence Jerome, "In evil promises, break faith; in a corrupt vow, change your resolve" (C.22 q.4 c.5).[104]

Note also that secondarily an oath which is made through false gods is prohibited here; this ought not to be made by Christians. Nevertheless I believe that where it is expedient, a Christian can receive an oath from a Saracen made through his gods. Note especially that swearing is not to be done by created things, except by certain ones, such as by the gospel, the altar, the cross, or the relics of the saints. One can also swear by the hand of the bishop (C.22 q.1 c.11 and q.5 c.2). Hence note that he who swears by a nonpermitted created thing ought to be harshly punished, as Raymond says.[105]

On the third commandment

The third commandment is, "Remember that you are to sanctify the day of the Sabbath."[106] Thus by this commandment it is commanded, primarily and principally, to observe the Lord's day, and as a consequence other solemn festivities are mandated which are found in D.3 de cons. c.1. They are these: Christmas; Saints Stephen, John the Evangelist, the Innocents, Sylvester; the Circumcision of the Lord; Epiphany; the Purification of the Blessed Virgin Mary; the Finding of the Holy Cross; Holy Easter with its week; three Rogation Days; the Ascension of the Lord; Pentecost; St. John the Baptist; the Twelve Apostles and especially Peter and Paul, who illuminated the whole world by their preaching; St. Laurence; the Assumption of the Virgin Mary, her birth, conception, and dedication; St. Michael; the dedication of whatever oratory or church; All Saints; St. Martin; and those feast days which each bishop and the clergy in his diocese commend for celebration, which are to be announced for local celebration but not

104. Gratian attributes this to Isidore.
105. Raymond of Penyafort, *Summa*, Bk I, 9, 1.
106. Exodus 20:8

to all in general. Yet understand this last category as saints canon-
ized by the Roman church, because a bishop cannot by himself
canonize anyone (X 3.45.1). The rest of the feast days are not man-
datory to keep but are prohibited. These things are written and set
out in the aforementioned canon, *Pronunciandum* (D.3 de cons. c.1).
Likewise Pope Eusebius ordered the feast of the Finding of the
Holy Cross to be solemnly celebrated on the seventh of May (D.3
de cons. c.19). Note also that in the aforementioned canon, *Pronunciandum* (D.3 de cons. c.1), no mention is made of the feast of
the Annunciation to Blessed Mary, nevertheless it is a solemn feast
and is to be celebrated.

But perhaps someone will say that this commandment concerning the Sabbath day does not mean the Lord's Day. As guidance
here, it is noted that in the old law there were some ceremonial
commandments and some moral ones. The ceremonial ones were
those that pertained to the specific worship of God, like that on
a certain day such and such a sacrifice should be made, and also
those that pertained to the ceremonies of that people, like that
they should wear certain clothes, etc. And these commandments
out of which Christ arose and the gospel was promulgated are not
to be observed; indeed the one who observes them sins mortally.
But the moral commandments were those which came from the
dictates of the law of nature, like to serve God, honor parents, and
the like. And these commandments still remain in force. Now the
commandment concerning the keeping of the Sabbath was moral
in part, in as much as a debt of honor is owed to God. This comes
from the dictates of the law of nature. But that such honor was
owed more on a set day than on other days was ceremonial in as
much as the rest of that day was a figure of that great Sabbath on
which God rested in the tomb. And therefore in as much as that
ceased, this commandment for the Sabbath day was changed to the
Lord's day, and for good reason. Indeed on this day the world began its beginning, Christ rose from the dead, death was destroyed,
and life received a new start. And this is the meaning of St. Paul in
Colossians where he says, "Let no one judge you in food or drink,

or in keeping festivals, omens, or Sabbaths, which are shadows of future things."[107] And about this, the Apostle argues much in Hebrews, chapters 3 and 4. And there are many chapters on this in D.3 de cons.

On feast days, people ought to devote themselves more than on other days to hymns, psalms, and spiritual songs,[108] and to other good works. Therefore they ought to abstain to a greater extent from all servile works, not only from sin, which is properly called servile because it makes one the servant of the devil, but also from crafts and secular business. Let neither a trade nor an agreement be made, nor anyone be sentenced to punishment or death, nor civil suits be sworn except to make peace (D.3 de cons. c.3). On these crafts and other secular duties, the Lord pronounced, saying, "Six days you will work, but on the seventh day which is the Sabbath of the Lord your God, you shall not do any work, you, your son, your daughter, your male servant, or your female servant, your beast and the newcomer who is within your gates."[109] Also note that on account of the danger of enemies or coming storms, crops may be gathered on Sundays and feast days, yet nevertheless, concerning these, let them consider to whom they belong and pay out greater alms. Also on these days scholars can write the readings which they heard during the week in their notebooks.

On the fourth commandment

The fourth commandment and the first of those which pertain to the neighbor is, "Honor your father and your mother."[110] Thus by this commandment it is directly commanded that we should honor our parents. And this should be understood not only to apply to the honor of reverence, such that the knees should bow before them and their hands should be kissed and the like, but also to the honor of help and provision, namely, that their needs should be provided for, according to each one's ability. And under the names of "father" and "mother" are to be understood the prel-

107. Colossians 2:16–17   108. Ephesians 5:19; Colossians 3:16
109. Exodus 20:9–10   110. Exodus 20:12; Deuteronomy 5:16

ates of the church and magistrates and temporal lords to whom due honor is to be shown. Also under the names of "father" and "mother" are to be understood all neighbors to whom works of mercy are to be shown. Among the works of mercy, some are spiritual and some are corporal. The spiritual ones are these: to instruct the ignorant, to correct offenders, to forgive wrongs, to console the sad, to support the needy, to pray for one's persecutors. Hence the verse:

> Consule, castiga, solare, remitte, fer, ora.
>
> Advise, castigate, console, forgive, support, pray.

The corporal ones are these: to feed the hungry, to give drink to the thirsty, to clothe the naked, to visit the sick, to redeem captives, to gather the homeless into shelter, to bury the dead. Hence the verse:

> Visito, poto, cibo, redimo, tego, colligo, condo.
>
> I visit, drink, feed, redeem, cover, gather, bury.

On the fifth commandment

The fifth commandment and the second toward the neighbor is, "Do not kill,"[111] with "unjustly" implied. By this commandment murder is prohibited. Under the name of "murder" understand all bodily injury which can be done against a neighbor. Here note that murder is twofold; some is spiritual, some is bodily. Spiritual murder is done in five ways. First, by hating. Hence John in his first letter, "The one who hates his brother is a murderer."[112] Then by detracting, by advising evil, by killing. Discussion of these three is found in D.1 de pen. c.14, c.25, and c.26. Or by taking away sustenance (D.86). "Feed the one dying of hunger; if you did not feed him, you have killed him."[113] And each of these kinds of murder, according to the doctors, is a mortal sin.

Bodily murder, according to the doctors, may be done in two

---

111. Exodus 20:13; Deuteronomy 5:17   112. 1 John 3:15
113. D.86 c.1

ways, by word or by deed. Murder by word may be done in three
ways, namely, by command, by advice, and by legal prosecution
(D.50 c.8; D.1 de pen. c.23). And any of these, if done unjustly, is a
mortal sin. Murder by deed may be done in four ways, namely, by
justice, by necessity, by accident, and by will. By justice, as when a
judge or civil servant justly kills one condemned to death. If this
killing is done out of malice or love of spilling human blood, even
though such a person dies justly because he deserved death, even
so the one who kills sins mortally on account of corrupt intention. But if it is done out of love of justice, the judge sins neither
in condemning him to death nor in handing him over to the servant who kills him, nor does the servant sin in carrying out the
order of the judge as long as he does so as a servant of the order
of law. This is proven by the word of the Apostle in the Epistle
to the Romans, "Let every soul be subject to higher authorities."
And then it follows, "For it is not without reason that he carries
a sword. For he is a minister of God; an avenger to execute wrath
upon whomever does evil."[114]

If murder is done by necessity, make a distinction because that
necessity was either avoidable or unavoidable. Suppose that it could
have been avoided without killing the person, then he is guilty of
murder and ought to do penance just as for a mortal sin. Or it was
unavoidable because he killed a person without planning the murder, but rather did it with sorrow of soul while defending or saving himself. In this case he is not said to sin nor is he bound to
penance. Nevertheless he ought to sorrow and reckon it among his
sins, because in such a case guilt can come where there is no guilt,
according to X 5.12.2.

But if murder is done by accident, make a distinction: either it
happened while acting lawfully or unlawfully. If it happened while
acting unlawfully, for instance, if he threw a rock in a place where
people were accustomed to travel, or if while he was stealing a
horse or an ox someone was struck and killed by the horse or the

114. Romans 13:1, 4

ox, etc., in this case, he is simply guilty of murder. But if he was acting lawfully, for instance, if he was cutting down trees he needed or was taking down hay from a wain or something similar, if he was as careful as he should have been, namely, looking around or shouting, not too late or too calmly but in good time and loudly, so that if someone was there or was coming he could have fled or watched out for himself, the killing will not be imputed to him. This is proved in D.50 c.50; X 5.12.25.

But if the murder was done willingly, without any distinction it is to be considered a most grave and enormous sin (D.50 c.44).

On the sixth commandment

The sixth commandment is, "You shall not commit adultery."[115] Thus by this commandment is prohibited all cohabitation, except with a lawful wife. And for what this is and how many kinds of cohabitation there are, see above in Part II, tract 3, chapter 9.

On the seventh commandment

The seventh commandment is, "You shall not steal."[116] Thus by this commandment are prohibited stealing, usury, fraud, pillage, deceit, and in general every illicit acquisition of another's goods by any means whether hidden or by agreement.

On the eighth commandment

The eighth commandment is, "Do not bear false witness."[117] Thus by this commandment, all lies are prohibited. About this, note that according to Augustine in his book, *On Lying*, there are eight kinds of lies.[118] The first is what is told against the doctrine of the faith and good morals, such as saying that Christ was not born of the pure Virgin Mary, or that he did not suffer on the cross, or something similar against the articles of the faith or good morals. The second is what aids no one and injures someone, such

115. Exodus 20:14; Deuteronomy 5:18   116. Exodus 20:15
117. Exodus 20:16; Deuteronomy 5:20
118. Augustine, *De mendacio*, c. 25 (PL 40:505); C.2 q.2 c.8.

as the lie of a detractor or false witness in a criminal case. The third is what aids one but injures another, like the testimony of a false witness in a monetary case. The fourth is what is done solely out of a desire for lying, without cause or usefulness. The fifth is what is done to satisfy greed, like the lie of a flatterer. The sixth is what injures no one but helps someone avoid danger to his wealth, as when someone, knowing that the wealth of another is about to be taken by a thief or robber, lies, swearing that he does not know where it is. The seventh is what injures no one and helps someone avoid personal danger, as when someone seeks to kill, and another person lies, swearing that he does not know where the person is. Eighth is what injures no one and helps protect someone from bodily impurity, as when someone lies to one wanting to corrupt a virgin by saying that she is married or that he does not know where she is, so that her virginity might be preserved.

Another distinction is offered by Augustine again, namely, that one type of lie is pernicious, and this includes five different kinds, and this is always a mortal sin (C.22 q.2 c.8). Another type is vicious, and this includes three different kinds beyond the first distinction, and this is a venial sin. Another type is jesting, and I believe that this also is venial. I take this to be when the one to whom it is told knows that it was said in jest and that it was not said out of a desire to lie. Concerning the lie of a flatterer, note that one can flatter another in three ways. In one way, by attributing to him good that he does not have. Some say that this is a mortal sin and others that it is venial. In another way, by making public the evil that he does have, and this is mortal sin according to all. In another way, by exaggerating the good that he does have, and this is venial according to all.

On the ninth and tenth commandments

The ninth and tenth commandments prohibit interior acts, namely, acts of will, namely, that no one covet the wife of another, and under the name of wife understand any woman, because as the Apostle says, "Anyone who will have looked at a woman, so as to lust after her, has already committed adultery with her in his heart,"[119] and that no one covet possession of the goods of another.[120]

And among the ten commandments of the law, some are affirmative and some are negative. And the difference between them is clear since the affirmative ones always obligate, not forever, but only for time and place; the negative ones obligate always and forever. Concerning these ten commandments there are these verses:

> *Unum crede deum, nec iures vana per ipsum.*
> *Sabbata sanctifices, et venerare parentes.*
> *Non sis occisor, fur, mechus testis iniquus.*
> *Vicinique thorum resque caueto suas.*

> Believe in one God, do not swear by him in vain.
> Keep the Sabbath holy, and honor your parents.
> Do not be a killer, thief, adulterer, or false witness.
> Beware of your neighbors' spouse and goods.

CHAPTER 4: On the gifts of the blessed

Because, by the testimony of Augustine, "No good will remain unrewarded, nor any evil unpunished," lastly the gifts of the blessed are to be considered, that is, the rewards which those who observe these commandments will have. Therefore note that the keepers of these commandments will be given seven gifts of glory in paradise, three on the part of the soul and four on the part of the body. The first gift on the part of the soul is the clear vision of God, namely, that we will see God clearly, without any veil; and all our beatitude consists in this vision. Hence Augustine, "The vision is the whole reward." And this clear vision succeeds the vision of faith, as the Apostle Paul says, "Now we see," that is, in this life, "in a mirror dimly," namely, by faith, "but then," namely, in paradise, "face to face."[121] The second gift on the part of the

119. Matthew 5:28   120. Exodus 20:17; Deuteronomy 5:21
121. 1 Corinthians 13:12

soul is a firm hold because we will hold God so firmly that we will not fear to lose him in any way. And concerning this hold, it says in the Canticle, "I held him, and would not let him go."[122] And this firm grasp succeeds the virtue of hope. The third gift to the blessed soul will be perfect enjoyment, because the blessed soul will perfectly delight in God and will cling to him and will be satisfied and take pleasure in him. Hence the Psalm, "I shall be satisfied when your glory appears, etc."[123] And this perfect enjoyment succeeds the love of charity. And concerning these three modes, Augustine says, "We will see, we will love, and we will praise." And this duty we will have in paradise, namely, to see, to love, and to praise God.

And after the resurrection we will have four gifts on the part of the body because our bodies will be agile, that is, they will move through any space whatsoever without any fatigue or labor. They will also be impassible because they will not be able to suffer anything. They will also be immortal because they will not be able to die in any way. They will also be brilliant; hence the Savior said, "The righteous will shine like the sun in the kingdom of my Father."[124] In whose kingdom may the King of kings and Lord of lords, Jesus Christ, make us fellow citizens. Amen.

Best wishes

I have written these things briefly concerning the office of curates, so that simple priests may be instructed in some things and the more advanced may labor toward higher things. I humbly ask that if in this little book the reader should find something useful, let him attribute it only to God, giving thanks that he deigned to impart to me, a sinner, some little spark of understanding. But ascribing to my ignorance and carelessness those things which are less well said, may he correct with charity and pour out prayers to God for me, a sinner.

122. Song of Solomon 3:4   123. Psalm 16:15
124. Matthew 13:43

Here begins the table of the book called
Handbook for Curates

In its first division, this book is divided into three principal parts. The first part deals with the sacraments and the things which pertain to the administration of the sacraments themselves. This principal part is divided into seven tracts.

Part two of this book, in which penitents and those things which pertain to the hearing of confession and the imposition of penances are dealt with, is subdivided into four principal tracts.

Chapter 5: On what ought to be confessed.

Chapter 6: What confession ought to be like.

Chapter 7: On repeating confession.

Chapter 8: How the priest ought to conduct himself toward the one confessing.

Chapter 9: On the questions to be asked during confession.

Chapter 10: On the power of the keys and the effect of confession.

Chapter 11: On the seal of confession.

Tract 4 is on satisfaction. It has six main chapters.

Chapter 1: What satisfaction is.

Chapter 2: On alms, and this chapter is subdivided into four chapters.

Chapter 1: From what alms ought to be given.

Chapter 2: Who can give alms.

Chapter 3: To whom alms ought to be given.

Chapter 4: How alms ought to be given.

The third principal chapter of this fourth tract is on fasting which is the second part of satisfaction, and it is subdivided into four chapters or considerations.

Chapter 1: How many types of fasting there are.

Chapter 2: When fasting was instituted.

Chapter 3: How many things are required for fasting.

Chapter 4: How many good things fasting accomplishes.

The fourth principal chapter of this fourth tract is on prayer which is the third part of satisfaction.

Chapter 5: What penance ought to be imposed for every sin and on the measure of penance.

Chapter 6: Whether one can satisfy for another.

The third principal part of this book in which the articles of the faith are dealt with and those things which pertain to the teaching of the people. It is divided into four chapters.

Chapter 1: On the articles of the faith.

Chapter 2: Containing three principal parts, it is on the petitions of the Lord's Prayer.

The book written by the most renowned man of the Lord, Guido of Monte Rochen, called *Handbook for Curates,* together with its table, ends here.

APPENDIX, BIBLIOGRAPHY
& INDEX

Authors and Sources Cited in the *Handbook for Curates*

ALBERT THE GREAT, ST. (Albertus Magnus; ca. 1206–1280): Dominican scientist, philosopher, theologian, and teacher of Thomas Aquinas who wrote extensively on a range of subjects. He was especially influential in his efforts to apply Aristotelian ideas to the study of Christian doctrine, which helped to lay the foundations of the Scholastic method.

AMBROSE, ST. (ca. 340–397): bishop of Milan, one of the four Fathers of the Latin Church, who gained fame for his preaching and ardent defense of Catholic orthodoxy. His list of writings is extensive, including sermons, scriptural commentaries, and letters. Guido explicitly cites his sermons on creation, *Hexameron*, and the Ambrosian missal. Since at least the eighth century, the liturgy and rites of the Church of Milan had been attributed to St. Ambrose; they encompassed a rich manuscript tradition, including a sacramentary and missal for the celebration of the mass.

AMBROSIASTER: name given to the author of a commentary on all but one of the epistles of St. Paul, possibly written in the late fourth century. Guido specifically cites the commentary on 1 Timothy and misattributes it St. Ambrose, as was the norm throughout the Middle Ages. Doubts about its authorship were not raised until the sixteenth century.

ANSELM OF CANTERBURY, ST. (1033–1109): theologian, philosopher, archbishop of Canterbury. A prolific author, Anselm examined the full spectrum of Catholic doctrine in his writings. His ideas and methods contributed to the development of Scholastic theology.

APOSTLES' CREED: early Christian profession of important points of doctrine that was widely believed to have been composed by the Apostles. Divided into three sections addressing God the Father, Jesus Christ, and the Holy Spirit, the Apostles' Creed became a standard statement of faith in the Latin West.

AQUINAS, ST. THOMAS (ca. 1225–1274): Dominican friar, theologian, and philosopher. Aquinas's masterwork was the theological summary, *Summa Theologiae*, which aimed to address all essential topics, human and divine, in an authoritative and systematic manner. Guido draws explicitly from Aquinas's *Summa* as well as from his *Quodlibets* and commentaries on Peter Lombard's *Sentences* (see below).

ARISTOTLE (384 B.C.E.–322 B.C.E.): Greek philosopher whose major works address logic, natural philosophy, metaphysics, and ethics. Latin translations of his writings became more widely available in the twelfth and thirteenth centuries in Western Europe and became a cornerstone of medieval intellectual life. Guido refers to him as "the Philosopher," and identifies three of his writings by name: *Metaphysics, Ethics,* and *On Plants* (the latter is a false attribution).

ARIUS (ca. 250–336): priest from Alexandria who taught that the Son (the second person of the Trinity) was created by God, not coeternal with God. "Arianism" denied the divinity of Christ. The Nicene Creed, promulgated in 325 by the first general council of the church, explicitly countered this belief (see below).

ATHANASIAN CREED: profession of faith stressing God's nature as a Trinity and the divine and human natures in Christ. Long attributed to Athanasius as part of his campaign against Arianism, it is now commonly believed to be of later origin.

ATHANASIUS, ST. (ca. 296–373): bishop of Alexandria, Egypt, and opponent of Arianism. Despite frequent clashes with imperial authorities, Athanasius committed his public career to defending the Nicene definition of Christ (see below).

AUGUSTINE OF HIPPO, ST. (354–430): bishop of Hippo, one of the four Fathers of the Latin Church, Western Christianity's most influential theologian on questions of ecclesiology, sacraments, morality, and grace and free will. Guido cites five texts by Augustine by name: *On Lying (De mendacio), On the Trinity (De trinitate), On Nature and Grace (De natura et gratia), On the Care of the Dead (De cura pro mortuis),* and *On True and False Penance (De vera et falsa poenitentia);* the latter is a false attribution.

BEDE (672/3–735): English Benedictine monk who produced many biblical commentaries and historical works, most famously *A History of the English Church and People* in 731, telling the story of the conversion of Britain and encouraging its allegiance to Rome. It became an authoritative source for early English history. His scriptural exegesis was also widely read. Guido cites one source by Bede by name, his homily on the circumcision of the Lord.

BELETH, JEAN (d. 1182): theologian and liturgist who wrote his best known work, *Summa de ecclesiasticis officiis,* while teaching in Paris in the 1160s. It enjoyed considerable success in manuscript and later in printed form. Guido cites it by name.

BENEDICT XI, POPE (1240–1304; pope from 1303): Dominican pope whose decretals were included in the *Extravagantes communes.*

BERENGAR OF LANDORRA (ca. 1262–1330): Master general of the Dominican Order and Archbishop of Compostella. Guido makes reference to Berengar of Landorra's *Quodlibets,* although the collection does not survive.

BERNARD OF AUVERGNE (Guido refers to him as Bernard of Gueraco and Brother Bernard; active late thirteenth and early fourteenth centuries): Dominican theologian and early supporter of Aquinas. Although he authored several works and sermons, his fame rested on his written refutations of *quodlibets* by Godfrey of Fontaines, James of Viterbo, and Henry of Ghent. Guido refers explicitly to the corrections against Henry of Ghent and Godrey of Fontaines.

BERNARD OF CLAIRVAUX, ST. (1090–1153): abbot of Clairvaux who became one of the most influential religious figures in twelfth-century Christendom. He was a prolific writer of theological treatises, sermons, and letters, known in particular for their emphasis on the need for all people to draw closer to God. Guido mentions Bernard's collection of eighty-six sermons on the Song of Songs by name *(Super cantica).*

BOETHIUS (ca. 480–ca. 524): Roman statesman and philosopher whose writings combined Greek philosophical traditions and orthodox Christianity. His translations of and commentaries on works by Aristotle became a key source of knowledge of Aristotle in the Latin West.

BONIFACE VIII, POPE (ca. 1234–1303; pope from 1294): trained as a canon lawyer, Boniface published an influential compilation of canon law, *Liber sextus,* during his papacy as a continuation and supplement to the *Liber extra* (see Pope Gregory IX below).

CHRYSOSTOM, ST. JOHN (c. 347–407): deacon, priest, and bishop of Constantinople who gained fame for his preaching (his name means "golden-mouthed"). His sermons were widely read, copied, and imitated for the quality of their biblical exposition.

CLEMENT V, POPE (1264–1314; pope from 1305): studied civil and ecclesiastical law before his election to the papacy. His decretals were added to the official body of canon law when they were promulgated by John XXII in 1317 as part of the *Clementinae* (see below).

DONATUS: appointed bishop of Carthage in 313 by a dissident faction within the local church. It argued that many church officeholders were morally unworthy of their offices, thereby invalidating their sacramental authority. Despite the spread of "Donatism," the orthodox view that the sacraments were valid in and of themselves held sway.

DUNS SCOTUS, JOHN (ca. 1265–1308): Franciscan Scholastic philosopher and theologian, known as the "Subtle Doctor" because his writings were difficult to understand. His works included two commentaries on the *Sentences* of Peter Lombard (see below), *Opus oxoniense* (or *Ordinatio*) and *Opus parisiense* (or *Reportata parisiensia*). Guido draws on the latter.

DURAND OF SAINT POURÇAIN (d. 1334): Dominican philosopher and Scholastic theologian; expounded scripture in Avignon for the papacy as Master of the Sacred Palace from 1313 to 1317; bishop of Le Puy-en-Velay and later of Meaux. Guido refers to Durand's "sacramentary," which is, in fact, his commentary on the fourth book of Lombard's *Sentences.*

DURANDUS, WILLIAM (also Duranti or Durantis; 1231–1296): jurist and canonist, bishop of Mende. He gained considerable fame in his lifetime for various works, including the *Rationale divinorum officiorum*, which details and interprets various aspects of the Mass of the Roman Rite, and several books on canon law. Guido cites one by name, *Repertory of Canon Law* (*Repertorium juris canonici*), a commentary on the decretals.

EBERHARD OF BÉTHUNE (fl. 1212): Flemish grammarian who wrote a popular grammatical treatise in hexameters, known as *Graecismus*, among other works.

GLOSSA ORDINARIA: widely used scriptural commentary (*glossa*) on the Vulgate compiled in the early twelfth century. Glossed in the margins and between the lines with comments drawn from the church fathers, it was a standard source for biblical study in the Middle Ages, hence its name, *ordinaria* (usual). However, although found in nearly every medieval library of any size, the *Glossa ordinaria* was not an official text and varied from copy to copy, sometimes inconsequentially, sometimes dramatically. Guido refers to it as "the gloss," as was typical at the time.

GODFREY OF FONTAINES (before 1250–ca. 1309): Scholastic philosopher and theologian whose major work are his *Quodlibets* addressing a range of contemporary ecclesiastical, doctrinal, and disciplinary disputes. He was embroiled in a public theological dispute with Bernard of Auvergne. Guido refers explicitly to one of Godfrey of Fontaine's *Quodlibets*.

GRATIAN (d. no later than 1159): canon lawyer who compiled a systematic collection of patristic texts, conciliar decrees, and papal pronouncements known as the *Decretum* (ca. 1140). It became the standard reference work for the study and practice of medieval canon law, upon which all subsequent collections built. Guido cites extensively from Gratian, often drawing his quotations from patristic authors (especially Augustine) from this collection.

GREGORY I, ST. (ca. 540–604; pope from 590): Benedictine monk and pope of Rome, last of the four doctors of the Latin Church. As pope, he played an instrumental role in shaping Christian doctrine, liturgy, and papal authority. He wrote prolifically on religious themes, including an extensive commentary on the book of Job. Guido refers to *On Job* (*Moralia in Job*) by name as well as to Gregory's *Dialogues* (*Dialogorum Libri*) which tell the stories of various saints. Guido also quotes a prayer (collect) attributed to Gregory, found in the so-called Gregorian sacramentary from the early Middle Ages.

GREGORY IX, POPE (ca. 1170–1241; pope from 1227): studied theology in Paris and canon law, most likely in Bologna, before his election to the papacy. His background as a canonist influenced his decision to create a more accessible and better organized collection of decretals. The result became known as the *Decretals of Gregory IX (Liber extra)*, officially published in 1234.

HENRY OF GHENT (Henri de Gand; d. 1293): secular theologian and philosopher who worked to restore Augustinianism to prominence in the Scholastic setting. He was the author of fifteen *Quodlibets* covering a broad range of subjects, from metaphysics to politics to ecclesiology.

HERVAEUS NATALIS (Hervé Nédellec; d. 1323): Dominican master of theology and master general of the Dominican Order. Guido refers to him as "Britone" (a nod to his place of birth) in connection with his earliest substantial work, a sentence commentary, dating to around 1303–1304.

HILARY OF POITIERS, ST. (ca. 315–ca. 367): bishop of Poitiers and leading opponent of Arianism, against which he penned his best known work, *De Trinitate*. In the Latin West, he became an equal to Jerome, Ambrose, and Augustine as a doctor of the church.

HOSTIENSIS (Henricus de Segusio; ca. 1200–1271): canonist who reached the rank of cardinal. His master work, which became known as the *Golden Summa (Summa aurea)*, displayed extensive knowledge of both Roman and canon law; Guido cites the *Summa* by name. The portion on the sacrament of penance was especially influential as Guido's use of it in his discussion of confession suggests.

HUGH OF SAINT VICTOR (d. 1141): philosopher, theologian, mystic. He composed many works, including the first major medieval theological summa, *On the Sacraments of the Christian Faith (De sacramentis Christianae fidei)*. Known for his deep knowledge of patristic authors, especially St. Augustine, Hugh forged new paths in the realms of theology, exegesis, and spirituality.

INNOCENT III, POPE (ca. 1160–1216; pope from 1198): theologian and canonist who worked to strengthen papal authority over the universal church. Among his most enduring achievements was the assembly of the Fourth Lateran Council in 1215. The council approved seventy decrees covering an array of theological, pastoral, and disciplinary issues, notably the obligation of all adult Christians to confess at least once a year to their own priest (*Omnis utriusque sexus*). Before becoming pope, Innocent wrote several works, including a treatise on the mass, *On the Sacred Mystery of the Altar (De sacro altaris mysterio)*, which Guido cites.

INNOCENT IV, POPE (d. 1254; pope from 1243): legal scholar and pope. His major work was a commentary on the decretals of Gregory IX *(Apparatus)*, considered a masterpiece of medieval canon law. His own decretals were issued by Boniface VIII in 1298 *(Liber sextus)*.

JEROME, ST. (340/2–420): one of the four Fathers of the Latin Church and early proponent of Christian asceticism. His many writings include biblical commentaries, letters, and translations. His translation of the Bible into Latin, known as the Vulgate, became the version most widely used in Western Europe.

JOHN XXII, POPE (1249–1334; pope from 1316): canon lawyer and papal reformer. In 1317, he issued the *Clementinae,* a body of laws drawn largely from the Constitutions of Clement V in the Council of Vienne (1311–1312). Two other collections, the *Extravagantes* of John XXII and the *Extravagantes communes,* contain his own judicial decisions as well those of various popes not found in earlier compilations.

JOHN OF DAMASCUS, ST., OR JOHN DAMASCENE (ca. 675–ca. 750): monk, theologian, musician known for his encyclopedic mastery of Greek patristic thought. His book, *Font of Wisdom,* became a standard textbook in philosophy and his sermons were also widely circulated.

JOVINIAN (d. ca. 406): Roman monk and writer who opposed the elevation of monasticism in Christian thought and practice as a higher spiritual state. Condemned as heretical, his views are known only through the writings of his opponents, notably St. Jerome and St. Ambrose.

LATERAN CREED, OR INNOCENTIAN CREED (1215): exposition of the Catholic faith promulgated in the first decree of the Fourth Lateran Council (*Firmiter credimus*). The decree was formulated to counter the growing threat of heresy; it reaffirmed the doctrine of the Trinity, proclaimed that no one could be saved outside the universal church, and sanctioned the doctrine of transubstantiation.

MANI (216–277): founder of a religious sect condemned by Christians as heretical. Mani and his followers embraced a dualistic notion of the universe in which God and spiritual enlightenment battled against Satan and the material world. According to Mani, human suffering did not stem from original sin, as orthodox Christians believed, but rather from humans' contact with matter.

MUHAMMAD (ca. 570–632): religious leader in seventh-century Arabia and founder of the religion of Islam. In about 610, Muhammad began to have visions, which he and his followers believed came directly from God. The revelations were preserved in writing to form the Muslim holy book, the Qu'ran. Although Muslims worship the same God as Christians (and Jews), they reject key elements of Christian doctrine, including the divinity of Christ. With the rise of the crusading movement in late eleventh-century Europe, Islam was routinely demonized as a religion of infidels.

NICENE CREED (325, 381): common statement of Christian faith issued by the ecumenical council of Nicaea to address a number of doctrinal issues, including the teachings of Arius (see above). The creed defines Christ as consubstantial with the Father, an explicit counter to Arianism. The version issued by the Council of Constantinople became the liturgical standard.

ORIGEN (ca. 185–ca. 254): philosopher and theologian who exerted a great influence on biblical exegesis with his allegorical approach to the interpretation of the Bible. His writings were extensive and drew on both Platonic philosophy and Christian theology. They were condemned as heretical in the fifth century for reasons that are not entirely clear.

OVID (43 B.C.E.–17 C.E.): Roman poet whose works were widely read and imitated in the Middle Ages for the quality of their verse and subject matter. Guido identifies one of Ovid's works by name, *Remedy of Love* (*Remedia Amoris*).

PELAGIUS (ca. 360–418): theologian admired for his deep knowledge of the scriptures and the writings of classical Greek and Latin Fathers. His guiding belief was in the absolute freedom of human will to act for good or for evil. This belief came under fire because of its theological implications, including the denial of original sin. Pelagius was excommunicated in 417 and Pelagianism formally condemned as heretical in the early sixth century.

PAUL, ST. (first century): early Christian leader who wrote many of the letters included in the New Testament. His letters, along with commentaries on them, helped to shape Christian theology on such topics as grace, redemption, and the Trinity. Guido often calls Paul "the Apostle."

PETER LOMBARD (ca. 1100–1160): theologian, bishop of Paris. He is best known for his work, *Sentences (Sententiarum Quatuor Libri)*, which expounds the entirety of Christian doctrine in four books. It had great influence because of the range of topics it addressed and its efforts to reconcile seemingly contradictory authorities. The *Sentences* became a standard university textbook; beginning in the mid 1240s, all masters candidates in theology were required to lecture on it.

PSEUDO-DIONYSIUS THE AREOPAGITE (fl. ca. 500): Greek Platonist author falsely identified as Dionysius the Areopagite, an early convert to Christianity (Acts 17:34). By the late sixth century, his writings were accepted as authoritative and orthodox in both the Eastern and Western churches. Guido cites one of the treatises by name, *On the Celestial Hierarchy.*

PLATO (ca. 429–348 B.C.E.): Greek philosopher whose ideas shaped early Christian and medieval thought. Many Christian writers saw an affinity between his views and Christianity, notably his belief that humans have immortal souls distinct from their bodies. At the same time, however, Christians' belief in the resurrection of the dead as something to look forward to was incompatible with Platonic philosophy.

PTOLEMY, CLAUDIUS (ca. 85–165): Greek astronomer and geographer who propounded the geocentric theory of the universe. His observations and mathematical calculations describing the rotations of stars, the sun, moon, and planets around a fixed earth were considered authoritative until the late sixteenth and seventeenth centuries.

RAYMOND OF PENYAFORT, ST. (1185–1275): Dominican friar and canonist. His *Summa* was an essential source for Guido, especially in the tracts on marriage and penance. At the request of Pope Gregory IX, Raymond also compiled and arranged a collection of papal decretals *(Liber extra)* that, along with Gratian, formed the foundation of the *Corpus iuris canonici.*

RICHARD OF MENVILLE (Richard of Middleton; b. ca. 1249): Franciscan philosopher and theologian. Guido cites his commentary on the *Sentences* by name *(Super Quatuor Libros Sententiarium)*, which Richard wrote while studying at the University of Paris in the early 1280s.

SABELLIUS: Roman theologian who was excommunicated by Pope Callistus I in ca. 220 for his teachings. His central belief rejected the doctrine that the Trinity was a single godhead comprising three distinct and enduring persons (Father, Son, and Holy Spirit).

SENECA, LUCIUS ANNAEUS (ca. 4 B.C.E.–65 C.E.): Roman philosopher whose writings included letters, plays, and moral treatises. They were especially valued by medieval authors as sources of ethical insight and guidance.

WILLIAM OF SAINT PATHUS: Franciscan, royal confessor, author of *Life of Saint Louis (Vie de Saint Louis)*. He wrote the book after the canonization of King Louis in 1297 and drew heavily upon the material collected during the canonization proceedings. Guido mentions the book by name while recounting its version of a popular story about St. Louis's encounter with a leprous monk.

Selected Bibliography of
Principal Works Cited

Primary Works

Aquinas, Thomas. *De articulis fidei et ecclesiae sacramentis.* In *Traités: Les raisons de la foi., Les articles de la foi et les sacrements de l'Église,* ed. Gilles Emery, 211–95. Paris: Cerf, 1999. Partial English translation available in *The Catechetical Instructions of St. Thomas Aquinas,* translated by Joseph Collins, 119–31. New York: Joseph Wagner, 1939.

———. *Scriptum super Sententiis.* Available online at http://www.corpusthomisticum .org/iopera.html.

———. *Summa Theologiae.* Available online at http://www.corpusthomisticum.org/ iopera.html. English translation available online at http://www.newadvent.org/ summa/.

Augustine. *De cura pro mortuis.* PL 40:591–610. English translation available online at http://www.newadvent.org/fathers/1316.htm.

———. *De mendacio.* PL 40:487–518. English translation available online at http:// www.newadvent.org/fathers/1312.htm.

———. *Liber de vera et falsa poenitentia.* PL 40:1113–30.

Beleth, Jean. *Summa de ecclesiasticis officiis.* Edited by Heribert Douteil. Corpus Christianorum Continuatio Mediaevalis, 41A. Turnhout: Brepols, 1976.

Bernard of Clairvaux. *On the Song of Songs.* Translated by Kilian Walsh. 4 vols. Spencer, Mass.: Cistercian Publications, 1971–1980.

Biblia Latina cum Glossa Ordinaria: Facsimile Reprint of the Editio Princeps Adolph Rusch of Strassburg 1480/81. 4 vols. 1480. Reprint. Turnhout: Brepols, 1992.

Cura pastoralis pro ordinandorum tentamine collecta. [Ulm: Johann Reger, ca. 1498–1499].

Duns Scotus, John. *Opera Omnia: Editio minor.* Vol. II/2, *Opera Theologica.* Alberobello: Editrice, 2001.

Durand of St. Pourçain. *Petri Lombardi Sententias Theologicas Commentariorum.* 1571. Reprint. Farnborough, Hants, U.K.: Gregg Press, 1964.

Eberhard of Béthune. *Graecismus.* Edited by J. Wrobel. Vratislaviae: G. Koebneri, 1887.

Friedberg, Emil. *Corpus iuris canonici.* 2 vols. Graz: Akademische Druck-und-Verlagsanstalt, 1959.

Gerson, Jean. *Opusculum Tripartitum.* In *Opera omnia,* ed. Louis Ellies Du Pin, vol. 1, col. 425–50. Antwerp: Sumptibus Societatis. 1706. Reprint. Hildesheim: Olms, 1987.

Godfrey of Fontaines. *Le huitième [-dixième] quodlibet de Godefroid de Fontaines.* Les philosophes belges: Textes et études, 4. Louvain: Institut supérieur de philosophie de l'Université, 1924.

Gregory I. *Liber sacramentorum.* PL 78:25–240.

———. *Moralia in Job.* PL 76:9–782.

Hostiensis. *Summa aurea.* 1537. Reprint. Aalen: Scientia, 1962.

Hugh of Saint Victor. *De sacramentis Christianae fidei.* PL 176:173–618. English translation, *On the Sacraments of the Christian Faith.* Translated by Roy J. Deferrari. Cambridge, Mass.: Medieval Academy of America, 1951.

Innocent III. *De sacro altaris mysterio.* PL 217:763–915.

Jacob of Voragine. *The Golden Legend: Readings on the Saints.* Translated by William Granger Ryan. Princeton, N.J.: Princeton University Press, 1993.

Lochmaier, Michael. *Parochiale curatorum.* [Nuremberg: Friedrich Creusner, ca. 1493].

Lombard, Peter. *Sententiarum Quatuor Libri.* Available online at http://www.franciscan-archive.org/lombardus/opera/ls4-01.html.

Manuale parochialium sacerdotum. [Strassburg: Printer of the 1483 "vitus Patrum," about 1485].

Mirk, John. *Instructions for Parish Priests.* Edited by Edward Peacock. Early English Text Society/Trübner & Co: London, 1868; rev. ed., 1902. The 1868 edition is also available online at http://www.archive.org/stream/instructionsfor00furngoog#page/n4/mode/1up.

The Missal in Latin and English. Translated and edited by J. O'Connell, H. P. R. Finberg, and R. A. Knox. Westminster, Md.: Newman Press, 1959. The section on the eucharistic service may also be found in Bard Thompson, *The Liturgies of the Western Church,* 54–91. Cleveland: Meridian Books, 1961.

Natalis, Hervaeus. *In quatuor Libros sententiarum commentaria.* 1647. Reprint. Farnborough, Hants, U.K.: Gregg Press, 1966.

Raymond of Penyafort. *Summa de poenitentia et matrimonio.* 1603. Reprint. Farnborough, Hants, U.K.: Gregg Press, 1967. English translation of Bk IV, *Summa on Marriage.* Translated by Pierre Payer. Toronto: Pontifical Institute of Mediaeval Studies, 2005.

Richard of Menville. *Super Quatuor Libros Sententiarum.* 1591. Reprint. Frankfurt: Minerva, 1963.

William of Saint Pathus. *Vie de Saint Louis.* Edited by H. François Delaborde. Collection des textes pour server à l'étude et à l'enseignement de l'histoire 27. Paris: A. Picard, 1899.

Secondary Works

Alston, R. C. *Books with Manuscript: A Short Title Catalogue of Books with Manuscript Notes in the British Library.* London: British Library, 1994.

Barney, Stephen A., ed. *Annotation and Its Texts.* New York and Oxford: Oxford University Press, 1991.

Baron, Sabrina Alcorn, Eric N. Lindquist, and Eleanor F. Shelvin, eds. *Agent of Change: Print Culture Studies after Elizabeth L. Eisenstein.* Amherst: University of Massachusetts Press, 2007.

Bast, Robert J. *Honor Your Fathers: Catechisms and the Emergence of a Patriarchal Ideology in Germany, 1400–1600.* Leiden: Brill, 1997.

Binz, Louis. *Vie religieuse et réforme ecclésiastique dans le diocèse de Genève pendant le grand schisme et la crise conciliare (1378–1450).* Geneva: Alex. Jullien,1973.

Boyle, Leonard E. *Pastoral Care, Clerical Education and Canon Law, 1200–1400.* London: Variorum Reprints, 1981.

————. "The Fourth Lateran Council and Manuals of Popular Theology." In *The Popular Literature of Medieval England,* edited by Thomas J. Heffernan, 30–43. Knoxville: University of Tennessee Press, 1985.

————. "The Inter-Conciliar Period 1179–1215 and the Beginnings of Pastoral Manuals." In *Miscellanea, Rolando Bandinelli, Papa Alessandro III,* 45–56. Siena: Accademia senese degli intronati, 1986.

Brundage, James A. *Medieval Canon Law.* London: Longman, 1995.

Clebsch, William A., and Charles R. Jaekle. *Pastoral Care in Historical Perspective.* New York: J. Aronson, 1983.

Dykema, Peter A. "Conflicting Expectations: Parish Priests in Late Medieval Germany." Ph.D. dissertation, University of Arizona, 1998.

————. "Handbooks for Pastors: Late Medieval Manuals for Parish Priests and Conrad Porta's *Pastorale Lutheri* (1582)." In *Continuity and Change: The Harvest of Late Medieval and Reformation History,* edited by Robert J. Bast and Andrew C. Gow, 143–62. Leiden: Brill, 2000.

Eisenstein, Elizabeth L. *The Printing Press as an Agent of Change: Communications and Cultural Transformations in Early Modern Europe.* New York: Cambridge University Press, 1979.

————. "AHR Forum: An Unacknowledged Revolution Revisited." *American Historical Review* 107 (February 2002): 87–105.

Evans, G. R. *Mediaeval Commentaries on the* Sentences *of Peter Lombard.* Vol. 1. Leiden: Brill, 2002.

Febvre, Lucien, and Henri-Jean Martin. *The Coming of the Book: The Impact of Printing, 1450–1800.* Translated by David Gerard. London: NLB, 1976.

Grafton, Anthony. "Is the History of Reading a Marginal Enterprise? Guillaume Budé and His Books." *Papers of the Bibliographical Society of America* 91 (1997): 139–57.

Guardiola, Conrado. "Los primeros datos documentales sobre Guido de Monte Roquerio, autor del 'Manipulus curatorum.'" *Hispania* 48, no. 170 (1988): 797–826.

Howsam, Leslie. *Old Books and New Histories: An Orientation to Studies in Book and Print Culture.* Toronto: University of Toronto Press, 2006.

Jackson, Helen J. *Marginalia: Readers Writing in Books.* New Haven, Conn.: Yale University Press, 2001.

Jensen, Kristian, ed. *Incunabula and Their Readers: Printing, Selling and Using Books in the Fifteenth Century.* London: British Library, 2003.

Johns, Adrian. "AHR Forum: How to Acknowledge a Revolution." *American Historical Review* 107 (February 2002): 106–25.

Jungmann, Josef A. *The Mass: An Historical, Theological, and Pastoral Survey.* Translated by Julian Fernandes. Collegeville, Minn.: Liturgical Press, 1976.

Kiermayr, Reinhold. "On the Education of the Pre-Reformation Clergy." *Church History* 53 (1984): 7–16.

Lemaître, Nicole. "Le catéchisme avant les catéchismes, dans les rituels." In *Aux origines du catéchisme en France*, 28–44. Paris: Desclée, 1989.

Lualdi, Katharine J. "Change and Continuity in the Liturgy of the *Prône* from the Fifteenth to the Seventeenth Century." In *Prédication et liturgie au Moyen Âge*, edited by Nicole Bériou and Franco Morenzoni, 373–89. Turnhout: Brepols, 2008.

Milway, Michael. "Forgotten Best-sellers from the Dawn of the Reformation." In *Continuity and Change: The Harvest of Late Medieval and Reformation History*, edited by Robert J. Bast and Andrew C. Gow, 113–42. Leiden: Brill, 2000.

Otero, Horacio Santiago. "Guido de Monte Roterio y el 'Manipulus curatorum.'" In *Proceedings of the Fifth International Congress of Medieval Canon Law, Salamanca, 21–25 September, 1976*, edited by Stephan Kuttner and Kenneth Pennington, 259–65. Vatican City: Biblioteca Apostolica Vaticana, 1980.

Reinburg, Virginia. "Liturgy and the Laity in Late Medieval and Reformation France." *Sixteenth Century Journal* 23, no. 3 (1992): 526–47.

Rosenthal, Bernard. *The Rosenthal Collection of Printed Books with Manuscript Annotations.* New Haven, Conn.: Yale University Press, 1997.

Rubin, Miri, and Walter Simons, eds. *Christianity in Western Europe, c. 1100–c. 1500*, vol. 4 of *The Cambridge History of Christianity.* Cambridge: Cambridge University Press, 2009.

Saenger, Paul, and Michael Heinlen. "Incunable Description and Its Implication for the Analysis of Fifteenth-Century Reading Habits." In *Printing the Written Word: The Social History of Books, circa 1450–1520*, edited by Sandra Hindman, 225–58. Ithaca, N.Y.: Cornell University Press, 1991.

Schabel, Christopher, ed. *Theological Quodlibeta in the Middle Ages*, Vol. 2: *The Fourteenth Century.* Leiden: Brill, 2007.

Sherman, William H. *Used Books: Marking Readers in Renaissance England.* Philadelphia: University of Pennsylvania Press, 2008.

Stansbury, Ronald J., ed. *A Companion to Pastoral Care in the Late Middle Ages (1200–1500).* Leiden: Brill, 2010.

Stoddard, Roger. *Marks in Books.* Cambridge, Mass.: Houghton Library, Harvard University, 1985.

Tentler, Thomas. *Sin and Confession on the Eve of the Reformation.* Princeton, N.J.: Princeton University Press, 1977.

Thayer, Anne T. "Learning to Worship in the Later Middle Ages: Enacting Symbolism, Fighting the Devil, and Receiving Grace." *Archive for Reformation History* 99 (2008): 36–65.

Tribble, Evelyn B. *Margins and Marginality: The Printed Page in Early Modern England.* Charlottesville: University Press of Virginia, 1993.

General Index

Abraham (Old Testament), 148, 252, 291

absolution, 85–86, 184; from God, 202; priest's granting of, 180–81, 194, 237, 238–41, 267

acolyte, order of, 11; character impressed on, 114; eucharistic role of, 111; marriage allowed, 147

Adam, 130, 160, 173–74, 182–83

adjuration. *See* exorcism

adoption, 143; as sons of God, 283

adultery, 206, 224, 230, 231; commandment against, 294, 303, 305; effects on marriage, 132, 144, 148–49; gravity of, 260, 261; penance for, 262–63; by priests, 262–63. *See also* fornication

adult baptism, 27, 30, 32, 33, 174

affinity: as circumstance of sin, 205, 262; definition of incest, 230; as impediment to marriage, 127, 140, 150–52, 155

Agnus dei (mass). *See* "Lamb of God"

Albert the Great, St.: on almsgiving, 251

Alleluia (mass), 88, 91

almsgiving, 245–54; effects of, 256, 267, 269, 290; on feast days, 300; how to give, 253–54; origin of term, 251; as penance, 203, 258, 265; what can be given, 246–49; who can give, 249–51; who can receive, 251–53

altars, 64, 65, 96, 111

Ambrites: errors of, 274

Ambrose, St.: on almsgiving, 252; on confession, 236, 238, 240; on orders, 115, 116; on passion of Christ, 60–61; on penance, 159, 160, 170, 260; on sacramental forms, 58–59, 119

Ambrosiaster, 115n211

Angel of Great Counsel, 87, 91

angels, 48–49, 110, 252, 276, 285; in the mass, 89, 94, 286, 289, 296

anger, sin of, 224–25, 227, 233

Annunciation to the Virgin Mary, 279, 299

anointing: in baptism, 34, 36; in confirmation, 40, 41–42; in extreme unction, 11, 122; in orders, 109, 113–14; repetition of, 13; of the sick, 118–19, 120–21

Anselm of Canterbury, St.: on sins, 177

antiphons, 65n100, 283n26

apostles, 3, 9, 10, 11, 18, 185, 187. *See also* disciples; *and individuals by name*

Apostles' Creed, 272, 273–74, 274–75, 276, 277

Aquinas, Thomas, St., xxv, xliv; on baptism, 26, 29; on confession, 189, 192; on confirmation, 37; *De articulis fidei et ecclesiae sacramentis*, xxiii; on extreme unction, 120, 123; on fasting, 256; on gaming, 248; "Lauda Sion," 63n92; on the mass, 57; on orders, 110, 113; on penance, 267; *Summa Theologiae*, xxiv, xxviii

archbishops: hearing confessions, 193, 195–96. *See also* bishops

Aristotle: on actions, 49, 114, 253–54; on forms, xxvii, 54, 124; on influence of particular places, 63

Index of Scripture

Old Testament

Genesis
1:1, 285
1:23–24, 160
2:17, 255
2:23–24, 130
3:9, 183
3:12–13, 213
3:19, 160, 290
4:13, 170
9:1, 130
15:5, 285
18:1–8, 252
18:20–21, 264
19:1–29, 230
19:24, 264
22:1, 291
28:12–13, 163

Exodus
3:13–14, 284
5:3, 163
12:11, 102
16:17–20, 67
20:2–27, 293
20:3, 294
20:7, 294, 297
20:8, 294, 298
20:9–10, 300
20:12, 253, 294, 300
20:13, 294, 301
20:14, 294, 303

20:15, 294, 303
20:16, 242, 294, 303
20:17, 294, 305
22:19, 230
28:2–3, 75
28:30, 271

Leviticus
18:6–18, 145

Numbers
1:53, 11
12:13, 262
22:28, 5

Deuteronomy
5:6–21, 293
5:16, 253, 300
5:17, 301
5:18, 303
5:20, 242, 294, 303
5:21, 294, 305
12:13–14, 63
16:20, 254
24:6, 165
32:6, 282

Joshua
7:19–26, 211

Judges
16:28–30, 24

Ruth
2:4, 89

1 Samuel
14:24–25, 256

2 Samuel
7:14, 281

2 Kings
1:10, 227
1:12, 227
25:1–10, 256

2 Chronicles
35:20–24, 24

Tobit
4:7, 246
4:9, 254
4:11, 245
6:8, 34
12:8, 254

Esther
5:1–3, 76
7:2, 75

Job
26:13, 220
31:18, 246

Psalms (Vulgate numbering)
2:7, 71, 281
6:3, 121
6:6, 171
6:7, 211
8:2, 286
8:8, 173
10:5, 285
16:15, 306
18:2, 289
19:2, 94
21:14, 69
21:15, 165
21:17, 69
24:7, 175
25:6, 76
31:5, 180, 202, 208
32:6, 285
33:2, 101
33:15, 288
35:9, 99
36:27, 288
40:3, 289
50:19, 165, 179, 245
55:9, 214

347

New Testament

Handbook for Curates: A Late Medieval Manual on Pastoral Ministry was designed and typeset in Centaur by Kachergis Book Design of Pittsboro, North Carolina. It was printed on 60-pound House Natural Smooth and bound by Sheridan Books of Ann Arbor, Michigan.